Studies i

Series Editors
Afua Twum-Danso Imoh ⓘ
University of Bristol
Bristol, UK

Nigel Patrick Thomas ⓘ
University of Central Lancashire
Preston, UK

Spyros Spyrou ⓘ
European University Cyprus
Nicosia, Cyprus

Anandini Dar
School of Education Studies
Ambedkar University Delhi
New Delhi, India

This well-established series embraces global and multi-disciplinary scholarship on childhood and youth as social, historical, cultural and material phenomena. With the rapid expansion of childhood and youth studies in recent decades, the series encourages diverse and emerging theoretical and methodological approaches. We welcome proposals which explore the diversities and complexities of children's and young people's lives and which address gaps in the current literature relating to childhoods and youth in space, place and time. We are particularly keen to encourage writing that advances theory or that engages with contemporary global challenges. Studies in Childhood and Youth will be of interest to students and scholars in a range of areas, including Childhood Studies, Youth Studies, Sociology, Anthropology, Geography, Politics, Psychology, Education, Health, Social Work and Social Policy.

Bengt Sandin • Jonathan Josefsson
Karl Hanson • Sarada Balagopalan
Editors

The Politics of Children's Rights and Representation

palgrave
macmillan

Editors
Bengt Sandin
Department of Thematic Studies—
Child Studies
Linköping University
Linköping, Sweden

Jonathan Josefsson
Department of Thematic Studies—
Child Studies
Linköping University
Linköping, Sweden

Karl Hanson
Centre for Children's Rights Studies
University of Geneva
Geneva, Switzerland

Sarada Balagopalan
Department of Childhood Studies
Rutgers, The State University of
New Jersey
Camden, NJ, USA

ISSN 2731-6467 ISSN 2731-6475 (electronic)
Studies in Childhood and Youth
Published with the support of the Swiss National Science Foundation
ISBN 978-3-031-04482-3 ISBN 978-3-031-04480-9 (eBook)
https://doi.org/10.1007/978-3-031-04480-9

© The Editor(s) (if applicable) and The Author(s), under exclusive licence to Springer Nature Switzerland AG 2023. This book is an open access publication.
Open Access This book is licensed under the terms of the Creative Commons Attribution 4.0 International License (http://creativecommons.org/licenses/by/4.0/), which permits use, sharing, adaptation, distribution and reproduction in any medium or format, as long as you give appropriate credit to the original author(s) and the source, provide a link to the Creative Commons licence and indicate if changes were made.
The images or other third party material in this book are included in the book's Creative Commons license, unless indicated otherwise in a credit line to the material. If material is not included in the book's Creative Commons licence and your intended use is not permitted by statutory regulation or exceeds the permitted use, you will need to obtain permission directly from the copyright holder.
The use of general descriptive names, registered names, trademarks, service marks, etc. in this publication does not imply, even in the absence of a specific statement, that such names are exempt from the relevant protective laws and regulations and therefore free for general use.
The publisher, the authors, and the editors are safe to assume that the advice and information in this book are believed to be true and accurate at the date of publication. Neither the publisher nor the authors or the editors give a warranty, expressed or implied, with respect to the material contained herein or for any errors or omissions that may have been made. The publisher remains neutral with regard to jurisdictional claims in published maps and institutional affiliations.

This Palgrave Macmillan imprint is published by the registered company Springer Nature Switzerland AG.
The registered company address is: Gewerbestrasse 11, 6330 Cham, Switzerland

Acknowledgements

The Politics of Children's Rights and Representation arises from a research project titled Children's Rights and Perceptions of Justice, Rights and Equality: The Challenge of Children's Representation. We are grateful to the British Academy for funding the program Tackling the UK's International Challenges of which this research project was a part. This research project would not have happened without the intellectual and organizational energies of Afua Twum-Danso Imoh who played a critical role in gathering together a group of research scholars from across the world to speak to this urgent issue. This group of scholars included Sarada Balagopalan, Karl Hanson, Jonathan Josefsson, Yaw Ofosu-Kusi, Didier Reynaert, Bengt Sandin, and Christopher Willman. This group shared initial versions of their chapters at a conference in Accra, Ghana, where we decided to expand the planned edited volume to include several other scholars whose research spoke to the various themes that emerged from our spirited and intense conversations both during and after conference hours. We thank Afua for her gracious hospitality and for sharing with us her love for Accra and the University of Ghana for hosting us. This conference and the coordination of meetings following this also owe a lot to the able efforts of Christopher Willman who served as a postdoctoral fellow on this grant and Edward van Daalen for his important role in helping organize the policy seminars. In addition, we are very grateful to all the contributors to this volume for their powerful contributions and willingness to work with the feedback they received from us. As fellow volume editors, we benefitted not only from our shared interests but also our different knowledges and perspectives. The volume is stronger as a result and the lively zoom calls made this project a pleasure to work on. We are also thankful for the insightful and supportive comments from the anonymous reviewers.

This book is published Open Access with the generous support of the Swiss National Science Foundation.

Contents

1 **Representing Children**   1
Jonathan Josefsson, Bengt Sandin, Karl Hanson, and Sarada Balagopalan

Part I   **Childhood Politics: From Rights and Participation to Representation**   29

2 **Recognizing Children's Rights: From Child Protection to Children's Human Rights—The 1979 Swedish Ban on Corporal Punishment in Perspective**   31
Bengt Sandin

3 **Adults in Charge: The Limits of Formal Child Participatory Processes for Societal Transformation**   59
Afua Twum-Danso Imoh

4 **Children's Participation in Their Right to Education: Learning from the Delhi High Court Cases, 1998–2001**   81
Sarada Balagopalan

5 **Representing the Child Before the Court**   105
Nataliya Tchermalykh

Part II Children's Representation and the International Politics of Children's Rights — 129

6 'Could It Be That They Do Not Want to Hear What We Have to Say?' Organised Working Children and the International Politics and Representations of Child Labour — 131
Edward van Daalen

7 "Children Without Childhood": Representations of the Child-Soldier as an International Emergency — 161
Jana Tabak

8 Children's Representation in the Transnational Mirror Maze — 181
Karl Hanson

Part III Children's Representation in Times of Inequalities and Injustices — 203

9 Deliberative Disobedience as a Strategy for Claiming Rights and Representation in the Family: The Case of Accra's Street Children — 205
Yaw Ofosu-Kusi

10 Combatting Child Poverty in the Childhood Moratorium: A Representational Lens on Children's Rights — 227
Didier Reynaert, Nicole Formesyn, Griet Roets, and Rudi Roose

11 Child Figurations in Youth Climate Justice Activism: The Visual Rhetoric of the Fridays for Future on Instagram — 251
Frida Buhre

12 Political Strategies of Self-representation: The Case of
    Young Afghan Migrants in Sweden   275
    Jonathan Josefsson

13 Political Representation of Aboriginal and Torres Strait
    Islander Youth in Australia   301
    Sana Nakata and Daniel Bray

Index   325

Notes on Contributors

Sarada Balagopalan is Associate Professor of Childhood Studies in the Department of Childhood Studies, Rutgers, The State University of New Jersey, Camden, USA. Her interdisciplinary research engages marginal children's experiences with compulsory schooling, labour, gendered school spaces, children's rights discourses and pedagogies of "citizenship". Broadly focused on postcolonial childhoods, her work is directed at both challenging the exclusionary logics that often underlie humanist efforts around marginal children, as well as productively drawing upon these children's lives to decentre hegemonic assumptions around childhood. Sarada's book *Inhabiting Childhood: Children, Work and Schooling in Postcolonial India* (Palgrave Macmillan, 2014) foregrounds the tension between children's work and schooling as a key site where discourses of colonial modernity, the "developmental" nation-state, late capitalism and current transnational efforts around children's rights play out. Sarada is an associate editor of the *SAGE Encyclopedia of Children and Childhood Studies (2020)* and serves as co-editor of the journal *Childhood*.

Daniel Bray is Senior Lecturer of International Relations in the School of Humanities and Social Sciences at La Trobe University, Melbourne, Australia. His research lies at the intersection of International Relations and Political Theory, focussing on pragmatist approaches to cosmopolitan politics, global governance and the theory and practice of representative democracy. His current research examines the representation of children and childhood in democratic politics. He is the author of two books, *Pragmatic Cosmopolitanism: Representation and Leadership in*

Transnational Democracy (Palgrave Macmillan, 2011) and *Global Democratic Theory* (with Steven Slaughter, 2015).

Frida Buhre is a researcher in rhetoric at the Department of Literature, Uppsala University, Sweden. She studies the political aesthetics of the youth climate justice movement, especially focusing on two areas: the mobilization of the Fridays for Future as well as youth and children as agents of change in the UN Climate Change Conferences. With a background in rhetoric and political philosophy, she has published on issues of political agency and power, temporality, pedagogy and knowledge regimes and Sami political mobilization. Her work has appeared in *Rhetoric Society Quarterly*, *Högre Utbildning*, in anthologies, as well as in *College Composition and Communication*.

Nicole Formesyn is policy officer at the Organisation for Community Development (SAAMO) East-Flanders. For more than 20 years, she worked with vulnerable people on their social rights. She was involved in projects on the right to housing, the right to education and child poverty.

Karl Hanson is Professor of Public Law and Director of the Centre for Children's Rights Studies at the University of Geneva in Switzerland. He obtained his doctorate in law in 2004 from Ghent University, Belgium, where he worked as a researcher at the Children's Rights Centre and as a senior researcher at the Human Rights Centre. His publications and main research interests are in the interdisciplinary field of children's rights studies and include theorizations on children's rights and childhood studies, child labour and working children, juvenile justice and the role of independent national children's rights institutions. He teaches at the University of Geneva in the *Master interdisciplinaire en droits de l'enfant* (MIDE). He is also the Programme Director of the *Master of Advanced Studies in Children's Rights* (MCR) and chair of the Steering Committee of the *Children's Rights European Academic Network* (CREAN). Karl Hanson is co-editor of the journal *Childhood*.

Jonathan Josefsson is Associate Professor in the Department of Thematic Studies—Child Studies at Linköping University, Sweden. His research focuses on young migrants' political activism, voting rights, age and democratization and the political representation of children and youth in global politics. Jonathan is the principal investigator for the research project: "Youth Representation in Global Politics: Climate, Migration and Health Governance Compared" (Riksbankens jubileeumsfond

2020–2023) and was a 2019 visiting fellow at the FXB Center for Health and Human Rights, Harvard University and the Department of Childhood Studies, Rutgers University. His most recent publications include "Empowered Inclusion: Theorizing Global Justice for Children and Youth" together with John Wall (Globalizations 2020), "Non-citizen Children and the Right to Stay: A Discourse Ethical Approach" (Ethics & Global Politics 2019) and "Age as a Yardstick for Political Citizenship: Voting Age and Eligibility Age in Sweden During the Twentieth Century" together with Bengt Sandin (2022).

Sana Nakata is Associate Professor of Political Science, co-director of the Indigenous-Settler Relations Collaboration and Associate Dean Indigenous in the Faculty of Arts at The University of Melbourne, Australia. She is a Torres Strait Islander woman, trained in law and political theory with research interests in the politics of childhood and, in particular, Indigenous childhood and its implications for democracy in contexts of ongoing colonization. She is the author of *Childhood Citizenship, Governance and Policy: The Politics of Becoming Adult* (2015) and co-editor of the book series *Indigenous Settler Relations in Australia and the World*.

Yaw Ofosu-Kusi is Professor of Social Studies with a PhD in Applied Social Studies from the University of Warwick, UK. He is currently the Dean of the School of Arts and Social Studies of the University of Energy and Natural Resources, Sunyani, Ghana. His research has primarily focused on the informal economy, children's mobility and street life as labour. His most recent works include: *The Challenge of African Potentials: Conviviality, Informality and Futurity*, Ofosu-Kusi, Y. & Motoji M. (eds.), Bamenda: Langaa RPCIG in association with Centre for African Area Studies, Kyoto University, Japan (2020); *Children, Childhood and the Future: Cross-Cultural Perspectives*, Kleeberg-Niepage, A., Ofosu-Kusi, Y., Rademacher, S. & Tressat, M. (eds.), Newcastle-upon-Tyne (2020). In 2017, he edited the volume, *Children's Agency and Development in African Societies*, Dakar: Council for the Development of Social Science Research in Africa (CODESRIA).

Didier Reynaert is Lecturer of Social Work and senior researcher at the EQUALITY//Research Collective of HOGENT University of Applied Sciences and Arts, School of Social Welfare. His expertise lies in the field of social work theory, social justice, human rights and children's rights.

Didier Reynaert is also Guest Lecturer of Social Work Theory at the HAN University of Applied Sciences (the Netherlands), Guest Professor of Ethics in Education at Ghent University and Guest Lecturer of Children's Rights at Odisee University of Applied Sciences

Griet Roets is Associate Professor of Social Work in the Department of Social Work and Social Pedagogy, Ghent University (Belgium). Her research interests include social work in relation to social inequalities of poverty, disability, gender, age and place/space, conceptualizations of citizenship and social rights, socio-spatial perspectives in social work and qualitative research methodologies.

Rudi Roose is Associate Professor of Social Work in the Department of Social Work and Social Pedagogy, Ghent University (Belgium). His research interest is focused on the development of socially just practices in the context of managerialism and the recognition of ambiguity on social work.

Bengt Sandin is Professor Emeritus in the Department of Thematic Studies—Child Studies at Linköping University, Sweden. Sandin's research has focused on children and childhood in a historical perspective, spanning the time from the early modern period to the late Swedish welfare state. His research—including studies of early modern education and state-building, child labour, nineteenth-century childhood, street children, educational media politics, welfare politics and welfare regimes—reflects an engagement in the social and cultural history of children and the construction of childhood. His current research deals with children's rights regimes in Sweden; voting restrictions and the political representation of children and youth in Sweden, 1900–2000; and the limit of state responsibility, redressing child abuse in out-of-home care. His recent publications include: *Schooling and State Formation in Early Modern Sweden*. Palgrave Macmillan 2020, "Child Rights Governance: An Introduction," with Anna Holzscheiter and Jonathan Josefsson, in *Childhood*, special issue: *Child Rights Governance*, ed. Holzscheiter, Josefsson, Sandin, 2019; "Historical Justice through Redress Schemes? The Practice of Interpreting the Law and Physical Child Abuse in Sweden," with Johanna Sköld and Johanna Schiratzki, in *Scandinavian Journal of History* 2018 and "Age as a Yardstick for Political Citizenship: Voting Age and Eligibility Age in Sweden During the Twentieth Century" together with Jonathan Josefsson (2022).

Jana Tabak is Assistant Professor in the Department of International Relations at the State University of Rio de Janeiro. She is the author of *The Child and the World: Child-Soldiers and the Claim for Progress* (2020). Her other publications include: a co-edited special issue of *Childhood: A Journal of Global Child Research*; a book entitled *Organizações Internacionais: História e Práticas*, 2nd edition, ed. with Monica Herz and Andrea Ribeiro Hoffmann (2015); and Modernity at Risk: Complex Emergencies, Humanitarianism, Sovereignty, with Carlos Frederico Pereira da Gama (2012). She is the author of articles in the journals *Contexto Internacional, Cultures et Conflits, Global Responsibility to Protect* and *The Hague Journal of Diplomacy*. She has taught in the areas of international organizations, peace and conflict studies and children and war.

Nataliya Tchermalykh is a postdoctoral teaching and research fellow in the Centre for Children's Rights Studies at the University of Geneva (Switzerland). She is a social anthropologist and holds a doctoral degree in sociology and anthropology from the Graduate Institute of International and Development Studies in Geneva. Her research interests encompass socio-legal studies, legal anthropology, visual anthropology and art. Her last research project, supported by the Swiss National Science Foundation, is called *Can a Child Sue a State? A socio-anthropological inquiry into prerequisites of children's access to international justice.*

Afua Twum-Danso Imoh is Senior Lecturer of Global Childhoods and Welfare at the University of Bristol. Drawing upon an interdisciplinary background, her research focuses on children's rights and social and cultural norms; parent-child relations and the implications for children's wellbeing and rights; the impact of historical developments and more recent social changes on constructions of childhood and child-rearing practices; and children's participatory rights with a focus on trying to move beyond voice. Much of this research has concentrated on Ghana and Nigeria and has received external funding from a number of sources. Specifically, out of the ten research and networking projects she has managed as principal investigator, eight have been funded by external bodies. Her work has been published in a number of edited collections as well as in peer-reviewed journals. She is also the lead co-editor of three edited collections: *Childhoods at the Intersection of the Global and the Local* (published by Palgrave Macmillan in October 2012), *Children's Lives in an Era of Children's Rights: The Progress of the Convention on the Rights of the Child in Africa* (December 2013) *Global Childhoods Beyond the North-South*

Divide (published by Palgrave Macmillan in 2018). She is currently an editor for the Palgrave Macmillan Study of Childhood and Youth Series and editorial board member for Third World Thematics and the Rutgers Series in Childhood Studies. Afua holds a BA (Hons) in History and Sociology (University of Manchester), an MSc in Development Studies (the London School of Economics and Political Science) and a PhD in African Studies (the University of Birmingham).

Edward van Daalen is a postdoctoral fellow in the Centre for Human Rights and Legal Pluralism (CHRLP) of the McGill University in Montreal, Canada, where he works on the intersections of international law and policy making, children's rights and social movements. He holds a PhD in international public law from the University of Geneva, Switzerland, for which he studied the role of organized working children in the development of international child labour law. He has published various innovative chapters and articles published in leading human rights journals, including the *International Journal of Human Rights* and the *International Journal of Children's Rights*. He is an organizing member of the Children and Work Network and founder of the Law and Cinema Club at the Sciences Po Law School in Paris.

CHAPTER 1

Representing Children

Jonathan Josefsson, Bengt Sandin, Karl Hanson, and Sarada Balagopalan

The Oscar winning documentary film *Born into Brothels*, written and directed by Zana Briski and Ross Kauffman, received critical public acclaim and was praised by many children's rights advocates at the time of its release in 2004. The film seductively weaves together a narrative of compassion together with showcasing the actions taken by Zana Briski, a New York-based photographer, to remove children of sex workers from Sonagachi, a red-light district in Kolkata, India, from their debilitating environments. Despite their alleged neglect by their sex worker mothers,

---

J. Josefsson (✉) • B. Sandin
Department of Thematic Studies—Child Studies, Linköping University, Linköping, Sweden
e-mail: jonathan.josefsson@liu.se; bengt.sandin@liu.se

K. Hanson
Centre for Children's Rights Studies, University of Geneva, Geneva, Switzerland
e-mail: Karl.Hanson@unige.ch

S. Balagopalan
Department of Childhood Studies, Rutgers, The State University of New Jersey, Camden, NJ, USA
e-mail: sarada.balagopalan@rutgers.edu

© The Author(s) 2023
B. Sandin et al. (eds.), *The Politics of Children's Rights and Representation*, Studies in Childhood and Youth,
https://doi.org/10.1007/978-3-031-04480-9_1

who are depicted as being both incompetent and indifferent to their offspring, the documentary does not represent children of sex workers as passive beings. Rather, Briski teaches them to use a camera and with this tool the children share their lives as active speaking subjects who, thanks to their own creativity and the lessons learned from Briski, make great photographs that document how they see their lives. Convinced of their potential, Briski takes the role of spokesperson for the children and explores possibilities of enrolling these children in a boarding school. Located at a safe distance from the red-light district of the city, this boarding school would help ensure that the children will not return easily to the brothels where their families live. A few years later, an alternative reading of the situation of children of sex workers from Sonagachi is presented in the 2011 documentary film *We are foot soldiers* (which is the English translation of 'Amra Padatik') directed by Debolina Dutta and Oishik Sircar who also published an article on their film in *Childhood* (Sircar & Dutta, 2011). Even if *Born into Brothels* portrays children as competent photographers, *We are foot soldiers* criticises the way the film represents children of sex workers primarily as helpless victims. The struggle over how these children get represented concerns how their portrayal in *Born into Brothels* relies upon the idea that a 'saviour from outside' is required to represent children's interests and ensure they get an education and thereby improve their future life chances. *We are foot soldiers* offers a counternarrative by representing children of sex workers as active agents rather than merely passive recipients of welfare interventions by others. Also, through sharing their daily practices of resilience and resistance, which they believe were not portrayed in *Born into Brothels*, they argue that the rights and interests of children of sex workers are better represented by an advocacy group run by children themselves. This advocacy group not only speaks and acts on behalf of themselves and other sex workers' children in Sonagachi to reduce the stigma that their mothers and they themselves face while enrolling in school, but they also work in solidarity with other children elsewhere in the world (Sircar & Dutta, 2011).

The struggle over the representation of children of sex workers denotes two central dictionary definitions of the word 'representation', namely, as 'a description or portrayal of someone or something in a particular way', and, as 'the action of speaking or acting on behalf of someone or the state of being so represented' (Oxford Languages, 2022). First, a key element of children's representation consists of how children as a group, or the child and childhood as a figure, is portrayed or described. Certain populations of children—like children of sex workers who live in a red-light district in a megacity in the Global South—often serve as iconic symbols of poverty with their descriptive, visual and portrayals reinforcing multiple stereotypes and attendant logics of compassion. As has been demonstrated by childhood scholars before, the aesthetic depictions and dominant discourses of children and childhood have throughout the history in various ways been deeply intertwined with major political, social, and cultural processes of change (Ariès, 1962; Balagopalan, 2014; Bessant, 2021, p. 1ff; Bernstein, 2011, James & Prout, 2015, p. 202; Hallett & Prout, 2003; Nakata & Bray, 2020; Sparrman, 2017; Higonnet, 1998; Rose, 2016; Hallberg & Sandin, 2021). The portrayals and depictions of children and childhood have in this way always been embedded in institutional and political practices to achieve political or organizational aims (Rose, 2016) and display how emotionally charged images of children can both mobilise popular support and reveal different and conflicting ways of representing children (Berents, 2020; Burman, 1994; Peacock, 2014). In the case of Briski's documentary, it demonstrates the ways that agential depictions of children also can be used to consolidate, rather than decenter, the victimization of children. Conversely, the portrayal of a group of actively engaged children such as the members of *Amra Padatik*, the collective of children of sex workers central in Sircar and Dutti's film, needs to take into account the social and economic conditions in the red-light district. Yet, the portrayal of children as subjects of rights does not erase their vulnerabilities.

Second, children's representation involves speaking or acting on behalf of children or children's state of being so represented and thus involves a performative act (Holzscheiter, 2016). Representation in its performative sense, that is, when people 'speak or act on behalf of' someone or something (Alcoff, 1991; Saward, 2010; Pitkin, 1967), can refer to formal and institutionalised structures as found in for example representative democracies (Urbinati, 2006) or international organisations (Holzscheiter, 2016), but can also be used in reference to family settings, NGOs and the realms of global politics and social media networks, to name a few (Disch et al., 2019; Saward, 2020). Children often rely on a person or a group of people who speaks on their behalf and who represents them, for instance, in legal or political affairs. Children's representatives can be influential (usually adult) individuals like Zana Briski but they can also be a group of children who represent other children, as in the case of the organization *Amra Padatik*. This aspect of representation is closely linked to children's rights and participation and to the shifting complexities and dynamics that mark the institutionalization and formalization of children's voices (James, 2007).

In addition, the two films' conflicting viewpoints of children and childhood also indicate the political dimension of children's representation. Put another way, representing children is not only linked to portrayals and performances, but also politics, where the act of speaking in and of children and childhood is both an act, and the result, of political struggle. Children's representation as portrayals and performances reflects existing formalized processes as well as long-term political changes and historical conflicts between different interests and ideologies (Berents, 2020; Holzscheiter, 2016; Peacock, 2014). Different actors struggle to claim the authority to define the portrayal of children as, for example, dependent or as autonomous subjects, or both, and use these for different political purposes with sometimes unintended consequences (Hallberg & Sandin, 2021). In the context of portraying children of sex workers, it is suggested that they should represent themselves rather than rely on a 'saviour from outside'. *We are foot soldiers* focuses on the political organization developed by children of sex workers. These children's efforts to politicize their struggle for dignity not only for themselves, but also for their mothers requires them to demand attention on distinctly different terms than those offered by the mainstream narrative of victimization. More generally, political conflicts, and for that matter, consensus building, around children and childhood illustrates how children recurrently play a constitutive role as temporary outsiders who present both risk and renewal to the demos (Nakata & Bray, 2020). Young people's involvement in social movements, mass mobilisation and extra-parliamentary action against inequalities and injustices have a long history and speaks to the importance of closer engagement with children's political representation for our understanding of politics as such (Bessant, 2021; Cummings, 2020; Dar & Wall, 2011; Hinton, 2021; Josefsson & Wall, 2020; Nakata, 2008; Wall, 2021). The struggles around securing more accurate or genuine representation of children and youth often entails organizing for self-representation to shift existing regimes of power. It further reveals the intimate interdependence between portrayals, performances, and politics in our understanding of children's representation.

THE CHALLENGE OF CHILDREN'S REPRESENTATION

The question of children's representation is particularly timely in today's world not only because of demographic shifts and the increase of the generation under 18 years of age but also because of the global challenges we face. Despite making up half of the world's population, children and youth have in many respects been denied the capacity to represent their interests, particularly on matters of political import. However, it is clear that young people in many contexts have been understood as either competent contributors to politics with a legitimate claim to represent themselves, or in other cases, have been regarded as posing a considerable risk to society and stability. Indeed, you would have to think very hard to come up with a political question that does not involve young people as central objects or agents of change. Whether it be young people organizing against the exploitative extraction of resources in indigenous areas in India (Gergan & Curley, 2021), Canada and the USA (Ibid), shaping the struggle for democracy as part of the Arab Spring (Honwana, 2019), unifying against climate change (de Moor et al., 2021) and migrant policies in Global North countries (Josefsson, 2017) and against gun violence, racism and policing regimes in the USA (Hinton, 2021), their increased participation in the political sphere has helped produce new, and emergent modes, of formal and informal representation within these global, national and local efforts.

However, these questions about children's representation, and in particular the politics involved, are not new. The debate on child labour, including how to depict or tell the story of working children as well as who is entitled to speak and act on their behalf, offers a telling example, from the late nineteenth century, of the close connection between portrayals, performances and politics of children's representation. In 1899, the newsboys of New York went on strike because the *Evening World* and *Evening Journal* had decided to lower the pay and the terms for the newspapers that the newsboys sold. The press at that time reported on the wage struggles but also illuminated the independent culture of this class of child workers and their vocal and prolific leadership in demanding their rights and fair pay. The voices of the children were, in these press stories, represented by children themselves (New York Times, July 25, 1899; New-York Tribune, July 21, 1899). At this same time, around the turn of the century, imageries of the street urchins became an important tool for the child saviours calling attention to the deplorable and degrading living conditions of street children and child labourers. Photos by Jacob Riis and later by Lewis Hines influenced legislation and reforms as well as nurtured the ambitions of generations of child saviours, professionals, philanthropists, non-governmental organisations and government agencies that spoke out and represented the interests of children in what Ellen Key described and hoped to be a century of the child (Riis, 1971; Dimock, 1993; Aronsson & Sandin, 1996; Platt, 2009). Whereas the newspapers depicted agentive young street vendors who could very well speak on behalf of themselves, iconic photographs of passive victims of child labour later offered visual justifications for well-meaning adult outsiders to act on behalf of children. Some hundred years later, at the end of the twentieth century, images of children as active citizens went hand in hand with the promotion of children's participation rights including in political matters. In 1996, in line with these changing childhood images, a group of Danish children aged 10–12 protested in front of a government commission against the implementation of an EU directive for newspaper delivery work that would outlaw child labour between 10–13 years of age. About 3200 children would lose their work. The delegates of the commission expressed their sympathy for the cause and agency of the children that wanted to work. However, different political arguments were deployed to limit children's representation as they declared that the Danish government was bound by a broader agreement with the EU that restricted their ability to meet the demands of the newspaper boys. The Danish parliament had no authority over the matter, they claimed, and could not politically represent the voices of these children given their international obligations (de Coninck-Smith et al., 1997, 7).

A well-known example from the Global South of contestations over the way how children should be represented is the leadership of young school children in protest marches against the South-African Apartheid regime during the 1976 Soweto uprising (See Twum-Danso Imoh, this volume). In this case, the South-African government at that time did not consider that the protesters had a legitimate political right to voice an opinion which questioned the regime's racist foundations. The protest was violently suppressed, and the participants were described as undisciplined troublemakers rather than as political activists. This view on the young activists radically changed once the Apartheid regime had ended and 16 June was declared a public holiday to commemorate the actions undertaken by the 'young heroes' during the 1976 Soweto uprising (Hanson & Molima, 2019). Since 1991, on the initiative of the Organisation of

African Unity (OAU), 16 June was proclaimed the Day of the African Child. Even though it commemorates the political courage of the school children who participated in the demonstrations held in 1976, it has been turned into a continent-wide advocacy event for the promotion of children's rights to education, rather than to recognise children's political representation.

Children's representation has, hence, developed into a site of contestation and power over who represents whom, what, when and where. The opposing viewpoints about representation that we have discussed above provide a point of departure to explore the linkage between children, representation, and politics, which is the focus of this book. The controversies around the representation of children actualise the political character of different means of representing children by different agents and institutions across multiple contexts and during various moments in time. Given the intimate entanglement between portrayals, performances, and politics in representing children, how do contemporary representations of children and childhood differ from, and build on, the past? What underlies the current political representational efforts of young people and what are their effects?

In this book, we offer an interdisciplinary analysis of the complexities, and affordances, that have marked, and continue to affect, children, childhood and representation as 'portrayals', 'performances' and 'politics'. It builds on the widespread recognition that traditional forms of democratic representation having excluded the participation of children (Bessant, 2021; Schrag, 1975; Wall, 2012, 2021), as well as acknowledges how depiction of children as right bearers and right subjects has influenced the political discourse about children. However, while new forms of representing children and their rights have certainly shaped new political avenues through which young people have been represented, these have also been deployed to control and govern the younger generation (Sandin, 2012; Holzscheiter et al., 2019; Wells, 2011). This tense interplay between young people who assert their political subjectivity, but who are simultaneously entangled in processes that seek to craft them into governable citizens reveals children's political representation less as a panacea and more as a fraught exercise. The book attempts to raise fundamental questions around earlier discursive constructions of young people's agentic actions by exploring children and childhood through the concept of representation.

This book claims that the lens of representation can bring new facets into our thinking that differ from the concept of children's rights and participation that have been dominant in childhood studies and other fields (Reynaert et al., 2009; Lundy, 2018; Tisdall, 2008). By treading on grounds well-travelled by scholars in Childhood Studies in its broadest sense including those within the disciplines of history, sociology, politics and children's geography we have assembled a set of different scholarly contributions to highlight the critical importance of representation to our understanding of children and childhood. Our interest in children's representation complements also a revitalized scholarly debate about the concept of political representation where theorists have been stretching out our concepts about when and how political representation take place (Brito Vieira, 2017; Disch et al., 2019; Saward, 2020; Urbinati, 2006). In these discussions, children as a category has been relatively absent in comparison with the interest in categories such as gender, ethnicity and class. As we argue, in times of societal and political transformations, these various forms of representing children have become central to offer visions and directions, as well as long-term legitimacy and sustainability. The representation of children and youth, however, does not only come with promises, renewals and hopes, but is also accompanied by risks, reproduction of existing injustices and instability. Given this, questions around who is representing young people and what claims are being made by these representatives become key.

In order to explore how the lens of children's representation might be used to enhance our understanding of children, youth and politics, we have collected a series of papers based on empirical and theoretical research in over seven countries. These chapters address a wide range of current social and political challenges where the representation of children and childhood has become sites of contestation that need further empirical and theoretical exploration. By collecting essays on several historical and contemporary subjects that affect children's lives, including migration, democracy, child labour, street children, poverty, welfare, education and child rights legislation, the volume engages with the very fundamental challenge of how to represent a group of people in democratic societies and global politics, and more specifically, how to represent children and young people.

The book is composed of thirteen chapters that are arranged in three sections. The chapters in the first section look back at the emergence of ideas around children's rights, participation and representation and studies how these concepts have been used, transformed and critiqued in various parts of the world. The chapters presented in the second section broadly trace the effects of the global circulation as well as limitations of children's rights discourses in international politics. Section three gathers chapters that are concerned with children's political representation in relation to structures, processes and experiences of inequalities and injustices.

CHILDHOOD POLITICS: FROM RIGHTS AND PARTICIPATION TO REPRESENTATION

Young people have over the last decades received significant attention in global politics. Mass mobilisation by children and youth in various parts of the world in recent years illustrate how young people are not only affected by political processes, but also actively shape these very dynamics (Bessant, 2021; Cummings, 2020; Josefsson & Wall, 2020). The engagement of, and for, children and youth in politics constitutes a continuum of longer and multifaceted historical processes where young people have claimed rights and also gained significant formal recognition as rights holders. In this sense the social, cultural, symbolic and political representations of young people during the twentieth century have made possible new systems of welfare and governance of rights for those under the age of majority (Holzscheiter et al., 2019; Nakata, 2015; Wells, 2011, 2021). Yet, as the contributions of this volume show, while this development clearly opened up new avenues for the protection of young people and their opportunities to participate in matters affecting them (see e.g. the chapters by Balagopalan, Josefsson, Sandin, Twum-Danso Imoh in this volume), the ways in which children and youth get represented have largely been shaped by the emergence of separate and exclusive domains for children and youth (Reyneart et al in this volume).

The adoption of the Convention on the Rights of the Child (hereafter: CRC) by the United Nations General Assembly in 1989 marked what commonly is referred to as a culmination of over 100 years of discourse on international children's rights (Stearns, 2017). The child rights movement has been led by charitable organisations and middle-class philanthropists and governments seeking to improve the conditions and welfare of children, initially in national and local contexts, and later, further afield with as part of a global outreach (Fass, 2011; Twum-Danso Imoh, 2012). The Convention represented a turning point in how children were perceived in international social policy by elevating children from 'objects of adult charity' to independent rights holders (Veerman, 1992; Twum-Danso Imoh & Ansell, 2014). Such discourses and policies developed in conjunction with a global history of colonial exploitation and expansion, two major world wars, the building of welfare states and rise of neo-liberal economies, the challenges of a post-colonial reconstitution of identities, societies and nations, both in the Global South and the Global North. Yet, the recognition of children as rights holders was also driven by fundamental regional, national and local transformations that developed distinctively before, and after, the breakthrough of the international discourse of children's rights in the latter part of the twentieth century (see Sandin and Twum-Danso Imoh in this volume). The development of welfare regimes of different characters including the growth of foreign aid, missions, philanthropies and management of distant domains to the liberation, control, and governance in the Global South are some examples of how the emergence of young people's rights, participation and representation are tied into specific historical and political processes (Balagopalan, 2019; Honwana, 2012; Kasanda, 2019; Marshall, 2004, 2013, 2014; Nehlin, 2009; Pickard & Bessant, 2018; Roberts, 2015, Twum-Danso Imoh & Okyere, 2020; Vallgårda, 2015).

Against this backdrop, we find good reasons to pay closer attention to how different historical trajectories have informed the growing responsibility of states to protect and represent children during the twentieth century. The role of the state to represent children and their rights evolved as a result of the interaction between social, legal and political spheres of public authority such as education, poor relief and social welfare, labour law, family law and criminal law. The emergence of childhood politics and the representation of children must be understood in relation to the role of parents and governments, as demonstrated in Bengt Sandin's chapter in this volume (Sandin, Chap. 2). Sandin shows how children's rights were redefined by Swedish legislators in different branches of government from the late nineteenth century and onwards, a redefinition that continued during the 1960s and 1970s with the prohibition of corporal punishment in the family in 1979. He argues that the adoption of the new legislation was a consequence of fundamental changes in the role of the Swedish state during this period in representing, protecting, and controlling children in institutions such as orphanages, reformatories, childcare and penal institutions under government responsibility as well as in schools and in the family. It was built on the concomitant establishment of a new type of relationship between children, the family and the state and on the advent of a multicultural society. In this sense, the chapter illustrates how state action to represent the voice and rights of others, in this case children, is always relational and intimately connected to the work of individuals, groups and various institutions. However, this means that different parts of the state apparatus or organisations outside the national state can act and have acted without coordination and with the aim of solving varying and sometimes conflicting political issues. It is this complex interaction between parental rights and responsibilities, children's autonomous rights and the responsibility of the state and government agencies that makes it necessary to examine representation as an important and transforming social phenomenon. Yet, the kind of national roots underpinning the issue of representing children and their rights in politics that Sandin describes certainly also ties into international relations, histories and orders of power.

The international diffusion of children's rights is an expression of the intricate interplay between political traditions of how to represent children by different modes of governance, legal traditions, gender relations and family roles. Children's rights and the representation of children must thus be understood as situated and as a resulting outcome of intermingling the notions of freedom, liberation and control of children innate in different forms of governance (Balagopalan, 2019; Fay, 2019; Hanson & Nieuwenhuys, 2013; Holzscheiter et al., 2019; Twum-Danso Imoh et al., 2019). A key component from the 1970s and onwards of the idea that children had fundamental human rights was expressed in the emphasis that children had the right to participate in matters that affect them. It was significant because earlier international children's rights discourses and programmes, it was argued, had mostly ignored children's voices or did not treat children's voices with sufficient deference, even in their efforts to ensure their welfare and well-being (Hallett & Prout, 2003; James, 2007; Lundy, 2018). The CRC aimed at responding to this deficit by not only including protection and provision rights within its contents, but by also providing for the participation rights of children. However, the limits of such participation rights become evident when we apply the lens of representation to the concept as Afua Twum-Danso Imoh does in her chapter in this volume (Chap. 3). Despite the vision behind the CRC and the excitement that the participation principle evoked around the world, it was, from the outset, limiting in its capacity for genuine transformational impact. This is primarily due to the fact that while the CRC foregrounds the importance of children's views and involvement in decision-making, it also ensures that adults remain in control in deciding the terms relating to who participates, how they participate, the topics on which they participate and ultimately, the outcome of participatory initiatives. Thus, in this way, the control of children's participation rights is firmly handed to the management of adults. As a result, what emerges within the CRC is a persisting understanding of children's rights as being a gift of adults which they then give to children—whether this gift is linked to children's care and protection rights or their participation rights. This limitation surely then raises questions about the extent to which the CRC, a treaty regarded as representing a landmark due to its perception of children as subjects—rather than objects—of rights, represents a genuine shift from earlier human rights laws and social policies which explicitly depicted children as objects of rights dependent on the charity of adults. In her chapter, Twum-Danso Imoh calls for the need to look outside this dominant child participation framework in search for examples of genuine forms of transformative child participation and representation. An example of the transformative impact of what may be considered non-CRC-framed children's participation is provided through an analysis of the role of children in the struggle to end apartheid in late twentieth century South Africa through actions for self-representation.

In the next chapter, Sarada Balagopalan explores the interrelationship between rights, participation and representation in the context of education in contemporary India. With several states in the majority world having passed legislation around free and compulsory education and millions of marginal children are now enrolled in schools, the question of how we frame children's participation in their right to education assumes considerable significance. By drawing together discussions around children's representations, participation and educational equity, Balagopalan critically opens up the particular dynamic that has helped produce educational equity as a continually deferable goal. In her chapter, she argues that the dominant representations of first-generation learners as economically marginal children are variously, as well as continually, leveraged to justify their presence within unequal and deeply segregated school spaces. To help problematize this narrative of assumed victimhood, she studies a set of court cases adjudicated in the Delhi High Court between 1997–2001 that foreground the state's role in perpetuating existing inequalities through highlighting the effects of these dominant constructions of the experiences of first-generation learners in school. By countering a simplistic narrative around these children's presence in schools as an adequate measure of their participation, these Delhi High Court cases help foreground the critical and structural role the state is required to assume to fulfil these children's equitable exercise of their right to education. Moreover, by highlighting their identity as learners, and not as marginal children who are recipients of state welfare services, these cases help expose how schooling for this population circulates as a critical compensatory technology that is no longer about guaranteeing educational equity.

In a related focus on courts and children's legal representation, though in a distinct geographical setting, namely Europe, Nataliya Tchermalykh's chapter focuses on the role of the courts and professional lawyers to critically engage with children's access to rights and justice. She notes how in the twenty-first century, despite the near-universal ascendance of children as independent actors and rights bearers, which have been reinforced by the CRC, children universally lack legal capacity to autonomously act upon these rights in a court of law. In this context, the indispensability of adult legal actors as conduits to children's access to justice is an undeniable reality. Through a set of court cases, Tchermalykh shows how the courtroom success of a case does not necessarily mean social justice for the aggrieved children; conversely, failure in the courtroom does not necessarily mean alienation and desperation. For children, legal experiences may play an emancipatory role, as it decentres and challenges the unidirectional model of the law (from state to citizen), delineating legal processes as merely top-down mechanisms for social control, that cannot be challenged from the bottom-up. An exercise in legal reasoning that challenges dominant discursive, epistemological, and political norms may, under certain conditions, lead to evidence that illuminate the potential reversibility of the processes of domination and exclusion, and demonstrate a more interactive approach to the law. Yet this should not be interpreted, according to Tchermalykh, as a statement that courts and litigation are the only, or even the central, means to achieve more justice for children. Rather, this chapter considers children's lack of legal standing as an important exclusionary factor, and therefore, frames children's representation by adequate legal professionals as one of the important dimensions of their access to justice. Furthermore, it considers legal professionals, representing children in both domestic and international arenas as active actors of the development and interpretation of children's rights.

Similar to the four chapters that constitute the bulk of this section of the book, several other chapters in the volume explore more closely the interrelationships between rights, participation and representation. The chapters discussed above are mainly based on local contexts and help demonstrate the intimate connection between rights, notions of child participation and forms of representation in specific historical processes. However, as we well know, these questions often intertwine with, and are seldom separable from, the global and transnational arena in which these discourses, policies and practices circulate, develop and in which the success of their national implementation get measured. The following section presents a set of chapters that focuses more distinctively on these processes of international politics of childhood and children's rights and discusses a few of its myriad effects on the portrayals, performances and politics of children's representation.

CHILDREN'S REPRESENTATION AND THE INTERNATIONAL POLITICS OF CHILDREN'S RIGHTS

In the 1960s and 1970s, a growing attention to children and youth as right subjects (Holt, 1974; Margolin, 1978; Schrag, 1975; Sandin's chapter in this volume) helped to drive the international diffusion of children's rights norms. This was followed by implementation of legislation, policies and institutions in the wake of the adoption of the CRC in 1989 (Holzscheiter, 2010; Holzscheiter et al., 2019). The international awareness of children as a distinct population of concern and the heightened attention devoted to their rights and interests at the time of the adoption of the Convention was certainly not new from a historical perspective. It can, instead, be traced back to the end of the nineteenth century and which later manifested in for instance the League of Nation's Child Welfare Committee in 1919 (Droux, 2016), the Geneva Declaration of 1924 and the UN Declaration on the Rights of the Child of 1959 (Fass, 2011; Moody, 2014). Yet, in the latter part of the twentieth century, a 'new' internationalism and international politics of children's rights emerged together with the institutionalization of political bodies with the purpose of representing specifically the rights of children and youth in national and international politics. When a new landscape of actors, sites and systems of child right governance emerged at the turn of the twenty-first century, this resulted in 'new defining features' of the linkage between the representative and the represented (Holzscheiter et al., 2019, See also Josefsson chapter in this volume). The political representation of young people evolved through a complex playing field involving professionals, NGOs, international organisations, corporations, a plurality of state agencies, families, and young people themselves; all of whom variously claimed to represent children and youth.

At the turn of the twenty-first century, a general opening up of global governance institutions to non-state actors (Tallberg et al., 2013) also had implications for the representation of children and childhood in international politics. With regard to children's rights, this paved the way for new actors who claimed to represent specific or larger populations of young people on a broad range of questions such as migration, environment, health, labour, peace and security and democracy. However, the international recognition of young people as actors and as rights holders became at the same time a productive tool for governance and the advancement of different political interests (Holzscheiter, 2016, Holzscheiter et al., 2019; Kwon, 2019; James, 2007, Josefsson, this volume; van Daalen, this volume). This resulted in challenges around how children and youth were depicted in international politics (Holzscheiter, 2010, Beier, 2020, See Tabak's chapter in this volume) and also produced contestations over who could claim the authority to represent the group of children and youth (Holzscheiter, 2016, see van Daalen this volume and Hanson this volume).

This latter point is developed in van Daalen's chapter that traces the struggle of working children's movements to have their views heard within more normative debates on child labour in the International Labour Organization (ILO). The persistence of these movements and the ILO's sustained non-representation, as well as misrepresentation, of their viewpoints highlights how the particular portrayal of child labour and the curated performance of a few adult and children's voices vehemently opposing child labour can stall, but does not necessarily erase, the efforts of more marginalized population of working children at gaining increased political representation. They ways in which young people seek to reframe the debate on child labour helps open up considerations around how changing the current normative framework that marks children's representations is critical especially if we seek to integrate the experiences of marginal children and youth across the world. Despite the success and the representational power that the campaigns of banning child labour 'in all its forms' have had in the shaping of the public imaginary, van Daalen argues that highly diverse and complex phenomena of child labour will certainly remain a controversial question in relation to children's representation in international politics for many years to come.

Normative framings of children and childhood that mark this global flow of ideas and images are explored in Jana Tabak's chapter which focuses on the ways legal and representational energies combine to produce an iconic image of the 'child soldier' as pathological. She challenges this normative framing by disclosing how apparently oppositional constructions of the child soldier as either innocent or monstrous share this 'discourse of the norm'. This representational logic of opposite extremes, as Tabak argues, operates to (re)produce child soldiers either as objects of exploitation or as objects of salvation with both representations producing them as targets of international intervention (or, protection) with no chance of autonomous decision-making.

Karl Hanson's chapter scales up this discussion by taking a critical stance towards organisations that claim to speak on behalf of children in transnational politics and global governance. In his chapter, he explores the close connection between international policymaking on children, childhood and children's rights, and how transnational campaigns and entities play a dominant role in shaping public discourse. By analysing two particular international campaigns, one about minimum age legislation for child soldiering, and a second about children and young people who have taken the lead to fight climate change via international legal procedures, he points to some of the current limits of representing children at the transnational level and thereby raises fundamental questions around who is speaking on behalf of children and where their representation is being performed.

All of the above chapters draw attention to the continued exclusions that mark the performance of representational power around children in international politics on their rights. In addition, they serve to foreground the reasons why a focus on representation and the international politics of children's rights may open up new thinking and avenues about how children and youth can assert their rights and be politically represented in international institutions in ways that go beyond the implementation of rights as individual entitlements. In the next section, we discuss in what way a move beyond a traditional liberal framework of individual rights can allow us to theorize children's political representation in the face of inequalities and injustices. The significance of this move reminds us of the need to continue to remain cautious about how political representation of young people may also risk reaffirming existing exclusions and orders of domination. How might we recognize young people's efforts to reframe and reimagine political representation while being careful about not reinforcing current geopolitical hierarchies that are based on normative assumptions around what constitutes 'ideal' political action?

Children's Representation in Times of Inequalities and Injustices

So far, we have discussed how children's representation can work as an analytical device to study the ways in which children and their rights have emerged historically and been shaped in close interrelationship with local, national and global contexts and processes. Yet, as we will point to in this section, children's representation also open up possibilities to scrutinize how children and youth gain recognition and access to schemes of justice, equality and rights through struggles, contestations and (re)claims of representation (Fraser, 2005; Saward, 2020; Josefsson & Wall, 2020). In times of inequalities and injustices, the chapters of this section suggest, the political representation of children and youth cannot be reduced to a matter of identifying and transmitting interests, rights or voices from a pre-constituted group as defined in international treaties, in domestic law or through policy processes. More than anything, children's representations become sites of contestation over portrayals and performances of children and childhood between various experiences, actors, spaces and temporalities associated with a considerable amount of social and political power (Disch et al., 2019; Holzscheiter, 2016; Saward, 2010, 2020). It is by exploring these sites of contestation that the studies in this last part of the book shed light on how children and youth claims of representation present both risk and renewal to social, legal and political orders (Nakata, 2008; Nakata & Bray, 2020).

The intimate interdependency and power dynamics between children and parents in times of inequalities is addressed by Yaw Ofosu-Kusi. In his chapter, he highlights how street children in Ghana deliberatively use disobedience as a strategy for claiming rights and representation in the family. A central trait in whatever form of childhood one experiences in Ghanaian societies and in many other African societies is the tradition of respect and obedience. The emphasis on such principles is that some adults are generally enabled to claim an almost religious authority over their children or other subordinates (Ikumola, 2017; Ofosu-Kusi, 2017). However, while the majority of children accept this authority in homes and schools, others are currently questioning its absoluteness by finding ways to constructively participate in decisions affecting them or assuming some degree of control over their lives. In the chapter, Ofosu-Kusi argues that some street children deliberately defy parents, disengage themselves from families, and assume proto-adult status as a way of claiming decision-making space in order to assert rights and self-representation in a context characterised by rapid urbanization, rising dysfunctionality in some homes and woeful economic conditions for increasing numbers of families.

In their chapter, Didier Reynaert, Nicole Formesyn, Griet Roets and Rudi Roose pick up the relationship between parents and children as an entry point to discuss children's representation and inequalities. In their study on child poverty in Belgium, they demonstrate how the creation of separate domains for children also effects the ways in which their claims for social justice are represented. In the chapter, which is grounded in Nancy Fraser's three domains of social justice, notably redistribution, recognition and representation, they discuss 'child poverty' in relation to children's rights. According to the authors, the childhood moratorium can be considered as a separate and exclusive domain for children with social provisions such as schools, youth work, youth care, etc. In this childhood moratorium, children are represented as the 'victims of poverty' and are thought of as the 'deserving poor'. In contrast, parents are represented as the 'undeserving poor', responsible for their own poverty situation and the poverty situation of their children. Based on in-depth interviews with 30 families living in poverty in Belgium, Reynaert et al argue that a segregated approach of the representation of children and parents in poverty can be considered as a problem of 'misrepresentation'. This injustice can have a negative impact on realising children's rights for children living in poverty due to the fact that such an approach narrows the social problem of poverty down to an educational problem.

The kind of misrepresentation that Reynaert et al depict in their chapter speaks to how children and young people's lives are constitutively marked by intersectional hierarchies including those of caste, class, gender, region and religion that affect their social, economic, cultural and political representation. The acknowledgment of the close and complex interdependence between children, parents and other groups in societies helps us to draw attention to the differences that frame young people's experiences and compels us to go beyond a more narrow liberal framework of rights. For example, the participation of children and youth in large-scale social movements in several countries of the Global South have produced intergenerational collectivities that give voice to their grievances and their distrust of the state (Baviskar & Sundar, 2008). These intergenerational articulations for social justice reflect a mode of organizing that exceeds a liberal exercise of 'individual rights' and alerts us a longer and more progressive history of people's political struggle and organizing (Escobar, 2018; Stephen, 1997). This volume's theorization of political representation works with the differences that mark young people's political organizing in different parts of the world, from experiences of today's democracies in the Global North to the longer history of civil disobedience movements within anticolonial struggles as discussed above through the example of the Soweto uprising.

Although this edited volume does not focus on these movements *per se* it works with the recognition that these movements to overturn imperial power often drew on non-liberal traditions to offer a future roadmap around democratic representation (see e.g. the chapter by Twum-Danso Imoh about the Soweto uprising). Several social movements organized by indigenous youth and other marginalized populations in the Global South are mostly anchored in this sense of interdependency and alternate understandings of selfhood. However, not all are non-violent, and our tendency to conflate young people's assertions around intergenerational interdependency with non-violence has steered discussions on youth political representation to exclude more violent intergenerational movements in the Global South in which youth play a major role.

In contrast, non-indigenous youth engaged in Climate Strikes and Friday for Future actions, as Frida Buhre's paper in this volume discusses, foreground environmental concerns through alerting their peers to a future plagued by the repercussions of rising temperatures. Buhre's paper focuses political aesthetic dimensions to children's representation in the global online participatory culture of Fridays for Future communities on Instagram. Interested in the forms of visual rhetoric employed by grassroot activists to gain visibility and the attendant forms of childhood political subjectivities these represent, her visual analysis highlights how their rhetoric emphasizes courage, the global reach of the movement and the competency of the strikers. She argues that this visual rhetoric and political aesthetics challenges passive and futurist figurations of children in climate discourse by emphasizing the present power of children and youth thereby inviting us to recognize the political subjectivity of these activists.

As Buhre's chapter clearly illustrates, to study both the changing portrayals and performances of children's representations consequently provide us with a critical analytical lens to understand how the figure of the child and young people's claims for justice border on other notions of how children and childhoods are defined and used by different actors in longer processes of social, cultural and political change (Ofosu-Kusi, this volume; Balagopalan, this volume), but also in times of crisis, emergency and radical ruptures (Josefsson, this volume; Buhre, this volume; Twum-Danso Imoh this volume). Further, it speaks both to the temporal and spatial dimensions of children's representation. The advocacy efforts of indigenous environmental protestors against the continued capitalist extraction of resources on their lands evoke their ancestral/spiritual connections to the land as well as a past history of sustainable practices. As the indigenous scholar Kyle Whyte (2017) shares in relation to postcolonial settler colonial contexts in the USA, Canada, Australia and New Zealand, indigenous people's exercise of self-determination against what he terms as 'industrial settler campaigns' reveals the need to historicize the recent focus on the Anthropocene as what these communities have encountered over several centuries. With settler colonial campaigns already having degraded, depleted and caused irreversible damage to ecosystems, plants and animals that, 'ancestors had local living relationships with for hundreds of years and that are the material anchors of our contemporary customs, stories, and ceremonies'" it is the past that gets foregrounded within the environmental campaigns led by indigenous youth. Like in childhood studies more generally, questions about children's representation must engage with children and childhood's past, present and future (Hanson, 2017).

Let us take another example of young people's struggle against injustices with global implications, migration. The global governance and restriction of migration, which has arisen as a top political priority over the past decades to protect the interests of nation states, has developed in tandem with the nearly universal ratification and global mainstreaming of universal human rights of children. The consequence, as Jonathan Josefsson suggests in his chapter, is that the portraying of young asylum seekers as particular vulnerable and in need of protection with reference to children's rights, has in public discourse and asylum processes turned into an efficient instrument for the state to legitimize restrictive border regimes and deportations. In the chapter Josefsson highlights the ways young Afghan migrants in Sweden make use of particular strategies of self-representation to contest state governance of migration in a struggle for their right to stay in the country. In dialogue with ongoing political theoretical debates around democracy and representation (Disch et al., 2019; Brito Vieira, 2017; Saward, 2020), Josefsson show how these young political actors reject and recast the ways in which they are politically represented by others to claim political space and a voice of their own.

Many of the chapters in this volume consider the historical dimension of children and childhood as key to our understanding of children's representation today. But as Buhre, Josefsson, and also Sana Nakata and Daniel Bray show in their respective chapters, future dimensions of time appear to be just as central to grasp children's representation. In their chapter, Nakata and Bray explore the opportunities of political representation of First Nation youth by connecting historical and contemporary injustices faced by Aboriginal and Torres Strait Islander children in Australia. The cases of First Nation youth in Australia are used to illustrate how children play a constitutive role as temporary outsiders who present both risk and renewal to the demos. The first case focuses on the Northern Territory Don Dale Youth Detention Centre that became a site of political controversy in 2016 for its mistreatment of youth detainees. The second case explores a 2020 campaign by the conservative Liberal National Party in a recent Queensland state election to implement a youth curfew in Townsville, a city with a high number of Aboriginal and Torres Strait Islander residents. As evidenced by these debates, about youth crime and incarceration, Nakata and Bray argue that Aboriginal and Torres Strait Islander children are often represented as a source of risk which lies in tension with the potential of representing indigenous children as sources of renewal. These cases reveal the representative terrain in which Aboriginal and Torres Strait Islander young people must resist and speak back to a white national imaginary that works to limit the possible futures that Aboriginal and Torres Strait Islander peoples imagine for themselves.

Conclusion

A central endeavour of this book is to engage in a discussion about how representation as an analytical prism can deepen conversations in childhood studies and neighbouring fields about children, rights and politics. As legal, social, and political traditions have evolved in different parts of the world, these have configured multiple representations of children and childhood. Sometimes these representations have converged into coherent modes of portraying children and speaking on behalf of children. Other times, the portrayals and performances of children and childhoods have evolved into more conflicting or ambiguous understandings of their representation, not least in contexts where young people have advanced claims to represent themselves.

Our interest in children's representation, as argued in this book, complements ongoing theoretical and empirical work in childhood studies and related fields and ties into broader revitalised scholarly debates in political theory about how, where and when political representation takes place. Such a turn, we hope, can help us to bridge scholarly divides and challenge limiting notions of children's representations. From the perspective of politics, which obviously constitutes a red thread throughout this book, we seek to critically engage with how the political representation of children and youth through parliamentary politics, legislation, child ombudspersons, administrative procedures, welfare systems and implementation strategies of children's rights mobilise policy agendas and schemes of governance. The different contributions pursue to offer new concepts, sites, routes, actors and networks of children's representation across various parts of the world and put these into conversation with each other.

The chapters presented are thus mindful of young people's uneven access to citizenship as well as to the need to open up our framing of contemporary youth political representations to a longer history of youth action and organizing and its ethico-political affordances. In recognizing the transformative possibilities of children's political representation, this volume offers in addition a critical reading of child rights regimes and the ways in which democracies are organized to disclose exclusionary, racialized and colonial pasts of international and national politics. Several chapters push back against the dominant representational politics of marginalized childhoods in the Global South. Their efforts to read the epistemological weight of a normative childhood against the grain is what constitutively frames this volume's overall approach. While we acknowledge the opportunities of young people's struggles to gain recognition through new modes of political representation, we treat political representation as an uneven and contingent terrain where the continued risk of reaffirming existing intersectional hierarchies, that for long have marked children's participation, is still very much alive.

The portrayals and depictions of children and childhood have always been embedded in institutional practices to achieve political aims. We can provide required analytic space only by our efforts to disaggregate, historicize and contextualize children and childhood. In that vein, we hope that the contributions in this volume will stimulate further explorations and scholarly interchange about the politics of children's rights and representation.

References

Alcoff, L. (1991). The Problem of Speaking for Others. *Cultural Critique, 20*, 5–32.
Ariès, P. (1962). *Centuries of Childhood: A Social History of Family Life.* Vintage.
Aronsson, K., & Sandin, B. (1996). The Sun Match Boy and Plant Metaphors: A Swedish Image of a 20th Century Childhood. In P. Hwang, M. E. Lamb, & I. E. Sigel (Eds.), *Images of Childhood* (pp. 185–194). Lawrence Erlbaum Associates.
Balagopalan, S. (2014). *Inhabiting Childhood: Children, Labour and Schooling in Post-colonial India.* Macmillan.
Balagopalan, S. (2019). Why Historicize Rights-Subjectivities? Children's Rights, Compulsory Schooling, and the Deregulation of Child Labor in India. *Childhood, 26*(3), 304–320.
Baviskar, A., & Sundar, N. (2008). Democracy Versus Economic Transformation? *Economic and Political Weekly*, November 15, 87–89.
Beier, J. (Ed.). (2020). *Discovering Childhood in International Relations.* Palgrave Macmillan.
Berents, H. (2020). Depicting Childhood: A Critical Framework for Engaging Images of Children in IR. In J. Beier (Ed.), *Discovering Childhood in International Relations.* Palgrave Macmillan.
Bernstein, R. (2011). *Racial Innocence: Performing American Childhood from Slavery to Civil Rights.* New York: New York University Press.
Bessant, J. (2021). *Making-up People: Youth, Truth and Politics.* Routledge.
Bourdillon, M. (2006). Children and Work: A Review of Current Literature and Debates. *Development and Change, 37*(6), 1201–1226.
Brito Vieira, M. (Ed.). (2017). *Reclaiming Representation: Contemporary Advances in the Theory of Political Representation.* Routledge.
Burman, E. (1994). Innocents Abroad: Western Fantasies of Childhood and the Iconography of Emergencies. *Disasters, 18*(3), 238–253.
Cummings, M. (2020). *Children's Voices in Politics.* Peter Lang.
Dar, A., & Wall, J. (2011). Children's Political Representation: The Right to Make a Difference. *The International Journal of Children's Rights, 19*(4), 595–612.
de Coninck-Smith, N., Sandin, B., & Schrumpf, E. (Eds.). (1997). *Industrious Children: Work and Childhood in the Nordic Countries 1850–1990.* Odense University Press.
de Moor, J., De Vydt, M., Uba, K., & Wahlström, M. (2021). New Kids on the Block: Taking Stock of the Recent Cycle of Climate Activism. *Social Movement Studies, 20*(5), 619–625.
Dimock, G. (1993). Children of the Mills: Re-Reading Lewis Hine's Child-Labour Photographs. *Oxford Art Journal, 16*(2), 37–54.
Disch, L., van de Sande, M., & Urbinati, N. (Eds.). (2019). *The Constructive Turn in Political Representation.* Edinburgh University Press.

Droux, J. (2016). A league of its own? The league of nations' child welfare committee (1919–1936) and international monitoring of child welfare policies. *The League of Nations' Work on Social Issues*, 89–103. United Nations.

Escobar, A. (2018). *The Making of Social Movements in Latin America: Identity, Strategy, and Democracy*. Routledge.

Fass, P. S. (2011). A Historical Context for the United Nations Convention on the Rights of the Child. *The Annals of the American Academy of Political and Social Science, 633*(1), 17–29.

Fay, F. (2019). Decolonizing the Child Protection Apparatus: Revisiting Child Rights Governance in Zanzibar. *Childhood, 26*(3), 321–336.

Fraser, N. (2005). Reframing Global Justice. *New Left Review, 36*, 69.

Gergan, M., & Curley, A. (2021). Indigenous Youth and Decolonial Futures. *Antipode*. https://doi.org/10.1111/anti.12763

Hallberg, M., & Sandin, B. (2021). Pictured Political Projects: Sunshine Over a Welfare State in the Shadow of War. *Journal of the History of Childhood and Youth, 14*(1), 85–112.

Hallett, C., & Prout, A. (Eds.). (2003). *Hearing the Voices of Children: Social Policy for a New Century*. Routledge.

Hanson, K. (2017). Embracing the Past: 'Been', 'Being' and 'Becoming' Children. *Childhood, 24*(3), 281–285.

Hanson, K., & Molima, C. (2019). Getting Tambo Out of Limbo: Exploring Alternative Legal Frameworks that Are More Sensitive to the Agency of Children and Young People in Armed Conflict. In M. A. Drumbl & J. C. Barrett (Eds.), *Research Handbook on Child Soldiers* (pp. 110–131). Edward Elgar.

Hanson, K., & Nieuwenhuys, O. (2013). *Reconceptualizing Children's Rights in International Development: Living Rights, Social Justice, Translations*. Cambridge University Press.

Higonnet, A. (1998). *Pictures of Innocence: The History and Crisis of Ideal Childhood*. Thames & Hudson.

Hinton, E. (2021). *America on Fire: The Untold History of Police Violence and Black Rebellion Since the 1960s*. William Collins.

Holland, P. (2004). *Picturing Childhood: The Myth of the Child in Popular Imagery*. I. B. Tauris.

Holt, J. (1974). *Escape from Childhood: The Needs and Rights of Children*. E. P. Dutton.

Holzscheiter, A. (2010). *Children's Rights in International Politics: The Transformative Power of Discourse*. Palgrave Macmillan.

Holzscheiter, A. (2016). Representation as Power and Performative Practice: Global Civil Society Advocacy for Working Children. *Review of International Studies, 422*, 205–226.

Holzscheiter, A., Josefsson, J., & Sandin, B. (2019). Child Rights Governance: An Introduction. *Childhood, 25*(3), 271–288.

Honwana, A. M. (2012). *The Time of Youth: Work, Social Change, and Politics in Africa*. Kumarian Press.

Honwana, M. (2019). Youth Struggles: From the Arab Spring to Black Lives Matter and Beyond. *African Studies Review, 62*(1), 8–21.

Ikumola, A. D. (2017). Child Fosterage Dynamics in Selected Markets in Lagos State, Nigeria. In *Children's Agency and Development in African Societies*. Council for the Development of Social Science Research in Africa. Dakar.

James, A. (2007). Giving Voice to Children's Voices: Practices and Problems, Pitfalls and Potentials. *American Anthropologist, 109*(2), 261–272.

James, A., & Prout, A. (2015). *Constructing and Reconstructing Childhood: Contemporary Issues in the Sociological Study of Childhood* (3rd Rev. and Updated ed.). Falmer.

Josefsson, J. (2017). 'We beg you, let them stay!': Right Claims of Asylum-Seeking Children as a Socio-Political Practice. *Childhood, 24*(3), 316–332.

Josefsson, J., & Wall, J. (2020). Empowered Inclusion: Theorizing Global Justice for Children and Youth. *Globalizations, 17*(6), 1043–1060.

Kallio, K. P., & Häkli, J. (2011). Are There Politics in Childhood? *Space and Polity, 15*(1), 21–34.

Kasanda, A. (2019). The African Youth Civic Movements and the Struggle for Peace: The Case of Balai Citoyen and Filimbi. *Critical Sociology, 45*(6), 859–870.

Kwon, S. A. (2019). The Politics of Global Youth Participation. *Journal of Youth Studies, 22*(7), 926–940.

Lundy, L. (2018). In Defence of Tokenism? Implementing Children's Right to Participate in Collective Decision-Making. *Childhood, 25*(3), 340–354.

Margolin, C. R. (1978). Salvation Versus Liberation: The Movement for Children's Rights in a Historical Context. *Social Problems, 25*(4), 441–452.

Marshall, D. (2004). Children Rights in Imperial Political Cultures: Missionary and Humanitarian Contributions to the Conference on the African Child of 1931. *The International Journal of Childrens Rights, 12*, 273–318.

Marshall, D. (2013). Children's Rights from Below: Canadian and Transnational Actions, Beliefs, and Discourses, 1900–1989. In D. Goutor & S. Heathorn (Eds.), *Taking Liberties. A History of Human Rights in Canada* (pp. 189–212). Oxford University Press.

Marshall, D. (2014). The Rise of Coordinated Action for Children in War and Peace: Experts at the League of Nations, 1924–1945. In D. Rodogno, B. Struck, & J. Vogel (Eds.), *Shaping the Transnational Sphere. Transnational Networks of Experts and Organizations*. Berghahn Books.

Moody, Z. (2014). Transnational Treaties on Children's Rights: Norm Building and Circulation in the Twentieth Century. *Paedagogica Historica, 50*(1–2), 151–164.

Nakata, S. (2008). Elizabeth Eckford's Appearance at Little Rock: The Possibility of Children's Political Agency. *Politics, 28*(1), 19–25.

Nakata, S. (2015). *Childhood Citizenship, Governance and Policy: The Politics of Becoming Adult*. Routledge.
Nakata, S., & Bray, D. (2020). The Figure of the Child in Democratic Politics. *Contemporary Political Theory, 19*(1), 20–37.
Nehlin, A. (2009). *Exporting Visions and Saving Children: The Swedish Save the Children Fund*. Diss., Linköpings universitet, Linköping.
Ofosu-Kusi, Y. (eds). (2017). *Children's Agency and Development in African Societies*. Council for the Development of Social Science Research in Africa. Dakar.
Oxford Languages. (2022). *English Dictionary*. Oxford University Press.
Peacock, M. (2014). *Innocent Weapons: The Soviet and American Politics of Childhood in the Cold War*. The University of North Carolina Press.
Pickard, S., & Bessant, J. (Eds.). (2018). *Young People Re-Generating Politics in Times of Crises*. Palgrave.
Pitkin, H. (1967). *The Concept of Political Representation*. University of California.
Platt, A. M. (2009). *The Child Savers: The Invention of Delinquency* (Expanded 40th anniversary ed.). Rutgers University Press.
Quennerstedt, A. (2013). Children's Rights Research Moving into the Future—Challenges on the Way Forward. *International Journal of Children's Rights, 21*(2), 233–247.
Reynaert, D., Bouverne-de-Bie, M., & Vandevelde, S. (2009). A Review of Children's Rights Literature Since the Adoption of the United Nations Convention on the Rights of the Child. *Childhood, 16*(4), 518–534.
Riis, J. A. (1971). *How the Other Half Lives: Studies Among the Tenements of New York: With 100 Photographs from the Jacob A. Riis Collection*. Dover.
Roberts, K. (2015). Youth Mobilisations and Political Generations: Young Activists in Political Change Movements During and Since the Twentieth Century. *Journal of Youth Studies, 18*(8), 950–966.
Rose, G. (2016). *Visual Methodologies: An Introduction to Researching with Visual Materials* (4th ed.). Sage.
Sandin, B. (2012). Children and the Swedish Welfare State: From Different to Similar. In P. Fass & M. Grossberg (Eds.), *Reinventing Childhood After World War II*. University of Pennsylvania Press.
Saward, M. (2010). *The Representative Claim*. Oxford University Press.
Saward, M. (2020). *Making Representations: Claim, Counterclaim and the Politics of Acting for Others*. Rowman and Littlefield.
Schrag, F. (1975). The Child's Status in the Democratic State. *Political Theory, 3*(4), 441–457.
Sircar, O., & Dutta, D. (2011). Beyond Compassion: Children of Sex Workers in Kolkata's Sonagachi. *Childhood, 18*(3), 333–349.
Sparrman, A. (2017). Visual Representations of Childhood. In M. Heather (Ed.), *Oxford Bibliographies of Childhood Studies*. Oxford.

Stammers, N. (2012). Children's Rights and Social Movements: Reflections from a Cognate Field. In K. Hanson & O. Nieuwenhuys (Eds.), *Reconceptualizing Children's Rights in International Development: Living Rights, Social Justice, Translations* (pp. 275–292). Cambridge University Press.

Stearns, P. (2017). History of Children's Rights. In W. Vandenhole, E. Desmet, D. Reynaert, & S. Lembrechts (Eds.), *Routledge International Handbook of Children's Rights Studies*. Routledge.

Stephen, L. (1997). *Women and Social Movements in Latin America: Power from Below*. University of Texas Press.

Tallberg, J. S., Squatrito, T., & Jönsson, C. (2013). *The Opening Up of International Organizations: Transnational Access in Global Governance*. Cambridge University Press.

Tisdall, K. M. (2008). Is the Honeymoon Over? Children and Young Peoples' Participation in Public Decision-Making. *The International Journal of Children's Rights, 16*(3), 419–429.

Tremmel, J. C. (2006). *Handbook of Intergenerational Justice*. Edward Elgar Publishing.

Twum-Danso Imoh, A. (2012). The Convention on the Rights of the Child: A Product and Facilitator of a Global Childhood. In A. Twum-Danso Imoh & R. K. Ame (Eds.), *Childhoods at the Intersection of the Local and the Global* (pp. 17–33). Palgrave Macmillan.

Twum-Danso Imoh, A., & Ansell, N. (2014). Realizing Children's Rights in Africa: An Introduction. In *Children's Lives in an Era of Children's Rights* (pp. 19–34). Routledge.

Twum-Danso Imoh, A., & Okyere, S. (2020). Towards a More Holistic Understanding of Child Participation: Foregrounding the Experiences of Children in Ghana and Nigeria. *Children and Youth Services Review, 112*, 104927.

Urbinati, N. (2006). *Representative Democracy: Principles and Genealogy*. University of Chicago Press.

Vallgårda, K. (2015). *Imperial Childhoods and Christian Mission: Education and Emotions in South India and Denmark*. Palgrave.

Vandenhole, W., Desmet, E., Reynaert, D., & Lembrechts, S. (Eds.). (2017 [2015]). *Routledge International Handbook of Children's Rights Studies*. Routledge.

Veerman, P. E. (1992). *The Rights of the Child and the Changing Image of Childhood*. Martinus Nijhoff Publishers.

Wall, J. (2019). From Childhood Studies to Childism: Reconstructing the Scholarly and Social Imaginations. *Children's Geographies*. https://doi.org/10.1080/14733285.2019.1668912

Wall, J. (2021). *Give Children the Right to Vote: On Democratizing Democracy*. Bloomsbury Academic.

Wells, K. (2011). The Politics of Life: Governing Childhood. *Global Studies of Childhood, 1*(1), 15–25.

Wells, K. (2021). *Childhood in a Global Perspective*. Polity.
Whyte, K. (2017). Indigenous climate change studies: Indigenizing futures, decolonizing the Anthropocene. *English Language Notes, 55*(1), 153–162.
Wall, J. (2012). Can Democracy Represent Children? Toward a Politics of Difference. *Childhood, 19*(1), 86–100.

Newspapers

Newsboys Act and Talk. (1899, Jul 25). *New York Times* (1857–1922), p. 3.
Newsboys Go on Strike. (1899, Jul 21). *New-York Tribune* (1866–1899), p. 10.
ww.nypl.org/blog/2012/05/25/extra-extra-read-all-about-newsboys-strike-1899?fbclid=IwAR1pGYmbbYG1Xvl_ByB-MYzw5V_70TltpY2EPJrnSC-sS0sMvI2iTUU9RJM

Open Access This chapter is licensed under the terms of the Creative Commons Attribution 4.0 International License (http://creativecommons.org/licenses/by/4.0/), which permits use, sharing, adaptation, distribution and reproduction in any medium or format, as long as you give appropriate credit to the original author(s) and the source, provide a link to the Creative Commons licence and indicate if changes were made.

The images or other third party material in this chapter are included in the chapter's Creative Commons licence, unless indicated otherwise in a credit line to the material. If material is not included in the chapter's Creative Commons licence and your intended use is not permitted by statutory regulation or exceeds the permitted use, you will need to obtain permission directly from the copyright holder.

PART I

Childhood Politics: From Rights and Participation to Representation

CHAPTER 2

Recognizing Children's Rights: From Child Protection to Children's Human Rights—The 1979 Swedish Ban on Corporal Punishment in Perspective

Bengt Sandin

Introduction

Sweden, together with the other Nordic countries, stands out as a land where the protection of children and children's rights has been significant both in developing the welfare state and in building a national identity (Holzscheiter, 2010; Lindkvist, 2018). It was the first country in the world, in 1979, to forbid parents to use corporal punishment on their children. The prohibition of physical punishment of children in families in 1979 is an important symbol of a larger commitment to children's rights in welfare societies during the late twentieth century. The history of this matter also reflects power relations and the governance of society in

---

B. Sandin (✉)
Department of Thematic Studies—Child Studies, Linköping University, Linköping, Sweden
e-mail: bengt.sandin@liu.se

© The Author(s) 2023
B. Sandin et al. (eds.), *The Politics of Children's Rights and Representation*, Studies in Childhood and Youth,
https://doi.org/10.1007/978-3-031-04480-9_2

conjunction with the formation of the welfare state (Holzscheiter et al., 2019). There is therefore good reason to consider more closely when and how this view of the responsibility of the state to protect children against abuse was established. These are questions with many historical, political, and legal dimensions. They relate to how definitions of children's rights evolved in the interaction between different spheres of public authority in the expanding welfare state. They also concern the right of the state and its representatives to use violence in the form of corporal punishment against children and young people.

This chapter takes as a methodological starting point that the definition of improper care and of children's rights is not something that *exists* but something that *is done* in political and social processes, in order to solve specific social and political problems (Bacchi, 2009). The analysis here will be based on the fact that corporal punishment and abusive treatment of children were brought to the fore by developments in the school system from the start of the twentieth century, in connection with the emergence of public child welfare and family law from the 1920s to the 1960s, and in relation to criminal law. This meant that these themes were recurrent throughout the twentieth century but in different spheres of politics and with different perspectives in different periods. In methodological terms, this means that I relate different definitions in legislation and parliamentary debates to each other in order to identify key changes in meaning and how a change in one area affected another. As a basis for the analysis, I have used laws and statutes, regulations and legislative history in family and criminal law, as well as school law and social law including the earlier poor relief. This means that this survey relates the analysis of corporal punishment of children in the family to the changes that took place in several different areas of legislation.

An explicit ban on parents' corporal punishment of their children in the home did not come until 1979 when Sweden banned corporal punishment in the Parental Code as a result of a process lasting more than a hundred years. During this period, the right of adults to beat their children and the right of children to be protected from corporal punishment and other abusive treatment had been renegotiated time and time again (Bahr, 2019; Sandin, 2018). By following the legislation on corporal punishment, one can obtain a picture of the change in children's rights in relation to the outlook on children, family, and the state in Sweden.

The overarching questions for this chapter are: What social and institutional changes drove these political processes? How was the role of the state in representing and protecting children redefined? And how did the resolution to limit and finally abolish the right of parents to discipline children physically influence the definitions of the nature of children's rights and the representation of children? My analysis of the advent of a legal ban on corporal punishment in Sweden demonstrates how the evolution of children's rights discourses has been impacted by being a developed welfare society with a large offer of institutional childcare arrangements outside the family. In addition, immigration policies and the ambition to influence supposedly violent or backward child-rearing practices amongst the immigrant population played an important role when the corporal punishment ban was passed in 1979. The ban hence appears partly as a reaction to the transformation of a relatively homogeneous society to a multicultural society and an increased sensitivity about the quality of family caring for smaller children. What can these shifting conceptions of children's rights teach us about children's representation as autonomous individuals rather than as family members or part of collectives of children in institutions?

To address these questions, I will examine in the first section how the age limits for who could suffer corporal punishment, and who could punish whom, were shifted during the first part of the period, from 1900 to 1930. In the following sections, I trace the changes in how the state's role in the protection and representation of children was redefined and lead to a clearer position on the meaning of children's rights.

Corporal Punishment and Abusive Treatment: Age, Class, and Gender—Regulations and Norms 1900–1930

The dramatic transformation of society in the late nineteenth century had a profound impact on the conditions in which children were brought up. This was the case with the schooling and education of both girls and boys in the upper and middle classes, and the elementary school that existed for the majority of the population. However, it was not only a matter of the organization and content of education for the younger generation. The conditions in which urban children grew up attracted critical attention among the ruling social classes and authorities, who doubted the ability of working-class families to care for their children and were concerned about what they perceived as increasing juvenile delinquency. Children and young people were at the centre of a broad discussion of how children could be rescued from deplorable conditions (Lundström, 1993; Sundkvist, 1994; Weiner, 1995).

It was a broad international phenomenon which had a global impact, but in different ways depending on the social structure and historical experiences. In Sweden, Ellen Key has become a symbol of this commitment, and its foundation in various philanthropic movements and government initiatives (Platt & Chávez-García, 2009; Sandin, 2017). There was also a counterpart in the increasing interest in studying children. The child studies movement drew attention to diverse aspects of children's upbringing and development. Sciences such as pedagogy and psychology began to shape their epistemological traditions concerning matters of normality, parent-child relations, and juvenile delinquency (Hall, 1904, 1911; Donzelot, 1980; Turmel, 2008).

It was also in the years after 1900 that states in Western Europe began to introduce various forms of legislation to improve children's social conditions. This included not only education and health care, but also poor relief, foster care, adoption, and other issues. Other legislation sought in various ways to improve the conditions in which children grew up, for example, by separating children from families, while legislation on foster care and adoption was a way for the state to create families on new legal grounds (Lindgren, 2006; Fass, 2013; Sköld et al., 2014).

The legislative process delimited and defined parenthood and the role of men and women, but also, to a large extent, children's rights. A characteristic of this period was that it witnessed a clarification in some sense of what can be considered children's social rights against the background of a definition of their needs and view of the family as an institution.

During this process, ideas were shaped on the role of the state in relation to the family, to school, and to institutions of other types. It is clear that institutions intended to support children also involved the control of children and parents alike. The normative regulation of the meanings of childhood under the responsibility of the state included demands on families. This applied to the laws on child welfare as well as to other laws on adoption and foster children, reformatory institutions, etc. Children's rights also entailed standards for the exercise of parenthood (Gordon, 2002; Sundkvist, 1994; Lundström, 1993). At the same time, this protection of children meant that they were given special rights as children to for example an amount of education and a family. Such rights came with obligations or normative regulation of families.

This illustrates the relational meanings of children's rights, which is an import facet of this chapter, and also the consequences of systems designed to control the population. Rights are the basis of the system of governance. This also means that children's rights can conflict with parental rights and family autonomy and have implications for how the government controls the family (Holzscheiter et al., 2019; Sandin, 2012, 2018). The right to bring up children, including the use of corporal punishment, was fundamentally perceived to belong to the family—the parents. When children went to school or were taken into institutional care for one reason or another, these authorities also acquired a share of this parental right. The right of parents to punish their children physically was so much taken for granted in the late nineteenth century that it was not regulated in penal law. The right to corporal punishment could also be transferred to others, voluntarily or forcibly, through what was known as "derivative parental rights" (Alfredsson, 2014; Larsson, 2018; Schiratzki, 2019).

At the same time, this raised questions about how these "derivative parental rights" should be exercised and by whom. This question was at the heart of discussions during and after the turn of the century 1900, and led to restrictions on who could be physically punished under this parental right taken over by the state, and what forms such punishment could take. The right to administer corporal punishment was increasingly regulated through legislation and was placed under public control. Previous research has shown that corporal punishment of children was already being questioned in the early twentieth century, and as a means of upbringing it was regulated according to gender, age, and institutional context. It mainly concerned older boys, over the age of about 12–14, being excluded from corporal punishment in schools and child welfare institutions, along with girls and children from the higher social classes. In practice, the right to administer corporal punishment appears not to have been exercised at institutions to any great extent (Sundkvist, 1994; Norburg, 2015; Sandin et al., 2021). The public debate in the following years, with criticism of the state child welfare institutions, drew attention to shortcomings and also continued to criticize the state's takeover of parental rights. Could the state both represent and protect children from abuse (physical and mental) while it simultaneously used disciplinary force and risked violating the integrity of children? This criticism led to a broader discussion about parental rights in child rearing.

State Responsibility: Punishment or Upbringing, Regulation and Prohibition 1930–1950

The Swedish Poor Law and Child Welfare Association (a civil society organization) campaigned in the 1930s against corporal punishment of children and tried to influence the discussion about corporal punishment in schools, and also when improper care impaired children's mental health. This campaign stressed that the public elementary schools (*folkskola*) should have the same educational models as grammar schools and secondary schools which had children of the same age and where corporal punishment was prohibited. It also underlined the importance of public education setting a standard for how people should raise their children. The question was also relevant for children placed in foster homes, an issue that was discussed internationally. The leading experts opposed corporal punishment as an educational instrument (Stéenhoff, 1932a, 1932b, 1933, 1936; Löw, 2020).

During the 1942 review of the 1924 Child Welfare Act, both the national Medical Board, the Social Welfare Board and local child welfare boards in Swedish big cities questioned the use of corporal punishment and argued that it could have negative mental health consequences. In the view of the Social Welfare Board, it was an inappropriate instrument to use for a public authority. Furthermore, corporal punishment, which was in fact seldom used, would have the opposite effect to the intention behind social welfare (Proposition 1942: 20, 12). On the other hand, in cases where children were taken into care by the board, acting *in loco parentis*, no change to the legislation was suggested (Proposition 1942: 20, 12–13).

The bill was approved by parliament and the right of child welfare boards to administer or order corporal punishment was revoked, but children in institutional care, government acting "in loci parentis" could still be beaten until the end of the 1940s. During the 1930s, however, the *skyddshem* (literally, "protection homes", for children who were delinquent but had not committed any crimes) were heavily criticized for their perceived abuses (Lindgren, 2001), and in this connection the various forms of punishment were also discussed. Since corporal punishment was allowed in elementary schools, it was considered impossible to abolish corporal punishment in homes for delinquent children where the disciplinary problems were supposed to be more serious. In 1937, however, it was ruled that corporal punishment should be prohibited from the age of 18 for boys and 15 for girls. For younger children, corporal punishment could only be used if a children was guilty of serious brutality, that is, excessive force against officials, mistreatment of peers and animals, or gross disobedience, and only if other measures could not have the same effect. Any measures taken must be carefully recorded (Kungl. Maj:ts stadga för skyddshemmen, 1937: 860). As part of the discussion, other disciplinary measures such as solitary confinement were also called into question (Norburg, 2015).

The restriction of corporal punishment in these institutions was followed in 1946 by the complete removal of corporal punishment from the statutes of approved schools (the *ungdomsvårdsskola* which had replaced the *skyddshem*). Other punishments were also forbidden if they could damage the physical and mental health of the children (Kungl. Maj:ts stadga, 1946: 582). Two years later, in 1948, the National Board of Social Welfare decided to ban the use of corporal punishment and other degrading punishment in children's homes under their supervision. With these decisions, the criticism of corporal punishment was explicitly broadened to include the psychological consequences and to extend public responsibility for children's moral, physical, and mental upbringing. The National Board of Social Welfare's publication "Råd och anvisningar i socialvårdsfrågor" ("Advice and Instructions on Matters of Social Welfare", Socialstyrelsen 1948: 49) contains very clear directives on what it was forbidden to do to children. The following forms of punishment were prohibited in this publication, which was distributed to all child welfare institutions and boards in the country:

- Physical punishment of children in the form of slaps, beatings and the like
- Locking children up or isolating them in a room or wardrobe
- Cold showers or forced showers
- Refusing meals to children
- Force-feeding if children refuse to eat
- Forcing children to do things that they should do voluntarily on a daily basis, such as making a child go to bed as punishment

Corporal punishment was thus strictly forbidden, and instead the importance of "natural" punishments was emphasized, so that children would learn to understand the consequences of their actions in almost Rousseauan terms.

The unsuitability of corporal punishment was thus specified for institutions under state responsibility, including elementary schools, although the ban there did not come until 1958. In 1936, the Elementary School Statute was revised to introduce seven years of compulsory schooling. The statutes emphasized that corporal punishment could only be used in the event of very serious offences and if other corrections were ineffective. Children with mental retardation or physical defects were not allowed to be exposed to corporal punishment. Nor was it permitted to subject children to hurtful and insulting treatment. The Swedish Poor Relief and Child Welfare Association would have preferred a total ban but declared that the legislation should in reality be interpreted as a ban (Stéenhoff, 1936; Alfredsson, 2014). A few years later, the issue was integrated into a larger political project to reform the school system (Betänkande med förslag angående folkskolans disciplinmedel m. m., 1950; Qvarsebo, 2006; Alfredsson, 2014).

Alongside this, there was a discussion about the right of parents to use corporal punishment on their children. The secretary of state in the Department of Justice stated in the bill for a new Parental Code that the suitability of corporal punishment as means of upbringing had generally begun to be questioned and it could not be transferred without restriction to anyone else, such as school staff. This view was broadly shared by the bodies to which the matter was referred for comment. The experts in the inquiry into a new Parental Code suggested replacing the right to *tukta* (chastise, punish) with the term *tillrättavisa* (reprove, reprimand) (Proposition, 1949:93: 7). The bill was tabled and passed, including the term *tillrättavisa* "reprimand":

> In the discussion in the chamber and in several motions, however, it was questioned whether this could be perceived as removing the right of parents to use corporal punishment. It was clearly still possible for parents to use corporal punishment on occasion. The Swedish parliament nevertheless approved the proposal. (Riksdagstrycket Proposition *Nytt juridiskt arkiv*, Avd. II 1950: 65)

The proposed wording in the completely new Parental Code appears to have been interpreted as a restriction on parents' right to use corporal punishment as a means of upbringing, but without an explicit ban being imposed. One of the members of parliament pointed out that it was undoubtedly inappropriate for parents to hit their children but that an outright ban would mean too much interference in the sanctity of the family (Protokoll Första kammaren protokoll 1949: 19, p. 82).

State Responsibility for Children in Institutional Care Versus Parental Rights 1950–1960

In 1953, the Criminal Justice Committee presented the revision of the 1864 Penal Code. The committee referred to the Parental Code and concluded that the Penal Code should not permit corporal punishment in the family in the provisions on assault and that even minor assaults on children could be prosecuted (SOU 1953: 14: 135–137). However, the committee's report stressed that the extended possibility to prosecute for assault should not lead to "uncalled-for interference in private circumstances" (SOU 1953: 14: 137). The ability to use criminal justice to intervene in the family's internal circumstances was limited in these particular cases, but this did not mean that the authorities should waive their responsibility for children's living conditions in the family. The municipal social welfare boards must play a central role here to oversee the upbring of children.

The bill to amend the penal law stressed that legislation on criminal justice made it difficult to intervene against child abuse because of the parental right to use corporal punishment. The bill referred to the change in the view of the suitability of corporal punishment in the 1949 Parental Code and in the bill for a new child welfare act. On 1 July 1957, impunity for the use of corporal punishment was revoked and prosecutors were thus able to intervene against corporal punishment/assault (Alfredsson, 2014; Riksdagstrycket Proposition, 1957:170). But the implications of the decision were not as far-reaching as they may sound. The provision in the new criminal code followed older law which meant that "assaults that were not serious and not perpetrated in a public place could not be prosecuted unless the plaintiff reported the crime or prosecution was justified from the public point of view" (Alfredsson, 2014). This meant that the possibility of prosecuting was in fact limited to aggravated assault or assault in a public place. This restriction was aimed at avoiding interference in private circumstances. It also presupposed that the question of prosecution was pursued by someone of legal age (Alfredsson, 2014). Because children were under age, they could not be plaintiffs themselves, that is to say, they could not bring a suit against a parent or guardian. The limit to the protection in criminal law that the state was prepared to give to children in the family was drawn at assault (corporal punishment) in a public place. The family was still a closed area and the ability of the state to represent children in cases of neglect and abuse was limited.

The decision did however lead to changes in the School Act and the Child Welfare Act. In the following year, 1958, corporal punishment was prohibited in the Elementary School Statute. Because corporal punishment was equated in criminal law with assault, it could no longer be considered an educational tool in school, as a public space. It was therefore not primarily considerations of school policy that led to the decision, but a shift in the arguments about criminal policy (Qvarsebo, 2006; Alfredsson, 2014). But there were considerations of school policy in the background. The creation of a basic comprehensive school for all social classes (*grundskola*) was the result of the decision on nine years of compulsory schooling and experiments with unitary school (*enhetsskola*) in 1952, although the final decision was not taken until 1962. The parallel school system organized by class and gender was abolished.

This meant that school forms in which corporal punishment had long since been prohibited would be merged with elementary schools with a broader social recruitment where corporal punishment had been permitted, albeit restricted since the 1930s (Sandin, 2012). At the same time, it is interesting to note that the Elementary School Statute went beyond simply prohibiting pupils from being subjected to corporal punishment or abusive treatment, but also stressed that: "The teacher shall promote wellbeing in school and ensure that pupils take pleasure in their work, try to gain the trust of the pupils and respect them as independent individuals" (Kungl. Maj:ts Stadga, 1958 års folkskolestadga 1959:399, 6 kap., 54 §). Here the children are held up as independent individuals with the right to be respected.

The 1960 Child Welfare Act also emphasized that children in public care should be offered good care and upbringing. It was stressed that it was not appropriate for the powers of the child welfare board to be the same as those conferred on parents, partly because the responsibility of the child welfare board comprised not only children but also young adults up to the age of 24. The child welfare board or its representatives (foster parents or children's home staff) no longer had the right to chastise children in care but instead had to safeguard the child's individual character and development, which could not be reconciled with corporal punishment (Barnavårdslagen 1960: 97). The new statutes made it clear that children should not be subjected to corporal punishment or other abusive treatment (Kungl. Maj:ts Stadga 1960: 728; 1960: 595; Proposition 1960: 10).

The ability of the state to represent and protect children thus meant that it no longer had the right to administer corporal punishment *in loco parentis*. At this stage, then, there was an explicit ban on corporal punishment in approved schools and reformatories. Children taken into institutional care were protected by criminal law from all forms of corporal punishment. Only if prosecution was called for in the public interest or if parents abused their children in public could prosecution be brought. Generally speaking, those who were tasked under social law or school law were deprived of the right to beat children before parents were. In other words, children in institutions and at school were protected from physical and psychological violence earlier than when they were at home with their parents.

This meant that when the expansion of the welfare state began in earnest in the 1960s and the early 1970s, with a common school system for children of all social classes, and with a far-reaching family policy and childcare, the family was the only social environment with responsibility for children where children could receive corporal punishment. Corporal punishment of older children was evidently not very prevalent in families, according to the few surveys carried out (Stattin et al., 1995; SOU, 2009: 99: 104–106), but attention was drawn to the fact that younger children suffered particularly from being exposed to physical and psychological abuse.

The Family Is Not Outside the Law: Parents' Right to Corporal Punishment Is Increasingly Questioned

In the early 1960s, the issue of corporal punishment of children was raised again both in the public debate and in parliament. The "battered child syndrome" had attracted the attention of doctors in the United States, and was discussed among paediatricians in Sweden, for instance in the medical journal *Läkartidningen* (Frisk, 1964). Against this background, the ambiguities of the legislation were criticized in a couple of parliamentary questions in 1964. The members raising the questions demanded action against child abuse. The responsible minister said that the problem mainly concerned the possibility of obtaining information that the child welfare boards could follow up. Abuse of the right to corporal punishment should be prosecuted. The minister argued that there was a national consensus on common values when it came to protecting the integrity of the individual, and this also applied to very young people. She also noted that the right to administer corporal punishment had been gradually restricted in public institutions, and that only parents now had the right to punish their children this way (Protokoll Andra kammaren 1964: 36: 93–104).

The Ministry of Justice returned with a proposal to amend the Parental Code. The basic stance was that corporal punishment should be avoided in principle. It was proposed that the Child Welfare Act be supplemented to report child abuse to the child welfare board (Promemoria, 1966:1). It was clear from the statement by the Ministry of Justice that they were not convinced that the prevalence of child abuse could be affected by legislation. However, the law should better correspond to the intentions of parliament by imposing a duty on the public to report child abuse to the child welfare board (Promemoria 1966: 1: 7–9).

The ambition of the ministry was thus limited to a statutory requirement to report abuse, but the parents' right to reprimand their children was not reformulated. In this context, "reprimand" must be seen as synonymous with mild corporal punishment. It was still possible according to the bill for parents to reprimand their children, but they were not allowed to use means of upbringing that were inappropriate in relation to the child's age and circumstances (Promemoria, 1966:1). This was a defensive formulation. It was a matter of public responsibility, but it was clearly not forbidden to punish children physically. The proposal to introduce a responsibility to report offences suggests a willingness to gain insight into internal family conditions. Seventeen years earlier, when parents' responsibility for corporal punishment was replaced by a right to reprimand, the opposite was underlined, namely, that this should not entail or be perceived as an interference with internal family matters. But that was what happened now.

The comments from the organizations to which the proposal was referred were generally in favour of it, but many were also critical of the lack of binding commitments and explicit prohibitions. In a comment which, as it turned out, influenced the further treatment of the matter, the Court of Appeal of Skåne and Blekinge argued that the state should take a clearer position, firmly repudiating all forms of violence against children. It was essential to intervene against the widespread habit of corporal punishment. They also questioned the parents' private power sphere in the family and control over the children:

> Parents cannot have any claim to rule over their children in this regard without transparency and control. In the case of far less important matters, such as the possession and use of property of various kinds, modern society has

rejected any claim by the individual to maintain a private power sphere vis-à-vis public measures in the common and general interest. In the case of children in particular, the individual citizen must be subject to general rules and act with accountability. (Regeringsakter, 1966:2)

Child rearing should not be about obedience and submission, but about creating healthy, independent, and mature young people. This stance was based on the declaration in the Elementary School Statute that children should be respected as human beings. According to the Court of Appeal, the problem with the Parental Code was its conflictual and outdated conception of the relation between parents and children (Regeringsakter, 1966:2).

The Standing Committee on Law noted that parents were not outside the rule of law and decided to make an important amendment to the text; parents' right to reprimand their children was removed. This was a crucial change (Första lagutskottet, 1966:32, Proposition, 1966:69). The right of parents to administer corporal punishment was replaced with "the duty to supervise the children appropriate to the child's age and other circumstances" (SFS 1966: 308 ändring av föräldrabalken 6 kap. 3§).

The justification for the proposal is interesting. The committee noted, first of all, that the children who had been abused were very young and lacked the ability to communicate which made it difficult to prevent this type of crime in the homes, "hidden from view" (Första lagutskottet, 1966:32). The crimes were not discovered until it was too late. Preventive measures and information were needed in order to achieve a sustainable long-term change in the perception of corporal punishment of children. On this point, the committee took the same view as the secretary of state at the ministry. But in the matter of whether corporal punishment of children was in accordance with the law, they took a different view. It was unsatisfactory that unlawful abuse was permitted if it was carried out by parents or guardians against children. The Parental Code must therefore be designed in such a way that the grounds for impunity for corporal punishment are completely removed (Första lagutskottet, 1966:32). The Parliament followed the proposal and as of 1 July 1966, parents did not have the statutory right to beat their children, but the provision was not entirely clear, it was later claimed in the debate on the Corporal Punishment Act in the 1970s (Sandin, 2018).

The discussion of the design of the laws did not say anything specific about the child's age or gender. But it is implicit that the problem discussed only concerns small children since corporal punishment was banned in the school system and in the expanding childcare system. The public discussion was also about "the battered child syndrome", which obviously concerned small children. The issue of corporal punishment thus took on a more limited and new age-related meaning compared to the discussions up until the late 1950s.

Corporal punishment of children had previously been within the family's autonomous remit and authority. It was precisely this right that was called into question both in the discussion of the duty to report abuse in the Child Welfare Act, and by the challenge to the integrity of the family as a sphere outside criminal law. At the same time, it is clear that these positions on the family's right to administer corporal punishment were already questioned in the 1940s when the National Board of Social Welfare clearly stated that corporal punishment and abusive treatment were unacceptable in the institutions under the authority of the state acting in "loci parentis". This meant taking a distinct step away from the "transfer" of parental rights, even though parents were still entitled to use mild physical punishments. The new Elementary School Statute from 1958, as we have seen, emphasized that children should be respected as independent individuals.

The debate on child abuse was made into a burning political issue by Save the Children as well as by the newly formed organization BRIS (that stands for "Barnens rätt i samhället" which means "Children's rights in society"). Important to notice is that it took place within the broader political context of the 1970s that also stressed the extension of childcare, women's gainful employment and gender equality. The expansion of the welfare state put the focus not only on gender equality, but also on the ability of parents to manage their duty as parents. The question of parental education had been raised in the 1960s and it became an important topic in the debates during the 1970s. Arguments about children's physical, mental, and emotional integrity were also heard in the public debate in the 1970s. An inquiry into children's rights was then set up. The need to clarify what the parliamentary decision of 1966 actually meant was occasioned by a couple of cases of child abuse, by the foundation of BRIS, by the general debate about the welfare state and family policy, and also by immigration politics (Littmarck, 2017; Sandin, 2018; Sköld & Osvaldsson, 2019).

A parliamentary inquiry on children's rights that was set up and began by discussing the conditions for a ban on corporal punishment. The members of the committee noted that it is difficult to determine what constitutes corporal punishment, and it is unclear whether it is possible to solve the problem through a legal regulation. But, still, children with disabilities could not be subjected to corporal punishment, they noted, and why would such limitations not apply to all children? The representative of BRIS argued that the law was needed when it comes to providing information on Swedish law, especially to immigrants, who perhaps have learned in their homeland that children should be brought up with corporal punishment. (Protokoll och minnesanteckningar, 6 June 1977, 5)

Another inquiry member concurred and added that one could differentiate between different groups among which maltreatment of children occurred. The first group considered it correct to use corporal punishment for the purpose of bringing up children; they were most often immigrants. The second and third group of parents acted under emotional stress or struck their children in the interest of protecting them from harm.

The children's ombudsman for Save the Children highlighted the question of immigration:

> In many cases they come from countries which allow parents and guardians to use the means of upbringing that they find suitable, even physical punishment. The question may then be posed as to whether they must change their methods of discipline. In most regards they should, of course, retain their culture and traditions as they wish. However, when the question is whether traditions and values are in conflict with the principles that are fundamental for Swedish democracy, those immigrants who come must accept that they cannot retain their traditions. One such regulation fundamental to Swedish democracy is that children should not be exposed to abuse or other treatment that could cause injury. (Protokoll och minnesanteckningar, 10 June 1977, 2–3)

Against the background of a discussion of children's rights, legal capacity and the implications of the concept of the best interests of the child, it was established early on that immigrants were a central problem when it came to child abuse. The discussion reflected the difficulties of defining abusive corporal punishment and understanding the relationship between the Penal Code and the regulations in the Parental Code which appear in the public debate.

The discussion also dealt with which term, *punishment* or *correction*, could best describe the ambitions of the legal ban. The chairman thought that the term "*punishment* rather than *correction* clarified that one did not smack one's child in the face", while others emphasized that the ban had to express a rejection of both physically and psychologically abusive treatment and that the same rules must apply to all families, immigrant and Swedish alike, which would be beneficial to the integration of the children in Swedish society (Protokoll och minnesanteckningar, 17 November 1977, 1–2)

The committee members from Save the Children and the Red Cross were the ones who took up the question of immigrants in the committee, but no other members disagreed, which implied that their views were generally shared. At this time, Save the Children also conducted a poster campaign against child abuse in areas where immigrants were concentrated (*Dagens Nyheter* 15 September 1977).

The committee argued that the legislation was urgent, judging from the notes from the meetings. In the introductory, tentative and broad discussions about the rights capacity and the meaning of the child's best interests, it was clearly suggested that there were no easy and immediate answers. But the committee quickly concluded that children had the same rights to physical and psychological integrity as adults. One should also listen to children, as is evident from the introductory discussion of principles (Protokoll och minnesanteckningar, 6 June 1977).

It was apparent that the acute situation was associated with the question of the immigrant population. In the discussion that was jotted down in the notes of the meeting it was not only a question of how to reach immigrants with information, but also how they themselves caused the problem.

The Human Rights of Children: The Official Government Report

The discussion of the parliamentary inquiry resulted in an official government report on corporal punishment in the family. It is a short report of 29 pages, in which the emphasis on the reasons for the decision is on children as individuals with their own rights. The demand to concentrate on information campaigns is a logical consequence of the investigations that demonstrated the general public's lack of knowledge concerning the fact that corporal punishment of children was not allowed. At the same time, the official report's brief format, including the proposals, raised questions concerning how the need for changes in the Parental Code could really be justified. In the report it was stated that society had changed and that:

> The idea that the child is an independent individual with its own rights has appeared all the more clearly. This places demands on raising the child which build on cooperation, care, and mutual respect. (SOU 1978: 10, 23)

Therefore the goals of, for example, preschool have changed toward developing children into open, considerate people with power of insight and the ability to cooperate with one another, but also to reach their own judgements and to solve problems (ibid.). It is thus the child's rights as individuals that require that the state become involved in order to represent and protect children (see also Sandin, 2012).

According to the official report, research had also shown how the use of physical punishment was unsuitable and exposed children to psychologically debilitating treatment. Increasing violence in society, even in the form of violent entertainment, was also an unsettling sign with possible implications for the future. The actual justification for the law, it was stressed, was the need to nurture independent democratic individuals and the consequences of subjecting children to corporal punishment that would underwrite society's general orientation towards violence. At this point, the official commission report did not mention child rearing in immigrant communities as a problem.

The report, however, also sketches the need for parental education and information activities for parents. It was especially emphasized that information should reach immigrants to Sweden. The respect for other cultures could not "accept deviations from the Swedish view" in this regard. It was a cultural conflict. On this point it was clearly necessary, one can conclude, to depart from the guiding principle in Swedish immigrant policy that was built on respect for cultural values in the immigrant communities. It also pointed out that Swedish society would not benefit from accepting an authoritarian way of upbringing which, the report conceded, could be logical in an authoritarian and patriarchal society, like the ones immigrants supposedly came from (SOU, 1978: 10, 27). It was imperative that immigrant groups should not be excluded from these efforts to expand parent education. The focus on parental education was aimed at all children and included immigrants without targeting them specifically. The cooperation and reciprocal exchange between different cultures could have positive repercussions for the individuals involved, the report concludes in a positive vein. A favourable outcome was obviously dependent on the Swedish way of child rearing being accepted (ibid., 28–29).

The official government report was published as described above and was sent to various organizations for comments. The parliamentary bill roughly followed the outline of the official report. In the presentation of the need for legislation, emphasis was placed on the idea that this report represented something new which was not included in the 1966 law. Child abuse was *now* actually to be forbidden. Corporal punishment was abuse, as was psychological maltreatment. The bill was introduced as the end of a long conceptual development which now made clear that "the child is an independent individual who can demand complete respect for his/her person". Both the child's integrity and inherent value had to be respected (Proposition, 1978/1979: 67, 3–8, quotation p. 6). The contrast to the changes in 1966 is clear. Those changes did not emphasize children as independent individuals but rather the object of parents' responsibility to do what was best for the child (Promemoria, 1966:1). The design in 1966 was more paternalistic, while that of 1977 was more emancipatory. Even if the conceptual journey from paternalism to emancipatory rights was mainly grounded in an increasing critical discussion of the general ability of families, given the challenges of modern society, to provide for their children, shifting immigration patterns and attitudes towards immigrants too have played an important role.

The comments by the referral bodies were generally positive to the proposal and supported the need for a sharper legal position. Arguments embraced the notion that children are individuals who have the same demands for protection and good psychological conditions as adults, and that the increasing immigrant population implied a challenge to these values. The argumentation about immigration concerned the fact that child rearing among immigrants was characterized by other norms and values, and also the need to convey information to immigrant parents.

In contrast to many others, neither Save the Children nor BRIS underlined the problem of immigration; BRIS even emphasized that Swedish cultural traditions also enshrined authoritarian fostering ideologies (BRISBRIS skrivelse 30 March 1978) This is a little surprising as it was the children's rights organizations that brought up the question of immigration in the commission and actually in other public contexts too. On the other hand, the notes from the commission were taken during meetings and had no official status, while the referral comment was an official statement from the organization, which may have resulted in a more nuanced argument.

A closer look at the final inquiry report reveals a similar downplaying of the problem of immigrant culture. The discussion of immigration was placed in its entirety in the section on the need for information campaigns. There is reason to believe that the inquiry decided that singling out immigrants would be too antagonistic a position to take given the political consensual traditions and the current legislation on immigration. The conclusions reached in the inquiry meetings ran contrary to the ambitions of the government that was in the process of laying the foundation for a new immigration policy. Labour immigration to Sweden of foreign citizens had begun on a small scale during the 1960s and increased markedly about 1970. The immigration policy taken by the parliament had established a position contrary to that of the child rights enquiry. Sweden should be open to allowing foreign citizens to retain their cultural identity and their values (Proposition, 1975: 26, 60; Dahlström, 2004). It was in this light that the urgency of the report could be understood. The acute media interest and public campaigns, along with the general debates about the role of the family, created a new focus on the need to reach the population with a foreign background, and change their culture. Children should be treated in the same (Swedish) way regardless of the parents' cultural background. As regards the question of corporal punishment and psychological abuse, there was no room for tolerance of the values of other cultures; this was the conclusion of the report, which ran contrary to the general policy on immigration. All children in Sweden had the right to the same respect for their physical and psychological integrity.

In Conclusion, Particular or Universal Rights

The regulation of corporal punishment during the early twentieth century related as explained not only to the child's age, gender, and class, but also to the offences for which a child could be beaten and the manner in which the punishment was administered, which had to conform to the rule of law. Institutional contexts such as school, child welfare authorities, and the family played a role in this. The picture is complex because the norm system has varied with age (corporal punishment was regulated first for older children and later for the younger ones), gender (for girls, the age limits for when corporal punishment could be used as a means of upbringing were set at a lower age than for boys), and social class (in schools attended by middle- and upper-class children, corporal punishment was banned earlier than in the public elementary schools).The state was responsible for the protection of children there, but government agencies also assumed the right to punish and discipline children. Corporal punishment of children meant that the public authority acted *in loco parentis* to correct the child's perceived moral deficiencies. At the same time, corporal punishment was not to involve public shaming; this was emphasized by the rule that punishment had to be administered in private and in regulated forms. It was therefore, from the beginning, not only about the physical effects but also the psychological consequences of the punishment. Throughout, the legislative regulations testify of a desire to create transparent procedures that can be evaluated and to establish clear accountability mechanisms for deciding on and implementing corporal punishment when administered under state responsibility; similarly, the regulations also reveal the existence of great hesitations about the practice. At this particular point in history, public child welfare was changing from being aimed at controlling children and protecting society towards being defined as protecting social rights, which could also mean increased control of families. Here the state began to waive its own right to chastise or beat children under its responsibility.

The right and obligation of parents to chastise was replaced by the term *reprimanding* at the end of the 1940s, while the National Board of Social Welfare also banned corporal punishment and abusive treatment in the institutions over which it exerted authority. The next step was to abolish the right of the authorities—that is, the school system as a whole, child welfare institutions, and child welfare boards—to punish children physically and with humiliating treatment. When corporal punishment was banned in the whole of institutionally organized childcare/educational structure outside the family, it became possible to ban it within the family as well. This took place in parallel to a shift of focus towards an interest in the upbringing and care of small children. It was at the same time that the state asserted its right to intervene to protect the rights of children within the family. In this process, children's rights were also redefined to emphasize their rights as individuals.

The broader political context, driven by the expansion of childcare, women's employment outside the home, and gender equality, formed the political background to the newly organized associations BRIS and Save the Children which were able to focus on the rights of children. Legal scholars also began arguing for the recognition of children's legal capacity, their rights to independent representation and the right to separation from their parents. The building of the welfare state transformed from focusing not merely on equality, but also on the parents' capability or inability to carry out the task of being parents (Jacobsson, 1978; Klinth, 1999, 2002; Littmarck, 2017).

The argumentation about the individual rights of children, which were considered equal to those of adults, and their physical, psychological and emotional integrity, including a right to an independent voice, was clearly encouraged the stand taken by the inquiry (Jacobsson, 1978; Sandin, 2012).

In connection with the revision of the law in 1966, reference was made in some of the replies to reviews to problems in socially vulnerable environments. In 1977, such comments recurred mainly with reference to the immigrant population's cultural values. In the notes from the 1977 committee immigrants' views on child rearing are presented as a problem that required the state to put its foot down. But that took the discussion several steps further. It helped to transform the discussion about what children's rights might be a with a; children were not only to be protected by the state but also to be regarded as having human rights. In that way, the discussion also anticipated the criticism against multicultural tolerance of cultural traditions of family violence which was brought to the fore during the 1980s and 1990s (Dahlström, 2004; Schiratzki, 2005).

In this process, it became evident that the human rights of children in families ought to be under the surveillance of government, irrespective of ethnic background. The focus on parental education was broad and included immigrants but without targeting them specifically and exclusively. This happened as a consequence of the general and increasing interest in developing welfare policies in support of all families in Sweden, though with divergent focus depending on the different political visions carried by the political left and the centrist and liberal parties (Littmarck, 2017).

The proposal for the new law meant that the values concerning raising children and the rights of children in Sweden appear fundamental as human rights in a democratic society. Swedish values concerning child rearing were placed in parity with universal democratic human rights. In the process studied here, children's rights in Sweden were transformed from emphasizing children's rights as a separate sphere of rights, to emphasizing children as possessing the same fundamental individual rights as adults—human rights protected by the state. This process includes elements of continuity of protection of social rights, but also of fundamental transformations of the nature of children's voices and participatory rights (Sandin, 2012).[1] As a consequence, it was now expected from government agencies to listen to children and account for children's perspectives in their work. The child ombudsman (BO) and the child and pupil ombudsman are institutions that were created later to protect against violations of children's rights by others, but also by the institutions and government agencies in Sweden and to represent the voices of children in interaction with the government.[2] The legislation on children's rights that banned corporal punishment indicated two avenues for the development of children's representation. The first avenue entails that children were represented by government agencies that were sensitive to children's voices and demands, such as the child ombudsperson. The second avenue implied that children could represent themselves as individuals. In Sweden, the emphasis remains on the representations of children through institutional paternalistic arrangements and less so on young people's representation as individual political agents (Sandin & Josefsson, 2022).

The consequences of the processes described in this chapter are not linear. The link between the analysis of the legal ban on corporal punishment and children's representations demonstrate a historical conflict over what government and civil society agencies and institutions that best represented the younger generation but also the complex relationship between different branches of government and the family. Those conflicts also entailed different understandings of how children were best represented and what rights of children should be protected. In this process, the right of government to corporal punish children in its care and the exclusive right of families to corporal punish, represent and protect children was questioned. Corporal punishment and humiliating treatment was simply not seen as consistent with the role to protect and represent and led to an emphases on children's rights to represent themselves. These conflicts consequently influenced the very transformation not only of different modes of representation but also the definitions of children's social and participatory rights.

The outcome is also not linear. It is clear that children's rights can obviously be a means to control immigrant families' child-rearing practices, and in other cases contribute to the emancipation of children from minority backgrounds. Children's rights can be used to protect children against group pressure and cultural norms but also to confirm and reinforce a child's belonging to a particular cultural group. The notion of the best interests of the child has had different consequences according to the social, cultural and temporal context, and has historically proven to be used in many different ways (Petterson, 2003; Sandin & Halldén, 2003; Schiratzki, 2003, 2005; Lindgren, 2006; Leviner, 2018; Ponnert & Sonander, 2019).

NOTES

1. In this chapter, the focus is on the conceptual development of rights and representation rather than the practical application in social or health services, welfare policy, or the school system. Clearly the Swedish government could not live up to the high ambitions sometimes expressed in the laws and regulations (Schiratzki et al., 2019; Sköld et al., 2020; Sandin et al., 2021).
2. https://beo.skolinspektionen.se/; https://www.barnombudsmannen.se/om-webbplatsen/english/.

REFERENCES

Alfredsson, E. (2014). Den rättsliga regleringen av barnaga under 1900-talet—en del i civiliseringsprocessen? *Examensarbete Juristprogrammet Juridiska Fakulteten, 54.*

Bacchi, C. L. (2009). *Analysing Policy: What's the Problem Represented to Be?* Pearson.

Bahr, J. (2019). Barns rätt att skyddas från fysiskt våld. In L. Ponnert & A. Sonander (Eds.), *Perspektiv på barnkonventionen: Forskning, teori och praktik.* Studentlitteratur.

Betänkande med förslag angående folkskolans disciplinmedel m. m. avgivet den 20 januari 1950 av 1947 års skoldisciplinutredning 1950. Stockholm.

BRIS skrivelse 30 Mars (1978). Regeringsprotokoll, 16 November 1978, Justitiedepartementet nr 19 (Riksarkivet, National Archives).

Dahlström, C. (2004). *Nästan välkomna: Invandrarpolitikens retorik och praktik.* Statsvetenskapliga institutionen, Univ.

Dagens Nyheter 15/9 1977.

Donzelot, J. (1980). *The Policing of Families.* Pantheon Books.

Fass, P. S. (2013). *The Routledge History of Childhood in the Western World.* Routledge.

Första lagutskottets utlåtande 1966:32. Parlamentary documents and laws. Retrieved September 19, 2022, from https://www.riksdagen.se/sv/dokument-lagar/

Frisk, A. (1964). Misshandlade småbarn. *Svenska Läkartidningen, 61*(41), 3005–3011.

Gordon, L. (2002). *Heroes of Their Own Lives: The Politics and History of Family Violence: Boston 1880–1960.* University of Illinois Press.
Hall, G. S. (1904). *Adolescence: Its Psychology and Its Relations to Physiology, Anthropology, Sociology, Sex, Crime, Religion and Education* (Vol. 2 vols). D. Appleton and company.
Hall, G. S. (1911). *Educational Problems.* D. Appleton and Company.
Holzscheiter, A. (2010). *Children's Rights in International Politics: The Transformative Power of Discourse.* Palgrave Macmillan.
Holzscheiter, A., Josefsson, J., & Sandin, B. (2019). Child Rights Governance: An Introduction. *Childhood*, 1–18.
Jacobsson, U. (1978). *Ett barns rättigheter.* Askild & Kärnekull.
Klinth, R. (1999). Mannen och den jämställda familjen: Mannen i familjen speglad genom utbildningsprogrammen i svensk radio och TV 1946–1971. In *Medier och modernisering: En antologi om utbildningsprogram och samhällsförändring* (pp. 371–393). Stiftelsen Etermedierna i Sverige.
Klinth, R. (2002). *Göra pappa med barn: Den svenska pappapolitiken 1960–95.* Boréa.
Kungl. Maj:ts stadga för skyddshemmen 1937:860
Kungl. Maj:ts Stadga (1946:582) för skolor tillhörande barn- och ungdomsvården
Kungl Maj:ts stadga (1958:399) för folkskolor, fortsättningsskolor och försöksskolor.
Kungl Maj:ts Stadga (1960:728) för ungdomsvårdsskolorna.
Larsson, G. (2018). *Förbrytelser och förvisningar: Bestraffningssystemet i de svenska läroverken 1905–1961.* Acta Universitatis Upsaliensis.
Leviner, P. (2018). Barnkonventionen som svensk lag: En diskussion om utmaningar och möjligheter för att förverkliga barns rättigheter. *Förvaltningsrättslig tidskrift, 2.*
Lindgren, A.-L. (2001). Stat och kommuner. Kollektiv och enskilda: 1930-talets skyddshemsdebatt och folkhemspolitiken. *Scandia, 67*(2), 239–267.
Lindgren, C. (2006). *En riktig familj: Adoption, föräldraskap och barnets bästa 1917–1975.* Carlsson.
Lindkvist, L. (2018). Rights for the World's Children: Rädda Barnen and the Making of the UN Convention on the Rights of the Child. *Nordic Journal of Human Rights, 36*(3), 287–303.
Littmarck, S. (2017). *Barn, föräldrar, välfärdsstat: Den politiska debatten om föräldrautbildning och föräldrastöd 1964–2009.* University of Linköping.
Löw, J. (2020). *Världen, Sverige och barnen: Internationell påverkan på svensk barnpolitik under välfärdsstatens framväxt i mellankrigstidens tidevarv.* Diss., Linköpings universitet, Linköping.
Lundström, T. (1993). *Tvångsomhändertagande av barn: En studie av lagarna, professionerna och praktiken under 1900-talet.* Stockholm Univ.

Norburg, U. (2015). *Fängelse, skola, uppfostringsanstalt eller skyddshem?: Åkerbrukskolonien Hall för pojkar år 1876–1940*. Linköpings universitet, Institutionen för Tema.
Nytt Juridisk Arkiv, Avd II 1950. *Tidskrift för lagstiftning m. m.*
Petterson, G. (2003). Med hänsyn till barnets vilja? Socialtjänstens barnperspektiv och den nya välfärdsstatens villkor. In B. Sandin & G. Halldén (Eds.), *Barnets bästa: En antologi om barndomens innebörder och välfärdens organisering* (pp. 139–176). Brutus Östlings bokförlag Symposion.
Platt, A. M., & Chávez-García, M. (2009). *The Child Savers: The Invention of Delinquency*. Rutgers University Press.
Ponnert, L., & Sonander, A. (2019). *Perspektiv på barnkonventionen: Forskning, teori och praktik*. Studentlitteratur.
Promemoria 1966:1, Justitiedepartementet, Promemoria med förslag till viss ändring av föräldrabalken (Ju 1966:1)
Proposition 1942:20, Parliamentary documents and laws. Retrieved September 19, 2022, from https://www.riksdagen.se/sv/dokument-lagar/
Proposition 1949:93, Parliamentary documents and laws. Retrieved September 19, 2022, from https://www.riksdagen.se/sv/dokument-lagar/
Proposition 1957:170. Parliamentary documents and laws. Retrieved September 19, 2022, from https://www.riksdagen.se/sv/dokument-lagar/
Propostion 1960:10, Parliamentary documents and laws. Retrieved September 19, 2022, from https://www.riksdagen.se/sv/dokument-lagar/
Proposition 1966:69. Retrieved September 19, 2022, from https://www.riksdagen.se/sv/dokument-lagar/
Proposition 1975:26, Parliamentary documents and laws. Retrieved September 19, 2022, from https://www.riksdagen.se/sv/dokument-lagar/
Proposition 1978/1979:67 Parliamentary documents and laws. Retrieved September 19, 2022, from https://www.riksdagen.se/sv/dokument-lagar/
Protokoll, Första Kammaren 1949:19. Parliamentary documents and laws. Retrieved September 19, 2022, from https://www.riksdagen.se/sv/dokumentlagar/
Protokoll, Andra kammaren 1964:36. Parliamentary documents and laws. Retrieved September 19, 2022, from https://www.riksdagen.se/sv/dokumentlagar/
Protokoll och minnesanteckningar 1977–1978, Kommittearkivet, vol. 1, Utredning om barnens rätt. Riksarkivet. National Archive, Stockholm.
Qvarsebo, J. (2006). *Skolbarnets fostran: Enhetsskolan, agan och politiken om barnet 1946–1962*. Institutionen för tema, Tema Barn, Linköpings universitet.
Regeringsakter, Statsrådsprotokoll, Kungl Justitiedepartementet D-nr 860/66, 25 mars 1966. Riksarkivet, National Archives, Stockholm.
Retrieved September 19, 2021, from https://beo.skolinspektionen.se/

Retrieved September 19, 2021, from https://www.barnombudsmannen.se/om-webbplatsen/english/

Sandin, B. (2012). Children and the Swedish Welfare State: From Different to Similar. In P. S. Fass & M. Grossberg (Eds.), *Reinventing Childhood After World War II* (pp. 110–138). University of Pennsylvania Press.

Sandin, B. (2017). The Parent: A Cultural Invention. The Politics of Parenting. *European Journal of Developmental Psychology, 14*, 733–746.

Sandin, B. (2018). Barnuppfostran, föräldraskap och barns rättigheter: En studie av diskussionen kring agalagen 1979. In V. Lundberg & C. Riving (Eds.), *Mellan Malmö och Minneapolis: Kulturhistoriska undersökningar tillägnade Lars Edgren*. Arkiv förlag.

Sandin, B., & Halldén, G. (2003). *Barnets bästa: En antologi om barndomens innebörder och välfärdens organisering*. Brutus Östlings bokförlag Symposion.

Sandin, B. Sköld, J., & Schiratizki J. (2021). Var går gränserna för statens ansvar? Ett historiskt perspektiv på hur barns rättigheter representerats i upprättelseprocessen för dem som vanvårdats i fosterhem och på institution. Statsvetenskaplig tidskrift nr 4.

Sandin, B & Josefsson, J. (2022), The reform that never happened: a history of children's suffrage restrictions, with Jonathan Josefsson in John Wall, ed., *Exploring Children's Suffrage*. Palgrave Macmillan 2022.

Schiratzki, J. (2003). Barnkonventionen och barnets bästa—globalisering med reservation. In B. Sandin & G. Halldén (Eds.), *Barnets bästa: En antologi om barndomens innebörder och välfärdens organisering* (pp. 25–52). Brutus Östlings bokförlag Symposion.

Schiratzki, J. (2005). *Barnets bästa i ett mångkulturellt Sverige: En rättsvetenskaplig undersökning*. Iustus.

Schiratzki, J. (2019). *Barnrättens grunder*. Studentlitteratur.

Schiratzki, J., Sköld, J., & Sandin, B. (2019). Redress in Context: The Swedish Redress Scheme for Historical Abuse of Children in Care—Re-introducing Inquisitorial Procedure? *Nordisk socialrättslig tidskrift, 10*(21–22), 97–118.

SFS (Svensk författningssamling) 1966:308, ändring av föräldrabalken

Sköld, J., Sandin, B., & Schiratzki, J. (2020). Historical Justice Through Redress Schemes? The Practice of Interpreting the Law and Physical Child Abuse in Sweden. *Scandinavian Journal of History, 45*(2), 178–201.

Sköld, J., Söderlind, I., & Bergman, A.-S. (2014). *Fosterbarn i tid och rum: Lokal och regional variation i svensk fosterbarnsvård ca 1850–2000*. Carlsson.

Sköld, Johanna & Karin Osvaldsson. (2019). 'Barnrättspolitik och vuxensyn. Stabilitet och förändring i BRIS utåtriktade arbete', Socialvetenskaplig tidskrift, 26, 109–129.

Stattin, H., Janson, H., Klackenberg-Larsson, I., & Magnusson, D. (1995). Corporal Punishment in Everyday Life: An Intergenerational Perspective. In

J. McCord (Ed.), *Coercion and Punishment in Long-Term Perspectives* (pp. 315–347). Cambridge University Press.
Stéenhoff, G. (1932a). Kroppsagan i folkskolan. *Tidskrift för barnavård och ungdomskydd*, 2(2), 68–69.
Stéenhoff, G. (1932b). Kroppsaga som uppfostringsmedel. *Tidskrift för barnavård och ungdomskydd, 1932,* 143.
Stéenhoff, G. (1933). Frågan om kroppsaga i folkskolan inför skolornas målsmän. *Tidskrift för barnavård och ungdomskydd, 1933*(4), 143–145.
Stéenhoff, G. (1936). Frågan om kroppsaga i folkskolan avgjord. *Tidskrift för barnavård och ungdomskydd, 1936*(4), 132–133.
Socialstyrelsen. 1948:49. 'Råd och anvisningar i socialvårdsfrågor'.
SOU 1978:10. Utredningen om barnens rätt. Barnets rätt. 1, Om förbud mot aga.
SOU 2009:99. Vanvård i social barnavård under 1900-talet. Stockholm: Fritzes
SOU. 1953:14. Förslag till brottsbalk. Avgivet av Straffrättskommittén. Stockholm: Norstedts.
Sundkvist, M. (1994). *De vanartade barnen: Mötet mellan barn, föräldrar och Norrköpings barnavårdsnämnd 1903–1925.* Hjelm.
Turmel, A. (2008). *A Historical Sociology of Childhood: Developmental Thinking, Categorization, and Graphic Visualization.* Cambridge University Press.
Weiner, G. (1995). *De räddade barnen: Om fattiga barn, mödrar och fäder och deras möte med filantropin i Hagalund 1900–1940.* Hjelm.

Open Access This chapter is licensed under the terms of the Creative Commons Attribution 4.0 International License (http://creativecommons.org/licenses/by/4.0/), which permits use, sharing, adaptation, distribution and reproduction in any medium or format, as long as you give appropriate credit to the original author(s) and the source, provide a link to the Creative Commons licence and indicate if changes were made.

The images or other third party material in this chapter are included in the chapter's Creative Commons licence, unless indicated otherwise in a credit line to the material. If material is not included in the chapter's Creative Commons licence and your intended use is not permitted by statutory regulation or exceeds the permitted use, you will need to obtain permission directly from the copyright holder.

CHAPTER 3

Adults in Charge: The Limits of Formal Child Participatory Processes for Societal Transformation

Afua Twum-Danso Imoh

Introduction

The Convention on the Rights of Child, adopted by the United Nations in November 1989, was intended to represent a turning point in depictions and perceptions of children in international law and social policy. In particular, the Convention took the position that children were rights-holders who have views and ideas about their own lives and have a right to genuine participation in decision-making affecting them. Its centrality to the Convention is evidenced by the fact that the concept of child participation is included not only within the body of the Convention, but also as one of its four guiding principles (UN, 1989).

However, despite the vision behind the Convention and the excitement that the participation principle evoked around the world at the time of its adoption in the late 1980s, it was, from the outset, I will argue, limiting in

---

A. T.-D. Imoh (✉)
School for Policy Studies, University of Bristol, Bristol, UK
e-mail: afua.twum-danso@bristol.ac.uk

© The Author(s) 2023
B. Sandin et al. (eds.), *The Politics of Children's Rights and Representation*, Studies in Childhood and Youth,
https://doi.org/10.1007/978-3-031-04480-9_3

its capacity for genuine transformational impact. This is primarily due to the fact that while the Convention foregrounds the importance of children's views and involvement in decision-making, it also ensures that adults remain in control in deciding the terms relating to who participates, how they participate, the topics on which they participate and ultimately, the outcome of participatory initiatives. An analysis of the structure and organisation of these participatory events and projects also reveal the extent to which these formal participatory processes remain tightly regulated and controlled by adults who then proceed to facilitate or cultivate the 'right' kind of participation from a select group of children within projects and programmes (Wyness, 2009a, 2013; Horgan et al., 2017; Gallacher & Gallagher, 2008). As a result, what becomes apparent from these formal participatory processes is the strong emphasis placed on the creation of an enabling environment, primarily by government agencies, NGOs, or a research community, for the facilitation of children's participation which is often seen as enabling them to be able to express their agency (Gallacher & Gallagher, 2008). In this way, the control of children's participation rights within institutions and organisations in particular is firmly handed to the management of adults. As a result, what emerges within the Convention is a persisting understanding of children's rights as being a gift of adults which they then give to children—whether this gift is linked to children's care and protection rights or their participation rights. This limitation surely then raises questions about the extent to which the Convention, a treaty regarded as representing a landmark due to its perception of children as subjects—rather than objects—of rights, actually represents a genuine shift from earlier human rights laws and social policies such as the 1924 Declaration on the Rights of the Child and the 1959 Declaration on the Rights of the Child which explicitly depicted children in a passive light.

Therefore, this chapter seeks to contribute to existing bodies of literature that critically examine the extent to which the Convention and its attendant initiatives and policies around the world focusing on child participation represent not only a genuine shift in depictions of children within international law, but also a framework for the achievement of societal transformation, especially in relation to the position of children in many societies which is characterised by what Fraser (2005) calls status inequality and misrecognition. Thus, the inability of dominant participation initiatives to address this misrecognition that children in diverse contexts experience has led to the persistence of their exclusion and indeed, misrepresentation, from participation in mainstream social and political interactions. Specifically, the argument underpinning this chapter is that the vision of child participation in the Convention, and which is subsequently reflected in the language and concepts articulated in the Convention as well as in the practices it has inspired, is limited in the extent to which it can initiate genuine transformational change in society in relation to how children and their participation within their families, communities and societies are understood. The chapter will then proceed to call for the need to look outside of this dominant child participation framework in search for examples of genuine transformative child participation which see children engage in acts of self-representation independently or alongside adults in struggles for not only recognition, but justice, be it economic, political or social and in the process, contribute to societal transformation at a local, national or global level. It is important to note that at the same time children's representation transforms societies, these actions also contribute to transforming children's representation through the impact these acts have on the status inequality and misrecognition that affect children (see Intro this volume). A notable example of what may be considered non-CRC-framed children's participation is provided through an analysis of one case study: the role of children in the struggle to end apartheid in late twentieth century South Africa. It will finally discuss the implications of such examples of children participating and transforming their society—either independently from adults or with adults—for dominant child participation and children's rights discourses.

From Objects to Subjects of International Social Policy: A Turning Point Influenced by the Convention on the Rights of the Child?

Since the concept of children's rights emerged and became widely recognised in the early twentieth century, the depiction of children in global social policy was primarily as objects who were dependent on adults to provide them with protection and care. These ideas are best reflected in the 1924 Declaration of the Rights of the Child and the 1959 Declaration of the Rights of the Child, which together, laid the foundation for the drafting and adoption of the Convention on the Rights of the Child. The adoption of the Convention by the UN General Assembly in November 1989 was seen to represent, by members of the international community, a new era in the perception and position of children in international law as it took the standpoint that children were rights-holders who can play an active part in the enforcement of their rights (Veerhellen, 1994; Sinclair Taylor, 2002: Alderson & Morrow, 2004).

Given this image of the child within discussions leading to the drafting of the Convention, the contents of the treaty placed particular importance on the concept of participation, most notably evidenced by its inclusion as one of the four principles of the treaty as well as articulated in numerous articles within the body of the Convention. However, the understanding of child participation within the Convention departed from earlier discourses. For instance, child liberationists in Western Europe and North America such as Holt (1974) and Farson (1974) have long argued that children, like all other members of society, 'should have the right to a relevant education, to a meaningful job, to a supportive home, to personal property, to sexual relationships of their choice, to all available information without censorship, to expression of political opinions, and suffrage' (cited in Margolin, 1978, p. 446; see also Grossberg, 2014). Thus, early understandings of child participation were both comprehensive in nature and reflected the encompassing nature of the common sense understanding of the concept.

However, with the adoption of the Convention on the Rights of the Child almost 33 years ago by the UN General Assembly, the concept of child participation was redefined in several respects. Firstly, the concept became centred on children's voices as is evidenced by the participatory-related articles in the Convention which refer to children's rights to influence decisions made on their behalf, express their views, have freedom of thought, conscience, and religion and also their right to form associations. Therefore, it has been argued that, although like its predecessors (the 1924 Declaration of the Rights of the Child and the 1959 Declaration of the Rights of the Child), the Convention recognises that children need protection as well as social rights more generally, it goes a step further to acknowledge that they also have strengths and are not merely dependents waiting for adulthood to become full human beings, and hence, eligible for participation (see e.g. Sinclair Taylor, 2002). Secondly, the concept of participation as articulated by the Convention foregrounds the belief that adults are ultimately responsible for deciding which views expressed by which groups of children are acceptable and which are not. Hence, despite the fact that the Convention foregrounds the importance of children's views and involvement in decision-making, it also ensures that adults remain in control of facilitating or cultivating the 'right' kind of participation from a select group of children within projects and programmes, the terms relating to who participates, how they participate, the topics on which they participate and ultimately, the outcome of participatory initiatives (Wyness, 2009a, 2013; Horgan et al., 2017; Gallacher & Gallagher, 2008). Thus, while child liberationists such as the aforementioned Holt and Farson adopted a more bottom-up or child-centred concept of child participation, the Convention's definition and understanding appears to centre adults more closely within the concept of child participation.

Since its adoption, the Convention's principles centred around the right of children to to self-determination and participation have gained enormous momentum in broader children's rights discourses and has influenced the policies and programmes of many governmental and non-governmental agencies (both local and global) and, indeed, academic research projects. The resulting outcome is that today almost all mainstream conceptualisations, models and interpretations of the notion of self-determination as it relates to children and children's participation rights largely link participation to the notion of children having a voice (see Hart, 1992; Lansdown, 2001; Chawla, 2001; Wyness, 2006, 2009a; 2009b, 2013; Gallacher & Gallagher, 2008; Wall, 2011; Kallio, 2012; Horgan et al., 2017; Twum-Danso Imoh & Okyere, 2020). In fact, as Wyness (2013, p. 342) states:

> The CRC has been the catalyst and subsequent framework for developing policy at national, local and institutional levels, influencing professional practice-based initiatives for promoting children's participation. (see also Horgan et al., 2017)

Thus, the years following the adoption of the Convention have witnessed numerous initiatives in countries around the world. For example, recent years have seen the introduction of children's parliaments and mayors, the use of consultations with children as a central part of NGO programming and the increasing visibility of children delivering keynote speeches at global events address (see e.g. Wyness, 2006, 2009a, 2009b; Wall, 2011; Maclure, 2011; Thew et al., 2021). The resulting outcome of these initiatives is that today, a strong emphasis is now placed, in the programmes of international agencies and NGOs as well as in research projects, on foregrounding children's voices and attempting to see the world from their perspective (Wyness, 2009a, 2009b; Horgan et al., 2017; Percy-Smith & Thomas, 2010; Percy-Smith, 2015; Kallio, 2012).

Despite the vision behind the Convention and the excitement that the participation principle evoked around the world at the time of its adoption, this treaty was, from the outset, limiting in its capacity for genuine transformational impact in terms of recognising children as agents in society (see Wyness et al., 2004: 83). This can be seen in a number of ways. Firstly, although numerous initiatives have been introduced to foster children's participation, many of these are centred on understandings of child participation as children having a voice. That these voice-based participation initiatives have a role to play in the realisation of children's rights is not in doubt given the subordinate position of children in many societies and their widespread exclusion from political discourses (see Gallacher & Gallagher, 2008; Wyness, 2009b, 2013; Horgan et al., 2017). However, in more recent years this voice—oriented understanding of child participation has increasingly become problematized (see e.g. Wyness, 2013; Larkins, 2014; James, 2007; Horgan et al., 2017; Percy-Smith, 2015; Twum-Danso Imoh & Okyere, 2020). For example, arguments have been put forward that maintain that focusing exclusively on voice while overlooking the multitude of ways in which children can, and do, already participate in the various contexts that exist in the Global South in particular creates 'standard' and 'deficit' models of participation (Wyness, 2013). This has led to a situation whereby the participatory activities of children from this part of the world are de-legitimised or considered deviant (Percy-Smith & Thomas, 2010).

A notable example is the idea of children having responsibilities to their families and communities which is especially evident in parts of the South. Specifically, at the same time as child participation as a concept has been promoted alongside the implementation of the Convention in diverse societies around the world, concerns have been raised about the responsibilities children have to their families and communities in parts of the South. For instance, in sub-Saharan Africa, the notion of children having responsibilities is a key component of the socialization process to ensure that children of different genders are equipped with the knowledge and skills to undertake the responsibilities expected of them as adult men and women in their communities (see Nsamenang, 2004; Lancy, 2012). However, these responsibilities children are expected to undertake are not allocated randomly. Chores are constantly monitored by adults within their family who gradually increase their responsibility as children prove their competence in a particular skill or task until it is clear that they are able to engage in work that is normally reserved for adults (see Nsamenang, 2004; Lancy, 2012). Despite the socialization rationale underpinning the notion of children having responsibilities in contexts across the continent, much of this work tends to be branded by international advocacy groups as exploitative and an abuse of power by adults which deprives children of their rights (Nsamenang, 2004). This perception stands in sharp contrast to the views of many children in these societies who see the undertaking of these responsibilities as a form of participation (see e.g. Twum-Danso Imoh & Okyere, 2020).

Secondly, even within this discursive notion of child participation, the limitations of the Convention are evident. For instance, while Article 12 stipulates that consideration must be given to the views of children, it also adds a *proviso* that this should depend on the age and maturity of the child. This effectively implies that interpretation of this article will depend greatly on how adults construct age, maturity, and capability in their particular social and cultural context. As Stasiulis (2005, p. 9) states 'concepts such as "capability of the child" and "maturity" are always subject to adult interpretation' (see also Wyness, 2006, 2013). Thus, in this way, the control of children's participation rights is firmly handed to the management of adults. As a result, what emerges within the Convention is a persisting understanding of children's rights as being a gift of adults which they then give to children, an accusation often levied at the 1924 and 1959 Declarations on children's rights. This limitation surely then raises questions about the extent to which the Convention, a treaty that is seen as game-changing due to its perception of children as subjects—rather than objects—of rights actually represents a genuine shift from earlier human rights law and social policies which explicitly depicted children as objects of rights dependent on the charity of adults (e.g. see 1924 Declaration on the Rights of the Child). Therefore, while participation is included in the four underlying principles of the Convention along with protection and is equally weighted, it can be argued that in reality that is not the case as the principle of protection clearly trumps that of participation.

In relation to the formal participatory processes that have been inspired by the Convention in recent years, it is evident that there is a strong emphasis placed on the creation of an enabling environment, primarily by adults (government agencies, NGOs, researchers) for the facilitation of children's participation which is often seen as supporting them to express their agency (Gallacher & Gallagher, 2008). This maintenance of the control of adults within participatory initiatives may be best reflected in the language used in the relevant literature. Specifically, there is evidence of expressions such as 'empowering' children through participatory initiatives, 'offering' children the opportunity to participate, 'enabling' children to exercise their participatory rights and 'enhancing' children's participation and empowerment. Even the definitions of child participation that have emerged in the years after the adoption of the Convention further indicate the underlying assumption in the language used that there is an expectation that adults are to retain control of participatory processes while at the same time ensuring that they provide or give opportunities to children. Overall, a review of a range of definitions provided by numerous commentators (Sinclair, 2004; Hart, 2007) point to an understanding of child participation which is founded upon adults giving children a voice or space to express their opinions. Van Beers (1995, p. 4), for instance, defines participation as:

> Listening to children, giving them space to articulate their own concerns and, taking into account the children's maturity and capacities, enabling them to take part in the planning, conduct and evaluation of activities, within or outside the family sphere, which may imply involving them in decision making.

Thus, central to this definition is the adult who plays a listening and facilitating role in fostering the participation of children in a given context. Research scholarship has not been immune to these assumptions. In an edited volume more recently produced by Campbell with her colleagues (Campbell et al., 2011, p. 5), they state in their introduction that each project described in the collection of chapters they had compiled 'attempted to facilitate or develop young people's capacity to exercise agency, by ensuring that to varying degrees their experiences and voices were represented and their participation encouraged' (see also Gallacher & Gallagher, 2008). Again, here, it is the adult researchers and their attempts to 'develop' and 'encourage' young people's agency which is centred.

The use of language in these ways in the literature appears to suggest that children's enactment of participation, or their potential to express agency, is not an act which they can initiate and drive themselves and instead, has to be elicited, facilitated, mediated, encouraged, structured, or cultivated by adults. This can partly be attributed to the emphasis placed on encouraging children's civic participation which largely takes places in the public sphere (Horgan et al., 2017), leading to their participation becoming institutional in nature. This, consequently, leads to a situation whereby adults are required to mediate or determine the framework of participatory initiatives due to the fact that in these spheres adults are in positions of power and responsibility (Wyness, 2013). This demonstrates that in an era dominated by the emphasis placed on child participation as voice which, in turn, has been foregrounded during a period, at least in international law and policymaking, centred around underscoring children's rights and the recognition of children as social actors, the approaches adopted assume that 'children require to be "empowered" by adults if they are to act in the world' (Gallacher & Gallagher, 2008, p. 503; see also Fuchs, 2019). The problem, Gallacher and Gallagher (2008, p. 503) argue, within participatory research processes where adults develop the participatory techniques to be employed bearing in mind their desire to facilitate children's effective participation is that such approaches risk 'perpetuating the very model that they purport to oppose'.

This underlying belief that adults, within institutions and organisations specifically, are required for children to enact agency or to be able to exercise their participatory rights results in adults being positioned as those who determine which children participate, how they participate and what impact their participation can have. In fact, it can be argued that through the formal initiatives developed to promote or facilitate the ability of children's participation, strategies are actually being developed to not only regulate and control children, but also work to limit and restrict them (Wall, 2011; Holzscheiter et al., 2019; Larkins, 2014). Larkins (2014, p. 9), for example, claims:

> Children's status as citizens is also undermined by social welfare interventions and laws that apply levels of control, limitations in rights and restrictions in access to certain public spaces, that are not imposed on adults.

Hence, through these formal processes of participation 'children are made subjects of governance' (Holzscheiter et al., 2019, p. 4; see also Sandin, 2014).

The tight regulation and control of participatory processes leads to questions about the extent to which participatory initiatives serve the interests of children in the long run. This is a point raised by Campbell and her colleagues (Campbell et al., 2011, p. 2) when they make the argument that it is essentially not possible to separate children's rights from those of adults. The resulting outcome, then, is that 'when adults invoke children's rights it is simply to promote adult agendas'. Wyness (2009b, p. 540) supports this when he also notes that despite the claims by adults of their advocacy efforts on behalf of children, there is the potential that it is the interests of adults that determine what are in the best interests of children. This situation comes about because of the very nature of advocacy efforts which mean that it is rare that children's voices are heard directly on issues that affect them. The logical question to subsequently pose is: what are these adult agendas that may be prioritised in participatory initiatives? A number have been pointed to explicitly or implicitly by commentators over the years. Gallacher & Gallacher (2008, pp. 503–504) specifically maintain that:

> In order to be effective, governmental power depends upon knowledge of the population being governed. We want to suggest that current enthusiasm for practical, 'policy-relevant' social research on children is closely connected to adult anxieties about young people: how to improve them, make them more employable, more productive and healthier; how to encourage and regulate their moral conduct and to participate in democratic politics.

One particular issue that ties these various desired outcomes that participation should inculcate is the notion of children as future citizens which is a clear thread in the literature as one key motivation underlying participatory processes (see Wyness, 2013; Horgan et al., 2017; Gallacher & Gallagher, 2008; Wyness et al., 2008). This links closely to what Jenks (1996) has called 'a vision of futurity'. This emphasis on developing future responsible citizens is evident in how both the academic and non-academic literature has talked about participatory processes. For instance, Partridge (2005) asserts that the process of participation itself can give children the chance to learn more about their environments, which ultimately benefits them as it increases their knowledgeable and facilitates their ability to become responsible inhabitants in their communities. In turn, Kirby and Bryson (2002) argue that children who are permitted to participate may be of greater benefit to the community itself as they tend to be in a better position to take up roles of responsibility upon maturity. Thus, this provides a rationale for the strong emphasis normative forms of child participation place on citizenship activities which are seen to prepare children for their role as full responsible citizens of society who will eventually be able to work and, of course, vote, and help to sustain law and order as well as democratic structures once they achieve adulthood (Wyness, 2009a, 2013). Interestingly, this rationale for participatory processes with children suggest that dominant understandings of child participation have become linked with notions of socialization whereby governmental or non-governmental agencies become agents of socialization working to prepare the child for responsibility and citizenship within society. While these processes emphasise the empowerment and inclusion of children, there is a hint, in these discourses, of traditional theories relating to socialization which were promulgated by scholars such as Talcott Parsons (see e.g. Parsons & Bales, 1956) which see the child as a rather passive being. This focus on children as producing future citizens within formal, dominant participatory processes is an indication that dominant understandings of child participation and childhood more generally may not be about, or for, children at all.

Decentring the Adult in Child Participatory Processes for Transformational Change

This critique about the limits of the transformational effects of Convention-inspired participatory definitions and processes builds upon existing critiques made by scholars from various disciplines who have long been concerned about the Convention's paternalist framing (see e.g. Stasiulis, 2005; Liebel, 2002; Hashim & Thorsen, 2011). Using these critiques as a foundation, the main argument underpinning this chapter is that we need to recognise that if we are interested in looking for transformative instances of child participation, which is inherently linked to acts of self-representation by children, the Convention's definition of participation and the attendant formal processes centred on the public sphere which it has inspired are not where we should focus our energies. These formal and public spheres of participation are limited in their transformational impact. Hence, in order to gain an insight into forms of child participation with transformative potential and impact, there is a need to go beyond the more formal initiatives which have hitherto been dominated not only by the notion of participation as voice, but have also been tightly regulated and controlled by adults. Instead, the suggestion here is that researchers and others need to cast their eyes elsewhere. The implications of this would require researchers to focus on bottom-up approaches to participation and the enactment of citizenship, possibly through small-scale everyday forms of persuasion and actions initiated by children themselves within the contexts in which they live their everyday lives.

This position garners support from a range of scholars coming from different perspectives. In line with their liberationist ideology, child protagonists suggest that true participation should be child-led as opposed to being determined by adults (Miljeteig, 2000). Participation under this ideology takes the view that children can act in their own names to defend their rights and they should, therefore, be given the chance to do so without restrictions. More recently, relevant scholarship has urged us to adopt an approach that foregrounds the everyday acts in which children engage by themselves, or with others, that are not under some regulation and control by adults. To do this we need to look at the mundanities of children's everyday lives and identify the 'routine, informal opportunities for meaningful participation' (Horgan et al., 2017, p. 276). The work of Larkins (2014, p. 9) who adopts a relational approach to this issue is especially significant. Specifically, she makes the case that children's citizenship is enacted in the home, school, leisure spaces, and is best reflected in transgressions and behaviours of resistance as well as through acts relating to 'negotiating rules of social coexistence, contributing to socially agreed good and fulfilling their own individual rights' (Larkins, 2014, p. 19). This then leads her to conceptualise children's activities as either 'acts or actions of citizens' leading to an emphasis on children's everyday practices of citizenship, which may have political significance even if they are not political in nature. This recognises the way children themselves enact citizenship instead of participating in the citizenship they are offered whether by NGOs or governmental agencies (see also Horgan et al., 2017).

Taking a Long Historical View to Understand the Transformational Potential of Children's Participation: The Case of the Soweto Uprising of 1976

History may provide us with lessons about such bottom-up forms of everyday participation in which children have engaged. In fact, history teaches us that those we consider to be children today have always participated in their societies, often in ways that have contributed to transformations of some kind. Examples from the contemporary period which illuminate this point is the role many children played in the civil rights movement in the USA and the anti-apartheid struggle in South Africa in the latter half of the twentieth century (see also Wall, 2011).

In relation to South Africa, the role of children is especially notable during the Soweto uprising of the second half of 1976 as it illuminates very clearly the extent to which the participation of Black African children and young people who were in primary schools (both junior and senior stages) and high schools and who were aged 20 years old and under resulted in a transformation which overhauled the political and social structures of South African society. This action by Black children and young people in this context was provoked by the apartheid government's decision that maths and social studies should be taught in Afrikaans in senior primary and junior secondary schools—a decision that the government had long planned, but started to put in place more concretely from 1968 onwards. This decision, which was eventually implemented in early 1976, was not popular with African adults and children alike, including teachers, many of whom did not speak Afrikaans and would, as a result, struggle to teach these subjects effectively to children, leading to a worsening of educational standards for Black children. In particular, teachers were concerned about the loss of critical thinking in students which would be replaced by a reliance on rote learning in Afrikaans due to their own lack of proficiency in the language (Ndlovu, 2004). There was also a concern that as teaching in English had also just been introduced in 1975 this meant that by adding Afrikaans as another foreign language Black children had to be taught in schools, this would lead to the loss of mother tongue language. Further, Afrikaans was also the language of the apartheid State and all its agents and thus, this decision:

> represented the state's assault on the language and culture of black people, on their future, and on their power and ability to effect changes in policies of immediate concern. In this case, the violence that was central to the practices and ideology of the authoritarian apartheid state had become central also to the lived experiences of historical actors during this time. (Pohlandt-Mccormick, 2000, p. 25)

As a result, children and young people, aged between 10 and 20, who were those most affected by these changes, sought to prevent them through low-key protests which took the form of class boycotts, school strikes and disruptions within schools in May and early June 1976. While parents and other adults did not support the imposition of Afrikaans in their schools, they sought to stop these actions and ensure children returned to school:

> Concerned parents held emergency meetings with school board and homeland representatives. On 22 May 1976, a meeting of parents, Orlando-Diepkloof Zulu school board members, and Inkatha ye Sizwe members, led by Gibson Thula, the urban representative of KwaZulu, held a meeting at Phefeni Junior Secondary School. The meeting decided that students should return to school while the matter received urgent attention. But the striking students largely ignored this plea. On 3 June 1976 pupils at Emthonjeni, Belle, Thulasizwe, and Pimville returned to class. They had been told apparently that lessons in mathematics and social studies would be suspended for the time being. But students from other schools steadfastly continued with their strike action. (Ndlovu, 2004, p. 335)

These early actions by children were dismissed and ignored by the State (Pohlandt-Mccormick, 2000), leading them to intensify their plans for protest and make their voices heard. Final plans for a three-day peaceful demonstration to start on 16 June were made on 13 June. Following the meeting, an inclusive action committee was established and consisted of higher primary, junior secondary and high school students. It was this group that is believed to have coordinated the demonstration on 16 June. Another student leader has since outlined the initial intentions for 16 June:

> Our original plan was just to get to Orlando West [Junior Secondary School], pledge our solidarity, sing our song and then we thought that is it, we have made our point and we go home…Neither did we expect the kind of reaction that we got from the police that day. (Ndlovu, 2004, p. 340)

In line with the plan they had developed, then, on 16 June thousands of children, some say 15,000 (Tin, 2001), others say 6000 (Pohlandt-Mccormick, 2000) started to march from their schools to central Soweto. As they marched, they sang, shouted, and waved placards with words such as 'Away with Afrikaans' and 'Afrikaans is the language of the oppressors' (Pohlandt-Mccormick, 2000). The police, who had been informed of their plans, deployed approximately 50 officers to the area to meet the procession of school children. The two groups met at 10.30 am on 16 June 1976 and tensions rose, leading the police to shoot into the crowd of children within one hour of the encounter, killing two children

(17-year-old Hastings Ndolovu and 13-year-old Hector Pieterson). Many other children were injured on that day. This reaction by the police sparked the uprising which continued consistently for six months and carried on sporadically, in certain areas, until 1978. The subsequent unrest was not only in Soweto, but also across the country, including city centres and rural homelands (see Pohlandt-Mccormick, 2000).

Schools were burnt down, forcing many to close. Other buildings associated with the apartheid State were burnt down such as those relating to the Bantu Affairs Administration Board, Urban Black Councils, and post offices (Tin, 2001). Beerhalls, *shebeens* and bottle stores, which served adults within their communities, were also burnt down and liquor was destroyed. Barricades were set up by children in order to keep out the police and stop commercial transport from coming into Soweto. Those buses that sought to leave the area to go to central Johannesburg were firebombed and stopped by children. Children also sabotaged railway lines and signals. Street battles took place between children and police. School children initiated 'stay aways' whereby they sought to persuade or coerce adults to stay at home instead of going to work from August to November 1976. On the first stay away on 4th August 60% of workers stayed away. This figure is said to have increased for the next two stay aways, but reduced by the fourth and last one on November 1st of that year (Lodge, 1983; Tin, 2001).

That children have always been the symbol of the Soweto uprising has not been in dispute, but the extent to which they initiated, led, and organised the demonstrations on 16 June 1976 and the subsequent uprising has been downplayed by various actors, including the ANC (African National Congress) in the decades since (see Pohlandt-Mccormick, 2000; Tin, 2001). Instead, as Tin (2001) argues, the children who led and drove the Soweto uprising are represented (or indeed, misrepresented) in anniversaries held to mark the period, as martyrs who had their childhoods taken away from them and not as actors or subjects who played a significant role in a process which, ultimately, resulted in the end of the apartheid State. Instead, some accounts place emphasis on adults such as workers and trade union groups and members of the Black Conscious movement as those who were instrumental in shaping or influencing the actions that children took on 16 June 1976 and in the following months. Tin (2001) explains that this is due to the disbelief amongst commentators that children could be so dangerous and effective in ways that previous protests such as those that occurred in Sharpeville, in March 1960 consisting primarily of adults, had not been. Thus, in this way children's self-representation for justice, which led to genuine transformative change for themselves and the wider society, had the consequence, arguably, of compounding their status inequality and misrecognition in their society in the immediate decades after, as efforts were made to downplay the agency they exhibited and, instead, foreground their passivity.

While indeed it is possible that some older children involved had been inspired by, most notably, the Black Consciousness Movement, which had had been gaining momentum in the country since the late 1960s and had found its way into some schools through a younger generation of teachers who were active in the movement (Moloi, 2011), it was children and young people who were in junior and senior primary schools and high schools who planned and organised and led the demonstration on 16 June, very often without their parents knowing (Ndlovu, 2004). As Tin (2001) asserts firmly, those who initiated and led the events of this period were clearly not university students. Instead, they were school pupils aged 20 and below. He points to photographs taken of the day of the demonstration on 16 June and claims that they show teenagers and school children wearing uniforms marching, shouting with clenched fists, waving placards and sticks. He goes further and claims that in these pictures from the first day no adults were present at all. Instead, it is only in pictures a few days later that adults start to be appear, but by this time everyone was on the streets and the adults captured in photographs were chasing school children with weapons (Tin, 2001). This centrality of children to the uprising is further supported by Pohlandt-Mccormick (2000) who states that according to the South African Institute of Race Relations, 89 of the dead in the West Rand area within the first two weeks of the uprising were under the age of 20, with 12 below the age of 11. This leads her to conclude that:

> The students mobilized themselves and then accepted the responsibility that the events thrust upon them to continue to expand the battles for change, with varied success and at a great cost in death, imprisonment, banning, and exile. Since 1976, the struggle against apartheid has been politically successful. In this, the historical actors of the Soweto uprising played a major part. (Pohlandt-Mccormick, 2000, p. 27)

While the children had support from some adults, it is important to recognise that the conflict that occurred was not only between the children and the apartheid State and its attendant agents, but also between children and adults in their community, especially their parents, who they felt had accepted their subservient status within the country and had submitted themselves to the apartheid State and its rules. Fathers, in particular, were symbols of this parental submission as the strategies they had developed to survive were interpreted as weakness by their children (Tin, 2001). The fact that key places attacked by children included *shebeens* and liquor stores, which primarily served African populations, is an indication of the anger children felt towards their parents and the strategies the latter had adopted to cope with life in South Africa at the time. This disregard for their parents' values was further illuminated by the fact that many children run away from home to join armed groups who were living in exile in countries such as Botswana without necessarily informing their parents (Lodge, 1983; Tin, 2001). Furthermore, attacks and threats children faced not only came from agents of State, but also from adults within their communities. For example, as a response to the stay aways children tried to impose on adults, an order from the Soweto Urban Black Council came which stated that children who stopped workers from going to work should be killed which was approved by the police. As a result, workers started carrying sticks and other such weapons to attack children who tried to stop them from going to work (Tin, 2001).

Such an example of children's participation and organisation demonstrates the transformation that children's collective actions can have on society. However, recognising this has to go along with acknowledging that such a bottom-approach centred on everyday acts of participation initiated by children themselves has its implications. In particular, such an approach means studying, and acknowledging, forms of child participation that do not always correspond with dominant children's rights discourses or even ideas about children's place and expected behaviours in society. Instead, such actions by children may include forms of participation that challenge adult authority and power at a state, community, and family level, thereby disrupting long-valued socialization processes and cultural norms that regulate adult-child relations as was the case during, and following, the Soweto uprising in South Africa. It also means recognising that child-driven participation processes may also be as unequal and exclusive as adult-controlled processes (see Wyness, 2009b)—something which is not too surprising as often, the interactions between children represents a microcosm of wider social relations. While this unbridled agency reflected in child-driven, bottom-up examples of participation may cause some concern to some, there is a need to recognise that processes for change are rarely smooth regardless of context. Conflict, rupture, and disruption are key features of any action for change, especially when it is both in response to social injustice and seeks an outcome which is genuinely transformational. This feature is constant regardless of whether the action for change is spearheaded by children, adults, or indeed, both, bearing in mind the interdependencies that exist between generations (Josefsson & Wall, 2020).

Conclusion

The key argument in this chapter is that while the Convention on the Rights of the Child did represent a turning point in representations and perceptions of children in global social policy, the fact that it places adults at the centre of determining which children participate and how they participate limits the transformational potential of any participatory processes that are inspired by the treaty. This is not to say there is no value in the, often public and formal, participatory initiatives the Convention inspires. It simply means that we cannot expect such efforts to engender significant changes to the status quo in terms of the status inequality and misrecognition that children experience in diverse societies, at least in relation to adults. This is largely due to the fact that child participatory processes, without genuine forms of representation, cannot result in a change that is transformative for children and their societies more generally. Therefore, such initiatives are limited in their transformational potential which fundamentally means that while some changes may be made here and there, the structures that ensure children's subordinate position, or indeed, status inequality as Fraser (2005) puts it, in society persists. For child participation that has the potential for genuine societal transformation, there is a need to conceptualise self-representation as a key element of participation. This involves de-centring the adult within the concept and practice of child participation and foregrounding the actions for self-representation exhibited by children and young people themselves. Alongside this is the need to recognise that children do not need to be provided with, or encouraged to, take up spaces for action. They do so anyway with, or without, adult support. Certainly, history, from sub-Saharan Africa and, indeed, elsewhere including in parts of the Global North, teaches us that those categorised as children today have long demonstrated the capacity for self-representation in their efforts to address any injustice, they and their communities experience. The fact that there may be consequences for society as a result of this action taken by children is part and parcel of processes of transformation as all actions seeking genuine transformative impact—whether they are initiated by adults or children—lead to consequences of some kind.

References

Alderson, P., & Morrow, V. (2004). *The Ethics of Research with Children and Young People: A Practical Handbook*. Barnardo's.

Campbell, K., Denov, M., & Maclure, & Inbal, S. (2011). Introduction. In M. Denov, R. Maclure, & K. Campbell (Eds.), *Children's Rights and International Development: Lessons and Challenges from the Field*. Palgrave Macmillan.

Chawla, L. (2001). Evaluating Children's Participation: Seeking Areas of Consensus. *Participatory Learning and Action Notes, 42*, 9–13.

Farson, R. (1974). *Birthrights*. Macmillan.

Fraser, N. (2005). Reframing Justice in a Globalizing World. *New Left Review, 36*, 69–88.

Fuchs, S. (2019). Towards the Democratization of the Future: The Struggle for Social Recognition and economic success of a West African Association of Working Children and Youth. *Childhood, 26*(2), 139–152.

Gallacher, L., & Gallagher, M. (2008). Methodological Immaturity in Childhood Research? Thinking Through "Participatory Methods". *Childhood, 15*(4), 499–516.

Grossberg, M. (2014). Liberation and Caretaking: Fighting Over Children's Rights in Post-war America. In P. Fass & M. Grossberg (Eds.), *Reinventing Childhood After World War II*. University of Pennsylvania Press.

Hart, R. (2007). Empowerment or Frustration? Participatory Programming with Young Palestinians. *Children, Youth and Environments, 17*(3), 1–23.

Hart, R. A. (1992). Children's Participation: From Tokenism to Citizenship. *Innocenti Essay* no. 4. Florence: International Child Development Centre.

Hashim, I., & Thorsen, D. (2011). *Child Migration in Africa*. Nordic African Institute and Zed Books.

Holt, J. (1974). *Escape from Childhood*. Dutton.

Holzscheiter, A., Joseffson, J., & Sandin, B. (2019). Child Rights Governance: An Introduction. *Childhood, 26*(3), 271–288.

Horgan, D., Forde, C., Martin, S., & Parkes, A. (2017). Children's Participation: Moving from the Performative to the Social. *Children's Geographies, 15*(3), 274–288.

James, A. (2007). Giving Voice to Children's Voices: Practices and Problems, Pitfalls and Potentials. *American Anthropologist, 109*(2), 261–272.

Jenks, C. (1996). *Childhood*. Routledge.

Josefsson, J., & Wall, J. (2020). Empowered Inclusion: Theorizing Global Justice for Children and Youth. *Globalizations, 17*(6), 1043–1060.

Kallio, P. (2012). Desubjugating Childhoods by Listening to the Child's Voice and the Childhoods at Play. *ACME: An International E-Journal for Critical Geographies, 11*, 81–109.

Kirby, P., & Bryson, S. (2002). *Measuring the Magic? Evaluating and Researching Young People's Participation in Public Decision-Making*. Carnegie Young People Initiative.

Lancy, D. (2012). The Chore Curriculum. In G. Spittler & M. Bourdillon (Eds.), *African Children at Work: Working and Learning in Growing Up*. Lit Verlag.

Lansdown, G. (2001). Promoting Children's Participation in Democratic Decision-making. *Innocenti Insights, no. 6*.

Larkins, C. (2014). Enacting Children's Citizenship: Developing Understandings of How Children Enact Themselves as Citizens Through Actions and Acts of Citizenship. *Childhood, 21*(1), 7–21.

Liebel, M. (2002). Child Labour and the Contribution of Working Children's Organisations in the Third World. *International Review of Education, 48*(3–4), 265–270.

Lodge, T. (1983). *Black Politics in South Africa Since 1945*. Longman Higher Education.

Maclure, R. (2011). The Dynamics of Youth Participation: Insights from Research Fieldwork with Female Youth in Senegal. In M. Denov, R. Maclure, & K. Campbell (Eds.), *Children's Rights and International Development: Lessons and Challenges from the Field*. Palgrave Macmillan).

Margolin, C. (1978). Salvation Versus Liberation: The Movement for Children's Rights in a Historical Context. *Social Problems, 25*(4), 441–452.

Miljeteig, P. (2000). Creating Partnerships with Working Children and Youth. *Social Protection Discussion Paper Series*, no. 21, World Bank, Washington, DC.

Moloi, T. (2011). Bodibeng High School: Black Consciousness Philosophy and Students Demonstration, 1940s–1976. *South African Historical Journal, 63*(1), 102–126.

Ndlovu, S. (2004). The Soweto Uprising. In The South African Democracy Educational Trust (Ed.), *The Road to Democracy in South Africa: 1970–1980*. UNISA Press.

Nsamenang, A. B. (2004). *Cultures of Human Development and Education: Challenge to Growing Up African*. Nova Science Publishers Inc.

Parsons, T., & Bales, R. (1956). *Family Socialization and Interaction Process*. Routledge & Kegan Paul.

Partridge, A. (2005). Children and Young People's Inclusion in Public Decision-Making. *Support for Learning, 20*, 181–189.

Percy-Smith, B. (2015). Negotiating Active Citizenship: Young People's Participation in Everyday Spaces. In K. Kallio, S. Mills, & T. Skelton (Eds.), *Politics, Citizenship and Rights. Geographies of Children and Young People* (Vol. 7). Springer.

Percy-Smith, B., & Thomas, N. (Eds.). (2010). *A Handbook of Children and Young People's Participation: Perspectives from Theory and Practice.* Routledge.

Pohlandt-Mccormick, H. (2000). "I saw a nightmare…": Violence and the Construction of Memory (Soweto, June 16, 1976). *History and Theory, 39*, 23–44.

Sandin, B. (2014). Children and the Swedish Welfare State: From Different to Similar. In P. Fass & M. Grossberg (Eds.), *Reinventing Childhood After World War II.* University of Pennsylvania Press.

Sinclair, R. (2004). Participation in Practice: Making It Meaningful, Effective and Sustainable. *Children & Society, 18*(2), 106–118.

Sinclair Taylor, A. (2002). The UN Convention on the Rights of the Child: Giving Children a Voice. In A. Lewis & G. Lindsay (Eds.), *Researching Children's Perspectives.* Open University Press.

Stasiulis, D. (2005). The Active Child Citizen: Lessons from Canadian Policy and the Children's Movement. *POLIS* 12 (numero special). Retrieved January 8, 2020, from http://polis.sciencespobordeaux.fr/vol12ns/stasiulis.pdf

Thew, H., Middlemiss, L., & Paavola, J. (2021). Does Youth Participation Increase the Democratic Legitimacy of UNFCCC-Orchestrated Global Climate Change Governance? *Environmental Politics, 30*(6), 873–894.

Tin, H. (2001). Children in Violent Spaces. Reinterpretation of the 1976 Soweto Uprising. In R. Kriger (Ed.), *Social Identities in the New South Africa.* Kwela Books.

Twum-Danso Imoh, A., & Okyere, S. (2020). Towards a More Holistic Understanding of Child Participation: Foregrounding the Experiences of Children in Ghana and Nigeria. *Children and Youth Services Review, 112.*

UN (1989). The Convention on the Rights of the Child, Geneva: The United Nations.

Van Beers, V. H. (1995). *Participation of Children in Programming.* Radda Barnen.

Veerhellen, E. (1994). *The Convention on the Rights of the Child: Background, Motivation, Strategies, Main Themes.* Garant Publishers.

Wall, J. (2011). Can Democracy Represent Children? Toward a Politics of Difference. *Childhood, 19*(1), 86–100.

Wyness, M. (2006). Children, Young People and Civic Participation: Regulation and Local Diversity. *Educational Review, 58*(2), 209–221.

Wyness, M. (2009a). Children Representing Children: Participation and the Problem of Diversity in UK Youth Councils. *Childhood, 16*(4), 535–552.

Wyness, M. (2009b). Adult's Involvement in Children's Participation: Juggling Children's Places and Spaces. *Children & Society, 23*, 395–406.

Wyness, M. (2013). Global Standards and Deficit Childhoods: The Contested Meaning of Children's Participation. *Children's Geographies, 11*(3), 340–353.

Wyness, M., Harrison, L., & Buchanan, I. (2004). Childhood, Politics and Ambiguity: Towards an Agenda for Children's Political Inclusion. *Sociology, 38*(1), 81–99.

Open Access This chapter is licensed under the terms of the Creative Commons Attribution 4.0 International License (http://creativecommons.org/licenses/by/4.0/), which permits use, sharing, adaptation, distribution and reproduction in any medium or format, as long as you give appropriate credit to the original author(s) and the source, provide a link to the Creative Commons licence and indicate if changes were made.

The images or other third party material in this chapter are included in the chapter's Creative Commons licence, unless indicated otherwise in a credit line to the material. If material is not included in the chapter's Creative Commons licence and your intended use is not permitted by statutory regulation or exceeds the permitted use, you will need to obtain permission directly from the copyright holder.

CHAPTER 4

Children's Participation in Their Right to Education: Learning from the Delhi High Court Cases, 1998–2001

Sarada Balagopalan

INTRODUCTION

On March 3, 2021 UNICEF unveiled its 'pandemic classroom' to remind the world of the number of students who had missed school during the past year. This 'pandemic classroom', a physical installation set up outside the UN headquarters in New York, consists of rows of neatly arranged new prefab chair-desks, 168 in total, each adorned with a bright blue school bag emblazoned with a white UNICEF logo. The affect of an eerily empty open-air classroom is powerfully achieved by an oversize blackboard on which, in uppercase letters, is written the following words: "Class attendance: Absent 168 million children".

COVID-19-related lockdowns have closed schools across the world and it is this unequivocal loss of schooling for 168 million children that the empty benches symbolize, one chair standing in for one million

S. Balagopalan (✉)
Department of Childhood Studies, Rutgers, The State University of New Jersey, Camden, NJ, USA
e-mail: sarada.balagopalan@rutgers.edu

© The Author(s) 2023
B. Sandin et al. (eds.), *The Politics of Children's Rights and Representation*, Studies in Childhood and Youth,
https://doi.org/10.1007/978-3-031-04480-9_4

children. The affective pull of the installation is empirically supplemented by a UNICEF report that discusses how children in different regions have been unevenly affected by these lockdowns. While the most severely impacted regions, in terms of overall percentages, include Latin America and the Caribbean, South Asia ranks high in terms of sheer numbers. Stating how "children unable to access in-person schooling fall further and further behind, with the most marginalized paying the heaviest price" the Report argues for governments to prioritize schooling in their 're-opening plans'. Fearing that these empty benches and attendant statistics may not do enough to convey the critical role that schooling plays in children's lives, the Report also shares how children worldwide "rely on their schools as a place where they can interact with their peers, seek support, access health and immunization services and a nutritious meal" and warns that "the longer schools remain closed, the longer children are cut off from these critical elements of childhood".

Explaining the exhibit, Henrietta Fore, UNICEF's Executive-Director, shares how "Behind each empty chair hangs an empty backpack—a place-holder for a child's deferred potential," adding that "shuttered doors and closed buildings" meant that "children's futures are being put on indefinite pause". This instillation was intended as a message to governments to not only prioritize reopening schools but to reopen them, "better than they were before". This grudging recognition of a deeper problem, which is almost hidden in the well-provisioned 'pandemic classroom', points to how this moment is being leveraged to openly conceal a parallel and more enduring "educational emergency". This is namely the scandalous irony that contemporary schooling efforts in the global south have effectively normalized the existing landscape of highly class, caste and racially segregated schools (Akyeampong, 2009; Srivastava & Noronha, 2016). Quite unlike the well-provisioned 'pandemic classroom', in these iniquitous and poorly provisioned classrooms, it is increased teacher surveillance, precarity and the unlikelihood of schooling translating into greater social mobility that are the experience of most first-generation school students. The UNICEF Report's narrative around what these students miss when school is closed reveals the dynamic that aids in the continued legitimization of these unequal school spaces. This is namely that with school closures these first-generation school attendees miss not only their peers but also their immunizations and a nutritious meal. The normalization of these socially and economically marginalized children within a victimhood narrative, in which the school space provides them a modicum of basic services, is also that which help defer, and effectively sideline, considerations of school quality and equity. While there is no denying that marginal children require these services, the pivoting of schools as spaces that primarily provide these services helps produce schooling for this population as a simplistic exercise, that is, the necessity of securing the presence of children in unequal and segregated school spaces is tied to the provision of these services.

This segregated landscape of schooling, which marks most children's exercise of their right to education in a majority of countries in the global south, fundamentally disrupts the traditional association of schooling with the equalizing of opportunity. Instead, it alerts us to schooling having emerged as a critical compensatory technology that helps maintain existing differences rather than mitigate them. This chapter problematizes how children's participation in their right to education in the Indian context has been overdetermined by victimhood narratives. I do this through sharing a set of court cases adjudicated in the Delhi High Court between 1997 and 2001. These cases helped foreground the state's role in perpetuating existing inequalities and thereby helped highlight the extent to which dominant construction of school participation for first-generation students is framed through a reassertion of their poverty and marginality. These cases, which precede India's adoption of the right to education, played a key role in several provisions of this legal act which went into effect in 2009. By anticipating and countering this more simplistic narrative around what constitutes marginalized children's participation in school, these Delhi High Court cases not only center the critical role that the materiality of school spaces exercise in children's learning, but also aid in recalibrating how these children should be signified within a school space. This is namely through their identity as learners and not as marginal children who are recipients of state welfare services. By shifting the onus away from the child and onto the school, these cases foreground the critical structural role the state is required to assume to fulfill these children's equitable exercise of their right to education. To better situate these cases, the chapter begins with a brief discussion around shifts that mark the broader theorization of children's participation and weaves into this discussion the critical need to open up children's participation to focus on the right to education. It then shifts focus to the Delhi High Court cases which, quite unlike several previous cases which had established the need to legalize the right to education, drew national attention to the harsh realities that confront marginal children *once they enroll in school*.[1] By making visible the material and social reality of first-generation school attendees' experiences in schools, these cases critically interrogate whether children's enrollment in unequal and largely segregated schools could serve as an adequate metric of children's participation. In addition, they importantly helped disclose how an underlying politics of representation reproduces, rather than redresses, the structural exclusions that marked them first-generation school attendees. This chapter's discussion of these court cases is organized around how these helped foreground the poor quality of schools together with revealing the dominant construction of these marginal children within these school spaces. Following this, the chapter concludes by analyzing what these cases add to existing theorizations on children's participation in their right to education.

From Children's 'Voices' to 'Citizenship': Situating the Right to Education Within Existing Conceptualizations Around Children's Participation

The global acceptance of the UNCRC (United Nations Convention on the Rights of the Child) as well as the parallel rise of social theory that view children as active agents has produced a plethora of research that centers, both methodologically and analytically, the importance of children's participation. Article 12 of the UNCRC which focuses on children's capabilities to form their own views and express them on all matters that affect them asserts children's right to have a voice in decision making. However, scholars recognize several contradictions that mark its working out. On the one hand, there has been a global shift in recognizing the importance of including children's viewpoints even though the extent to which these are listened to or included within the global policy regime remains ambiguous (Prout & Hallet, 2003). On the other hand, given the parallel rise of children's rights and neoliberal economic regimes across the globe, the amplification of children's voices has also served as a highly effective smokescreen to mask worsening inequalities. Prescient to these complexities, Allison James (2007) warned of the dangers of privileging 'children's voices' through highlighting the problems posed by authenticity, singularity and paternalism risked in this inclusion. Concerned around the "why and how" of children's participation, James views this as a critical epistemological issue that includes issues of representation and methodology. She foregrounds a range of other problems—specifically those of translation, interpretation and mediation (ref). By flagging concerns around translation, interpretation and mediation, James helps foreground how children's interests come to be represented, and recognizes the potential of children's voices being used to confirm existing agendas. Authenticity for James is about foregrounding the terms under which children's voices materialize. Moreover, she highlights how the inclusion of children's voices, by privileging the 'child' as a singular category risks 'glossing over' intersectional differences between children including those of class, race, culture and gender, to name a few. She says that this singular focus risks disempowering children further while giving them greater visibility.[2]

James' warnings broadly resonate with the experiences of scholars and practitioners who work on children's participation, who've created and tweaked models and programs in order to ensure that these risks are increasingly mitigated. With Hart's (2008) conceptualization of a linear ladder of participation having been dismissed as overtly reductionist and simplistic (Carpentier, 2016; Larkins et al., 2014), scholars have offered other models that attend to the power dynamics and complex intersectionalities that mark children's lives. Some of these include Larkins et al.'s (2014) conceptualization of children and young people's participation in research as a 'lattice'; Lundy's (2007) incorporation of space, audience, voice and influence as the four key components of children's participation; and Johnson's (2017) change-scape which acknowledges wider contextual issues and how processes of participation change over time.

Barry Percy-Smith and Percy-Smith, B., & Thomas, N. (2010) in their Introduction to their handbook on children's participation, acknowledge how critical scholarship on children's participation recognizes this as open-ended and multiply enacted and not as a singular and uniform set of actions undertaken by children and youth. This recognition around how differences in context and everyday material realities make it difficult to clearly define children's participation has prompted them to conceptualize children's participation as closely linked to their exercising citizenship. They state,

> If children are to achieve real benefits in their own lives and their communities, and create a better future, they can only do this by being active citizens, articulating their own values, perspectives, experiences and visions for the future, using these to inform and take action in their own right and, where necessary, contesting with those who have power over their lives. (p. 3)

Their turn toward citizenship as an indicator of participation understands children neither as pre-political beings nor as 'not-yet-citizens' but as politically marginalized subjects (Moosa-Mitha 2005). Further disaggregating this overarching framing to include how intersectional differencesIntersectionalities/intersectional differences, asymmetries of power and the strong traces of a more exclusionary past constitutively produce children's exercise of citizenship as a disparate, and far from uniform, terrain, would allow us to more critically analyze participation in terms of a more politicized framing.

Given the generalized condition of neoliberal economics that marks contemporary global capitalism, this imperative to learn from the pitfalls of children's participation has become even more urgent. This is especially true if one also keeps in mind what Jessica Whyte (2019) discusses as the parallel histories of human rights and neoliberalism, or the role that human rights have played within neoliberal attempts to develop a moral framework for a market society. With several countries in the global south having set in place a legal guarantee around children's right to education, there appears to be a shared agreement around the critical significance of this right. However, unlike other rights, whose exercise and violation are easier to assess, what exactly constitutes children's participation in their right to education is particularly complex. For example, it is easy to identify actions that violate children's participation in their right to freedom of thought and expression (Saunders, 2012). When it comes to the right to education, however, what counts as children's participation in, or exercise of, this right is more ambiguous as schooling is a complex and multifaceted experience, that involves control, compulsion, disciplining and, at times, material rewards.

As a valuable experience in and of itself, as well as a preparation for other activities, children's participation in their right to education has thus far been complexly entangled within a neoliberal terrain has produced a dilution of structural issues. David Harvey (2005) discusses neoliberalism as being in ascension since the 1970s and setting in place processes of deregulation, privatization and the withdrawal of the state from the provision of social welfare services. Neoliberalism constructs human well-being as best advanced "by liberating individual entrepreneurial freedom and skills within an institutional framework characterized by strong private property rights, free market and free trade" (Harvey, 2005, p. 2). In the Indian context, more recent efforts to democratize schooling, which resulted in the legalization of free and compulsory elementary education in 2009, emerged in the early 1990s with the liberalization of country's economy and more specifically with the government's acceptance of the structural adjustment program (SAP) of the International Monetary Fund and the World Bank (Balagopalan, 2022; Kumar et al., 2001; Mukhopadhyay & Sarangapani, 2018). Tempered by lessons learnt from Latin America and Africa, the World Bank had by the early 1990s already targeted school education as a critical safety net while it simultaneously dismantled other measures of social welfare. In fact, the legalization of the right to education in many countries of the global south coincides with the rise of neoliberal policies which produced this right within a politics of enumeration, increased privatization and deferment of equity (Balagopalan, 2018).

Promoted by transnational organizations and postcolonial states, the enumerative politics around the right to education excessively rely on enrollment numbers, with organizations like UNESCO, for example, having naturalized this logic to shape the narrative on the success of this right. This technocratic landscape—in which longer national and local histories and complexities of educational exclusion get erased within an universal language of numbers—devastatingly aids in the parallel masking of an increasingly segregated landscape of schooling. Stephen Ball (2012) powerfully contextualizes this politics of enumeration within global policy-setting's efforts to conceal the unevenness of compulsory schooling. He links this normalization of metrics to the World Bank's structural adjustment programs and neoliberal economic policies as well as the parallel technocratic investments in privatization by state and non-state actors. His work resonates strongly with that of other scholars who've discussed how governments by disinvesting in education as a public good appeared to support moves that allow them to relinquish their responsibility around guaranteeing the necessary financial and social investments required to realize all children's right to education (Fredman et al., 2018; Unterhalter, 2007).

Moreover, this landscape of enumeration coexists with the global affirmation of this right within a highly speculative dynamic. This is namely parallel efforts within global policy discourse that amplify the individuated and aspirational 'futures' that schooling will make possible (Balagopalan, 2022; Huijismans et al., 2021). Untethered from more substantive structural and equity concerns in education and with schooling, in effect, no longer being about the equalizing of opportunity through state provisioning, this speculative dynamic resonates with what Gill-Peterson (2015) in the context of racialized schooling practices in the United States has discussed as the restaging of education as 'entrepreneurial labor'. This is in stark contrast to what the first UN Special Rapporteur on children's right to education, Katarina Tomasevski, had advocated in terms of the four A's needed for the proper realization of this right. Tomasevski (2003) argued that the right to education consisted of schooling being available, accessible, agreeable and adaptable. By framing these 4 A's around substantive 'input factors' that foreground the need for systemic change, and not just the kind indicated in the UNICEF report on schooling during the pandemic, it is particularly timely to theorize what constitutes children's participation in their right to education now that this right is globally guaranteed.

Within existing research, rights-based approaches to educational policy have challenged dominant political and economic ideologies of neoliberalism and economic austerity that promote the commodification of education (Greany, 2008; Spreen & Vally, 2006). Their arguments around the inseparability of education from deepening poverty and inequality foreground state obligations to ensure this fundamental human right. They help re-emphasize how the protection and exercise of this right is intimately linked to the exercise of citizenship and depends on the state fulfilling certain conditions under which this right can be meaningfully claimed (Thapliyal et al., 2013). By combining this human rights framework with Amartya Sen's human capabilities approach they help reinforce the critical role the state exercises in guaranteeing this right; a role that is irreconcilable with the increased privatization of education (McCowan, 2011).

Adding to this, the following cases heard before the Delhi High Court serve as a cautionary note around the underlying material and social conditions required to facilitate the meaningful educational participation of first-generation school attendees. By insisting that these children's primary identities in school are as 'learners', these cases help foreground considerations of school equity as urgent and central to children's exercise of their right to education. This is quite unlike the UNICEF report which views these same children's presence in school primarily in terms of their 'marginal' status. The latter is what is used to legitimize all schools, irrespective of whether they are of questionable quality or deeply segregated, as always an improvement on these children's existing lives. Serving less as a space in which the state attempts to set in place the necessary measures for achieving educational equity, these schools instead aid state efforts to provide a modicum of essential services. In contrast, the effort in these cases to foreground these children's entitlements as citizens helps unpack the power dynamics that underlie dominant representations of first-generation school attendees as 'marginal children' (Balagopalan, 2022).

Delhi High Court Cases, 1998–2001

The lawyer Ashok Agarwal, a key figure in filing these public interest litigation (PIL) cases,[3] began his career as a labor lawyer. The backstory of how he became interested in schooling is noteworthy because he began by advocating against tuition hikes in private schools on behalf of middle-class parents.[4] Approached by the Delhi Abhibhavak Mahasangh, a parent coalition, in December 1997 to file a case against the massive increase (113% in some cases) in school fees in Delhi's private schools, it was while fighting this case that his attention was drawn to government primary schools in the capital. Run by the Municipal Corporation of Delhi these 1776 schools which enrolled 800,000 of the city's children were, according to Mr. Agarwal, largely responsible for the increase in private school fees. What he meant was that the poor state of these municipal schools left middle-class parents with no choice but to enroll their children in private schools. After receiving a court injunction to cap the fee hike at 40%, he shifted his attention to the MCD schools and began to file PILs in Court under the All India Lawyer's Union (AILU). From 1997 onward he filed several cases including those involving issues of school infrastructure, teacher recruitment, transparency in exam evaluation, distribution of the mid-day meal and school uniforms, banning of corporal punishment, to name a few. In this section, I share details from a few court cases, adjudicated by the Delhi High Court between 1998 and 2001, that focused on two separate, though inter-related, concerns. The first set of cases problematized enrollment as an inadequate measure of children's participation in schools by through amplifying the state's grossly inadequate provision of school infrastructure, while the second case focused specifically on upholding the dignity of marginal children as 'learners' within school spaces. Read together these cases help highlight the complexities that frame marginalized children's right to education including the critical role of the state and the enduring effects of a representational politics that constructs these first-generation school attendees primarily as marginal children rather than as citizens who have recently gained their right to an equitable education.

Equity as indexed in the materiality of school spaces: Focused on the 'lack of basic amenities' in the city's MCD schools, this sub-section discusses two cases which drew heightened media attention and produced a robust and very public investigation of Delhi's school infrastructure. The first case was filed on behalf of the family of a seven-year-old boy, Anshu Sharma, student of MCD Primary School in southwest Delhi who was crushed to death on December 23, 1997, while crossing the road during school hours to get a drink of water. His death raised a public outcry as it happened within months of the first PIL filed by the AILU to highlight the 'deplorable' state of MCD schools.[5] This case focused attention on the absence in MCD schools of basic amenities like drinking water, electricity, fans, toilet blocks, desks, playground, play material and the lack of pucca buildings, boundary walls and black boards. The AILU utilized reports filed by MCD's public works department, several years preceding Anshu's death, which had already declared as 'dangerous' 64 primary school buildings with 327 classrooms.

With no action having been taken to demolish and re-construct these structures and to provide an alternate learning space for children, Anshu's death served as a grim reminder of the everyday conditions that marginal children faced in school.[6] Moreover, through deploying statistics that brought the city's entire municipal school system under media scrutiny, these cases exposed how 54 MCD schools with an average of 600 students in each had no water connection, that as many as 137 primary schools in Delhi were being run in tents, that 65 primary schools had no toilet blocks and that another 83 primary schools had no electricity connections. With winter temperatures falling as low as 6 degree Celsius, this PIL additionally disclosed the Municipal Corporation of Delhi using better resourced school buildings as local offices. All of these disparate statistics around the deplorable state of school infrastructure in the nation's capital helped construct a very public narrative that contradiced the MCD's version of events around the 'accidental' death of seven-year-old, Anshu.[7]

The MCD's response was to provide the Court with figures, aggregate numbers on the facilities that did exist as well as the money that had been spent on improving schools. The MCD also worked to counter the reports on dilapidated schools by blaming these existing conditions on children and their families. The MCD's defense included brazen attempts to justify the dilapidated infrastructure by highlighting how the majority of nine lakh enrolled students were children of construction workers and slum dwellers. These children, according to the MCD, were being raised in an environment in which the basic sense of individual safety, hygiene and personal conduct is not very well developed. They argued that given the very low literacy levels of parents, disciplining these children had proved to be a very difficult exercise as a majority of children who had grown up in construction sites as infants demonstrated an entrenched habit of recklessness and rash disregard for danger to their own person and towards their peers. This 'deficit framing' of the poor was, however, something that the Court refused to legitimize. Instead, the Court directed the municipal authorities to improve the provision of water in schools stating, "Water sustains life and the importance of provision of drinking water in a school cannot be over emphasized. To deny water is to deny adequate sustenance. Provision for wholesome potable water in schools is part of right to life enshrined under Article 21 of the Constitution".[8]

This right to life, or Article 21, was again invoked in 1999 after the death of another child, Mehnaz, who was 16 years of age. On February 5 Mehnaz, a ninth-grade student who attended the Government Girls Senior Secondary School in Brahmpuri, Delhi, was shot dead in the middle of the school day by a boy who had walked into the school with a gun and had managed to reach the second floor of the building where Mehnaz was seated. Though her assailant was arrested and Mehnaz survived the immediate attack, she died a week later in hospital. Ashok Agarwal, as part of the Social Jurist filed a case to get Mahnaz'z parents compensation as their child's death on school premises was a violation of Article 21. This case also helped amplify the gendered toll exerted by the absence of security in schools. In this particular case not only was the main gate and boundary wall of the school broken and no security guard in place but the gate was seldom shut on a regular basis. By invoking the constitutional duty of the school to take care of its students, this case was extended to include the prevailing state of security in other girls' schools in the capital. Facts and photographs were provided as evidence on the despicable state of building infrastructure that affected 3000 schools that had a shift-system (where girls attended in the morning and boys in the afternoon) with the absence of adequate security measures exposing girls to the constant risk of being harassed and attacked.

The Court in its judgment stated, "The State must by its acts show that it cares for its citizens and values life…. Such disregard for the security of the girl students negates Article 21 of the Constitution".[9]

In addition, Social Jurist, the non-profit that emerged out of this increased interest of a group of lawyers in elementary education, mobilized municipal school children to write postcards to all of the High Court judges around the general condition of their schools. Kusum Kumari, a 11-year-old girl wrote, "Our school has no rooms. In the winter we sit in a tent and we fall ill. There is no electricity. I have no shoes," and her letter was used by the newspapers with dramatic effect to discuss increased state investment in schools as a concrete step in the right direction. In its verdict around these set of cases, the High Court in February 2003, observed:

> It is a very sorry state of affairs that in the capital of the country, despite the petition being filed by a citizen, required actions have not been taken up by any of the authorities and school children are required to sit either under tin sheds or in open for the purpose of education.... Court has to interpret so as to advance the provisions made in the Constitution. If the children who are attending the schools are not provided a good class-room with sitting arrangements or a playground, it would not be possible for the students to get proper education. Other facilities such as sanitation and pure water are also required to be provided by the school authorities. *In absence of adequate facilities, if the children are sent to the schools, it means torture on them.* They are not expected to do any hard work at this age. *But they are expected to be trained with love and affection and by providing necessary infrastructure so that they can have love and affection for the school/Institute and they attend the school regularly and drops out are minimized.* It is for this reason the government should provide adequate facilities.

Before these cases were adjudicated, the dominant discourse on marginal children and schooling was their lack of access to school, a viewpoint promoted nationwide by the Indian government's District Primary Education Program. Within this metanarrative of access less was said on the quality of the government schools in which these marginal children were enrolled. The Delhi High Court cases interrupted this narrative by making available for public consumption a devastating catalogue of what 'access' had meant in the lives of children who had diligently attended school. Through tactically deploying statistics, photographs and narratives of children, these cases disaggregated 'access' to disclose children's less than ideal participation in these school spaces. As the evidence shared and the judges verdicts made clear, the state received a strong rebuke for its apathy and its efforts to legitimize decrepit school spaces.

Though this criticism, directed at the state, appears at face level to be an assertion around increased equity and accountability in schooling, the outcome of these cases was far more complex. This was because the disapproval directed at the state resonated more broadly with the rise of a more technocratic imagination in these years in which the liberalization of India's economy was in full swing. Echoing judgments passed by the High Court in several other cases, the underlying pattern of these was to expose the state's managerial inefficiencies in order to legitimize technocratic and corporatist solutions that moved in the direction of privatizing state infrastructure. This move was evident, for example, a slew of cases aimed at evicting the poor from residing in 'unauthorized' slums (Ghertner, 2011) and in what Ghertner has analyzed as "green evictions" or efforts of middle-class housing associations to have more control over land use in the city by citing concerns around security and the environment.

Benefitting middle-class and elite interests had not been the intent of the cases taken up by the Social Jurist. However, the media attention these cases received helped produce broad based public support around the need to open-up government schools to technocratic and corporatist remedies. These technocratic efforts would set in place a range of pedagogic interventions to address school quality without any radical redistribution of resources to improve school infrastructure nor address entrenched and enduring segregation of schools. These interventions skillfully leveraged the continued victimization of the marginal child producing school improvement as best addressed by corporatist and private technocratic interventions. In the case of government schools, these corporate interventions reiterated the ruse around the 'urgency' of schooling as that which could transform the lives of poor children and recalibrated discussions away from infrastructural provisions to focus on entrepreneurialism instead (Subramanian, 2020).

Maintaining the dignity of the schooled child as learner: This case concerned the distribution of 'essential items' to marginal children in school. In the complaint filed with the National Human Rights Commission in 2001 the Social Jurist stated that distribution of blankets, sweaters and other essential items to these children in "full public view" constituted a human rights violation.[10] The complaint was filed after a member of the team noticed a newspaper report in a leading regional language daily that contained a photograph and a caption of a high-ranking official of the Delhi local government distributing winter clothes among marginal children enrolled in one of the city's more elite government schools.[11] Stating that the photograph depicted the government official handing out these clothes in a very public ceremony, the lawsuit went on to confirm that this mode of distribution was the norm within these educational spaces. They cited two more media images from another vernacular newspaper that contained similar photos of high-ranking political party officials and other government functionaries handing out these "essential items" to marginal students within the school space.[12] The case stated that this "routine practice" of handing out these items were a "mode of propaganda" and strongly denounced this practice as "derogatory to the dignity of the school children most of whom belong to lower strata of society but also tantamount to violation of human rights of these children" (Agarwal, unpublished, p. 68). The case did not contest the distribution of these "essential items" but rather foreground that what made this humiliating to the children involved was the fact that it was done in "full public view". The complaint also cited Articles 39 and 40 of UNCRC. Though these provisions specifically refer to the child victim and the child in violation of the law, they were invoked more because they discuss the need for the child to be in "an environment which fosters the health, self-respect and dignity of the child" and "be treated in a manner consistent with the promotion of the child's sense of dignity and worth".

By framing the performative distribution of essential items as a violation of these provisions, the lawsuit urged the Government of Delhi and Municipal Corporation of Delhi to immediately ban such practices. That this case went beyond the three mediatized images and school sites to include all marginal children in the city was made clear through language that reiterated how "a majority of children of poor parents who go to school in this country are being educated in 7.5 odd lakh government schools. It is estimated that in Delhi alone, more than 20 lakh children are studying in schools run by Delhi Government and Municipal Corporation of Delhi". Stating that their being from the "lower strata of society" made it all the more urgent, "to adopt even more careful attitude towards these to instill in them the sense of pride and dignity" the lawsuit went on to detail how these children might suffer from a "sense of insecurity" within these spaces as they lack many of the "facilities which children of the rich enjoy". It went on to declare that, if such practices are encouraged, their self-respect will be adversely affected and it would be very difficult to bring them at par with the rest of the society. Facilities of free education, food, shelter, writing material, uniform etc. to the children should be encouraged but not at the cost of their self respect and dignity. Even otherwise, the provisions of free education, food, books, bags, clothing etc. are made at the cost of national exchequer and there is no provision which allows these schools to use these facilities for their publicity benefits.

This self-respect was tied to children believing that they were being singled out because they were poor. If the child "from the beginning is condemned to a mere beggar," the complaint added, not only will this affect their psychological development but will severely misrepresent the fact that they are in school as a matter of right and not charity. The National Human Rights Commission agreed with the complaint filed and directed the government of Delhi to take appropriate actions.[13] Around a year later, by February 28, 2002, the Directorate of Education issued an order to all schools banning the practice of distributing "essential items" "in full public view" and also prevented schools from inviting notable individuals who were interested in encouraging this form of publicity. This case helped recalibrate dominant representations that constructed first-generation school students primarily through their marginal status. It helped explain the psychological toll that these representations can have on children and the critical importance of recognizing them as learners who have a right to schooling. Rather than attempting to stop the distribution of these much needed items this case emphasized the importance of maintaining children's dignity while addressing their needs. Schooling as a process hinged to the preservation, and not the erosion, of children's dignity, can only unfold within equitable learning spaces in which these children are valued as learners and not constructed as recipients of charity.

Both of these cases variously highlight the role of the state in both guaranteeing educational infrastructure and protecting the dignity of children who are first-generation learners. Bluntly speaking these cases helped demonstrate 'access' and enrollment as inadequate measures of children's participation. Instead, these cases moved the focus away from marginal children as charitable objects to their role as subjects, as learners within these spaces and thereby helped frame their school participation within a more robust interrogation of equity in government schooling. This much-needed public scrutiny, however, unfolded within the larger context of India's economic liberalization and paradoxically aided processes already underway to privatize schooling and further dilute infrastructural concerns.[14] With calculations around school quality increasingly constructed as having less to do with addressing inequity and more to do with pedagogical innovations a rising technocratic class reframed the concerns raised by these cases in terms of a corporatist 'ethics of privilege' (Balagopalan, 2014; Sadgopal, 2010; Subramanian, 2020). Corporate interest in government schools, along with the state's willingness to cede control through 'public-private partnerships', drastically redrew the template of educational justice for the marginal child. This increasing marketization of school choice and the parallel rise of low-fee private schools rendered government schools as a less desirable choice. However, several of these provisions that these Delhi High Court cases helped establish around educational equity were included in India's 2009 Right to Education Act (Juneja, 2014).[15]

Conclusion

As a result of these processes, in India we have a situation in which a strong law around all children's right to education coexists with the reality of deeply segregated and increasingly privatized school spaces. With the state intentionally ceding its role, as evidenced most starkly in the reduction of budget allocations for elementary education, the implementation of this right is paradoxically marked by parallel processes that erase, mystify and continually defer concerns around educational equity. The representational logics that underlie UNICEF's pandemic report serves as a good example of this obfuscation of equity. Instead of utilizing the loss of schooling that marginal children experienced during the pandemic to draw urgent global attention to disparities in learning outcomes as that which precedes this more recent disruption and is tied to the increasing normalization of segregated and iniquitous schooling for first-generation learners across the global South, the report instead constructs this urgency around schools serving as a site that provides a range of compensatory services to marginal children. Children's participation in their right to education rests upon the image of a child signified primarily in terms of their enduring poverty. The dominance of this representation produces these children's educational participation within a dialectic that combines victimhood and futurity (Balagopalan, 2021, 2022). First, they overarchingly construct all schools, including poor quality and highly segregated schools, as virtuous spaces in which marginal children have much-needed access to compensatory services. And second, by positioning schools as the only spaces through which marginal children can access an improved future of social mobility they broadly affirm the importance of equity and quality schooling while simultaneously managing to construct these as less urgent concerns. This dynamic produces a self-sustaining logic in which the accountability of international organizations and nation-states is indexed in a fluid and continuously deferrable set of criteria (as reflected in the SDG and MDG goals) with this being justified through children's access to compensatory services within these highly unequal spaces of instruction.

Rather than fundamentally challenging the Indian state's steady withdrawal from guaranteeing this right, UNICEF's representational logics appear to ventriloquize the mystification of concerns linked to equity. This underscores what this chapter has discussed regarding children's participation in their right to education as that which is seldom separable from the power dynamics within which they are represented. This resonates strongly with what several scholars have analyzed in relation to representations of marginal populations. In her work on young Black mothers in the UK, Anne Phoenix (1993) used the term "normalized absence, pathologized presence" to mark how these mothers were represented within social commentary and academic research. In a similar manner, Daniel Bray discusses how the "*partial or incomplete* conception of an object, which is subsequently used as the basis for representative activity" produces certain 'constitutive effects' (Nakata, 2015, p 8). Broadly speaking these analyses help foreground how, "representative claims concern more than the act of representation; they produce power relations by constituting the content, value and meaning of the represented. In short, representative claims are intended to have certain effects on politics" (ibid.).

Similarly, representations of marginalized children's exercise of their right to education get produced through an amalgam of 'constitutive effects' that primarily work to sediment their pathologized presence as marginal children and not as learners. The Delhi High Court cases not only helped draw attention to this representational politics but also alerts us of the need to set in place a more robust idea of children's participation that prioritizes educational equity (McCowan, 2010, 2011). This is a framework that constructs these children first and foremost as learners who have a right to school and not as recipients of charity within school spaces. By bringing into public conversation the abysmal experiences of first-generation learners in school, these cases helped rethink existing assertions that upheld schooling as the self-apparent resolution to their current marginality. Building on these cases to develop a counterintuitive view of children's participation in their right to education requires us to destabilize the prevailing commonsense of educational equity as a continually deferrable goal. Pivoting the discussion around citizenship would allow us to push back against the depoliticized social optimism that marks the parallel construction of schools as sites for the distribution of basic welfare services to marginal children. However, by foregrounding citizenship, this counterintuitive framing of children's participation does not at all believe that the marginal status of first-generation school attendees can be magically erased or overturned. Rather, by underscoring the strong resonances between earlier moments of casteist and capitalist exploitation and the present educational crises that we currently inhabit, we can begin to think about alternatives that holistically center these first-generation students as learners and citizens.[16] As the Delhi High Court cases remind us, this centering could be both shaped and challenged by a vision of social justice that values substantive educational equality as a central criterion for these children's exercise of citizenship and not as a goal that can be perpetually deferred.

Notes

1. These cases include the *Mohini Jain vs State of Karnataka* (1992) and the *J.P Unnikrishnan vs State of Andhra Pradesh* (1993), both of which pushed for the right to education to be made legally enforceable. In the former case, India's Supreme Court ruled that the framers of the Constitution had intended to guarantee all children's right to education by including a Directive Principle and tied this right to the fulfillment of Article 21 or the 'right to life'. This obligation of the state as part of the fulfillment of Article 21 was reasserted the following year in the *Unnikrishnan* case, with the judges clearly stating that free and compulsory education until 14 years of age should be made legally enforceable.
2. In addition, James also interrogates the extent to which children as co-researchers within projects, and particularly children's rights projects, also risk generating a form of paternalism either by overlooking power differentials between adult and children researchers or by providing provided children with a significant role in carrying out the research, *simply because they are children*.
3. According to Ashok Agarwal the PIL, or public interest litigation, was adopted by the Supreme Court of India in 1976. It refers to: "PIL can be defined as a forum of litigation where the petitioner is not the aggrieved party but a public spirited persons taking up the cause of other person/persons who are unable to approach the court for enforcement of his/their rights due to reason of poverty, illiteracy, backwardness etc." (Agarwal, unpublished manuscript, p. 14).
4. For someone who started his career in litigating education cases by taking on a case for the parents of private schools it is quite poignant that the

same parents would later come to oppose him quite bitterly and side with school authorities around a case that required these private schools to reserve seats for economically backward children in lieu of the subsidized land they had received from the state.
5. These cumulative figures included documentation on the number of primary school buildings (1310), total numbers of classrooms (17,209), number of 'Lavatory Blocks' (2675) and boundary walls (1298), as well as an affidavit that stated that the MCD 'repair and maintenance budget' had been enhanced from Rs. 1.5 crore to Rs. 15 crore that year, in addition to which Rs. 30 crores was being made available for the construction of buildings and new rooms, with 400 pucca rooms and 400 semi pucca rooms already underway.
6. In Shahadara in northwest Delhi, the Delhi Corporation had displaced 700 children and in Krishna Nagar students were denied access to the playground.
7. Given that this case preceded the 2009 Right to Education Act, the law that the AILU cited included the 1957 MCD Act which made the maintenance and running of primary schools the responsibility of the Corporation in the 12 zones of the city. In addition, it also cited Rule five of the 1973 Delhi School Education Rules which stated that the MCD will impart free education for all children until the eighth grade or until they reached 14.
8. While in this particular utterance the judges were linking undrinkable water to marginal children's "right to life", it isn't unusual for the court to invoke Article 21 of the Indian constitution in relation to education. This is because the Supreme Court had in the *Unnikrishnan* case (1993) had declared that every child in the country up to the age of 14 had a fundamental right to education as part of their right to life. However, this was the first case in which schooling was being disaggregated to include key infrastructural provisions as part of this fundamental right.
9. The case was made that girls are usually subjected to harassment at the hands of local boys who are often members of local gangs and who have free reign of the school space because of the total lack of security personnel. These boys at times make it difficult for these girls to attend school and might also be used as a reason by the girls' family to stop sending her to school.
10. *Social Jurist vs. Government of NCT and Others* (Complaint to NHRC), date of complaint: 02.03.2001.
11. This appeared in the popular Punjabi newspaper *Punjab Kesari* on January 23, 2001, along with a photograph that showed the Deputy Speaker of Delhi Assembly handing out woolen clothing among economically marginalized schoolgirls of Sarvodaya Vidyalaya.

12. These appeared in the popular Hindi newspaper *Dainik Jagaran* on January 21, 2001, and January 27, 2001. While the first image depicted high-ranking members of the youth wing of the Bharatiya Janata Party distributing pullovers among the poor students in another Sarvodaya Vidyalaya school in the city, the second showed a Municipal Councilor and a Member of Education Committee distributing the same at an MCD school.
13. The NHRC did not take much time at all to attend to this complaint and issued its order on March 30, 2001.
14. This haphazard approach to school infrastructure was also affected by the success of government-run one-room schools in rural areas of the country and the emergence of low-fee private schools. Both types of schools got presented as robust and cheap alternative to the heavy burden of reforming government schools. These newer spaces of schooling had rebuffed infrastructural norms and their modular template circulated as more easily replicable than the repair of existing government infrastructure signaled by the Delhi High Court.
15. This chapter does not have the space to discuss this important case but it did insert a key provision in Section 12 c of the 2009 Right to Education Act that requires private schools to reserve 25% of their annual admission for economically and socially marginalized children from the neighborhood.
16. Schooling is a complex endeavor and in thinking about it holistically we would also need to rethink the curriculum that first-generation learners get taught within these spaces as well as become more aware of the racial, caste and class habitus that marks school spaces even when they are segregated. The contents of this curriculum, language used in the classroom, the privileging of upper-caste worldviews in a school's ethos while neglecting Dalit lifeworlds—all of this would need to be taken into account to make schooling a meaningful exercise for first-generation learners.

References

Akyeampong, K. (2009). Revisiting Free and Compulsory Education (FCUBE) in Ghana. *Comparative Education, 45*(2), 175–195.

Balagopalan, S. (2014). *Inhabiting 'Childhood': Children, Labour and Schooling in Postcolonial India.* Palgrave.

Balagopalan, S. (2018). 'Afterschool and during vacations': On Labor and Schooling in the Postcolony. *Children's Geographies, 17*(2), 231–245.

Balagopalan, S. (2021). The Politics of Deferral: Denaturalizing the 'economic' value of children's labor in India. *Current Sociology, 70*(4), 496–512.

Balagopalan, S. (2022). Introduction: Modernity, Schooling and Childhood in India: Trajectories of Exclusion. *Children's Geographies.* https://doi.org/10.1080/14733285.2022.2073196

Ball, S. (2012). *Global Education Inc.: New Policy Networks and the Neo-liberal Imaginary.* Routledge.

Carpentier, N. (2016). Beyond the Ladder of Participation: An Analytical Toolkit for the Critical Analysis of Participatory Media Processes. *Javnost - The Public, 23*(1), 70–88.

Fredman, S., Campbell, M., & Taylor, H. (Eds.). (2018). *Human Rights and Equality in Education: Comparitive Perspectives o the Right to Education for minorities and disadvantaged groups.* Bristol: Policy Press.

Ghertner, A. (2011). Green Evictions: Environmental Discourses of a "slum-free" Delhi. In R. Peet, P. Robbins, & M. Watts (Eds.), *Global Political Ecology.* Routledge.

Gill-Peterson, J. (2015). The Value of the Future: The Child as Human Capital and the Neoliberal Labor of Race. *Women's Studies Quarterly, 43*(1/2), 181–196.

Greany, K. (2008). Rhetoric Versus Reality: Exploring the Rights-Based Approach to Girls Education in Rural Niger. *Compare: A Journal of Comparative and International Education, 38*(5).

Hart, R. (2008). Stepping Back from 'the ladder': Reflections on a Model of Participatory Work with Children. In A. Reid, B. B. Jensen, J. Nikel, & V. Simovska (Eds.), *Participation and Learning.* Springer.

Harvey, D. (2005). *A Brief History of Neoliberalism.* Oxford University Press.

Huijismans, R., Ansell, N., & Froerer, P. (2021). Introduction: Development, Young People and the Social Production of Aspirations. *European Journal of Development Research., 33*, 1–15.

James, A. (2007). Giving Voice to children's voices: Practices and problems, pitfalls and potentials. *American Anthropologist, 109*(2), 261–72.

Johnson, V. (2017). Moving Beyond Voice in Children and Young People's Participation. *Action Research, 15*(1), 104–124.

Juneja, N. (2014). India's New Mandate Against Economic Apartheid in Schools. *Journal of International Cooperation in Education, 16*(2), 55–70.

Kumar, K., Priyam, M., & Saxena, S. (2001). Looking Beyond the Smokescreen. *Economic and Political Weekly, 36*(7), 560–568.

Larkins, C., Kiili, J., & Palsanen, K. (2014). A Lattice of Participation: Reflecting on Examples of Children's and Young People's Collective Engagement in Influencing Social Welfare Policies and Practices. *European Journal of Social Work, 17*(5), 718–736.

Lundy, L. (2007). 'Voice' is not enough: Conceptualising Article 12 of the United Nations Convention on the Rights of the Child. *British Educational Research Journal, 33*(6), 927–942.

McCowan, T. (2010). Reframing the Universal Right to Education. *Comparative Education*, 46(4), 509–525.

McCowan, T. (2011). Human Rights, Capabilities and the Normative Basis of 'Education for All'. *Theory and Research in Education*, 9(3), 283–298.

Moosa-Mitha, M. (2005). A difference-centered alternative to theorization of children's citizenship rights. *Citizenship Studies*, 9(4), 369–88.

Mukhopadhyay, R., & Sarangapani, P. 2018. Introduction: Education in India Between the State and Market–Concepts Framing the new Discourse: Quality, Efficiency, Accountability. In *School Education in India*, edited by M. Jain, A. Mehendale, R. Mukhopadhyay, P. M. Sarangapani, and C. Winch, 1–27. New Delhi: Routledge.

Nakata, S. (2015). Representing Indigenous Australian Childhoods. *Indigenous Law Bulletin*, 8(17), 7–10.

Percy-Smith, B., & Thomas, N. (2010). *A Handbook of Children's and Young People's Participation: Conversations for Transformational Change*. Routledge.

Phoenix, A. (1993). The Social Construction of Teenage Motherhood: A Black and White Issue? In A. Lawson & D. Rhode (Eds.), *The Politics of Pregnancy: Adolescent Sexuality and Public Policy*. Yale University Press.

Prout, A., & Hallet, C. (2003). *Hearing the Voices of Children*. Routledge.

Sadgopal, A. (2010). Right to Education vs Right to Education Act. *Social Scientist*, 38(9/12), 17–50.

Saunders, K. (2012). The Framers, Children, and Free Expression. *Notre Dame Journal of law, Ethics and Public Policy*, 25, 187–236.

Spreen, C., & Vally, S. (2006). Education Rights, Education Policies and Inequality in South Africa. *International Journal of Educational Development*, 26(4), 352–362.

Srivastava, P., & Noronha, C. (2016). The Myth of Free and Barrier-Free Access: India's Right to Education Act. *Oxford Review of Education.*, 42(5), 561–578.

Subramanian, V. (2020). Parallel Partnerships: Teach for India New Institutional Regimes in Municipal Schools in New Delhi. *International Studies in the Sociology of Education.*, 29(4), 409–428.

Thapliyal, N., Valy, S., & Spreen, C. (2013). "Until we get up again to fight": Education Rights and Participation in South Africa. *Comparative Education Review, 57 (2)*.

Tomasevski, K. (2003). *Education Denied: Costs and Remedies*. London: Zed Books.

Unterhalter, E. (2007). *Gender, Schooling and Global Social Justice*. Routledge.

Whyte, J. (2019). *The Morals of the Market: Human Rights and the Rise of Neoliberalism*. Verso.

Open Access This chapter is licensed under the terms of the Creative Commons Attribution 4.0 International License (http://creativecommons.org/licenses/by/4.0/), which permits use, sharing, adaptation, distribution and reproduction in any medium or format, as long as you give appropriate credit to the original author(s) and the source, provide a link to the Creative Commons licence and indicate if changes were made.

The images or other third party material in this chapter are included in the chapter's Creative Commons licence, unless indicated otherwise in a credit line to the material. If material is not included in the chapter's Creative Commons licence and your intended use is not permitted by statutory regulation or exceeds the permitted use, you will need to obtain permission directly from the copyright holder.

CHAPTER 5

Representing the Child Before the Court

Nataliya Tchermalykh

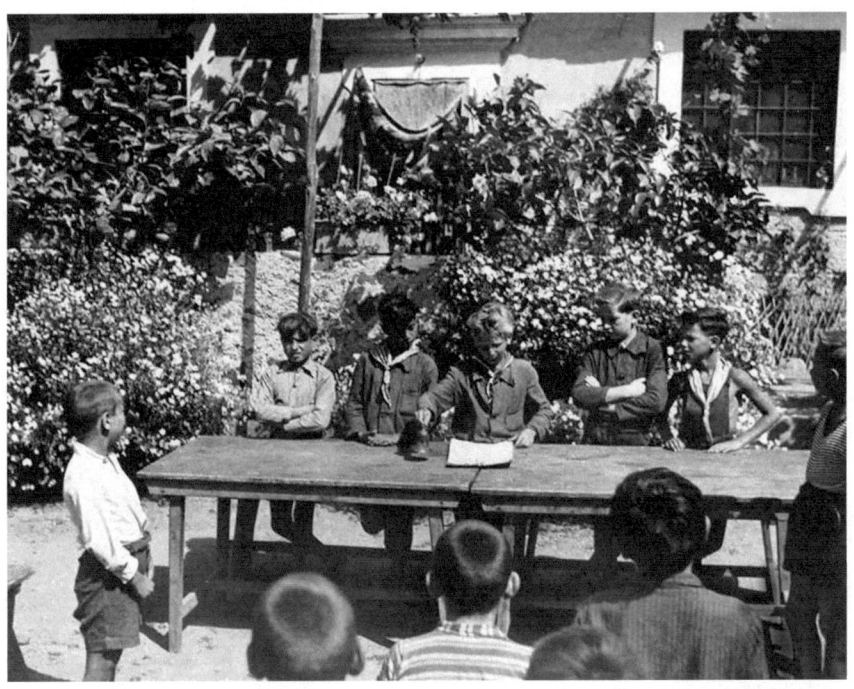

N. Tchermalykh (✉)
Centre for Children's Rights Studies, University of Geneva, Geneva, Switzerland
e-mail: Nataliya.Tchermalykh@unige.ch

© The Author(s) 2023
B. Sandin et al. (eds.), *The Politics of Children's Rights and Representation*, Studies in Childhood and Youth,
https://doi.org/10.1007/978-3-031-04480-9_5

Introduction

In *L'internationale des républiques d'enfants*—a recent book, in which historians of childhood narrate the now-forgotten social experiment in "children republics", that emerged in different parts of Europe between 1939 and 1955—one picture attracted my attention. It is an old, black-and-white photograph. In a garden full of sun, children are performing court proceedings. There are those who seem to be child-attorneys, a child-defendant and a child-plaintiff, and no adults. A no-more-than-ten-year-old judge is reading the court decision. Other children—all boys—are listening to him, standing without motion, their postures translating a state of inner tension, rather than play[1] (Boussion et al., 2020).

This scene, where all power roles seem to be occupied by children, creates a rather disturbing feeling in the observer. In this image of the child-driven legal world there is something artificial. Is it because, I first asked myself, the idea that children are incapable of making justice for themselves is so hegemonic that we interiorized it entirely, and the whole proceeding appeared as a masquerade?

But later I realized that this is precisely *not* what adequate justice for children would look like. What we seek for children is not an artificial place where some child-law might be enacted, because their "jurisdiction" would extend only to the limits of this thoroughly circumvented microsociety, without a real impact on the broader one, the world of the adults. Rather, we seek their fuller and more immediate inclusion in the legal sphere that adults share with children. In practice, as Boussion et al.'s historical research demonstrates, in these places, called Children Villages, disenfranchised kids, some of whom had just escaped the Nazi concentration camps, were merely performing the democratic fantasies of their adult beneficiaries.

In the twenty-first century, despite the near-universal ascendance of children as independent actors and rights bearers, reiterated by the UNCRC (UN Convention on the Rights of the Child), children universally lack legal capacity to autonomously act upon these rights in a court of law. In this context, the indispensability of adult legal actors as conduits to children's access to justice is an undeniable reality. This chapter interrogates the meaning of children's professional representation in courts for a broader theoretical reflection on children's representation in the legal realm. How could we adequately and, more importantly, realistically model the child-adult nexus in the process of justice-making for children?

Some international bodies of children's rights governance suggest that the significant barriers faced by children on their ways of approaching the law can be overcome by means of rendering justice "more accessible", "more friendly" or more "child-centered". This chapter takes a different approach. Rather than assuming that children's access to justice is contingent on the "friendliness" of the systems of justice they face, I argue that it is contingent on their capacity to act upon these systems, while exercising their right for independent legal counsel. This argument bridges the justiciability of social and political grievances, as part of active citizenship, with Fraser's reflections on representation as a third necessary dimension of social emancipation, alongside redistribution and recognition (Fraser, 2005).

The arguments in this chapter should not be interpreted, however, as a statement that courts and litigation are the only, or even the central, means to achieve more justice for children. Rather, this chapter considers children's lack of legal standing as an important exclusionary factor, and therefore frames children's representation by adequate legal professionals as one of the important dimensions of their access to justice. Furthermore, it considers legal professionals, representing children in both domestic and international arenas, as significant actors in the development and interpretation of children's rights.

The argumentation in this chapter is organized in two sections. In the first section I provide a frame to the discussion of children's representation in courts by delineating such adjacent concepts as children's legal capacity and legal standing, highlighting the pitfalls of the narrative on child-friendly procedures, and discussing the ways to adequately model the avenues through which children access justice. In the second section I move to a nuanced description of the professional world of lawyers, adjudicating children's social, economic and political rights in different jurisdictions, including the European Court of Human Rights. In the second section of the chapter, I ask: how do lawyers, defending children in courts, position themselves vis-à-vis their clients, the state, the legal and moral systems they operate within? Do they think only individually and locally, or also collectively and globally? To what extent their practice may effectively contribute to the advancement of social justice for children?

In this chapter, I outline the main challenges of child professional representation, stressing that while it does not escape the reproduction of social hierarchies and epistemological domination, it cannot be reduced to them, leaving some hope for mutually significant alliances between children and their adult defenders in the courtroom, and beyond. I conclude by proposing a tripartite model which is a synthesis of three available formats of child representation in courts. Drawing on empirical material collected through interviews and fieldwork observation, this chapter interrogates the meaning of children's professional representation in courts for a broader theoretical reflection on different instances of children's representation that are brought together in this volume.

SECTION 1

Understanding Children's Access to Justice: From an "Artificially Constructed Incapacity" to Effective Legal Assistance

Childhood is a large and complex category that serves descriptive, normative and regulatory purposes. Despite the remarkable ascendency of children's rights as an international legal norm, substantiated in a near-universal ratification of the CRC, Pupavac (2001) pointed out an inherent paradox in legal reasoning, manifested in CRC, that separates the child, as a rightholder, and the moral agent who is empowered to act upon these rights. Children do not hold office (create law), do not vote (validate law, or elect others to create new law) and only rarely bring cases to court (action existing law in their interests). In other words, in the eyes of the States *children* remain *de jure* subordinate and without authority for most purposes. This paradox helps highlight how, despite the recent advancements, it is the adults, with political power and access, not the children, who identify and turn into law children's existence, needs and authority. Adults—parents, guardians *ad litem*, community members, NGO representatives, lawyers— are also the main actors who take action on their behalf through legal avenues, as the first and foremost precondition for "getting a foot in the door" of the legal system is one's *legal capacity*, that depends on age, as a central definitional variable.

The countries of the world overwhelmingly enshrine a general rule that individuals under the age of 18 lack the standing to approach courts by themselves and, in many cases, must rely on their parents or legal guardians to initiate proceedings on their behalf. The absence of a clear position on legal capacity as a form of emancipation may be interpreted as a blind spot in the reasoning of the UNCRC: Although it recognizes procedural rights of the child in addition to substantive rights, it remains silent on the fundamental right to an effective remedy and does not invoke directly the issues of legal standing, leaving this matter for national legislations (Daly, 2017). Whereas some countries may adopt a graduated approach, granting children some standing before the court during their adolescence, or allow the courts to grant such standing via an ad hoc decision, even in these jurisdictions the logic assigned to the different age restrictions is not fully transparent, and often internally inconsistent. This inconsistency was termed by Nolan as "artificially constructed incapacity" (Nolan, 2011).

Does "Child-Friendly" Bring More Justice to Children?

Meanwhile, within the rhetoric of international bodies of children's rights governance there is a well-established consensus about the fact that "children's access to justice" is the fundamental prerequisite for the realization of their rights. At the same time, international actors reflecting on, implementing or facilitating the coming of children to the various legal loci agree that children face significant barriers in their paths to approaching the law—in which lack of legal capacity is listed as one point among other factors, such as socio-cultural, material, emotional and mental obstacles.

Some optimistically argue that the conundrum of children's access to justice can be overcome by means of rendering the justice "more sensitive", "more friendly" and more "child-centered", contributing to the inflation of such concepts as "child-friendly" or "child-centered" justice that proliferate in the rhetoric of international organizations and children's rights forums (Mahmoudi et al., 2015). Whereas according to the UN these strategic targets are supposed to be achieved by 2030, it would not be an exaggeration to call children the world's least litigious demographic (United Nations, 2015).

The Council of Europe defines as "child-friendly" the legal system that "guarantees effective implementation of all children's rights at the highest attainable level", emphasizing that "particular attention needs to be paid to the delivery of child-friendly information, adequate support for self-advocacy, appropriately-trained staff, design of courtrooms, clothing of judges and lawyers, sight screens, and separate waiting rooms" (Guidelines of the Committee of Ministers, 2011).

The limit of this definition is well demonstrated in Susan J. Terrio's ethnography of children in the American immigration courts. One of the judges she spoke to (who, incidentally, granted asylum in very few cases) reported a case that "broke his heart", involving an 11-year-old boy who had fled Haiti for the United States. Overcoming parental abandonment and abuse in a group home, he became a scholar-athlete in college. He happened to be with his older brother, a drug dealer, during a police force bust, and both were convicted of selling illegal substances. Although he had no prior record and was a stellar student, his conviction for an aggravated felony was a deportable offense. "He had a good immigration attorney", the judge recalled, "but there was nothing I could do" (Terrio, 2015).

This decision could have been delivered by a judge without a robe, and in a relaxed atmosphere of a "child-friendly" courtroom, equipped with sight screens and waiting rooms full of toys—all these parameters, however, would not significantly alter the violence of the final decision, translating the "highest attainable level" of justice for the child, labeled as "non-citizen migrant". Similarly, in several European countries the deportation of a family happens in several stages: first one parent, then the other, then finally the child(ren). Once the whole family is expelled, the children are deported based on their "best interests" and their "right to family life", and in apparent accordance with Art.9 of the UNCRC, stating that "a child shall not be separated from his or her parents".

There is no doubt that the international elaboration of "child-friendly justice" contributes to building a common aspirational horizon for further developments of justice for children and sets a universal standard for such developments within the policy-making domain. However, social scientists, including children's rights scholars, have critiqued and warned about the immediate appropriation of concepts, developed by policymakers, into the realm of social research, as they might be inadequate for a realistic description of a given social reality (Liebel, 2007; Holzscheiter et al., 2019). And more importantly, not all operational categories of practice are useful as categories of theorization (Brubaker, 2013; Brubaker & Cooper, 2000).

To put it differently, adding the modifier "child-friendly" to our discussions of complex, and often conflictual, social processes apparent in the courtroom, is by no means a plausible way to deconstruct the existing power hierarchies underlying the court procedures. On the contrary, the uncritical recourse to "child-friendly" as a ready-made solution may provide a friendly facade to instances of social injustice that conceals and camouflages the lack of substantive rights and, as in the previous examples, the extreme violence of existing power relations. When speaking about how to render law truly more "child-friendly", the first question to ask, perhaps, is "how often is justice the child's friend?"

Modeling Children's Access to Justice

If one admits that the mere mention of insufficient "child-friendliness" or "sensitiveness" lacks the theoretical productivity to adequately address children's sinuous path to justice, how then might we examine children's access to justice in its broadest sense, including processes accompanying justice-making with and for children?

In the conventional sociological literature, the main way to acknowledge obstacles and barriers to effective litigation is represented by the metaphoric image *of the dispute pyramid* (Miller & Sarat, 1980). This pyramid represents the ways to justice not positively (how does a case reach the court?), but negatively (why does it not?), and illustrates the attrition at each stage of the process from the wide variety of "unperceived injurious experiences" (the base of the pyramid) to the small percentage of claims that are actually adjudicated (its tip). Whereas this model efficiently visualizes how litigation is grounded in people's attitudes toward law, it is also criticized for presenting a legalistic vision of justice-making that excludes informal social claiming and, as a result, misrepresents a substantial portion of the ways in which people respond to injuries and a sense of injustice more generally.

This pyramid is far from being the best to represent children's access to justice, as the foundational plateau of unperceived experiences would be too large in relation to the claims that end up being lodged and adjudicated—and the result would not even look like a pyramid at all. Children very rarely bring their injurers to court, due to a multiplicity of factors, besides the lack of legal standing: such as cost, lack of information, cultural obstacles, fear, stigma and lack of trust in the legal system. It is important to stress, however, that a large part of children-related disputes is settled differently, outside the court system. Representing the ways of children to justice in the classical way, as a pyramid of legal action, would conceal more than it reveals of child-related justice-making.

More recently and replying to a decade-long criticism of the inconsistencies of the pyramidal model, in a widely cited article "The Dispute Tree and the Legal Forest", Albiston, Edelman and Milligan proposed to replace the mathematically inspired metaphor of the pyramid by an organic, or botanical one, represented by the dispute tree. The tree, with some ordinary-looking branches, and some "truncated branches for injuries named and blamed but not claimed, and fruitless tips for grievances that were pursued without remedy then abandoned", is supposed to represent "the life of the law" (Nader, 2005)—or plural approaches to dispute-resolution—in a more realistic fashion.

Extending this metaphor to the area of children's rights and their adjudication, which kind of tree could one imagine? Is it a flowering tree that might be beautiful, but does not provide sustenance? Or is the child too rare a visitor of the "legal forest" to be able to "enjoy their flowers, eat their fruit, climb them, sit in their shade, jump from branch to branch"? These are questions that need further empirical consideration, that exceeds the scope of this chapter. However, what one can advance with confidence is that courtroom justice for children is quite a high-hanging fruit, that one is not able to reach with the help of a "ladder" (additional financial resources), but only if an adult sits them on their shoulders. In other words, so long as the branches of the children's rights tree do not bend downward, then children, in order to efficiently enter and act upon a legal arena, are supposed to form alliances with adults, those who are their parents or complete strangers, who belong to the professional world of law. The real question is then who they are, how they are chosen, how they act—and how, and to what extent, they represent children.

Section 2

Professional Legal Representation as a Fundamental Part of Access to Justice

Socio-legal scholarship recognizes that full participation in the legal process—or the act of recognizing an injury, holding another responsible for it, and seeking a legal remedy (sometimes rephrased as "naming, blaming, and claiming" injuries (Felstiner et al., 1980), or as "justiciability of a case or a right")—makes an individual a willful participant in governance rather than an object of government. To put it differently, in modern liberal democracies, the articulation of citizenship, legality and state governmentality implies, among other avenues, the capacity of citizens to actively seek redress for injustice, through available procedures. Although it is true that the state is authorized to enforce law and rights on its own initiative, extensive evidence indicates that the state only rarely exercises this authority, especially in civil and welfare cases, because the legal systems are structured to respond to citizen-initiated complaints.

Arguing for representation as a third necessary dimension of social justice, alongside economic redistribution and cultural recognition, Fraser defines representation as a set of processes that structure public contestation within the society—in other words, how members of the political community "air their claims and adjudicate their disputes" (Fraser, 2005, p. 75). By interrogating children's legal representation, the abstract Arendtian concept of the "right to have rights", inscribed in the political membership to a nation-state, can be bridged with more empirically informed dimensions of citizenship, such as political participation, legal capacity, and access to rights and social justice (Lister, 2007). Consequently, children's pathway to justice could be traced, and theoretically framed in a much more realistic way, moving beyond the "implementation gap" (Vandenhole et al., 2015), or the "child-friendly" packaging of the existing set of laws and procedures.

It must be noted that in modern liberal democracies there is no substantiated discussion about how to render justice more "adult-friendly", primarily because adults are viewed as universal legal subjects—even though the whole legal process appears as impenetrable for an outsider, adults and children alike. By contrast, it is widely approved that the most significant aspect of due process (for adults) is the right to independent legal counsel, and a choice among different modes of representation, as the right to be heard may be rendered meaningless without sufficient legal knowledge. This statement equally applies to children, who, as legal subjects, but especially as a politically (and economically) disadvantaged category, need independent counsel and professional representation in courts, without necessarily being fully aware of such a necessity.

One parameter too often overlooked in both international reports and academic accounts is the availability of adequate legal professionals in the field, as an essential variable defining children's access to justice (Sandefur, 2008, 2009, 2019). In fact, these legal professionals must not only be available, but also willing to initiate and litigate a court procedure on behalf of a child, given that free legal aid for children outside the criminal justice system is guaranteed only in specific matters (Albiston & Sandefur, 2013). Children easily provoke empathy and collect financial donations, but this does not make them desirable as clients for all legal professionals. Whereas the children-oriented NGO sector proliferates worldwide, the same observation can't be made about legal firms or independent counselors.

The legal representation of children is a complex area in both children's rights and socio-legal studies that remains under-documented and under-researched. Whereas states keep accurate records of how many children were convicted in juvenile courts, and for which reasons, the information about how many cases were lodged by children or on behalf of them remains scarce and not easily accessible.

In this sense, the further examination of the child-attorney nexus is crucial in order to understand justice-making for children that contributes theoretically to the understanding of children's representation in society. Lawyering-for-children is a vast, disparate and fluid professional activity that is not easy to classify. Lawyers, who represent children across ages, cases and jurisdictions, have multiple, and sometimes even conflicting, notions of justice for children, as well as the best ways to achieve it. What brings them together is that most of the lawyers systematically engaged in children's defense would define their practice as unconventional—at least to a certain degree—this aspect being defined by the "unconventionality" of their clients, who, on the one hand, do not always have the necessary capacity to fully understand the risks and benefits at stake, and on the other hand, are in a critically disempowered position vis-à-vis the legal systems they operate within (Appell, 2007, 2005). What follows is not an attempt at a comprehensive "taxonomy", but rather a cartography of this under-examined professional area that, however, shapes the advancement of children's rights in a crucial way.

On the following pages, I will describe a recent case brought to the European Court of Human Rights by a Swiss lawyer, acting on behalf of a young girl from Roma community, a case that encapsulates several important aspects of lawyering-for-children, and will serve as a basis for further discussion on different approaches and modalities of children's representation in courts of different jurisdictions—domestically and internationally.

Lăcătuş v. Switzerland: *Bridging the Local to the Global*

On an ordinary evening of an especially cold day, I was among the passersby hurrying back home to escape the *bise*—a bone-chilling wind, blowing from the Geneva Lake. At the doorsteps of one of the many small shops, marking the immigrant area, where I live, I noticed a young woman. She was sitting on the pavement, her legs tucked under her. In her hand she was holding a plastic cup, where a few coins were clinking. As I was passing by, I gave her a coin, and heard a well-recognizable refrain: "bonjour madame s'il vous plaît madame merci madame"—a few words that the members of the Roma community know of French. Once back home, from my window I could see some other people that looked new to the area: an older man with a cardboard sign was standing next to the Swiss bank, and several people were sitting at the bench of a nearby bus station. The bus arrived and left, but they went on sitting, snacking and chatting cheerfully with their children running around. The snow started falling, and something imperceptibly changed in the familiar neighborhood.

These encounters surprised me. I knew that Geneva explicitly prohibits street-begging, by means of one short and bold sentence "Celui qui aura mendié sera puni de l'amende" (Whoever begs will be punished with a fine) that can be found in A.11 of its Penal Code. How could they be here again—so present, so visible? Did they know what they were risking? But the explanation was not slow in coming: a few hours later I learned that the European Human Rights Court issued a decision, *Lăcătuş v. Switzerland*, leading to the invalidation of this law, and providing arguments for further decriminalization of street-begging everywhere in Europe (Lăcătuş v. Switzerland, 2020). The reconfiguration of the urban landscape, or rather its repopulation with members of a particularly marginalized community that I could observe from my window, was an immediate and quite extraordinary effect of a decision taken by a geographically remote high court.

This decision was the culmination of a career-long effort of a human rights lawyer, practicing in Geneva in favor of Roma populations, aimed at proving through legal action that the criminalization of street-begging was in direct conflict with human rights doctrine. The lawyer behind the Lăcătuş case is a paradigmatic example of a "cause lawyer" for whom bringing a grievance to the court is a moral, social and political cause broader than the immediate interests of their clients. In socio-legal scholarship "cause lawyers" is a generic term, describing legal professionals who deploy their legal skills to challenge prevailing distributions of political, social, economic, and/or legal values and resources in order to transform some aspect of the status quo in each society—or, more recently, within the international legal arena (Hilbink, 2004).

Such forms of unconventional, or unorthodox lawyering, received multiple names and designations. They are described as rebellious, progressive, transformative, radical, critical, socially conscious, alternative, political, visionary and activist lawyers. These designations describe those who apply their skills in the service of social change, social justice and equality of judicial treatment. As these causes are much broader than the immediate interests of their clients, these lawyers sometimes choose clients and cases not neutrally, but according to their own political and redistributive projects. In this, a large part of lawyers, representing children, may fall into the category of the so-called cause lawyers.

Lawyering for Children: Protection or Redress?

More broadly, one should distinguish two main approaches in children-rights advocacy and representation. The protective approach, or lawyering-for-relief, proposes individualized solutions that leave the *status quo* in place—by accommodating one person, or making an exception to a general rule. This approach can be defined as "humanitarian" lawyering, according to the anthropological definition of humanitarianism, perceived as the imperative "to assist fellow human beings and to alleviate suffering", without "necessarily act[ing] to defend violated rights" (Wilson & Brown, 2009, p. 11). A paradigmatic example of "humanitarian" lawyering is the legal assistance provided by NGO workers, preparing undocumented children-migrants for interviews aimed at defining their age. Whereas the assistance of a legal professional provides immediate positive results for asylum decisions, it does not always leave space for a critique of the necessity to conduct such interviews in the first place.

Should Violeta-Sibianca, the protagonist of the Lăcătuş case—a Romanian national of Roma origin, born in a poor family and who to the present date can't read, nor write—have met a lawyer, engaged uniquely in the "lawyering-for-relief" activity, her story would never have reached Strasbourg.

After 2007, following Romania's admission to the European Union, Violeta-Sibianca could travel to different European cities, including Geneva. When staying in the city, she was living in extremely precarious conditions, without benefiting from any form of social aid or support, sleeping under the bridges by night and begging on the streets by day. During the daytime, she was systematically intimidated by police officers: cumulatively over three years, she received 900 CHF of fines, her meager belongings were systematically confiscated, and she was once even imprisoned for not being able to pay the forfeits.

Despite these precarious conditions, her lawyer did not seek temporary housing and financial support from the Swiss welfare system or regularization in Geneva—that was in any case almost impossible to achieve and not necessarily desired by the client—but was rather focused on Violeta-Sibianca's primarily bread-winning activity and her humiliating interactions with the police.

In other words, the lawyer opted for a proactive approach, or *lawyering-for-redress*, that consisted in framing combative or innovative lawsuits challenging the prevailing institutional treatment of her clients—in this case, the explicit criminalization of street-begging. This approach includes acting upon the legal arenas to contest ill-founded accusations, obtain compensations for grievances, or making those responsible for them accountable. Lawyers opting for this approach often aim to promote change through expanding, challenging or changing substantive law, litigating matters to create new laws or push the existing boundaries of children's rights.

Children's Representation as a Local and Global Practice

To complexify the picture even more, one should add that the legal representation of children does not only happen within their respective legal and political systems, defined by the state boundaries, but also in the international courts following the pluralization of the legal fields involving children. Here, one could distinguish lawyers who think locally, within national boundaries, and engage in the practice of "expanding lawyering", consisting in "paving new ways for the law to come to children". In other words, they elaborate new and enlarge existing child-oriented legal infrastructures—avenues that bring professional legal services closer to children. This includes free legal aid offices, "legal buses", telephone hotlines or apps, as well as the *pro bono* representation of disadvantaged children, or participation in professionally led movements for gratuity of all legal services for children.

The professional activity of Lăcătuş' lawyer *started* exactly like this—first in her office, when she once received a client of Roma origin, assisted by a benevolent translator—but later developed in a transnational practice. Lawyers who operate at the transnational level think globally, transcending the national boundaries and aiming at supranational legal bodies. They engage in what might be called "ascending lawyering", that may happen both nationally and internationally. This technique consists in upscaling a case in order to get decisions in courts of higher jurisdiction—in this particular case, to reach the two chambers of the Swiss Supreme Court, the negative decision of which can be challenged by a lawsuit at the European Human Rights Court.

This activity creates new legal frameworks, as law can be a mechanism both for increasing rights and for challenging laws that serve as markers of subordination and inferiority of children and contribute to the development of new legal norms—as, for example, the decisions of the EHRC are considered as parts of human rights doctrine. These legal techniques are located on different scales that move horizontally within and across national borders as well as vertically among local, national, regional and international domains. In order to make an individual story successfully "travel" through these disparate and fragmented legal channels, a significant intellectual effort of interpretation, translation and framing is necessary from the lawyer's side.

Children's Representation and the State: Socio-economic Rights or Civil Liberties?

The very practice of children's representation is contingent upon conflictual discrepancies within the conception of children's rights that are inherited from human rights doctrine. On the one hand, advocating for civic or political rights for children positions the child *against* the state and its coercive institutions—as it was clearly the case in Lăcătuş, or in the case of Palestinian children, accused of violence against armed soldiers, debated in Israeli courts,[2] or in a recent case of a group of adolescents, accused of terrorist acts against the Russian state, committed in the space of the popular videogame Minecraft.[3]

On the other hand, lawyers, targeting the welfare, or socio-economic rights, implying more protection coming *from* the state institutions—as for example, advocating for unconditional admission of undocumented migrant youth in state-subsidized shelters—tend to (or must follow strategically), dominant norms of child welfare in each society, in a manner consistent with the societal demands. As Boon has noted, "the lawyer in a liberal state ostensibly pursues the same ends as the state itself…. But lawyers hold the state to its promises" (Boon, 2001, p. 153). Ending this phrase by "without asking for more" would not be inconsistent. In a similar vein, Nolan makes an explicit argument against the courts as spaces of contestation of socio-economic rights for disadvantaged children, arguing that the judicial system is too partial to attack the broad and deep origins of poverty, and despite individual successes in the courtroom, the underlying problem will remain largely unmediated and unaddressed (Nolan, 2011).

Over several years of tight legal battles with the Swiss system, Lăcătuş' lawyer developed a sophisticated argumentation in the spirit of the European Convention on Human Rights that *de facto* prioritizes civic and political rights of peoples over their social, economic and cultural rights. According to this framework, her lawsuit presented the act of collecting money in public places as part of the right to respect for private and family life, freedom of expression and non-discrimination, alleging, *inter alia*, that Lăcătuş had been the victim of discrimination on account of her social and financial situation and her origins. Whereas the Supreme Court of Switzerland rejected all these allegations in block, the European Court of Human Rights ruled unanimously in favor of the case, admitting that the facts infringed the applicant's "right for private and family life", encompassing the right for human dignity and the right to seek relief in a situation of distress. The decision mentioned explicitly that the rights of the applicant were infringed on the grounds of A.11 of the Geneva Penal Code, which led to the subsequent abrogation of the article, and simultaneously opened new avenues to destigmatize everyday activities of street children and challenge their intimidation by the police, at least in European countries. It should be noted that the initial sum of 16.75 CHF confiscated by the police was restituted to Lăcătuş after more than ten years, and she received 900 CHF as compensation for moral damage.

Replying to the Court's argumentation in Lăcătuş, the Swiss Government invoked such reasons for the prohibition of street-begging as public order and safety, the economic well-being of the country and the protection of the rights and freedoms of others, as those who beg in public harass passers-by, bother restaurant patrons and dissuade shoppers, and incite violent reactions from those they inconvenience. It also invoked the potential harm to the tourist attractiveness of the city of Geneva. The Government submitted that this law exists primarily for reasons of protection, as those who beg are commonly exploited by criminal enterprises, especially where children are concerned. Additionally, the Government mentioned that Lăcătuş had never addressed Swiss social services to seek a solution to her situation. As for the "freedom of expression" (of distress), invoked by the lawyer, the Government mentioned that Lăcătuş, when begging, never tried to speak up about the condition of the Roma population, nor made any specific political argument toward the Geneva community.

Overall, the efforts of the state were aimed at the reconceptualization of the case as an individual, domestic and narrowly economic issue—whereas the effort of the lawyer, sustained by the Court, was presenting, or rather "translating", it in the human rights language, as a collective civic and political case of transnational significance for Roma community that includes, but is not limited to, children and youth involved in street-begging.

In the case of *Lăcătuş v. Switzerland*, despite its undoubtedly progressive nature in terms of recognition of rights of children and disadvantaged minorities, the argument of EHRC followed the lawyer's translation of Lăcătuş' grievances for police ill-treatment as a violation of her right for "private and family life" (Art.8), a right sufficiently vast to encompass "human dignity". A concurrent opinion of one of the judges interpreted her activities as the "right to express distress", perceived as a derivative of the freedom of expression, and another one again indicated that it was not a case of "human dignity", but that of a "human autonomy".

This decision disregarded, however, such important aspects of informal economic activities, elaborated by children's rights scholars, as the right to work in decent conditions, freedom of entrepreneurship, or even, arguably, cultural rights, leaving them outside of the legal debate. Additionally, the Court did not make any statement regarding the racial discrimination of Roma minorities. While interviewing the lawyer behind this case, I realized that all these dimensions were of equal importance to her; however, "they never passed through", as she framed it—or, in other words, they were never picked up by the Court in her attempts to advocate for this. This positioning results from an artificially constructed dichotomy that opposes civil and political rights on the one hand, and socio-economic and cultural rights on the other hand, which in the current configuration of international justice cannot be addressed and debated together.

Lawyering for Children as Interpretation, Translation and Transmission

Here, the lawyer acted as a translator, who connected transnationally circulating discourses to particular socio-legal contexts and adapted international documents into terms relevant to localized political struggles, enabling injured individuals to see the human rights violations against them. These processes of "translation", "transformation" and "interpretation" between everyday reality and the legal categories are already present in legal work—and, more philosophically, legal reasoning. In her seminal theorization of global and local processes in law, explained through a linguistic metaphor of "vernacularization", legal anthropologist Sally Engle Merry emphasized that a key dimension of human rights, perceived as a transnational field of practice, is the work of intermediaries—"the people in the middle"—who translate between abstract human rights concepts and specific situations (Merry, 2006).

Such intermediaries take stories of particular injuries and translate them into human rights violations so that global audiences will pay attention. Particular experiences are translated into the more generic terms of human rights violations so that they can circulate along transnational corridors. As Lăcătuş' success demonstrates, what once were tragedies, or failed cases in the eyes of the judges and civil society, are now also potentially violations of international law. The everyday grievances of children, documented by NGOs, may also constitute evidence of such violations that may be presented to international bodies (Hanson & Nieuwenhuys, 2012).

With the pluralization of legal regimes, representing a shift from the centrality of the state as the source of legal ordering, the legal work came to signify not only the reformulation of children's grievances in legal terms, but also the interpretation thereof within the frameworks of rights, associated with the functioning of supranational courts, and the transnational legality more generally. Within this new pluralization of law and heightened contest between local and global orders, state sovereignty emerges as an increasingly complex phenomenon, constrained by multilateral treaties and engagements (Fraser 2005).

Considering the above, one can delineate three modes of professional representation of children, based on the premises of lawyer-client interaction, that are not mutually exclusive, and may complement one another, stretching from the most conventional formats to the most unconventional ones, and apply to both international and domestic aspects of representation:

- Lawyering *on behalf* (or *in lieu*) of the child, when the legal representative defines the child's best interests, and develops the strategy according to her knowledge, experience and expertise in the field.
- Lawyering *for* the child, aiming at improving the conditions, protecting rights and solving problems, following the interests expressed by the child, that may not necessarily coincide with the lawyer's personal views.
- Lawyering for *the children*—as parts of marginalized communities, or as a group, that includes proactive litigation in national and international courts, and legal advancements, aimed at the development of children's rights law.

Ultimately, *Lăcătuş v. Switzerland* is an interesting example that synthetizes all three modes of representation and demonstrates how a lawyer, by writing down the story of an illiterate girl, actioned it at the international level to abrogate a law that *both*—the lawyer and the client—found discriminatory and unjust, however for different reasons. To my question about the meaning of the case for Lăcătuş herself, her lawyer replied: "For *this* applicant the decision was meaningful. Firstly, it meant less police harassment on the streets. Secondly, and most importantly, the meaning stemmed from her feelings of gratitude towards me, as I represented her community for over a decade. She knew that the decision was important for *me*, and therefore it was for her". And while in this case the decision did have a tangible effect on their everyday lives (i.e., the repealing of the law immediately provided access to previously restricted areas), the average Roma individual does not perceive international legal action, and the EHRC, as a reliable source of justice-making for the community. Indeed, it is evident that social suffering is never immediately alleviated by these victories, due to structural inequalities, and most importantly the disjointed temporalities of the law and everyday life. Nor do these decisions provide immediate political solutions, as their rhetoric has first to be picked up and utilized as arguments in political struggles by those who have a more direct access to polity.

Epistemological Challenges of Power Delegation in Courts

Whereas the Lăcătuş case is illustrative of an interesting form of intergenerational and trans-class solidarity between a socially sensitive legal professional and her disadvantaged client, it should be noted that all complex transnational processes that involve children only at the very first stages of the legal action do not come without significant challenges. Such challenges are associated with any form of representation, as the privileged access to legal knowledge *per se* places lawyers in a heightened position of dominance vis-à-vis their clients. This epistemological inequality, that in critical legal studies is sometimes defined as "epistemological imperialism"—the power to define which grievance may potentially become justiciable and how, or "legal extractivism", the power to access to and use someone's distress for a reason—is perhaps even more palpable in the courtroom, where those with legal education play the role of experts, and others the roles of complete outsiders (Madhloom & McFaul, 2021).

As experts, lawyers may construct their own notion of substantive justice and fail to search for the child's view. They may also lack information or imagination of how those rights will affect the client and children more generally. The attorney has relatively free reign to identify and shape the child's interests and little accountability when acting within this relationship. As Mnookin noted, rightly, "wherever power is delegated, there is always the potential and incentive for the agent to put his own interests ahead of those of his client. The problems infect almost every human relationship" (Mnookin, cited in Minow, 1990). The first and foremost risk, jeopardizing adequate representation of children in courts, is a marked tendency of individual adults, groups of advocates, and even the state institutions, to treat children as vessels for various sets of privately and publicly held values that children are not fully aware of. Sometimes, this leads to symbolic "usurpation" of a child's agency in a particular legal or political situation, when the child's voice, identity, grievances or political opinions serve solely to promote the cause, formulated by the attorneys "over the heads" of their clients—however noble this cause might be.

Whereas in European scholarship the notion of lawyering "in the best interest of the child" became hegemonic, contingent to the view expressed in the UNCRC (Freeman, 2006), in the American context scholars have argued about whether lawyers should advocate for the "best interests" or rather for the "expressed interests" of their clients, who are children. The doctrine of the "expressed interests" has been largely advanced by the progressive and advocacy-oriented members of the bar, who criticized the "best interest approach" firstly for ethical reasons, as it allocates too much of the decision-making power to the attorney, and secondly for theoretical ones, since the notion of the "best interest" when it comes to the client-attorney relationship is based on a legal fiction that may overshadow the legally codified spectrum of rights, and the client's wishes (Artwood, 2008). Some commentators even propose to convey an independent advocate to articulate the child's "best interests" position, leaving to the attorney the representation of what the child wants, despite the possible inconsistencies in the child's reasoning.

Conclusions: Toward a Mutually Significant Alliance?

The child imagines the law not as a written doctrine, but as a chain (network) of objects and persons, who impersonate power or mediate knowledge; the legal personhood of a child is constructed by interaction with these elements, constituting their cultural repertoire. The sound of the police siren that suspends the flow of time on the street, "you are under arrest!", the cuffs, but also random representations of legal process provided by popular culture, the officially stamped documents, or lack thereof, experienced by both the child and her relatives—the encounters with these disparate elements push children to reflect on, and position themselves in relation to such abstract concepts as "order" and "disorder", "justice", and "injustice", and the dialectical relationship between them. This is how the legal landscape emerges in the child's consciousness—and it can be either menacing or meaningful, or even captivating for some.

For legal anthropologists, law manifests itself not only as a material ensemble of codified norms and statutes, validated by a set of linguistic and social practices, but as a cognitive and semiotic construction mediated by immediate experiences: it is not something that happens outside the society, but within people's lives. Indeed, as Silbey puts it, law is deeply entrenched within the "tapestry of the everyday and ordinary events". Long before the codification of their rights, children had legal lives (Hanson & Nieuwenhuys, 2012). They had to, and still have to, navigate complex legal worlds with or without external guidance. From this viewpoint, disadvantaged children, who are often described as totally estranged from the legal sphere, may have in practice a more precocious and intimate relationship with the legal system than their more privileged counterparts (Balagopalan, 2019, 2014). Mostly illiterate Roma children, engaged in informal activities in the streets, are better informed about the everyday practices of law-enforcement than most legal professionals.

These interactions are also one of the first places where a child encounters the notion of social power and engages with legal and political authority. This power may be quite abstract, but it is substantially linked to such ideological and cognitive constructions as "the state", "bureaucracy" and finally "the law". The legal consciousness of an adult does not emerge magically when she turns 18, but is acquired gradually, as part of an individual's cultural repertoire and is shaped by various experiences, be they positive, negative or ambivalent.

Notwithstanding all these risks and perils, the experience of invoking the law, while being assisted by a competent legal professional, plays an important, formative role in the way children perceive justice and authority. As shown above, a courtroom success does not necessarily mean social justice; conversely, a courtroom failure does not necessarily mean alienation and desperation. For children, legal experiences may play an emancipatory role, as it decenters and challenges the unidirectional model of the law (from state to citizen), delineating legal processes as merely top-down mechanisms for social control, that cannot be challenged from the bottom upward. An exercise in legal reasoning challenging dominant discursive, epistemological and political norms may, under certain conditions, bring evidence about the potential *reversibility* of the processes of domination and exclusion, and demonstrate a more interactive (rather than subordinate) approach to the law.

In this sense, the experience of legal representation can be perceived as a mutually significant exchange between a child and her legal representative—a form of alternative legal pedagogy—that opens a window toward more legal literacy, and finally leads to a deeper understanding of democratic processes, such as plurality, adversariality and, more importantly, the possibility, and even necessity, to appeal the decisions taken without due consultation—including that of inadequate representation. The three formats of legal representation outlined in this chapter—lawyering *on behalf* (*in lieu*) of the child, that leaves the courtroom agenda to the discretion of the attorney; lawyering *for* the child, that follows the interests, views and opinions, expressed by the child; and lawyering for *the children*, aimed at achieving social justice for children as a social group—may be counterbalanced by a fourth—lawyering *with the child*, a practice based on the premise that every child is competent, capable of autonomy and needs more legal information, unless the contrary is proven. Whereas such conscious collaboration is desirable, it appears almost utopian, or at least exceptional at this juncture, as it does not realistically represent the structural premises of the professional legal field and its rigorous hierarchies of power, that are based on, among other things, epistemological privilege of access to legal knowledge.

Notes

1. Children's tribunal of Repubblica dei ragazzi de Civitavecchia around 1948, in Boussion, Gardet and Ruchat (2020, p. 77). Photographic albums of Carroll-Abbing, archives of l'Istituto internazionale per lo studio dei problemi della gioventù contemporanea, Città dei ragazzi, Rome.
2. https://www.dci-palestine.org/military_detention.
3. https://www.themoscowtimes.com/2020/11/23/siberian-schoolkids-charged-with-terror-over-minecraft-plot-reports-a72120.

References

Albiston, C. R. and Sandefur, R. L., (2013). Expanding the Empirical Study of Access to Justice. *Wisconsin Law Review, 1*, 101–120.

Appell, A. R. (2005). Children's Voice and Justice: Lawyering for Children in the Twenty-First Century. *Nevada Law Journal, 6*, 692.

Appell, A. R. (2007). Representing Children Representing What: Critical Reflections on Lawyering for Children. *Columbia Human Rights Law Review, 39*, 573.

Artwood, B. (2008). The Uniform Representation of Children in Abuse, Neglect, and Custody Proceedings Act: Bridging the Divide Between Pragmatism and Idealism. *American Bar Association* (No. 1, Spring), pp. 63–101.

Balagopalan, S. (2014). *Inhabiting "Childhood" Children, Labour and Schooling in Postcolonial India*. Palgrave Macmillan.

Balagopalan, S. (2019). Why Historicize Rights-Subjectivities? Children's Rights, Compulsory Schooling, and the Deregulation of Child Labor in India. *Childhood, 26*, 304–320.

Boon, A. (2001). Cause Lawyers in a Cold Climate: The Impact(s) of Globalization on the United Kingdom, in Sarat, A. & Scheingold, S.A. (Eds.) Cause lawyering and the state in a global era. Oxford University Press, 143–185

Boussion, S., Gardet, M., & Ruchat, M. (2020). *L'internationale des républiques d'enfants (1939–1955)*. Anamosa.

Brubaker, R. (2013). Categories of Analysis and Categories of Practice: A Note on the Study of Muslims in European Countries of Immigration. *Ethnic and Racial Studies, 36*(1), 1–8.

Brubaker, R., & Cooper, F. (2000). Beyond "identity". *Theory and Society, 29*(1), 1–47.

Committee of Ministers of the Council of Europe. (2011). Guidelines of the Committee of Ministers of the Council of Europe on child-friendly justice. Strasbourg: Council of Europe Publishing.

Daly, A. (2017). *Children, Autonomy and the Courts: Beyond the Right to be Heard*. Brill Nijhoff.

Felstiner, W., Abel, R., & Sarat, A. (1980). The Emergence and Transformation of Disputes: Naming, Blaming, Claiming …. *Law & Society Review, 15*(3/4), 631.

Fraser, N. (2005). Reframing Global Justice. *New Left Review, 36*, 69–88.

Freeman, M. (2006). *A Commentary on the United Nations Convention on the Rights of the Child*. Brill Nijhoff.

Hanson, K., & Nieuwenhuys, O. (Eds.). (2012). *Reconceptualizing Children's Rights in International Development: Living Rights, Social Justice, Translations*. Cambridge University Press.

Hilbink, T. M. (2004). You Know the Type…: Categories of Cause Lawyering. *Law & Social Inquiry, 29*, 657–698.

Holzscheiter, A., Josefsson, J., & Sandin, B. (2019). Child Rights Governance: An Introduction. *Childhood, 26*, 271–288.
Lăcătuş v. Switzerland 2020. European Court of Human Rights.
Liebel, M. (2007). Paternalism, Participation and Children's Protagonism. *Children, Youth and Environments, 17*(2), 56–73.
Lister, R. (2007). *Why Citizenship: Where, When and How Children?* Theoretical Inquiries in Law 8.
Madhloom, O., & McFaul, H. (2021). *Thinking About Clinical Legal Education*. Taylor & Francis Group.
Mahmoudi, S., Leviner, P., Kaldal, A., & Lainpelto, K. (Eds.). (2015). *Child-friendly Justice: A Quarter of a Century of the UN Convention on the Rights of the Child*. Brill Nijhoff.
Merry, S. E. (2006). Transnational Human Rights and Local Activism: Mapping the Middle. *American Anthropologist, 108*, 38–51.
Miller, R.E. and Sarat, A. (1980). Grievances, Claims, and Disputes: Assessing the Adversary Culture. *Law & Society Review, 15*(3/4).
Minow, M. (1990). *Making All the Difference: Inclusion, Exclusion, and American Law*. Cornell University Press.
Nader, L. (2005). *The Life of the Law*. University of California Press.
Nolan, A. (2011). *Children's Socio-Economic Rights, Democracy and The Courts*. Bloomsbury Publishing.
Pupavac, V. (2001). Misanthropy Without Borders: The International Children's Rights Regime. *Disasters, 25*, 95–112.
Sandefur, R.L. (2008). Access to Civil Justice and Race, Class, and Gender Inequality. *Annual Review of Sociology, 34*(1), 339–358.
Sandefur, R. (2009). Access to justice. Bingley, UK: Emerald Jai.
Sandefur, R.L. (2019). *Access to What? Daedalus, 148*(1), 49–55.
Terrio, S. J. (2015). *Whose Child Am I?: Unaccompanied, Undocumented Children in U.S. Immigration Custody*. University of California Press.
United Nations. (2015). Resolution A/70/L.1. Transforming our world: the 2030 Agenda for Sustainable Development.
Vandenhole, W., Desmet, E., Reynaert, D., & Lembrechts, S. (Eds.). (2015). *Routledge International Handbook of Children's Rights Studies*. Routledge.
Wilson, R. and Brown, R.D. (2009). *Humanitarianism and suffering: the mobilization of empathy*. Cambridge University Press.

Open Access This chapter is licensed under the terms of the Creative Commons Attribution 4.0 International License (http://creativecommons.org/licenses/by/4.0/), which permits use, sharing, adaptation, distribution and reproduction in any medium or format, as long as you give appropriate credit to the original author(s) and the source, provide a link to the Creative Commons licence and indicate if changes were made.

The images or other third party material in this chapter are included in the chapter's Creative Commons licence, unless indicated otherwise in a credit line to the material. If material is not included in the chapter's Creative Commons licence and your intended use is not permitted by statutory regulation or exceeds the permitted use, you will need to obtain permission directly from the copyright holder.

PART II

Children's Representation and the International Politics of Children's Rights

CHAPTER 6

'Could It Be That They Do Not Want to Hear What We Have to Say?' Organised Working Children and the International Politics and Representations of Child Labour

Edward van Daalen

Introduction

In the fall of 2017, I travelled to Buenos Aires to participate in the International Labour Organisation's (ILO) 'IV Global Conference on the Sustained Eradication of Child Labour' (hereafter: IV Global Conference). The aim of the IV Global Conference was to take stock of global progress made, and to set out an agenda to achieve the eradication of child labour in all its forms by 2025.[1] Kailash Satyarthi, who became known as the face

---

This chapter was elaborated within the framework of research project P2GEP1_191426 funded by the Swiss National Science Foundation.

E. van Daalen (✉)
Faculty of Law, McGill University, Montreal, QC, Canada
e-mail: edward.vandaalen@mail.mcgill.ca

of the Global March Against Child Labour and who together with Malala Yousafzai was awarded the Nobel Peace Prize in 2014, was one of the keynote speakers during the opening ceremony of the conference.

Satyarthi started his speech by insisting that the, at the time, estimated 152 million child labourers worldwide are not just figures in report, but that each of these children has "a beating heart and a divine soul".[2] He brought some of these children to life in the minds of the conference participants through a series of personal anecdotes. Satyarthi told a story of how he met with a Syrian refugee in Turkey who had lost a child which was probably trafficked. The man was now desperate to marry off his 12-year-old daughter before she too got stolen or sold. This was followed by an account of a group of trafficked child labourers in Delhi that were recently rescued from a jeans factory by Satyarthi's organisation. These children, he emphasised, had not seen daylight for three years, and would not dare to dream to one day wear those jeans.

Not long after Satyarthi's speech ended, I received a text message from Maria, one of the young representatives of the *Movimiento Latinoamericano y del Caribe de Niñas, Niños y Adolescentes Trabajadores* (Latin American and Caribbean Movement of Working Children and Adolescents; hereafter: MOLACNATs), the umbrella organisation of Latin American working children's movements. As will be detailed later on in this chapter, members of working children's movements defy and challenge the narratives of working children as passive victims waiting to be rescued. Instead, they assume their identity as workers and claim the recognition of their right to dignified work. Maria and I had met at a conference on working children that was held in Bolivia several weeks prior. There she had explained to me that MOLACNATs had explicitly requested access for working children to the IV Global Conference, but that the organisers had let them know that due to security measures nobody under the age of 18 would be welcome. In response, MOLACNATs sent a delegation to Buenos Aires to demonstrate against their exclusion. Maria's text informed me that the protest would be held on the third day of the conference, at the *Plaza del Congreso* in front of Argentina's National Parliament. Maria and other representatives of MOLACNATs were joined by members of *Asamblea Revelde*, a local working children's movement founded in one of the poorer suburbs of Buenos Aires. After some ice-breaker activities to get everybody's attention, two of the MOLACNATs delegates read out loud the letter of complaint they had sent to the United Nations (UN) Committee on the Rights of the Child:

Seeking to exercise our rights as per Article 12 of the Convention on the Rights of the Child, we asked the organisers to let us participate in the IV Global Conference [...]. Not only was this right to participate denied to us, but it was denied to anyone under 18 years of age, "for security reasons". Without fully understanding the reasons for this violation of our rights, we ask ourselves: Do they want to protect us or do they want to protect themselves against us? Could it be that they do not want to hear what we have to say?[3]

Talking to the working children and their supporting adults at the protest, it became clear to me that the prevailing belief was indeed that the ILO simply did not want them there, and was not interested in what they had to say. This belief had been strengthened by an article in the German periodic *Der Spiegel*, for which one of the ILO's child labour experts, Jose Maria Ramirez, was interviewed. When asked about the claim of organised working children to have a say in the IV Global Conference, Ramirez explained that allowing them to do so would be like inviting people to talk about the advantages of eating meat during a vegetarian dinner.[4] In other words, their presence and discourse was perceived to be incompatible with the representations of 'child labourers' as passive and vulnerable victims who are not able to speak for themselves.

This is problematic because even by the ILO's own legal definition, 'child labour' is a broad concept which constitutes much more than the so-called 'worst forms of child labour' such as slavery and trafficking as depicted by Satyarthi during his speech. Current global challenges such as the ongoing climate crisis and the Covid-19 pandemic result in growing numbers of working children who deserve policies, programmes and solutions that are substantiated by a plurality of experts, including working children themselves. To better understand how we arrived as this impasse and how we can move forward, I will use this chapter to reconstruct, analyse and problematise the institutional and geo-political developments that have resulted in the current status quo. It will bring to light how a select group of individuals and organisations came to hold the power to represent child labour as a form of modern slavery, while other actors and approaches, in particular organised working children and their claims for better working conditions, are excluded from global policy making. This reconstruction is based on: primary sources retrieved from several archives, including the ILO archives in Geneva, the International Institute of Social History in Amsterdam, and the Netherlands National Archive in The

Hague; semi-structured interviews with current and former (staff) members of governments, international organisations, NGOs and working children's movements conducted between 2015 and 2019; and additional secondary literature.

In the following section "Shifting Priorities in Child Labour Policy", I will detail the institutional developments inside the ILO between 1979 and 1996 which resulted in the decision to adopt a new ILO convention on the worst forms of child labour. In the section "We Do Not Want *Them* to Represent *Us*" I will then discuss the working children's movements and their efforts to participate in international events aimed at producing recommendations regarding the aim and scope of the new convention. The recognition of a paradox inherent in the notion that children have a right to participate in global governance helps to make sense of the finding that while this process provided the opportunity for organised working children to participate on the international level, it simultaneously resulted in their further exclusion. The penultimate section of the chapter, the section "Convention 182 on the Worst Forms of Child Labour", revolves around the role played by Satyarthi and the Global March Against Child Labour in the drafting and promotion of the new convention that was eventually adopted in 1999. I will engage with the theoretical concepts of 'mutual legitimation' and 'representational power' to elucidate how the ILO—and in particular the group of trade unions inside the organisation—and Satyarthi's Global March made strategic use of each other to feign democratic legitimacy and to uphold an effective, but self-serving, advocacy strategy in which working children are narrowly represented as helpless and voiceless victims of modern slavery. In the concluding section of the chapter "Concluding Remarks" I will make the case for why this representational strategy is problematic and why working children's movements are to be considered important stakeholders in the search for evidence-based programmes and policies that revolve around a more holistic understanding of working children's rights and wellbeing.

Shifting Priorities in Child Labour Policy

Reconsidering Convention 138

Central to the ILO's global campaign to eradicate child labour is its Minimum Age Convention 138 (hereafter: C138), which was adopted in 1973 to replace all earlier sector specific child labour conventions. It is important to make clear how C138 defines 'child labour', as this legal framework provides the basis for the statistical structure which is used to estimate and monitor how many children are in 'child labour' world-wide.

Whereas its preamble states that C138 has the objective to achieve "the total abolition of child labour", the actual text of the convention makes clear that this certainly does not mean all work done by children, as defined as persons under the age of 18 years.[5] While it sets a general minimum age of 15 years for all employment and work, it also provides many significant exceptions to this standard. The first concerns so-called 'light work', meaning work which is not likely to be harmful to health or development and which does not hinder school attendance. This type of work can be done by children of 13 years and older. The second main exception concerns so-called 'hazardous work', "which by its nature or the circumstances in which it is carried out is likely to jeopardise the health, safety or morals of young persons".[6] No person under the age of 18 is allowed to be engaged in such work. C138 provides further special exceptions for countries "whose economy and educational facilities are insufficiently developed", or in other words: developing countries.[7] They are allowed to exclude non-hazardous work from the scope of C138 if it is done within "family and small-scale holdings producing for local consumption and not regularly employing hired workers", and to lower all these minimum age standards by one year, except for hazardous work.[8] Despite these specific exceptions for developing countries C138 remained highly unpopular during the first years after its adoption, being ratified by only a handful of countries.

During the UN International Year of the Child in 1979, the ILO introduced the so-called 'two-plank' policy in an attempt to mitigate the initial failure of C138 to protect working children. In short, this policy encouraged countries to focus on protecting working children by regulating and 'humanising' their work in the short term, while aiming for ratification of C138 and the abolition of all child labour in the long term (van Daalen & Hanson, 2019). For a decade or so the ILO merely encouraged and applauded such programmes. Yet at the beginning of the 1990s, it started to implement its first technical assistance programmes, of which the 'Smokey Mountain' project was the most significant and would set the course for the ILO's future anti–child labour campaign.

Smokey Mountain

The project ran from 1989 to 1992 and was primarily aimed at helping children and their families that worked on and around the large garbage dump known as 'Smokey Mountain' in Manila, the Philippines. Whereas the outcomes of the project were considered a relative success by those directly involved (Gunn & Ostos, 1992), it served yet another goal for those overseeing the ILO's broader campaign on child labour, namely raising awareness and funding. As explained by a former ILO official:

> I was interested in that project really for two reasons. One is that a few [children] would benefit from some nutrition support and from some educational support on a part-time basis. It does not really change substantially their lives, but it helps. But there was a more fundamental reason. When that project was done, it happened to attract international media attention. Imagine from a media point of view, these children working on this mountain of garbage that is smoking and burning all the time, under very, very difficult conditions. After that, it was easy for us to mobilize resources for the International Program on the Elimination of Child Labour, IPEC, and later on of course for the new Convention on the Worst Forms of Child Labour.[9]

The ILO had commissioned a photographer to take pictures of children working on Smokey Mountain that were used in ILO publications and advocacy documents, which thus aided the ILO in its efforts to raise funds and awareness. In 1992, the year the Smokey Mountain project officially ended, the ILO kick-started its International Programme on the Elimination of Child Labour (IPEC) which continued to focus on projects similar to Smokey Mountain, loosely applying the same methodology. During the first years of its existence, most of IPEC's country projects were aimed at improving the working conditions of children working under very harsh and hazardous conditions. At the same time, awareness was generated by publishing reports about these projects (ILO, 1993). This pragmatic approach led to internal discussions about the viability and desirability of the thus far ineffective C138 and its general prohibition of all forms of work under the different minimum ages.

Targeting the Intolerable

More than two decades after it was adopted in 1973, C138 had been ratified by only 45 member states, amongst which were only very few developing countries. It was telling that out of the ten countries in which IPEC had implemented its programmes, only Kenya had ratified the convention (ILO, 1995). It was believed that the work done by IPEC on projects concerning child workers at great risk should inform national and international policy to reach such children more effectively. The former Deputy Director General of the ILO, Kari Tapiola, explained that as a result, many inside the ILO considered C138 "to be unwieldy or even obsolete" (Tapiola, 2018, p. 15). Yet this line of reasoning ran into stiff opposition from the Workers' Group inside the ILO, led by the International Confederation of Free Trade Unions (ICFTU).[10] Fearing a 'race to the bottom' during the years of increasing globalisation and the moving of production processes to countries with lower labour standards (Nieuwenhuys, 2007), the ICFTU was one of the fierce proponents of including a so-called 'social clause' in the General Agreement on Tariffs and Trade (GATT), which in 1995 would become the World Trade Organisation (WTO) (Vandaele, 2005). The social clause would link the international trade regime to the human rights regime by establishing minimum labour standards for workers in all member countries, and a child labour-free production process was one of the proposed standards. When it became clear that a social clause would not be adopted by the WTO, the ICFTU turned to the ILO and advocated for strengthening instead of weakening the ILO's commitment to abolish all forms of child labour (van Daalen & Hanson, 2019). The solution to this internal divide was found in the adoption of a new child labour convention. This new convention was to prioritise action against what would become known as the worst forms of child labour, while at the same time it was to reconfirm that the ratification of C138 and its objective to abolish all forms of child labour would remain the fundamental long-term goals.[11]

In a 1996 report the ILO made public its strategy to adopt a new convention and what was to be understood by 'the worst forms of child labour':

> [G]ive priority in the first instance to abolishing the worst and intolerable forms of child labour such as slavery and slave-like practices, all forms of

forced labour including debt bondage and child prostitution, and child work in hazardous occupations and industries. (ILO, 1996, p. 115)

In this report, the ILO also presented its first global estimates of child labour. Based on findings of experimental surveys in four countries it was estimated that about 250 million children were economically active in developing countries. While this figure was only a very rough estimate and said nothing about the type of work done by children or the conditions under which it was undertaken, its association with phenomena such child slavery and prostitution significantly shaped the public imaginary. In the words of former ILO-IPEC director Frans Röselaers, "The number drew international attention to the magnitude and scope of the child labour problem worldwide. It was widely publicised; hardly any article on child labour failed to mention it" (IPEC & SIMPOC, 2002 Preface).

Discussion: The Paradox of Institutionalisation

This section has made clear how the institutionalisation of a pragmatic policy to mitigate the early failings of C138—by prioritising the protection of working children and the improvement of their working conditions—paradoxically resulted in shifting priorities that would come to drown out arguments in favour of this policy.[12]

When in 1979 it was understood that C138 and its abolition objective—even with its many exceptions and flexibility clauses—was too ambitious to be ratified and implemented by developing countries, the ILO believed to have found an intermediary solution. It encouraged countries to improve the working conditions of children for whom working under the hazardous conditions was unavoidable. An ILO report published in 1989 noted a "remarkable surge" in "creative projects" conducted by governments and NGOs with the objective to "prevent the abuse of child labour and to protect and assist those children who do work" (ILO, 1989, p. 30). Only a year later the ILO initiated the Smokey Mountain project and got its own hands dirty.

While children and their families were provided with practical assistance and viable alternatives, ILO policymakers recognised the larger instrumental potential of the project. The shocking images and narratives of young children working on Smokey Mountain resulted in increased media attention and facilitated the mobilisation of resources. That the ILO still believes in the power of such representation is confirmed by the fact that,

20 years later, the cover page of the report in which the ILO the presented its 2021 global estimates of child labour features a young boy scavenging on a garbage dump (ILO, 2021).

When IPEC continued to implement and assist projects aimed at the protection of children working under the worst conditions—often by improving their working conditions—serious questions were raised about the viability of C138 and its abolition objective, not in the least place because it was still very poorly ratified by those countries it was designed for. Options that were explored for the further institutionalisation of IPEC's pragmatic policy ran into stiff opposition with the ILO's powerful block of trade unions. For reasons that were primarily related to the global political economy and the labour position of Western unionised workers, the trade unions had no intentions on weakening the ILO's commitment to the abolition of child labour, and in fact sought ways to reinforce this normative project. The solution to this internal divide was found in the adoption of a new instrument—one that prioritised the abolition of the so-called worst forms of child labour, including child slavery, child trafficking and child prostitution. After the Smokey Mountain project, the ILO understood the strategic force of representing child labour by means of these disturbing, but ultimately fringe, phenomena, in particular when combined with publicised global estimates of hundreds of millions of children in 'child labour' as broadly defined by C138.[13] This emotive advocacy campaign heavily influenced the public imaginary and allowed for the further mobilisation of resources. At the same time, the focus on the worst forms of child labour projected an ideology that would come to obscure and exclude the more pragmatic and creative approaches that laid at the foundation of the ILO's initial shift in addressing child labour. This becomes clear from the following section, which details the efforts of working children's movements to have influence over the process of discussing and drafting the new convention.

"We Do Not Want *Them* to Represent *Us*"

Working Children Get Organised

The first working children's movement is generally considered to be the *Movimiento de Adolescentes y Niños Trabajadores Hijos de Obreros Cristianos* (Movement of Working Adolescents and Children of Christian Workers; hereafter: MANTHOC) that was founded in 1978 in Lima, Peru

(Chacaltana, 1998; Taft, 2019b). One of the central objectives of MANTHOC, and most other working children's movements that followed, is to secure work with dignity for children, and the societal recognition of their status and value as workers with rights of their own. In the wake of MANTHOC, working children started to organise in other countries in Latin America, and in Africa and Asia as well. In Brazil, the *Movimento Nacional de Meninos e Meninas da Rua* (National Movement of Street Boys and Girls; hereafter: MNMMR) was formed in 1985 (Swift, 1997). Two working children's organisations, *Bhima Sangha* and the *Bal Mazdoor Union*, were founded in India during the late 1980s, and in Africa the *African Movement of Working Children and Youth* (AMWCY) saw the light of day in 1994 (Liebel, 2001; Swift, 1999). Although these different movements each have their own specific origin story owing to the different political, economic, and cultural circumstances in the respective region, they do have much in common (Nieuwenhuys, 2009; van Daalen, 2020). All of them are locally organised grassroots organisations of working children supported by adults and local NGOs that provide a platform on which working children can come together to strive for the improvement of their lives as children and workers.[14] Central to the philosophy of all these movements is the idea of *protagonismo infantile* (children's protagonism; hereafter: *protagonismo*). While definitions and interpretations vary, it roughly translates to a viewpoint that foregrounds children as having the agency to create social change, to make decisions for themselves, to claim their own rights, and to represent themselves (Taft, 2019a). One of the ways in which the movements seek to exercise *protagonismo* is by trying to influence policies and programmes on different levels, from the local to the national and international, where they seek self-representation through elected delegates (van Daalen & Mabillard, 2019). With the funding and support of several international child rights NGOs, representatives of the above-mentioned movements came together for the first time in 1996 in the town of Kundapur on the west-coast of India.[15]

The Kundapur Meeting

Confronted with the news about the creation of a new ILO child labour convention, the representatives of the different movements decided they wanted to have influence over its drafting. They believed it was important to break the pattern of others, adults, "talking and talking about *our* problems, as they have been doing for so many years without finding solutions".[16] Based on their discussions and experiences during the Kundapur meeting, they drafted a manifesto consisting of ten points that formed the basis of their joint international campaign. This list would become known as 'the Kundapur Declaration' and consisted of, amongst others, the following demands:

We want respect and security for ourselves and the work that we do.
We want an education system of which the methodology and content are adapted to our reality.
We want to be consulted in all decisions concerning us, at local, national, and international levels.
We are in favour of work with dignity and appropriate hours, so that we have time for education and leisure. (IWGCL, 1998)

The Kundapur Declaration was primarily a call to recognise working children as workers with rights to a safe and developmental working environment. Similar to the conventional trade unions, they also demanded influence in decision-making processes that affect them. The opportunity to do so presented itself in the form of two ILO 'preparatory conferences' to which NGOs and researchers were invited to come up with recommendations regarding the aim and scope of the new convention. The first was held in Amsterdam, the second in Oslo.

From Amsterdam to Oslo

The NGOs supporting the movements lobbied the Dutch government and the ILO to invite the movements of working children to the Amsterdam Child Labour Conference (hereafter: Amsterdam Conference). It was conveyed that the movements not only requested to participate, but that they claimed 'equal representation', meaning that if there are 20 ministers invited, there should be 20 working children present as well. The movements explained that "We will have discussions with our ministers, but we do not want them to represent us".[17] The organisers finally agreed to invite eight representatives of the different working children's movements who had participated in the Kundapur meeting: three from Latin America, two from West Africa and two from Asia. Eight, because eight ministers from developing countries were invited to the conference, by which the organiser believed they had respected the working children's demand for equal representation.[18] During the conference, the working children's representatives were able to attend all the discussions of the different panels and workshops, and on day one of the conference they were assigned their own plenary panel session.[19] During this panel session, the representatives presented the Kundapur Declaration and were asked to respond to a set of questions, including: Why do children work in conditions that are exploitative and dangerous? Vidal of MANTHOC argued that the ILO's general abolitionist approach pushes children to the more dangerous margins of the informal economy and should therefore be considered as one of the causes. Work, he explained, is one thing; bad working conditions are another. He urged the conference delegates not to confuse the two. At the end of workshop in which all of the working children participated, the conference participants adopted a recommendation that explicitly called for the participation of NGOs and working children's movements in the further development of international law and policy on child labour. However, in the official conference report, this specific recommendation was rendered more general and only made mention of 'civil society' (SZW, 1997). Despite such small setbacks, the delegation of working children's representatives felt strengthened by the experiences in Amsterdam and was confident they would be allowed to participate in a similar fashion in Oslo. There, however, things turned out to be more challenging than expected.

Having witnessed how the movements participated in Amsterdam and how their presence and claims for work with dignity attracted much media attention (ILO, 1997a), the trade unions united in the ICFTU pressured the Norwegian Government and the ILO to exclude organised working children from participating in the Oslo Conference.[20] The trade unions believed that their presence and diverging discourse would undermine the objective of the conference and of the new convention, that is to abolish all of child labour by starting with the worst forms. In response to their exclusion, the movements decided to organise a parallel 'shadow conference' elsewhere in the city in an attempt to influence the debates from the outside, for which they received support and funding from Save the Children Sweden and the Dutch Government.[21] But things took a turn several weeks before the start of the conference. General elections had provided Norway with a new government that proved much more receptive to the idea of children's participation, and at the last minute the movements were informed they could send three representatives to officially participate in the Oslo Conference. Furthermore, all of them were allowed to attend the closing ceremony on the final day. Despite these commitments by the organisers, the three working children's representatives that were elected by their peers to participate in conference concluded that, unlike the Amsterdam Conference, Oslo was not an appropriate space for the voices of working children to be heard.[22] No special arrangements had been made and they had not been invited to participate in any of the panel discussions. The delegation of Latin American movements' representatives therefore decided to demonstrate in front of the main entrance of the conference building with tape over their mouths as a symbol of their marginalisation. Their sense of being silenced was reinforced by the publication of the official conference report, in which not a single mention of their participation was made (ILO, 1997b).

Notwithstanding, they had succeeded in participating in both preparatory conferences and remained determined to continue their collective mission to directly contribute to the drafting of the new convention during the 1998 International Labour Conference (ILC).[23] Together they wrote a letter to the Director-General of the ILO:

> Dear Sir,
> We would like to make a request concerning the International Labour Conference scheduled to be held in Geneva; especially regarding point 6 on the agenda, the proposed new convention on the 'most intolerable forms of child labour'. In 1997, we, the representatives of working children's movements, participated in two Conferences where this proposed convention was discussed. Eight of us were at the Amsterdam Child Labour Conference, and four of us were at the Oslo Child Labour Conference. As you know, we are for a Convention that truly protects children from what the ILO calls the intolerable forms of child labour. But as the persons the convention will most affect, we are concerned its provisions be realistic and helpful. For that reason, it is important that the working children's own thinking should be heard from the mouths of their own democratically elected representatives […] We, the movement of working children want to be able to benefit from the 'self-representation' principle so fundamental to the ILO, and from Article 12 of the [UN]CRC because we are democratically elected and given a mandate by our movements which exist in more than 40 countries in Asia, Africa and Latin America. In this view we would like to be fully represented in the debate regarding the proposed convention.[24]

Discussion: The Paradox of a Children's Right to Participation

As will be discussed in the following section, the movements would never receive an answer from the ILO and were excluded from the further deliberations and drafting of the convention on the worst forms of child labour. Ironically, while the series of international events that were held in preparation of the new convention presented them with the opportunity to influence this process of global governance, their presence and participation ultimately resulted in their exclusion from future international discussions concerning child labour. This can be understood as the result of an inherent paradox that lies in the notion of a children's right to participate in global governance, which sees children lose effective control over the exercise of this special right as soon as they enter the international political arena.

The claim of the working children's movements that they had a right to participate in Amsterdam, Oslo and Geneva was certainly not baseless. The practically globally ratified 1989 UNCRC addresses the complex issue of a child's right to meaningful (political) participation.[25] The obligation of states to respect the views of children has been identified by the UN Committee on the Rights of the Child as one of the four 'general principles' of the UNCRC.[26] This general principle is not captured by one comprehensive article, but by a cluster of articles enshrined inside the UNCRC: Article 12 (right to be heard), Article 13 (freedom of expression), Article 14 (freedom of thought, conscience and religion), Article 15 (to freedom of association and to freedom of peaceful assembly) and Article 17 (right to access to information). State parties are obliged to take all appropriate legislative, administrative and 'other' measures (e.g. social and educational) to ensure the implementation of these articles. By means of the 2002 General Assembly Special Session on Children (UNGASS), the UN put in practice its obligation as intergovernmental organisation to indeed seek out and respect the views of children in international matters affecting them. In the preparatory process leading up to the UNGASS, more than 40,000 children from 72 countries were surveyed about their realities and their rights and obligations as children. During the UNGASS itself, hundreds of children—including representatives of working children's movements—were invited to participate in the different events of the special session and were asked to provide recommendations for the outcome document, 'A World fit for Children' (Skelton, 2007). In this document, world leaders reaffirmed their commitment to the UNCRC and to facilitate the participation of children in international law and policy making concerning them.[27] But as the examples in this chapter have shown, this was—and remains—anything but established practice.

Based on discourse of *protagonismo* and claims of their special children's right to participate, the representatives of working children's movements succeeded to gain access to the preparatory conferences in Amsterdam and Oslo and thereby to a process of global governance. However, as soon as they did, they lost effective control over the exercise of this right and were dependent on governments and the staff of international organisations when it came to the level of influence and self-representation they could practically exert. This is primarily due to the fact that the sphere of international law and policy making remains governed by interests and politics instead of by an adherence to rules and principles. Despite historical precedent of NGO involvement in international affairs that started centuries ago (Charnovitz, 1996), there still is no general theory and little empirically grounded accordance on what the exact role of civil society in global governance is or should be (Alston, 2005). For the Amsterdam Conference, the Dutch Government was not persuaded by arguments that the movements had a right to participate in the event, but agreed to their demands of full and 'equal' participation because of the threat of bad publicity if they would not allow them to do so. One of the civil servants in charge of organising the conference explained how she discussed this with her responsible Minister:

> I said, 'Yes, we have to do this. It is politically not feasible to just exclude the working children now. We will be crushed in the newspapers and this conference is doomed to fail if we do not accommodate these particular civil interests.'[28]

Regarding the Oslo Conference, the working children's representatives initially remained excluded from participating not because they were not well organised, but because the ICFTU held significant influence over the organisation of the conference and the trade unions simply did not want them there. After having witnessed how in Amsterdam the working children challenged the discourse on the worst forms of child labour by expressing their pride as workers and by demanding better working conditions and adapted education, it was considered that their presence in Oslo would undermine the purpose of conference. That it took an actual change in government for the movements to be allowed to participate shows just how erratic and unpredictable the state of international law and policy making remains, and how overtly dependent children are on other, more powerful, actors for the effective exercise of their participation rights. While the ICFTU and the ILO thus had to stomach the physical presence of three working children's representatives in Oslo, it was made sure that their presence and discourse on work with dignity would not be acknowledged in the official conference report. This was only a harbinger for the ensuing events in Geneva where the ILO held complete control over the drafting process of the new convention, and over which civil society organisations (CSOs) were included or excluded. In a strategic move to provide the ILO with the appearance of being a democratic institution that is open to working children's participation, Kailash Satyarthi and his Global March Against Child Labour (hereafter: Global March) were co-opted in the process of drafting and promoting the new convention on the worst forms of child labour.

Convention 182 on the Worst Forms of Child Labour

The Global March Against Child Labour

Whereas the official request of the working children's movements to participate in the ILO conference in Geneva remained entirely ignored, on the 2nd of June 1998 Kailash Satyarthi and dozens of children of his Global March were invited to the UN's *Palais de Nations* for the grand opening of the conference.

Satyarthi had made a name for himself in India as a radical raid and rescue activist during the 1980s. By founding Rugmark (now known as GoodWeave International, which provides certifications for 'child labour free' carpets and other woven goods produced in South Asia) (Chowdhry, 2003) he also became an influential international actor. He was furthermore involved in the drafting of the so-called 'Harkin Bill' (officially called the Child Labor Deterrence Act) which was unsuccessfully proposed to the US Congress by Senator Tom Harkin on several occasions since 1992, with the aim of imposing an import ban on products produced by child labour.[29] But Satyarthi gained real world-wide recognition as the founder and public face of the Global March. The Global March was modelled after a march against child slavery and servitude that was previously organised by Satyarthi throughout India, and which revolved around small rallies in towns and cities. Children that were rescued by Satyarthi's organisation featured prominently in these rallies, voicing their stories of neglect and abuse (Rotthier, 1995). From this experience sprung the idea for a global march that consisted of different marches crossing Asia, Africa, Latin America and Europe. In the periphery of the aforementioned 1997 Amsterdam Conference, Satyarthi organised a meeting of NGOs during which the Global March was officially founded. The objective of the Global March was simply to raise global awareness of child labour and to promote education for all.[30] After this meeting, a large-scale network and media campaign followed, with information letters sent to hundreds of NGOs all around the world, asking for their support and participation by organising events to coincide with the Global March, which was planned to symbolically end in Geneva to coincide with the 1998 ILC.[31]

Similar to the march in India, the Global March rallies were characterised by the presence and testimonies of rescued or former child labourers. The detailed accounts of anthropologist Susan Levine (1999), who attended the regional Global March events in South Africa, provide a window into why and how the Global March selected those children for the final march in Geneva. One of the organisers explained why he believed that a girl named Noluthando would be a suitable candidate:

> You can tell by her shyness that she is quite traumatized by the experience of work. She feels inferior to the other kids here who do not work.... And I think the fact that she cannot speak English works to our advantage for Geneva. We want people to see how work damages children, that they are illiterate because of work and are emotionally traumatized. (Quoted in: Levine, 1999, p. 151)

This strategy was also reflected in the information brochures about the core marchers that were distributed to journalists during the Global March events on the different continents. The list with the names, ages, nationalities and languages of the former or rescued working children was accompanied by a myriad of testimonies, many of them describing incidents of physical and psychological abuse in situations of slavery, servitude and bondage.[32]

The Worst Forms of Child Labour

As addressed in the section "Shifting Priorities in Child Labour Policy", through the Smokey Mountain project and the 1996 global estimates of child labour, the ILO had understood the power of advocacy based on disturbing images and narratives of victimhood. Witnessing the wide support and media attention that the Global March had rallied based on a similar strategy, the ILO engaged in talks with Satyarthi on how it could play a role in the ILC in Geneva and the discussions on the new convention. This would not have been possible without the approval of the workers' group led by the ICFTU. Whereas the trade unions are generally fiercely opposed to the participation of other (non–trade union) organisations in ILO matters—as these are generally perceived as competition for influence—they too understood that Global March would be a strategically valuable partner. With the consent of the workers' group, it was agreed that the Global March would be invited to the opening ceremony of the ILC as described above. The former Executive Director of the ILO, Kari Tapiola, explained that "some tweaking of established procedures was needed to enable this unique demonstration" (Tapiola, 2018, p. 17).

The role of Satyarthi and the Global March in the ILC went beyond their symbolic presence and support. During the negotiations about the final text of the convention, the Vice-Chairperson of the ILO's workers' group emphasised the special relationship between the Global March and the trade unions as he explained that "the organisers of the Global March had been in constant discussion with the Worker members about reaching an agreement on language acceptable to them" (ILO, 1999).

In the end, the members of the ILO's drafting committee agreed on the final text of ILO Convention 182 on the Worst Forms of Child Labour (hereafter: C182) which was officially adopted during the 1999 ILC. In its preamble it is clearly stated that C182 was devised to complement C138, which remains "the fundamental instruments on child labour".[33] In its central article, Article 3, C182 reconceptualises the concept of 'hazardous work' as 'the worst forms of child labour' and explicitly states that grave acts such as child slavery, child trafficking, forced child soldiering, child prostitution and pornography are to be considered as such forms, and that members states should prioritise eradicating them first. C182 thus does not impose any new standards and is *de facto* more of a soft law than a legally binding instrument. This helps explain its enormous success in terms of ratifications. Within only two years, C182 had been ratified by

116 countries, steadily growing to 187 out of the 187 ILO member states by 2020 and so becoming the first globally ratified ILO convention and the spearhead of the ILO's ongoing global anti–child labour campaign, in which Satyarthi and the Global March continue to play prominent roles.

Discussion: Two Lovers Locked in Romance

As was made clear in the previous section, states and intergovernmental organisations remain in strict control of the space for participation by CSOs in global governance, and decisions are often politically and instrumentally motivated. This was the case for the Amsterdam and Oslo conferences, and so it was in Geneva. But CSOs, like the Global March, are political entities as well. They aim to benefit from participating on the international level in a way that goes beyond exerting influence over global governance. This can be understood as a process of 'mutual legitimation'.

Kenneth Anderson contends that much more than merely a pragmatic choice to benefit from the expertise of (I)NGOs, their involvement provides "some veneer of democratic legitimacy" as they are generally perceived as baring a connection with 'the people' (Anderson, 2000, p. 95). NGOs in their turn receive legitimacy and credibility from participating on the highest political echelon. Anderson compares this situation to that of "two lovers locked in romance" in which they offer each other "love tokens of confirmations of legitimacy and eternal fealty" (2000, p. 117). The co-optation of Satyarthi and the Global March provided the ILO with a three-fold package of short- and long-term strategic benefits. First, the fact that the Global March initially presented itself as the representative of a large network of NGOs made its association with the ILO and the development of C182 a clear symbolic democratic affair. It helped the ILO to deflect criticism of it being an unfavourable environment for CSO participation.[34] Second, the presence of former and rescued working children that had been selected by the Global March to walk into the halls of the ILC projected onto the ILO the democratic legitimacy of the participation of children and relieved it from the pressure imposed by NGOs and organised working children to allow the latter to participate in ILO matters. Third, in terms of advocacy and fund raising, Satyarthi and the children of the Global March reinforced the proven effective strategy of representing of child labour as being a form of modern slavery and of working children as helpless victims waiting to be rescued. What Satyarthi and the Global March gained in return was 'representational power' on the highest echelon of international politics concerning child labour.

In a series of articles on the international politics of child labour, Anna Holzscheiter (2016, 2018) theorises representational power as meaning both acting on behalf of another (thing, person, group, etc.) and creating a discourse while doing so. Holzscheiter differentiates between, on the one hand, the 'power to represent', and on the other, 'the power over representation'. Having the power *to* represent in processes of international law and policy making means to be acknowledged as the legitimate representative of those affected. The power *over* representation refers to the discursive practices through which NGOs advocate for others by constructing identities and narratives about those they claim to represent. The ILO provided Satyarthi and the Global March the power to represent working children, who in turn are represented as victims who are not able to speak for themselves. Satyarthi is, in Holzscheiter's words, "caught between a rock and a hard place" (2016, p. 226), by which she means that he has to support the institutionalised discourse on children's right to participation while at the same time benefits from representing children as vulnerable victims in service of his own representational power.

Representatives of working children's movements were not given any formal representational power to represent themselves because they would destabilise the delicate process of mutual legitimation between the ILO and the Global March, and the strategic representational campaign from which they both benefit. That the movements therefore presented a real threat to the ILO's global campaign was understood and addressed when the final text of the convention was presented. A member of the drafting committee made explicit the paternalistic approach that had prevailed, and insisted to not take seriously the existence and claims of the absent working children's movements:

> To conclude, ignore those who talk of children's rights to work. Remember their right to learn and play, and our responsibilities as adults to choose for them a better life. There is a burden on our shoulders. It does not hurt like a load of bricks on the shoulders of a child, of a child labourer, nor as rape hurts a child forced into sex work. But it is a burden we must carry.[35]

Concluding Remarks

The year during which this chapter was elaborated, 2021, was declared the UN International Year on the Elimination of Child Labour (IYECL).[36] The main objective of the IYECL was to raise awareness and accelerate progress towards the global goal of eradicating all forms of child labour by 2025. This latter objective has been adopted by all UN member states as part of Target 8.7 of the 2015 Sustainable Development Goals (SDGs).[37] Target 8.7 is the latest policy instrument in the ILO's global anti–child labour campaign, and in the light of the above discussions on the worst forms of child labour, it may be no surprise that the target furthermore calls for the abolition of modern slavery, trafficking and forced labour. During the IYECL, Satyarthi, who has remained the public face of the ILO's anti–child labour campaign ever since the adoption of C182, was appointed as one of 17 special 'UN SDG Advocates' whose task it is to raise global awareness about the SDGs, and about Target 8.7 in particular. This, again, is hardly surprising. To gauge how effective the campaign on the worst forms of child labour with Satyarthi as public face and voice has been, one only needs to type 'child labour' into any online image search engine, and an array of very young Brown and Black children meet the eye; all seemingly living in the Global South, all performing activities that resemble slave-like conditions, all waiting to be rescued from peril. While it might be intuitively and emotionally appealing, there are a couple of serious problems with this strategy.

First, while these representations do certainly allude to the harsh, dangerous and often immoral situations in which real children find themselves, critical researchers have shown the ambiguity and nuances of the different realities that are captured by container terms such as child slavery, trafficking (Howard, 2017) and marriage (Horii, 2020). Such studies show that children involved in such practices are often exercising agency and that the situations they find themselves in are not always so straightforwardly 'wrong' as campaigns make them out to be. Second, representing child labour by these forms obscures the fact that behind the broad category of 'child labour' lies an immensely diverse phenomenon, and numerous empirical studies have highlighted the heterogeneous experiences of children that work for many different reasons, be it economic, cultural, social or emotional, under many different conditions.[38] As mentioned earlier on, in many countries in the Global South, C138 allows children to work full-time the day they turn 14 years, while an 11-year-old that is helping a parent tend their land or at a local market for one hour per week is considered to one of the 160 million children that the ILO estimates were in child labour in 2020 (ILO, 2021). The ILO's own figures furthermore suggest that the vast majority of working children combine some form of formal education and work, and that most children considered to be in child labour work in non-hazardous work which can have beneficial effects as well (Bourdillon et al., 2010). Third, for reasons alluded to above, this one-dimensional representation of child labour which has come to dominate the public discourse not only obscures, but also excludes representations of more diverse experiences and approaches, as the working children's movements experienced in their own quest for representational power on the international level; during the 1990s in Amsterdam, Oslo and Geneva, but also more recently in a process revolving around a new law in Bolivia in the drafting of which organised working children were involved (van Daalen & Mabillard, 2019), and in Buenos Aires during the ILO's IV Global Conference as described in the introduction. As Noah Peleg (2018, p. 430) has noted:

> It seems that the organisers of the 2017 IV World Conference on the Sustained Eradication of Child Labour in Buenos Aires had not 'security concerns' but rather stability concerns. Enabling the participation of the working children's movements would have destabilised their agenda and their paternalistic approach.

Working children's movements certainly do not represent all working children, and their demands and solutions should be as critically scrutinised as should the ILO's mainstream abolitionist approach. But they certainly do represent many of the diverse realities that working children experience and the problems they encounter. Furthermore, they have shown to be ready to step up and transform insights based everyday experiences and into a discourse and agenda that lends itself to international law and policy making. Child labour will not be abolished by 2025, nor will it probably ever be. If we may believe the ILO's (2021) latest global estimates, 160 million children are currently working in some form or another, and it is predicted that the effects of the worsening climate crisis and the current Covid-19 pandemic will add millions more to the under-18 work force. These children deserve creative and effective local programmes and policies guided by a sensible and evidence-based international framework infused with children's own experiences and based on a more holistic understanding of their rights and wellbeing. The past has shown that the exceptions and flexibility clauses of the C138 can accommodate such an approach, and working children's movements would make for valuable actors in a reconceptualisation of the ILO's global approach to child labour. For this to happen the ILO needs to first untangle itself from the locked-in romance with the Global March and instead prioritise those who it claims to want to protect.

Notes

1. This agenda was published as the Buenos Aires Declaration and can be accessed here: https://www.ilo.org/global/about-the-ilo/newsroom/news/WCMS_597667/lang%2D%2Den/index.htm (accessed on 11 January 2022).
2. The opening ceremony was recorded and can be viewed in full here: https://www.youtube.com/watch?v=mMMd6gsnGcc (accessed on 11 January 2022).
3. The full letter can be found on https://www.opendemocracy.net/en/beyond-trafficking-and-slavery/secretariat-of-movement-of-latin-american-and-caribbean-working-children-and-adolescen/ (accessed on 13 December 2021). At the time of writing this chapter no answer has been received from the Committee on the Rights of the Child.
4. The full article can be found here: www.spiegel.de/international/tomorrow/child-labor-in-bolivia-is-legally-permissable-a-1130131.html (accessed on 11 January 2022).
5. The text of C138 is available from: https://www.ilo.org/dyn/normlex/en/f?p=NORMLEXPUB:12100:0::NO::P12100_ILO_CODE:C138 (accessed on 11 January 2022).
6. C138—Article 3 (1).
7. C138—Article 2 (4).
8. C138—Article 5 (3). For a more elaborate discussion of these and other exceptions provided by C138, see: Hanson and Vandaele (2003); Nieuwenhuys (2007).
9. Interview with former ILO staff member, 30 November 2016.
10. Unlike other UN agencies, the ILO is a tripartite organisation which is composed of member states as well as of representatives of trade unions, the so-called 'worker's group', and of employers' organisations. In 2006 the ICFTU merged with the World Confederation of Labour (WCL) and became the International Trade Union Confederation (ITUC).
11. In addition, the ICFTU managed to secure the inclusion of the 'abolition of child labour' in the ILO Declaration on Fundamental Principles and Rights at Work, which placed a moral obligation on all member states to adhere to

these principles and rights to whether or not they have ratified the related conventions. For a critical discussion on the Declaration and its moral force, see: Alston (2004).
12. In his book on social movements and human rights, Neil Stammers (2009) addresses and theorises 'the paradox of institutionalisation' by pointing out how power and interest distort the codification and institutionalisation of natural rights.
13. Ironically, while the recurrent global estimates have since been closely associated with images and narratives about the worst forms of child labour, these figures do not actually include any data on practices such as slavery, prostitution or soldiering, as these remain outside the scope of what can be learned through the household surveys on which the global estimates are based. For a critical discussion of the global estimates, see: Janzen (2018).
14. For an insightful discussion about the dynamics between adult and working children in the Peruvian context, see: Taft (2015).
15. The main facilitator of the Kundapur meeting, and the movements' international campaign that followed, was the International Working Group on Child Labour (IWGCL). The IWGCL was created as a collaboration between two international child rights NGOs, the International Society for the Prevention of Child Abuse and Neglect (ISPCAN) and Defence for Children International (DCI) and existed between 1992 and 1997. For more information on the IWGCL and the different projects it initiated, see: IWGCL (IWGCL, 1998).
16. IWGCL, '1st International Meeting of Working Children Kundapur (India)' (Archive Defence for Children International Nederland, Inventory Number ARCH03007, International Institute of Social History, Amsterdam, 1996).
17. Ibid.
18. Letter from the Dutch Government to the IWGCL (Archive Defence for Children International Nederland, inventory number ARCH03007, International Institute of Social History, Amsterdam, 24 January 1997).
19. Unless stated otherwise, the following accounts are descriptions of video recordings of these preparatory meetings, that were retrieved from the archives of DCI-Netherlands in Leiden. The videos are on file with the author.
20. Interview with former ICTFU staff member, 14 December 2015.
21. Ministry of Foreign Affairs the Netherlands, 'Agreement Concerning: Working Children's Meeting, Oslo, 23 October—1 November 1997 (Activity No. WW128501)' (Archive Inventory 21586, Inventory Number 1950, National Archive, The Hague, 13 October 1996).
22. International Save the Children Alliance, 'Report on the Working Children's Forum Oslo, Norway 21 St October—2nd November 1997 and the International Conference on Child Labour 27th—30th October 1997' (Save the Children Resource Centre, 1998).

23. The ILC is an annual forum during which ILO delegates identify and discuss social questions and draft, adopt and monitor international labour conventions.
24. Letter to the ILO Director-General (Archive Defence for Children International Nederland, inventory number ARCH03007, International Institute of Social History, Amsterdam, 10 March 1998).
25. The United States is the only UN member state to have not ratified the UNCRC.
26. The other general principles are: 'non-discrimination', 'best interest of the child' and 'the right to life, survival, and development'. For a critical discussion of the general principles, see: Hanson and Lundy (2017).
27. Shortly after UNGASS, UNICEF (2003) published its 'State of the World's Children 2003' which sets out why it is important to listen to the views and opinions of children in global policy making.
28. Interview with former Dutch civil servant, 29 June 2016.
29. While the Harkin Bill never came became law, its mere submission had a deleterious effect in Bangladesh where thousands of children were abruptly dismissed from garment factories, many of whom ended up in much worse conditions (Hertel, 2006; Rahman et al., 1999).
30. Satyarthi would also become one of the public faces of the global Education for All campaign (Miles & Singal, 2010).
31. Novib, 'Global March Against Child Labour Report of The Hague Workshop' (Archive Defence for Children International Nederland, inventory number ARCH03007, International Institute of Social History, Amsterdam, 1997).
32. Global March Against Child Labour, 'Core Marchers Coming to the Netherlands 21–24 May, 1998' (Archive Inventory 2.15.86, Inventory Number 1950, Nationaal Archief, The Hague, 1998).
33. The text of C182 is available from: https://www.ilo.org/dyn/normlex/en/f?p=NORMLEXPUB:12100:0::NO::P12100_ILO_CODE:C182 (accessed on 11 January 2022).
34. For more on this critique and the difficult relationship between trade unions and other CSOs, see: Thomann (2008).
35. https://www.ilo.org/public/english/standards/relm/ilc/ilc87/com-chid.htm (accessed 11 January 2022).
36. General Assembly resolution 73/327, *International Year for the Elimination of Child Labour, 2021*, A/RES/73/327 (25 July 2019), available from https://digitallibrary.un.org/record/3814287?ln=en (accessed 11 January 2022).
37. For the full text of Target 8.7, see: https://www.alliance87.org/target-8-7/ (accessed 11 January 2022).
38. See for instance the work of Olga Nieuwenhuys (1996) and Tatek Abebe (2007), to name just a couple.

References

Abebe, T. (2007). Changing Livelihoods, Changing Childhoods: Patterns of Children's Work in Rural Southern Ethiopia. *Children's Geographies*, 5(1–2), 77–93.

Alston, P. (2004). 'Core Labour Standards' and the Transformation of the International Labour Rights Regime. *European Journal of International Law*, 15(3), 457–521.

Alston, P. (2005). The 'Not-a-Cat Syndrome: Can the International Human Rights Regime Accommodate Non-State Actors. In P. Alston (Ed.), *Non-State Actors and Human Rights* (pp. 3–36). Oxford University Press.

Anderson, K. (2000). The Ottawa Convention Banning Landmines, the Role of International Non-governmental Organizations and the Idea of International Civil Society. *European Journal of International Law*, 11(1), 91–120.

Bourdillon, M., Levison, D., Myers, W., & White, B. (2010). *Rights and Wrongs of Children's Work*. Rutgers University Press.

Chacaltana, J. (1998). A Case Study of Manthoc, the Movement of Working Children in Peru. In D. Tolfree (Ed.), *Old Enough to Work, Old Enough to Have a Say*. Rädda Barnen.

Charnovitz, S. (1996). Two Centuries of Participation: NGOs and International Governance. *Michigan Journal of International Law*, 18, 183.

Chowdhry, G. (2003). *Postcolonial Interrogations of Child Labor: Human Rights, Carpet Trade, and Rugmark in India*. Routledge.

Gunn, S., & Ostos, Z. (1992). Dilemmas in Tackling Child Labour: The Case of Scavenger Children in the Philippines. *International Labour Review*, 131, 629.

Hanson, K., & Lundy, L. (2017). Does Exactly What It Says on the Tin?: A Critical Analysis and Alternative Conceptualisation of the So-called "General Principles" of the Convention on the Rights of the Child. *The International Journal of Children's Rights*, 25(2), 285–306.

Hanson, K., & Vandaele, A. (2003). Working Children and International Labour Law: A Critical Analysis. *The International Journal of Children's Rights*, 11(1), 73–146. https://doi.org/10.1163/092755603322384038

Hertel, S. (2006). New Moves in Transnational Advocacy: Getting Labor and Economic Rights on the Agenda in Unexpected Ways. *Global Governance*, 12(3), 263–281.

Holzscheiter, A. (2016). Representation as Power and Performative Practice: Global Civil Society Advocacy for Working Children. *Review of International Studies*, 42(2), 205–226.

Holzscheiter, A. (2018). Affectedness, Empowerment and Norm Contestation–Children and Young People as Social Agents in International Politics. *Third World Thematics: A TWQ Journal*, 3(5–6), 645–663.

Horii, H. (2020). Walking a Thin Line: Taking Children's Decision to Marry Seriously? *Childhood, 27*(2), 254–270.

Howard, N. (2017). *Child Trafficking, Youth Labour Mobility and the Politics of Protection.* Palgrave Macmillan.

ILO. (1989). *Still So Far to Go: Child Labour in the World Today. Special Report on the Occasion of the Tenth Anniversary of the International Year of the Child.* International Labour Office.

ILO. (1993). *IPEC Implementation Report 1992–93.* ILO.

ILO. (1995). *Implementation Report: Review of IPEC Experience 1992–95.* International Labour Office.

ILO. (1996). *Child labour: Targeting the Intolerable.* ILO.

ILO. (1997a). *Amsterdam Child Labour Conference: Press Clippings 26–27 February 1997.* ILO.

ILO. (1997b). *Oslo International Conference on Child Labour. Final Report.* ILO.

ILO. (1999). *Report of the Committee on Child Labour, 87th Session, Geneva, June 1999.* ILO.

ILO. (2021). *Global Estimates 2020, Trends and the Road Forward.* ILO.

IPEC, & SIMPOC. (2002). *Every Child Counts: New Global Estimates on Child Labour.* International Labour Office.

IWGCL. (1998). *Working Children: Reconsidering the Debates. Report of the International Working Group on Child Labour.* IWGCL.

Janzen, S. A. (2018). Child Labour Measurement: Whom Should We Ask? *International Labour Review, 157*(2), 169–191. https://doi.org/10.1111/ilr.12041

Levine, S. (1999). Bittersweet Harvest: Children, Work and the Global March Against Child Labour in the Post-Apartheid State. *Critique of Anthropology, 19*(2), 139–155. https://doi.org/10.1177/0308275X9901900201

Liebel, M. (2001). 12 Rights, and Making Their Own Way: The Working Youth of Africa Organise Themselves. In M. Liebel, B. Overwien, & A. Recknagel (Eds.), *Working Children's Protagonism: Social Movements and Empowerment in Latin America, Africa and India.* IKO-Verlag für Interkulturelle Kommunikation.

Miles, S., & Singal, N. (2010). The Education for All and Inclusive Education Debate: Conflict, Contradiction or Opportunity? *International Journal of Inclusive Education, 14*(1), 1–15.

Nieuwenhuys, O. (1996). The Paradox of Child Labor and Anthropology. *Annual Review of Anthropology, 25*(1), 237–251. https://doi.org/10.1146/annurev.anthro.25.1.237

Nieuwenhuys, O. (2007). Embedding the Global Womb: Global Child Labour and the New Policy Agenda. *Children's Geographies, 5*(1–2). https://doi.org/10.1080/14733280601108312

Nieuwenhuys, O. (2009). From Child Labour to Working Children's Movements. In J. Qvortrup, W. A. Corsaro, M.-S. Honig, & G. Valentine (Eds.), *Handbook of Childhood Studies*. Palgrave.

Peleg, N. (2018). Illusion of Inclusion: Challenging Universalistic Conceptions in International Children's Rights Law. *Australian Journal of Human Rights, 24*(3), 326–344.

Rahman, M. M., Khanam, R., & Absar, N. U. (1999). Child Labor in Bangladesh: A Critical Appraisal of Harkin's Bill and the MOU-Type Schooling Program. *Journal of Economic Issues, 33*(4), 985–1003. https://doi.org/10.1080/00213624.1999.11506225

Rotthier, R. (1995). *Kinderen van de krokodil. Slavenarbeid in India (The Children of the Crocodile. Slave Labour in India)*. Atlas Contact.

Skelton, T. (2007). Children, Young People, UNICEF and Participation. *Children's Geographies, 5*(1–2), 165–181.

Stammers, N. (2009). *Human Rights and Social Movements*. Pluto Press.

Swift, A. (1997). *Children for Social Change: Education for Citizenship of Street and Working Children in Brazil*. Educational Heretics Press.

Swift, A. (1999). *Working Children Get Organised*. International Save the Children Alliance.

SZW. (1997). *Combating the Most Intolerable Forms of Child Labour: A Global Challenge. Amsterdam Child Labour Conference*. SZW. https://www.ilo.org/public//english/standards/ipec/conf/amsterdam/report.pdf

Taft, J. (2015). "Adults talk too much": Intergenerational Dialogue and Power in the Peruvian Movement of Working Children. *Childhood, 22*(4), 460–473.

Taft, J. (2019a). Continually Redefining Protagonismo: The Peruvian Movement of Working Children and Political Change, 1976–2015. *Latin American Perspectives, 46*(5), 90–110. https://doi.org/10.1177/0094582X17736037

Taft, J. (2019b). *The Kids Are in Charge. Activism and Power in Peru's Movement of Working Children*. NYU Press.

Tapiola, K. (2018). *The Teeth of the ILO—The Impact of the 1998 ILO Declaration on Fundamental Principles and Rights to Work*. ILO.

Thomann, L. (2008). The ILO, Tripartism, and NGOs: Do Too Many Cooks Really Spoil the Broth? In J. Steffek, C. Kissling, & P. Nanz (Eds.), *Civil Society Participation in European and Global Governance: A Cure for the Democratic Deficit?* (pp. 71–94). Springer.

UNICEF. (2003). *The State of the World's Children 2003*. UNICEF.

van Daalen, E. (2020). Working Children's Movements. In D. Cook (Ed.), *SAGE Encyclopedia of Children and Childhood Studies*. Sage Publications.

van Daalen, E., & Hanson, K. (2019). The ILO's Shifts in Child Labour Policy: Regulation and Abolition. *International Development Policy, 11*, 133–150. https://doi.org/10.4000/poldev.3056

van Daalen, E., & Mabillard, N. (2019). Human Rights in Translation: Bolivia's Law 548, Working Children's Movements, and the Global Child Labour Regime. *The International Journal of Human Rights, 23*(4), 596–614. https://doi.org/10.1080/13642987.2018.1541890

Vandaele, A. (2005). *International Labour Rights and the Social Clause: Friends or Foes*. Cameron May.

Open Access This chapter is licensed under the terms of the Creative Commons Attribution 4.0 International License (http://creativecommons.org/licenses/by/4.0/), which permits use, sharing, adaptation, distribution and reproduction in any medium or format, as long as you give appropriate credit to the original author(s) and the source, provide a link to the Creative Commons licence and indicate if changes were made.

The images or other third party material in this chapter are included in the chapter's Creative Commons licence, unless indicated otherwise in a credit line to the material. If material is not included in the chapter's Creative Commons licence and your intended use is not permitted by statutory regulation or exceeds the permitted use, you will need to obtain permission directly from the copyright holder.

CHAPTER 7

"Children Without Childhood": Representations of the Child-Soldier as an International Emergency

Jana Tabak

INTRODUCTION

In February 2021, Dominic Ongwen was found guilty by the International Criminal Court (ICC) for a total of 61 cases comprising crimes against humanity and war crimes. Committed in Northern Uganda between 1 July 2002 and 31 December 2005, these crimes included murder, rape, sexual slavery, forced marriage, torture, conscription, and use of children under the age of 15 in the armed conflict. Ongwen is a case in point as he himself was abducted at the age of about 9 on his way home from school and became a senior commander in the Ugandan irregular armed group, the Lord's Resistance Army (LRA). As such, he is the first person to be convicted by the ICC for a crime of which he was a victim himself. According to a *Globe and Mail* article from 2008 entitled "The Making of

J. Tabak (✉)
Department of International Relations, State University of Rio de Janeiro (UERJ), Rio de Janeiro, Brazil
e-mail: jana.tabak@uerj.br

a Monster?" "He [Ongwen] is known as the most courageous, loyal and brutal of the men who serve Joseph Kony, the LRA's charismatic and ruthless founder." The ICC verdict comes after a trial that lasted more than four years, was spread across 231 hearing days, and involved the testimony of 130 witnesses and experts, including numerous insiders, and the participation of 4065 victims through their legal representatives. Although for the many victims justice has been a long time coming, the reaction to the verdict among members of the affected communities and the public debate has been mixed in face of Ongwen's dual identity as victim-perpetrator.

According to Kony, Ongwen is "a 'role model' among the child soldiers" (Nolen & Baines, 2008). After this description, the article poses the following question: "How, in 11 years, did Dominic Ongwen turn from a *boy too small to walk* to the rebels' camp into one of their *fiercest, most senior fighters*?" (emphasis added). Incapable of answering it, the newspaper article retains the question mark in its title: Was Ongwen really turned into a monster? Or is he a child victim of war, like other child-soldiers who, as the article tells us, are "hauled into violent conflict before their own moral compass has developed [so that] they become unable to discern right from wrong"? In its decision, the ICC Trial Chamber acknowledged that the LRA abducted Ongwen as a child and that he experienced significant suffering in his childhood and youth as a result. However, the Court made a clean break between Ongwen's victimhood in early life and his perpetration of atrocity crimes as an adult: "this case is about crimes committed by Dominic Ongwen as a *fully responsible adult* and as a *commander* of the LRA in his mid to late twenties" (emphasis added). As Nortje argues, "He [Ongwen] was a victim of crimes under international law for the duration of his tenure as a child soldier in the LRA *until he turned 18*. Since then, he has become a perpetrator, a feared man across Uganda" (2017, p. 197; emphasis added).

The story of Ongwen's childhood that we know is very similar to the narratives about (mostly) African boys holding weapons taller than themselves, like AK-47s. These narratives have attracted enormous media attention and have also become a priority in the humanitarian field. Although the constructions and imageries vary, the representation of the child-soldier, especially as articulated in the humanitarian field, produces a relation between extremes with a clear message: childhood is facing a serious *crisis*. Graça Machel, in her report on the impact of wars on children, defines warfare in postcolonial states, where the majority of child-soldiers are found, in terms of the "abandonment of all standards" and a "sense of dislocation and chaos" (Machel, 1996, p. 9). As well as the armed conflict in Uganda, the war in Liberia is used as an illustrative example to emphasize the abandonment of standards that has brought human rights violations against women and children, including the recruitment of children into armed forces and groups. In February 2004, BBC News published a story about the need to disarm and rehabilitate child-soldiers in Liberia, which was understood as a critical step toward establishing peace in the country. The photograph posted next to the text was of a boy pointing a weapon toward the viewer: he was alone or abandoned, without family or state support, and he was not wearing a military uniform, but old clothes and flip-flops. Also, he was carrying a pinky fluffy backpack in the shape of a teddy bear, whose contents were unknown to us, the viewers: might it be food, clothes, toys, or bullets to reload the weapon? The single caption, placed underneath the image, read: "The prolonged civil war has damaged a whole generation." According to the journalist, "entering the world of Liberia's child soldiers is a *disturbing experience. Normal moral values are put to one side*" (emphasis added).

In the end, what do we know about Dominic Ongwen and the Liberian boy? Despite repeated references to the fact that Ongwen was recruited by the LRA on his way home from school, nothing is said to give a hint about what experiences he had while engaged in war besides the crimes he committed and how his life was as a child before being abducted by the armed group. Regarding the Liberian boy, the readers are none the wiser about him either: who he was, his age, how he became a soldier, what experiences he had while engaged in war, or if he was still alive. We know that both children were in an extremely vulnerable situation—they were "out of place," not protected, but, rather, subject to violence—but we are not able to glean anything about any specific circumstances. And yet, from that it becomes clear that, while we have been told very little, we actually *know quite a lot*—they were *just* a "child-soldier" or, in other words, a "child without childhood," for when being a soldier begins, the child drops out of childhood,[1] understood and promoted as a carefree, secure, and happy phase of human existence.

If, on one hand, according to the BBC story, the Liberian boy-soldier does not so much stop being a child, but loses his childhood—something rather more abstract and, arguably, somewhat more precious, that *must* be saved with the help of international organizations. On the other hand, Ongwen, according to the ICC verdict, is a soldier, not a child anymore, who was, first, "robbed of childhood," but then, as an adult, was capable of making voluntary choices in full cognizance of dangers, evaluating the risks and of committing violent acts that children are not. In both cases, the "child" can be rescued from the pathological child-soldier. That is, the idea of the child is still kept in the role of the irrational, innocent minor incapable of taking responsibility for his/her actions. Specifically in the case of Ongwen, the idea of the child is saved when the *Ongwen-adult* is found guilty. Both narratives—as a "child, not a soldier" and as a "soldier, not a child" respectively—are authorized by and, at the same time, reproduce the representation of the child-soldier as an *international emergency*, essentially deviant and pathological, understood as "exceptions to normal social life and global order: sudden, unpredictable, and carried strong moral imperatives for immediate action" (Calhoun, 2008, p. 96). As I argue throughout this chapter, the logic of opposite extremes—to be a child-soldier is to be an innocent victim and/or to be a feared irrational perpetrator—operates to (re)produce children as targets of international intervention (or, protection) with no chance of autonomous decision-making. Child-soldiers are either the objects of exploitation or the objects of salvation.

To consider these representations of the child-soldier, this chapter is divided in three parts. The first two parts explore the two main discourses that articulate and authorize the limits that (re)produce the child-soldier as an international emergency, setting boundaries within which only certain subjects, narratives, and responses are admitted: (1) the discourse of the law, that is, international practices that articulate children's participation in war as something that is wrong and must be banned under international law; and (2) what I call the "discourse of the norm," which is analyzed through the three contrasting images of the child-soldier as dangerous and disorderly, the hapless victim, and the resilient redeemed hero, as identified by Myriam Denov (2010) (Tabak, 2020). The discourse of the norm, in particular, makes visible child-soldiers as a pathology, excluding their aspects of disorder, dysfunction, and risk from the accepted boundaries of what is to be a child and its childhood. In this case, it is not only that children's participation in wars is wrong, but it is absolutely *abnormal* once every quality applied to a "normal," civilized childhood are absent in the lives of child-soldiers. In the third part, by challenging the idea of vulnerability, understood as victimization and invariably a site of inaction, I offer some reflections that aim to provide an alternative to framework for exploring children as political subjects (Marshall Beier, 2020) whose everyday lives within conflict zones destabilize the pervasive representations of both the child-soldier and the ordered world which claims to save him/her.

Within Boundaries: Banning the Use of the Child-Soldier

In 1996, Graça Machel, an expert appointed by the Secretary-General of the UN and a former Minister of Education of Mozambique, presented a report to the United Nations General Assembly entitled the *Promotion and Protection of the Rights of Children: Impact of Armed Conflict on Children*. In it, she indicates the inclusion of the issue of child-soldiers on the international agenda as a matter of concern:

> It is unconscionable that we so clearly and consistently see children's rights attacked and that we fail to defend them. It is unforgivable that children are assaulted, violated, murdered and yet our conscience is not revolted nor our sense of dignity challenged. This represents a *fundamental crisis of our civilization* [...] Each one of us, each individual, each institution, each country, must initiate and support global action to protect children. (Machel, 1996, p. 73; emphasis added)

The essential quality of child-soldiers, according to Graça Machel, is their vulnerability once they are dependent, exploited, and powerless. In order to internationally deal with the child-soldier emergency, there has been a high investment in the construction of international legal standards, which aims to build an insurmountable barrier between child and soldier, making the military recruitment of children *wrong*—or an international crime (Drumbl, 2012; Tabak, 2020). This section focuses specifically on the "response" to the child-soldier problem via the rights-based approach—or what I call the discourse of the Law. To use Holzscheiter et al.'s (2019) classification, the child-soldiers' protection and regulation, identified through children's rights, may be associated with the idea of *child rights governance*. As such, throughout this section, the discourse of the law must be understood as "an explicit instrument, not only to protect and emancipate children from oppression, but also to govern, regulate, and control children and childhoods" (Holzscheiter et al., 2019, p. 272).

Specifically, I analyze here how international legal standards articulate children's participation in armed conflicts as wrong and something that must be outlawed internationally. The discourse of the Law includes the 1977 Additional Protocols to the Geneva Conventions, the 1989 UN Convention on the Rights of the Child (UNCRC), the 1998 Rome Statute, the 1999 International Labor Organization Worst Forms of Child

Labor Convention, and the 2000 Optional Protocol to the Convention on the Rights of the Child on the Involvement of Children in Armed Conflict (hereinafter Optional Protocol). In addition, there are two international instruments adopted by UNICEF that have a key role in the debates on the definition of the category child-soldier—the 1997 Cape Town Principles and the Paris Principles.

Although children have always been present in the battlefields (Marten, 2002; Rosen, 2005), their international treatment has changed considerably since the end of the Cold War. The high number of state ratifications of the UNCRC and the World Summit for Children in 1990 has inaugurated a time in which the protection of children has come to occupy a central place in the international human rights and security agendas alike. In addition to that, the accumulation and publicization of atrocities, such as the murders, mutilations, abductions, and rapes committed in the so-called "New Wars" (Kaldor, 1999), has done much to lend urgency to the expansion of the international movement toward the elimination of the participation of children in any kind of regular or irregular armed group (Macmillan, 2011). The first systematic attempt to directly address the issue of child combatants can be found in the 1977 Additional Protocols to the Geneva Conventions. Since then, the governance of child's rights regarding children's participation in armed conflicts has been sustained by two main pillars, which articulate the ban on the involvement of children in armed conflict. First, there is the idea of "militarization," which can be understood in a more restrictive sense, considering only children's direct participation in hostilities, or, from a broader perspective, embracing not only combatant children in state and non-state forces, but also non-combatant children's involvement in supporting roles, working as spies, cooks, porters, messengers, and so forth. Secondly, there is the *age of the child*, which serves as a parameter for defining whether they are capable of playing certain social roles. Specifically, on the age issue, it is important to explore how this is also related to contemporary debates on the possibility of children taking responsibility for their actions versus their presumed ignorance, either because they are too young to commit such violent acts or because they just do what they are told to by adults. In one sense, it takes us back to the ICC verdict about Dominic Ongwen that excludes the "*boy* that is too small to walk the rebel's camp" in order to make its case against the "fiercest most *senior* fighter."

In regard to the first pillar, the militarization of children, the UNCRC (specifically, Article 38), and the Optional Protocol reproduce the 1977

Additional Protocols present the exact same vocabulary by affirming that children should "not take direct part in hostilities", which means active combat, but excludes other military activities, such as spying, supply transportation, and cooking. However, the Optional Protocol actually parallels Additional Protocol II insofar as its strongest restrictions are directed against non-state armed groups: "armed groups, distinct from the armed forces of a State, should not, *under any circumstances,* recruit or use *in hostilities* persons under the age of *18 years*" (United Nations General Assembly, 2000, Art.4; emphasis added). In this sense, this particular agreement reproduces two conceptions of the child-soldier: children cannot participate directly in hostilities as combatants on the behalf of State parties, while irregular armed groups are prohibited to use children "in hostilities" (Tabak, 2020).

For its turn, the Rome Statute, which is considered one of the most significant recent legal developments in limiting the use of child-soldiers, adopts a broader idea of militarization by abandoning the use of the term "direct." Specifically, Article 8 defines the use of children to "participate actively in hostilities" as a war crime. In the same vein, the ILO Worst Forms of Child Labor Convention includes, in its Article 3, among the worst forms of child labor the "forced or compulsory recruitment of children for use in armed conflict" regardless of the child's role in an armed conflict. However, the ILO convention is not as far-reaching, as its focus is only on children's forced involvement in hostilities.

A broader concept of child-soldiers in terms of "militarization" is finally articulated by the two international agreements regarding the interdiction of the involvement of children in armed conflict: the Cape Town Principles (1997) and the Paris Principles (2007). As the result from a symposium organized by UNICEF and the NGO Working Group on the UNCRC, the Cape Town Principles expanded the concept of "child-soldier" and adopted a more inclusive terminology of "children associated with armed forces or armed groups," which refers to "any person under 18 years of age who is part of any kind of regular or irregular armed force or armed group in *any capacity*" (1997, p. 12; emphasis added). Then, a decade later, UNICEF organized a review of the Cape Town Principles, which resulted in the Paris Principles and Guidelines on Children Associated with Armed Force and Armed Groups, which serves as the basis for the programs developed by the UN. The Paris Principles formally abandoned the concept of child-soldier in favor of the concept of a "child associated with armed group or armed force" in order to include all children who were military recruited regardless of taking direct part in hostilities.

Regarding the second pillar—the issue of age—we might say that the definition of the child-soldier contradicts somewhat the internationally accepted definition of the child established under the terms of the UNCRC. Although the UNCRC defines the 18th year of life as the transition point to adulthood, its Article 38 repeats the language of Additional Protocol I, establishing the temporal threshold for military recruitment at the age of 15. As such, Article 38 is the only provision of the Convention that does not contain the general age limit of 18 years. The Optional Protocol is, then, adopted as a way of fixing what was considered a major flaw in the treaty for those advocating against the use and recruitment of child-soldiers. However, the Optional Protocol does not eliminate the contradiction surrounding the age of child-soldiers as it raises the age to 18 of possible recruitment by irregular armed forces at the same time that states, in Article 3, that children who are 15 or over may be *voluntarily recruited* into the armed forces of a nation-state, provided that "such recruitment is done with the informed consent of the person's parents or legal guardians." The so-called "straight-18 position" was strengthened by the adoption of the ILO's Worst Forms of Child Labor Convention, which defines children as all persons under the age of 18 (Article 2). Also, according to the UNICEF principles, the age limit to participate in war must be 18. Nevertheless, it is worth noting that international humanitarian law is still guided by the Rome Statute, which defines, in Article 8, "conscripting or enlisting children under the age of fifteen years" as a war crime.

Over the course of 40 years, the participation of children in armed conflicts has been transformed from a practice loosely regulated and focused on children's role as combatants to one that is problematized and subject to greater control. While an international legal consensus about the age and military activities that define the child-soldier has yet to be reached, the way children's participation in wars is internationally governed produces—and at the same time is legitimized by—certain narratives about a *correct* idea of childhood and how a *normal* process of child development must be lived outside war. As such, child rights governance has become an integral part in the governance and regulation not only of the child-soldier, but also of their families and societies around the world (Holzscheiter et al., 2019).

Within such a formulation, there is no room left for considering children's own motivations, or their ability to understand their own circumstances and express their own views regarding their participation in hostilities or the local social constructions of the roles suitable to children according to their gender and age. After all, the view of the child-soldier as "out of place" is (re)produced through the same mechanisms that are meant to protect them. As such, the next section turns to the assumptions and categories that give social coherence to the representation of child-soldiers not only as a practice to be banned by the Law, but as an apparent pathology that needs to be kept under control. Through the analysis of three images or "frames" (Berents, 2020) that permeate and articulate the bounded category of the child-soldier as deviation—the victim, the monster, and the exceptional and resilient redeemed hero—I explore the multiple ways in which this normative discourse circulates.

The Governed Childhood and Its Many Exclusions: (Re)presenting the Pathological Child-Soldier

In her article "Human Rights, Child-Soldier Narratives, and the Problem of Form," Maureen Moynagh (2011) argues that "There is, it seems, a place already prepared in the Western imagination for the African child soldier as a subject of violence in need of human rights intervention and rehabilitation—intervention that threatens to mimic colonial infantilizing of Africans as needing the 'protection' of European powers" (p. 41). The boundaries of this "place" mentioned by Moynagh (2011), I contend, are articulated by particular frameworks that represent child-soldiers as an international emergency, whose life experiences—narrated through static, but not fixed, images of victim, monster, and redeemed hero—challenge the limits of the childhood's spaces *per* se, that is, home, school, and recreational centers (Rasmussen, 2004). These narratives, combined with the discourse of the Law, compose a general discourse, which is dominated by a problem-solving logic that defines children's participation in armed conflicts as both wrong and abnormal and because of that in urgent need of a solution.

To critically analyze these three images, this section is based on Denov's work (2010) in exploring the way the world's media and policy discourse construct child-soldiers in largely contrastive ways. According to Denov, "While these children are frequently constructed through the logic of extremes (as either extreme victims, extreme perpetrators or extreme heroes), in reality, the lives, experiences and identities of these children fall within the messy, ambiguous and paradoxical zones of all three" (Denov, 2010, p. 2). Furthermore, instead of understanding these images through static categories, I follow Berents' argument (2020) in working with these narratives as *frames*, which "allows the unpacking of the assumptions and stereotypes that inform images (...) Understanding these as frames allows a critical questioning of how we see what is *framed* as victimization or delinquency" (pp. 48–49; emphasis in the original). When it comes to images of children in context of wars, there is no doubt that it is the frame of the exploited victim that prevails. This representation revolves primarily around forced recruitment or abduction; children being forced to kill or slaughter, especially a family member; children witnessing extreme acts of violence, especially against other children; children being the object of humiliation, brutal beatings, rape, sexual slavery, slave labor, and hunger; and children unprepared for involvement in combat. Most of the reports by humanitarian organizations end up stating that all that these children want is to get back their "lost childhood," of which peace and school are crucial ingredients (Martins, 2011). As such, the correspondence between childhood, vulnerability, and victimhood is clearly articulated. For example, a Human Rights Watch report (re)produces this frame through children's testimonies:

> Early on when my brothers and I were captured, the LRA explained to us that all five brothers couldn't serve in the LRA because we would not perform well. So they tied up my two younger brothers and invited us to watch. Then they beat them with sticks until two of them died. They told us it would give us strength to fight. My youngest brother was nine years old. (2003, p. 2)

Paralleling these accounts, Roméo Dallaire, a distinguished human rights activist, depicts the child-soldier as an "end-to-end weapon system" and a "tool"; what is more, children are "vulnerable and easy to catch, just like minnows in a pond," while the adults involved are described as "evil" (2010, p. 3, 12, 15, 150). Children are, thus, depicted as hapless victims who are essentially irrational and are thus unable to understand or identify the risks of entering combat. Terms like "used as/for," "forced to," "brainwashed," and "manipulated" appear frequently in these narratives, articulating and authorizing this idea of the child whose agency is completely silenced. Considering Dominic Ongwen's case and his verdict, it is worth noting the former UN Special Representative for Children and Armed Conflict Radhika Coomaraswamy's argument when the Optional Protocol was adopted: "even when children behave like 'adults' during war their emotional and psychological vulnerability and the forced nature of their acts should be taken into account" (2010, p. 545). As a child-soldier, Ongwen was an exploited victim, but as an adult-soldier, he was mature enough to *voluntarily* adopt certain types of corrupt and destructive behavior. Another element that plays a major role in the articulation of the child-soldier as a hapless victim is the use of drugs and how this relates to children's irrationality. In a report on the armed conflict in Mali, the NGO Watchlist on Children and Armed Conflict emphasized that armed groups gave illicit drugs to children, who, according to one witness, behaved in a "'high' manner, including shooting their guns up in the air 'just for fun'" (2013, p. 19).

At the end of the day, as Lee-Koo (2013) summarizes, the frames of the child-soldier as a hapless victim revolve around three themes: protection/rescue, innocence, and degeneracy. As such, not only are child-soldiers constructed as passive objects within this international gaze, but their communities and nation-states are pathologized as dysfunctional and are politically delegitimized for their supposed inability to protect their most "precious resource." Together, Lee-Koo argues, "these three themes provide a moral foundation for conflict and project a familiar yet powerful metaphor for the claim that international order is the product of strong states, which protect vulnerable populations from abusive and ultimately illegitimate states" (2013, p. 483).

In stark contrast to the discourse of child-soldiers as victims is framing them as dangerous and evil beings or simply as monsters, permanently lost in an endless cycle of unrelenting violence and irrationality (Denov, 2010). It is as if by failing to meet the criterion of "innocence," these children are not only marginalized, but actually demonized (Tabak, 2020). Despite their small size and "childish" biological features, the still uncivilized child-soldiers are, according to the former French foreign minister Philippe Douste-Blazy, a "time bomb that threatens stability and growth in Africa and beyond" (BBC News, as cited in Denov, 2010, p. 7). A case in point is the framing of Omar Khadr by the international media, which tends to represent him either as an "innocent child" or as a "monster terrorist" (Foran, 2011). Khadr is a Canadian citizen who was held in Guantanamo Bay for eight years for allegedly throwing a grenade that killed a US soldier in Afghanistan in 2002, when he was fifteen years old. Khadr is the first child in US history to be tried for war crimes, including murder, conspiring with Al Qaeda, providing material support for terrorism, and spying on US military convoys in Afghanistan. Again, the same dilemma as the one in Ongwen's case: "Who is the real Omar Khadr? Murdering jihadist, victim of circumstance or model-citizen-in-the-making?" (Friscolanti, 2010). Regardless of the ambiguities and complexities of childhood experiences, the Ongwens and Khadrs of the world and countless other "dangerous children"—or, monsters—are only seen for how they differ from the "correct child." As children who have *deviated* from the "normal" course of development and have been transformed into fierce combatants, child-soldiers are a threat to social stability.

In one sense, these discourses that articulate the child-soldier either as a victim or as a feared perpetrator take us back to the image of the boy-soldier from Liberia (Doyle, 2004) introduced at the beginning of the chapter: the picture of the "vulnerable child" with no military uniform carrying a pink, fluffy, teddy-bear backpack merges with the picture of the dangerous being pointing a weapon toward the viewer. Together, such accounts stand on and lay claim to a binary relationship between adulthood and childhood, which operates as a symbol and pillar of the modern social order. Hence, when child-soldiers mess up the ordered universalized narrative about the protected territory of childhood and, in doing so, destabilize the boundaries that differentiate adults from children, the stability of a larger social order is threatened by the foreclosure on the child's future. That is, rather than offering a promise of a peaceful future, children engaged in armed conflict have the potential to put national and international progress in jeopardy by failing to take the steps prescribed in the model of child development. In this sense, it is worth noting how the child-soldier is represented not only as being threatened by war and adult abuse, but also as constituting a threat to the stability of the social order. This particular understanding of the child-soldier is shaped in a very specific way, suggesting that they are an international *emergency*, an exception to normal social life that disrupts, disquiets, and disturbs the everyday. Within this representation, the need to control them and the desire to restore them to their converse—the "normal" child—becomes, then, a matter of urgency (Tabak, 2020).

Finally, the image of the "redeemed hero" is pinned on a group of children, once victims and/or monsters, who have had the chance to overcome extreme violence and great adversity, survive war, cast off the child-soldier, and reintegrate into civilian life. These children are framed as "exceptional," who, as Berents has argued, exceed what is expected of them as children (2020): they survived the circumstances of war, were able to overcome their memories of fighting, and were thus able to "reset" their "natural" developmental course as children. An obvious example of this construction—from victimization to the recognition of their *exceptionalism* and *resiliency*—is the case of the former child-soldier Ishmael Beah from Sierra Leone: "while Beah's book has not been viewed as a simple, heroic tale, Beah's journey in and out of armed violence was documented by some journalists as a heroic transformation from violence to redemption"(Denov, 2010, p. 9).

Within this formulation, one attribute of the child stands out: children's capacity to recover from adverse situations. For example, Coomaraswamy concludes her statement at the Paris International Conference "Free Children from War," in 2007, by referencing to Beah's resilience:

> Terrible things have happened to children, but children are also resilient. They need encouragement, guidance and support; and with the proper care they can become outstanding members of society. Ishmael Beah, who is with us today, is a perfect example of this. This young man, a former child soldier from Sierra Leone, adopted by an American mother, went to school and university in the United States, graduating with honors.

The implication, however, as Marshall Beier (2020) reminds us, is that those who fail to be resilient or when less successful in withstanding adverse circumstances are framed as "failed subjects." For Dominic Ongwen, who failed to leave the LRA, the international response was to keep him under control behind solid boundaries of the ICC prison, excluded from "civilized" society.

While some of the former child-soldiers are called upon to be resilient, they are still framed as powerless to resolve the sources of insecurity they experience and because of this continue to be viewed as a target of intervention, but this time one that is envisioned by international actors as being in the "best interests of the child." Put another way, with "proper care" and international guidance, former child-soldiers are able to recover from war and, like Beah, go to school and graduate with honors. As I have previously argued, while intervention in child-soldiers as victims or/and monsters is read as a form of "exploitation and abuse" by the adult recruiters, for the former child-soldier as the redeemed hero, (international) intervention operates as the only form of redemption and thus offers a rapid solution to the emergency (Tabak, 2020).

Following on these narratives, it is possible to see how this representation of the child-soldier as an emergency is constructed through a process of differentiation that is structured through a dichotomous logic. That is, the child-soldier is constructed through a logic of exception: whatever qualities apply to a "normal," ordered childhood are absent in the lives of child-soldiers. However, in virtue of the "ambivalence" (Bauman, 1991) of the child-soldier as both the victim and the monster, this international problem cannot be depicted only as a human rights violation, in which there is a clear divide between victim and perpetrator, but, as an *emergency* that evokes fear, uncertainty, revulsion, horror, and sorrow. Then, against this undecidability, Bauman argues, "we experience ambivalence as discomfort and a threat. Ambivalence confounds calculation of events and confuses the relevance of memorized action patterns" (1991, p. 12). Thus, the typically modern effort of exterminating ambivalence—that is, to eliminate everything that could not be precisely defined (Bauman, 1991)—is put into action. By itself, the child-soldier phenomenon connects the *urgency* of the crisis triggered by the threat posed by the dangerous armed child with a heightened sense of *moral obligation* on the part of international organizations, governments, diplomatic corps, and (adult) citizens of the world to "save" the endangered child with arms caught up in these violent situations.

If, on one hand, the last two sections problematized the images of child-soldiers we are seeing, on the other hand, the next—and concluding—section invites us to briefly follow Berents' proposal to consider the images of children we are *not seeing*: "when certain images of certain children gain preeminence there are other children whose experiences are marginalized or erased" (2020, p. 53). Between the child-soldier as a *hapless victim*, the child-soldier as a *monster* and a risk to the world, and the former child-soldier as a *resilient redeemed hero*, there are a great many children who participate in wars, whose different stories of oppression and resistance, of who they are and who they might become, do not necessarily fit into the trajectory of redemption envisioned by the international community on behalf of humanity. By insisting in the perpetual (re)negotiations of children's pasts, presents, and futures, we might find spaces to critically reflect about children not only as the objects of exploitation and/or the objects of salvation, but also as political subjects.

Final Thoughts

The representation of the child-soldier as an international emergency cannot fully understand the complex experiences of "children with guns" who challenge the limits of the "normal" child and of the world that claims to save him/her. In order to consider the persistent everyday lives of those within conflict zones without reducing them to either "victim" or "monster," I prefer to speak of child-soldiers as "children who soldier," who are multiple, complex political subjects (Tabak, 2020). As sites of contestation and power, representations offer new avenues of articulating childhoods and children in different, but not essentialized, ways. In particular, this reconceptualization—or representation—of the child-soldier emphasizes "to soldier" as a verb and children as subjects in action. In doing so, I believe it opens room to explore the extent to which children are potentially competent and significant social actors and "active in the construction of their own lives, the lives of those around them and of the societies in which they live,"(James & Prout, 1991, p. 8) complicating both the normalized idea of both the child as the generalized form and its negative, voiceless counterpart, that is, the child associated with armed groups.

The idea of children as political subjects turns out to be very important for this analysis, since it enables us to challenge what Nick Lee (1999) calls the "vulnerability complex" in which children and, more specifically in this study, child-soldiers, are continuously placed. According to Lee, children's innocence is equated with being inherently vulnerable, which authorizes and legitimates children's political exclusion and adults' right to talk on behalf of them. At the same time, children's exclusion is linked to their lack of voice, taken here as a sign of their incompetence rooted in their biological and psychological immaturity rather than the outcome of any political process. Our aim is not to abandon the concept of vulnerability, but to question who is constructed as essentially vulnerable and what that is taken to mean—after all, "to greater or lesser extents, everyone, child and adult alike, is vulnerable" (Marshall Beier, 2020, p. 236). The alternative suggested here is to expand our political vocabulary to meet the challenge to think about ways of reconciling subjecthood and vulnerability and to reflect about—and with—children as significant social actors. In doing so, we could think of children who soldier as "subjects in (in)security" (Marshall Beier, 2020) whose vulnerability is not understood as its agency's polar opposite but as constituting a force capable of making these children to resist and to do something about their worlds under varied circumstances of age, race, class, and gender understood as systems of powers that structure their social lives. After all, child-soldiers—as every human being—are many and one and a static representation cannot reflect all that a subject can be. As such, thinking of child-soldiers as "subjects in (in)security" invites us to consider the vulnerabilities, dangers, and risks that limit and structure their lives and autonomy without falling back on essentialized accounts of children and their childhood, for that which there is no surprise because we seem to already know who they are, how they must behave and who they must become.

Within the story of child-soldiers as "children without childhood," very limited space is left for thinking about and exploring the nuances of children's agency in conflict once that child becomes the perfect (passive) victim of that "loss," and responsibility falls upon concerned adults to redeem them and restore the conditions of childhood (Berents, 2019). However, analyzing children's varied experiences as soldiers—providing care for their family and community members, running households, providing income for their family, joining (and escaping) armed forces, resisting political oppression, mourning and grieving for loss, and building networks with other children across conflict fault-lines—can tell different stories of oppression, participation, and resistance, which offer a more robust and nuanced understanding not only of how children survive in conflicts, but also of their capacities and competencies to navigate insecure contexts and help rebuild their own societies (Lee-Koo, 2018).

Despite this, as it was argued throughout the chapter, child-soldiers' agency is largely absent in their representation as an *international emergency*. The logic of opposite extremes—to be a child-soldier is to be innocent or to be feared—and the idea of the "normal" child combine and operate to (re)produce children as targets of intervention with no capacity for rational reasoning. Their undoubted need for protection and support dominates discussions of children's rights, reproducing the central tension between children's participation and child protection in the "discourse of the Law," where children's capacity to participate in identifying their own concerns and solutions is limited by the normalized and universalized ideas of the child's innocence, vulnerability, and irrationality.

Finally, labeling child-soldiers as extremely vulnerable is central to this process as it becomes part of the governing of this group (Lind, 2019). Through the "discourse of the norm," the ambivalent approach to the child-soldier, combining vulnerability and risk, obscures and homogenizes the complexity of the lived experience of children in war. In the two frames—the innocent victim and the dangerous monster—their representation as extremely vulnerable "becomings" authorizes the urgent need of their protection and control: they cannot become a threat to the world. For its turn, the frame of the resilient redeemed hero operates as the promise of a good future, or as the promise of *un*making the child-soldier. Their vulnerability connected to their resiliency articulates the narrative that emphasizes *exceptional* agency, which reinforces the implied incapacity of other children and strengthens certain expectations that this trajectory of redemption be followed in a specific way (Berents, 2019). Considering insecure contexts, Marshall Beier, then, argues: "In this way the resilience work of children, while highly politicized, is delegated to children who remain relatively powerless and constrained from meaningfully exercising autonomous political subjecthood" (2020, p. 228). At the end of the day, when seeing those images of Ongwen, Beah, Khadr, and the Liberian boy-soldier (whose name we don't know), we still have very little information about them, but *we know quite a lot*: as child-soldiers, they are an international emergency that feeds the fear of a world *at risk*.

Note

1. This sentence makes reference to Graça Machel's report on the Impact of Armed Conflict on Children (1996), which sets forth the main ideas that constitute the discourse about the child-soldier. There, the author says: "Children [child soldiers] are dropping out from childhood" (p. 57).

References

Bauman, Z. (1991). *Modernity and Ambivalence*. Polity Press.
Berents, H. (2019). "This is my story": Children's War Memoirs and Challenging Protectionist Discourses. *International Review of the Red Cross, 101*(911), 459–479.
Berents, H. (2020). Depicting Childhood: A Critical Framework for Engaging Images of Children in IR. In J. Marshall Beier (Ed.), *Discovering Childhood in International Relations* (pp. 41–64). Palgrave Macmillan.
Calhoun, C. (2008). The Imperative to Reduce Suffering: Charity, Progress, and Emergencies in The Field of Humanitarian Action. In M. Barnett & T. Weiss (Eds.), *Humanitarianism in Question: Politics, Power, Ethics* (pp. 73–97). Cornell University Press.

Coomaraswamy, R. (2010). The Optional Protocol to The Convention on the Rights of the Child on the Involvement of Children in Armed Conflict – Towards Universal Ratification. *International Journal of Children's Rights, 18*(4), 535–549.

Dallaire, R. (2010). *They Fight Like Soldiers, They Die Like Children: The Global Quest to Eradicate the Use of Child Soldiers.* Walker & Company.

Denov, M. S. (2010). *Child Soldiers: Sierra Leone's Revolutionary United Front.* Cambridge University Press.

Doyle, M. 2004, February 2. Call to Help Liberia's Child Soldiers. *BBC.* Retrieved March 20, 2013, from http://news.bbc.co.uk/2/hi/africa/3450263.stm

Drumbl, M. A. (2012). *Reimagining Child Soldiers in International Law and Policy.* OUP Oxford.

Foran, J. E. (2011). Interrogating 'Militarized' Images and Disrupting Sovereign Narratives in the Case of Omar Khadr. In J. Marshall Beier (Ed.), *The Militarization of Childhood: Thinking Beyond The Global South* (pp. 195–216). Palgrave Macmillan.

Friscolanti, M. (2010, November 9). Who Is the Real Omar Khadr? Murdering Jihadist, Victim of Circumstance Or Model-Citizen-in-the-Making?. Retrieved April 6, 2017, from *Maclean's.* http://www.macleans.ca/news/canada/who-is-the-real-omar-khadr/

Holzscheiter, A., Josefsson, J., & Sandin, B. (2019). Child Rights Governance: An Introduction. *Childhood, 26*(3), 271–288.

Human Rights Watch. (2003). Forgotten Fighters: Child Soldiers in Angola. *Human Rights Watch, 15*(10) https://www.hrw.org/reports/2003/angola0403/Angola0403.pdf

James, A., & Prout, A. (1991). A New Paradigm for the Sociology of Childhood? Provenance, Promise and Problems. In A. James & A. Prout (Eds.), *Constructing and Reconstructing Childhood: Contemporary Issues in the Sociological Study of Children* (pp. 7–34). Falmer Press.

Kaldor, M. (1999). *New and Old Wars: Organized Violence in a Global Era.* Stanford University Press.

Lee, N. (1999). The Challenge of Childhood: The Distribution of Childhood's Ambiguity in Adult Institutions. *Childhood, 6*(4), 455–474.

Lee-Koo, K. (2013). Not Suitable for Children: The Politicisation of Conflict-Affected Children in Post-2001 Afghanistan. *Australian Journal of International Affairs, 67*(4), 475–490.

Lee-Koo, K. (2018). 'The Intolerable Impact of Armed Conflict on Children': The United Nations Security Council and the Protection of Children in Armed Conflict. *Global Responsibility to Protect, 10,* 57–74.

Lind, J. (2019). Governing Vulnerabilised Migrant Childhoods Through Children's Rights. *Childhood, 26*(3), 1–15.

Machel, G. (1996). *Promotion and Protection of the Rights of Children: Impact of Armed Conflict on Children*. Report of Graça Machel, Expert of the Secretary General of the United Nations, Nova York, A/50/60.

Macmillan, L. (2011). Militarized Children and Sovereign Power. In J. Marshall Beier (Ed.), *The Militarization of Childhood: Thinking Beyond The Global South* (pp. 61–76). Palgrave Macmillan.

Marshall Beier, J. (2020). Subjects in Peril: Childhoods Between Security and Resilience. In J. Marshall Beier (Ed.), *Discovering Childhood in International Relations* (pp. 219–242). Palgrave Macmillan.

Marten, J. (2002). *Children and War: A Historical Anthology*. New York University Press.

Martins, C. (2011). The Dangers of the Single Story: Child-Soldiers in Literary Fiction and Film. *Childhood, 18*(4), 434–446.

Moynagh, M. (2011). Human Rights, Child-Soldier Narratives, and the Problem of Form. *Research in African Literatures, 42*(4), 39–59.

Nolen, S., & Baines, E. (2008, October 25). The Making of a Monster?. *Globe and Mail*. Retrieved May 14, 2017, from https://canadiancrc.com/newspaper_articles/Globe_and_Mail_The_Making_of_a_Monster_child_soldier_25OCT08.aspx

Nortje, W. (2017). Victim Or Villain: Exploring the Possible Bases of a Defence in the *Ongwen* Case at the International Criminal Court. *International Criminal Law Review, 17*, 186–207.

Rasmussen, K. (2004). Places for Children – Children's Places. *Childhood, 11*(2), 155–173.

Rosen, D. (2005). *Armies of the Young: Child Soldiers in War and Terrorism*. Rutgers University Press.

Tabak, J. (2020). *The Child and the World: Child-Soldiers and the Claim for Progress*. University of Georgia Press.

United Nations Children's Fund (UNICEF). (1997). *Cape Town Principles*. UNICEF. http://www.unicef.org/emerg/files/Cape_Town_Principles(1).pdf

United Nations General Assembly. (2000). *Optional Protocol to the Convention on the Rights of the Child on the Involvement of Children in Armed Conflict*, May 25. http://www.refworld.org/docid/47fdfb180.html.

Watchlist on Children and Armed Conflict. (2013). *Where Are They…? The Situation of Children and Armed Conflict in Mali*. Watchlist on Children and Armed Conflict.

Open Access This chapter is licensed under the terms of the Creative Commons Attribution 4.0 International License (http://creativecommons.org/licenses/by/4.0/), which permits use, sharing, adaptation, distribution and reproduction in any medium or format, as long as you give appropriate credit to the original author(s) and the source, provide a link to the Creative Commons licence and indicate if changes were made.

The images or other third party material in this chapter are included in the chapter's Creative Commons licence, unless indicated otherwise in a credit line to the material. If material is not included in the chapter's Creative Commons licence and your intended use is not permitted by statutory regulation or exceeds the permitted use, you will need to obtain permission directly from the copyright holder.

CHAPTER 8

Children's Representation in the Transnational Mirror Maze

Karl Hanson

INTRODUCTION

The chapter takes a critical stance towards organisations that claim to speak on behalf of children in transnational politics and global governance. Global power is exercised by a diffuse set of actors who exercise multiple types of power that interact in numerous ways and that have varying degrees of impact (Barnett & Duvall, 2005; Moon, 2019). Given their embeddedness in transnational politics and world affairs, international intergovernmental as well as non-governmental organisations participate in global governance and wield important portions of transnational public power, including on matters against which they are struggling. Take for instance the International Labour Organization (ILO) that occupies a central role in the global child labour regime (van Daalen & Hanson, 2019). In its vast transnational advocacy campaign to abolish child labour, the ILO claims to be speaking on behalf of children and to defend their rights and interests on the transnational arena of which it forms itself part.

K. Hanson (✉)
Centre for Children's Rights Studies, University of Geneva, Geneva, Switzerland
e-mail: Karl.Hanson@unige.ch

© The Author(s) 2023
B. Sandin et al. (eds.), *The Politics of Children's Rights and Representation*, Studies in Childhood and Youth,
https://doi.org/10.1007/978-3-031-04480-9_8

However, social movements of working children contest ILO's abolitionist perspective and find that the organisation merely defends the interests of its constituents, which are composed of representatives of governments, workers and employers, but does not represent positions taken by organised working children who see the ILO as their opponent rather as their spokesperson (see also van Daalen, this volume). This does not imply that you should retreat from speaking for others; such a position not only undercuts political effectiveness, but also stands in opposition to social justice ideals of collaboration and solidarity (Alcoff, 1991). The example does, however, point at current limits of representing children at the transnational level.

The dynamics at work in children's representation at the transnational level evokes a story told by Charlie Chaplin who was not only a famous filmmaker, actor and composer but also a great visionary and talented supplier of metaphors. In his 1928 film *The Circus*, the Tramp character escapes the police and takes cover at the local fancy fair in a mirror maze. The maze's interlocking mirrors and glass panes make it difficult for the little fellow to hide from the police or to find his way out of the maze but also for the police to catch him. Do persons or groups who in transnational arenas speak on behalf of children merely confirm global power imbalances between adults and children who are deemed not to be able to defend themselves? Or are children's spokespersons indispensable to advocate for their rights on complex and multi-layered international political stages? Like in a mirror maze, which obfuscates rather than enlightens where a person stands and how to move ahead, you cannot simply take for granted whose interests are represented nor the aims and direction of interventions and discourses on behalf of children.

The chapter will critically analyse the performances of children's representation in the transnational political arena: who is representing children and where are such representations enacted? To do so we will look at two largely advertised international struggles in favour of children's human rights. The first concerns international advocacy around minimum age legislation for child soldiering, a campaign led by transnational advocacy networks that claim to represent children and young people's rights and interests but in which child combatants do not take part. The second is about children and young people who have taken the lead to fight climate change via international legal procedures. Both cases illustrate the tension between transnational approaches that favour a 'global childhood' and national and other interests at stake in childhood politics. In our conclusion, we will consider possible strategies for children's representation to escape the mirror maze.

A World Coalition Against Child Soldiering

Like other situations where children 'don't do the right thing' such as marry young, commit offences or work (Hanson, 2016), the main idea defended in transnational children's rights advocacy concerning child soldiering is that a high minimum age is needed to respect children's fundamental rights. In international legislation concerning child soldiering, Article 38 of the 1989 Convention on the Rights of the Child (hereafter: CRC) had set the minimum age for the direct participation in hostilities and the recruitment into the armed forces at fifteen years. This minimum age limit, which was compatible with the then applicable international humanitarian law, has been criticised since its adoption and has sparked a large coalition of NGOs and States to engage in an international advocacy campaign in favour of a 'straight-eighteen' position on child soldiering and to raise the minimum age of child soldiering to eighteen years (Hanson, 2011). The coalition's successful lobbying efforts resulted in the adoption, in 2000, of the Optional Protocol to the CRC on the involvement of children in armed conflict (OPAC) that raised the minimum age to eighteen years for children's direct participation in hostilities and for their compulsory recruitment, whereas the minimum age for voluntary recruitment is set at sixteen years for the national armed forces of the State and at eighteen years for armed groups distinct from the armed forces of a State. The minimum ages set in OPAC are close to the advocated 'straight-eighteen' position. The only exceptions concern absence of a minimum age provision for indirect participation in hostilities, the exemption of military schools to fulfil the minimum age requirements and the remaining option for States to voluntary recruit young people below eighteen years in their national armies. OPAC's supporters hence acclaim the protocol as 'a significant milestone in the international community's halting journey towards the adoption of a policy that would see the cessation of all forms of recruitment and participation of children in armed conflict' (Sheppard, 2000, p. 63).

The optimistic assessment of the international community's virtues is tempered when looking at how the provisions dealing with children's voluntary recruitment in the national armed forces have distinctively been implemented in different nations. Art 3(2) OPAC prescribes that upon ratification, States must submit a binding declaration in which they indicate the applicable minimum age for voluntary recruitment into their national armed forces, which should be at a minimum sixteen, and the safeguards it has adopted to ensure that such recruitment is not forced or coerced. Whereas most ratifying countries have set at least eighteen years as minimum age for voluntary recruitment, four out of the five permanent members of the UN Security Council do not comply with the 'straight-eighteen' standard. China, France and the United States of America have declared seventeen, and the United Kingdom of Great-Britain and Northern Ireland sixteen as the minimum age for voluntary recruitment in their national armies. In its concluding observations on the reports submitted by these countries, the Committee on the Rights of the Child that has played a pivotal role in the straight-eighteen campaign recommends these countries review and raise their voluntary recruitment ages to eighteen years by referring to the 'spirit and principles' of the OPAC and of the CRC (Hanson & Molima, 2019). It is revealing to look at the explanations given by the UK, the country with the lowest minimum age, for recruiting persons as of sixteen years in its national army. The UK State Party report of 2007, which was submitted to the Committee on the Rights of the Child that is charged with monitoring compliance with OPAC, for instance, elaborates on the reasons why young people are attracted into pursuing careers in the armed forces (Committee on the Rights of the Child, 2007a). These deal with the country's need to dispose of necessary manpower to maintain its defence commitments in a competitive labour market as well as with the educational opportunities offered by the armed forces that turns many of its young recruits, including from disadvantaged backgrounds, into a highly trained and capable workforce. The 2007 UK report observes that this gives young people 'a sense of great achievement and worth, as well as benefiting society as a whole' (ibid., para 18). Taking a stance against what is understood as being a worldwide opinion, including the CRC Committee and almost all children's rights organisations large and small, the country maintains, together with all but one of its colleagues at the Security Council, that it is beneficial not only for the country and its army but also for the young people concerned to start voluntary recruitment below eighteen years. China equally argues that voluntary enlistment in the army, from seventeen years onwards, is an aspiration and an honour for many young people and also gives them a competitive advantage in the job market (Committee on the Rights of the Child, 2013). France, like China and the United States, which allows young people to be recruited from seventeen years onwards, also received criticism from the Committee on the Rights of the Child for the lack of a clear objective in complying with the internationally championed 'straight-eighteen' doctrine (Committee on the Rights of the Child, 2007b). Interestingly, besides justifying its own national minimum age for recruitment in the national army, France also highlighted, in its initial report under OPAC, its international activism concerning the situation of children in armed conflict, including its funding of NGOs that advocate for the protection of child soldiers and have adopted a 'straight eighteen' approach (Committee on the Rights of the Child, 2006).

Transnational advocacy undertaken by large NGO coalitions in the field of child soldiering has been instrumental, as mentioned above, to raise minimum ages in international law that in turn has impacted national legislation in most countries. As shown in earlier research (Hanson & Molima, 2019), asymmetries continue to exist in international policy regarding the recruitment of young people into the armed forces. On the one hand, established democracies and permanent members of the Security Council do not feel obliged to adapt their national practices and give in to pressure from transnational advocacy campaigns to raise their minimum age for voluntary recruitment to eighteen. Similar to social developments in the UK and the United States, which—due to a situation of persistent need for military manpower—have stepped up their efforts to attract young people to future military careers, China, for example, claims that the needs of the armed forces hamper raising the age for military recruitment to eighteen. On the other hand, newer democracies and less powerful regimes are more willing to show the international community that they endorse 'global opinion' and more easily adopt an unconditional 'straight-eighteen' position on child soldiering. In their discussions with supranational entities like the Committee on the Rights of the Child, powerful countries like the UK or France contest the standpoints of transnational advocacy networks by ultimately relying on their national sovereignty. Reversely, in the transnational political arena, and especially vis-à-vis politically less powerful countries, they no longer put at the centre the national sovereignty of other states but refer to humanitarian concerns on child soldiering that rely on the presumed vulnerability and weakness of children and young people. A totally different position is taken by younger nations, for instance, the Democratic Republic of the Congo, a fragile state that distinguishes between internal and external uses of international legislation. To the international community, the Democratic Republic of the Congo presents itself as a State that follows the generally accepted international rules, and hence aligns its legislation with the 'straight-eighteen' position on child soldiering and young people's perceived vulnerability. For internal purposes, the country is less inclined to follow the same path but instead takes as a point of departure the nation's national interests.

Two more general insights can be derived from this case. First, the global humanitarian campaign for a universal 'straight eighteen' position towards child soldiering is an enterprise entirely run by well-meaning outsiders without the direct or indirect participation of children and young people. It is ironic that in what some advocates have called a 'war against the use of child soldiers' (Sheppard, 2000, p. 46) the concerned children and young people, who have first-hand experience in fighting battles, have no place in 'the arsenal of weapons to be employed'. The successful global advocacy efforts to increase the minimum age for child soldiering provide a blueprint of the idea and practice that children are not needed for the advancement of children's rights. To advance the cause, children are represented by 'others' who in the transnational political arena speak and act in the name of children and young people. Moreover, the absence of 'children's voices' in these debates is not even questioned; the legitimacy of a transnational coalition of faith-based groups, humanitarian organisations, large children's rights entities to represent children's rights and interests in political debates about child soldiering seems self-evident. The example illustrates, as is the case for many other transnational advocacy campaigns in the children's rights field, that children's representation can be performed without involving children (see also Tabak, this volume).

Second, the discussion of minimum ages related to child soldiering illustrates the importance of national sovereignty for national and global representations of children (Hanson, 2021). Notwithstanding transnational networks' considerable influence on global childhood discourse, States continue to exercise a dominant share of the political power for elaborating national childhood and youth policies. In discourses for national audiences, States do not necessarily observe globalised ideas around vulnerable childhoods but refer to the Westphalian political order, especially in matters pertaining to their national armed forces, which lends them the sole power over their territories and justifies state sovereignty. For international audiences, discourses differ depending on a State's relative position in the transnational political arena. Permanent members of the Security Council can, as we have seen, assume out loud on the international scene that their national interests prevail over global childhood ideals, and at the same time ask other States to always give preference to global childhood ideals. Less powerful States are keen to show in transnational realms that they follow up on that request and adhere to universal, Western representations of childhood vulnerability, even if for national audiences they continue to give precedence to their national interests over globalised childhood ideals. What you see in the transnational mirror is hence not necessarily what you see in the national one. More powerful states, who are keen to preserve their own national sovereignty and promote international norms, tend to accept the double image projected by less powerful states. Global discourses about vulnerable childhoods on the international level go hand in hand with state sovereignty discourse at the national level. In other words, on the international plane countries from the global South need to show obedience to global childhood ideals but have a greater margin of autonomous action once they turn to their internal affairs. Out of genuine self-interest to preserve their own sovereignty claims as much as possible, powerful States accept the autonomy of less powerful states. Doing otherwise would undermine the idea of their own sovereignty.

There are many passages crossing the maze. Notwithstanding globalisation, political debates on children's representation in global affairs do not only take place on indeterminate transnational political spaces, but also, at the same time, at national political levels. It is important to reflect not only on who speaks or acts on behalf of children, but also on the political forums where this speaking and acting take place. In the following section I turn to a second case that focuses on an international legal procedure on climate change which has been introduced by young people. In this case, children and young people represent children's rights and interests in a transnational matter that is discussed as part of an international legal procedure.

THE CHILDREN OF THE WORLD VS. CLIMATE CHANGE

The urgency to curb further global warming and to fight the global consequences of climate change has given rise to introducing environmental protection cases that concern the rights of children and of future generations before courts in a wide range of countries including Germany, South Africa, Peru and South Korea (Nolan, 2021). Wewerinke-Singh (2021) observes that as of October 2021, eighty-three cases have been filed before domestic courts concerning States or corporations' inadequate climate action, whereas nineteen such cases have been introduced before regional and international judicial bodies. Amongst the latter is a communication submitted in 2019 to the UN Committee on the Rights of the Child by sixteen children from twelve different nationalities. Their claim is directed against five respondent States (Argentina, Brazil, France, Germany and Turkey) who have ratified or accessed the 1992 United Nations Framework Convention on Climate Change. All these States are member of the 2014 Optional Protocol to the Convention on the Rights of the Child on a communication procedure (OPIC) and have hence agreed that individuals or group of individuals may submit communications concerning the violation, by the concerned State, of any of the rights contained in the CRC or its Optional Protocols. The child petitioners, who at the time of the communication were between eight and seventeen years old, assert that each of the five respondent States helped cause the climate crisis, and, despite the knowledge that this endangers children's fundamental rights, is still perpetuating the crisis by undermining the global collective effort to solve it. In their communication, the complainants state that

> By recklessly causing and perpetuating excessive levels of carbon emissions, the respondents are failing to prevent the deadly and harmful impacts of climate change, and are violating the petitioners' rights to life, health, and culture, and failing to have the best interest of the child be a primary consideration in their climate actions. (Communication to the Committee on the Rights of the Child, 2019, para. 258)

A remarkable role in support of this petition was played by UNICEF who called this a 'landmark case' that was announced at a press conference hosted at UNICEF Headquarters in New York. The press release for this event cites UNICEF Deputy Executive Director Charlotte Petri Gornitzka who refers to 'the world's children' who are said to be holding, through this petition, 'the world' and its leaders accountable to their commitment for children's rights by having adopted, thirty years earlier, the CRC (UNICEF, 2019). During the press conference, one of the young petitioners, youth climate activist Alexandria Villaseñor from the United States, confirms that the group of children who claim that their rights have been violated stand here 'as citizens of the planet' who are victims of enduring pollution.

UNICEF's support of a small group of children to file a complaint to a human rights treaty body in the name of the 2.3 billion children of the world replicates the popular idea that children represent the present and future citizens of a single Planet Earth. This position is reminiscent of cosmopolitanism that considers all human beings, irrespective of their social or political affiliation, as belonging to a universal community of world citizens (Kleingeld & Brown, 2019), and which is widespread in discourses on children's involvement in environmental movement struggles (see e.g. Buhre, this volume Chap. 11). The argument made, in short, is that global climate change is a worldwide problem that, unconstrained by national borders, impacts every person on the planet. Global environmental challenges call for global political reactions. Political responses to solve the current environmental crisis cannot therefore be limited to nation states but need to be devised at the universal level. The prevalence of cosmopolitan worldviews on both environmental concerns and children's rights allows investigating from a different angle the two central questions being discussed in this chapter, namely, *who* can be seen as representing the children of the world and *where* do we locate power in transnational policy making.

Who can legitimately claim to represent the children of the world? In the complaint procedure on global warming, UNICEF does not explain why or how these sixteen young individuals, and not others, have been selected to speak on behalf of the world's children. The petitioners have not been elected by the planet's children to represent them nor have they been designated based on their expertise in environmental matters or particular vulnerability for the impact of climate change. As I have observed elsewhere (Hanson, 2015), the OPIC procedure has mainly been established for strategic litigation purposes as an additional advocacy instrument to raise international awareness for specific concerns. In this case the sixteen child petitioners appear as symbolic victims of violations of children's rights who have been selected for reasons undisclosed by unidentified entities, with the support of UNICEF, to initiate a case before an international treaty monitoring body. The question of how representative this small number of children is for all victims of climate change is similar to points that need to be resolved by any social movement which strategically makes use of individual legal procedures to draw attention to broader problems.

In a recently published practical guide for lawyers who defend children in conflict with the law, Defence for Children International (DCI)—

Belgium (2018) gives legal practitioners advice on the use of strategic litigation for the promotion of children's rights. Besides suggesting that they must be careful while deciding which international procedure to engage with, that it is important to cooperate with NGOs and that an individual case should sufficiently reflect a structural problem, the publication sees the choice of individual children for a case as a matter of ethics. Before starting a strategic legal procedure, the child must give its authorisation and also the best interests of the child need to be considered. These recommendations are in line with the rules of procedure to bring a communication before the Committee on the Rights of the Child in Article 3 OPIC that includes safeguards to ensure that those who are acting on the child's behalf are not manipulating children. Whether an individual child has been forced or instrumentalised against its will to represent a larger group of children deals with child protection and is a negative question. Children should be protected from being manipulated to act as spokespersons for a global cause, including the defence of human rights or the environment. Critics of children's involvement in social movements often mobilise the argument that children, because of their deemed incompetency to make autonomous political decisions, are manipulated by others as a means to delegitimise their arguments. In the present case on children's rights implications of climate change, we assume that the young people have not been manipulated and that these ethical considerations are being respected. We have no reason to believe that these child petitioners have been prompted to submit the communication or are being instrumentalised for a cause that is not theirs. Many petitioners comprising Alexandria Villaseñor from the United States, Ridhima Pandey from India, Greta Thunberg from Sweden and Ayakha Melithafa from South Africa are internationally known leaders of young people's environmental social movements, and it is difficult to imagine that their engagement with this international legal procedure would be the result of manipulation.

But what do the world's children think of their sixteen representatives? It is not because the rights of the representatives are protected that also the rights of those who are being represented have been considered. Here, the aim is to find out who might legitimately act on behalf of the world's children to fight climate change, which is a positive question. Questions related to children's legal representation in strategic litigation as in the case above are part of a more general 'crisis of representation' (Alcoff, 1991). The problem of speaking for others is salient not only for children but also arises in discussions on the legitimacy of political representation in liberal democracies and on representativity of social movement leadership in human rights advocacy. Speaking on behalf of others is part of the everyday work of many human and children's rights advocacy NGOs, such as Amnesty International, Human Rights Watch or Defence for Children International (see e.g. Jo Becker, 2012, 2017). The campaign to raise the minimum age for child soldiering discussed above is an illustration of a case where transnational advocates claim to represent children's rights and interests without involving the concerned child soldiers. According to Neil Stammers (2013) who speaks of 'the problematic of representational power', 'there is not necessarily a problem with NGOs speaking on behalf of the oppressed and those whose rights are being violated or threatened, those NGOs must ensure that they properly represent the interests, views and demands of those they claim to be representing' (p. 283). What are, in any context where the problem of speaking on behalf of others arises, the communication channels, participation methods and the means of representation between spokespersons and the people they claim to speak for? Are the spokespersons appointed through elections, by virtue of their communication skills or expertise on the themes being advocated? Or have they been chosen because they display some form of charismatic authority? And how do these questions play out in children's rights advocacy, where more often than not adults speak on behalf of children?

Even if children speak on behalf of other children (see also Holzscheiter, 2016), we cannot simply assume that sixteen children have received a mandate to speak on behalf of 2.3 billion others. Who would the world's children designate as their representatives to speak on their behalf? In addition, the successful designation of legitimate representatives, on whatever grounds chosen, does not resolve once and for all the problem of speaking for others. What is being expressed will remain under constant scrutiny, for the simple reason that the act of representation is not based on a single discovery of the truth but will continuously be mediated as they are the product of interpretation (Alcoff, 1991). Processes of mediation and interpretation in the field of children's rights can be captured by using the notion 'translation' (Hanson & Nieuwenhuys, 2013). The claims made by one person or group in the name of another person or group are not simply transferred but they are translated, an activity that involves an active stance of re-production and change that can be critically scrutinised (Freeman, 2009). The question *who* represents the world's children hence needs to be complemented by asking *how* these representatives translate the ideas and opinions of such a large group of people.

The international procedure submitted under OPIC by a group of children is not looking to be perceived as representative of the planet's youngest occupants but is about creating a discursive space in the transnational political arena to put the spotlight on climate change. This becomes clear in the decision adopted by the Committee on the Rights of the Child (2021) in response to the communication submitted by the sixteen young climate activists. The Committee finds that the complainants have successfully established jurisdiction and recognises their victim status but dismisses the case on the ground that the complainants have not exhausted the legal remedies available at the domestic level. Notwithstanding that no substantive redress has been granted, commentators have hailed the decision as 'ground-breaking' and 'historic' precisely because of its political success in raising awareness about how climate change has an impact on children's rights (Wewerinke-Singh, 2021). The Committee transcends standard limitations of international jurisprudence by using this individual communication procedure as a catalyst for the development of its own new General Comment on children's rights and climate change. Instead of giving redress to the alleged victims of the case, the Committee invites the young authors of the communication to share their views during the upcoming General Comment's drafting process (ibid.). The discourse so produced on the impact of climate change on children's rights is hence undoubtedly a political event, not only for the young climate activists but also for its supporters, including UNICEF and the Committee on the Rights of the Child. The latter was called upon to make a ruling on a conflict opposing the young complainants and the alleged States. However, it does not adjudicate the case in favour of the plaintiffs but acts as a transnational advocacy entity by lending its support for the political cause of climate change. As in a maze, rather than offering a clear answer to the claim, the path followed is a puzzling one.

In addition to asking who speaks and what is said and translated, a further relevant question on children's representation is where the conversations take place. Even if the child-led communication procedure on climate change under OPIC deals with a planetarian problem, it is directed against five individual States and not against transnational entities such as multinational corporations or large private investment funds that all bear responsibilities for the state of the world's climate. The nation States, the principal duty bearers for policies on children's well-being and rights, are also the entities that strategically, financially and administratively govern UNICEF, that can achieve its mandate to protect children's rights and help meet their basic needs only by collaborating with sovereign nation-states (Hanson, 2021). UNICEF is 'controlled by national governments that ultimately respect each and every other country's sovereignty to develop childhood and youth policies. The champion of the world's children, rather than being a cosmopolitan government for all children, is bound hand and foot by nation-states who remain in charge' (Hanson, 2021, p. 6). It is hence remarkable that UNICEF encourages children to submit a complaint before an international adjudicating body, not against transnational actors but against nation States about the impact on children of climate change for which both nation States and transnational actors bear responsibility.

A similar observation can be made regarding the Committee on the Rights of the Child, the entity that is the recipient of this Communication. The Committee has not been created as an international political body but as an entity devolved to monitoring State compliance with the CRC through the country report procedure as well as through the settling of individual communications. Its experts are designated by the member States of the CRC, an international treaty that relies mainly on national governments for its implementation and fully recognises State sovereignty. Within the existing international political system, policies for dealing with the well-being and rights of the world's children are, notwithstanding widespread cosmopolitan beliefs, the primary responsibility of nation-states, not of supranational entities (ibid.). The headlong rush of the Committee to call upon the authors of a communication directed against States—a communication that the Committee ultimately decided to dismiss—to participate in the development of a politically sensitive General Comment on children's rights and climate change is surprising. Like in a mirror maze, the apparently random mix between glass panes and mirrors makes it hard to find a way out; we are no longer sure by whom children should be represented in transnational matters nor where these representations are to be performed.

How to Escape the Mirror Maze?

Why is everything so complicated and often misleading in children's transnational representation? Fraser (2009) can be helpful here as she distinguishes social justice claims between claims that deal with redistribution (of material and immaterial goods between individuals, groups or generations), recognition (of a person's or a groups unique viewpoint on the world) and representation (who, how and where are questions related to just distribution and to representation discussed). The distinction between the three claims for social justice transpires in the field of childhood and children's rights studies.

Over the last thirty years, global children's rights discourse has been confronted with a proliferation of portrayals of appalling situations of children in the global South, pointing, for instance, at child exploitation, trafficking, child soldiering, violence against children that all emphasise children's victimhood and vulnerability. The large-scale trend of moralisation of discourse and policy in the field of children's rights and human rights (Poretti et al., 2014) has diverted attention away from questions about the economic and structural inequalities and unjust distribution that have caused children's hardship. Notwithstanding the weight attached to the moral arguments of its advocates, the children's rights framework cannot by itself satisfactorily act in response to the impact of large social and economic developments on the lives of children, including the consequences of globalisation. For example, according to the ILO News Room (2020) there has been between 2000 and 2016 a 40 per cent decrease of child labour and its worst forms, an evolution for which the organisation points at the ratification of its own Conventions on the worst forms of child labour and on minimum ages to work, as well as at the adoption of effective national laws and policies. Without entering into a discussion about the extent of this decrease or how it has been measured, it is remarkable that the ILO nowhere mentions macro-economic changes that have occurred during the same period, including overall economic growth and the halving of the number of low-income countries (Steinbach, 2019). To explain changes in the prevalence of child labour by giving credit only to moral persuasion and legislative changes, and by hiding profound concomitant economic changes, seems a distortion rather than a faithful mirror of reality.

It is tempting to think of the world as ultimately obeying to a set of moral values expressed in international human rights law. The children's rights framework provides an appealing blueprint for how a better future would look like, and many consider the implementation of international norms and programmes as the golden road to make that future come closer to reality. Contrary to the decline of claims for just distribution, claims for children's recognition have been on the rise and have dominated discussions on children's rights advocacy. The demand for the recognition of children involves asking us to acknowledge children's special status and their identity and subjectivities. Notwithstanding growing respect for children's subjectivities and rights 'as children', there are also risks involved in advancing claims for children's recognition. The 'straight-eighteen' position in child soldiering for instance comes down to the essentialisation of an iconic figure, the child soldier, whose history and location have been erased (see also Tabak, this volume).

Fraser distinguishes a third set of social justice claims that deal with questions of representation, which come close to demands for the realisation of children's rights to participation in decision making. Here, a distinction needs to be made between two levels where claims for representation play out. A first level discusses representation of children, including the absence thereof, within the Westphalian political order. Central themes in the discussion are about children and young people's right to vote, political participation or other forms of representation. Children's political representation within the national political space is far from complete compared to the representation of adults who in general have access to designated forms of participation such as voting rights in democratic elections. However, both children and adults suffer from forms of misrepresentation and democratic deficit, expressed by the rise of anti-democratic political parties, protest voters or the many initiatives for intensifying local citizenship and new forms of direct democracy. Within this context, the question how to represent children in national political arenas and decision-making processes needs to be further explored and experimented. The question of children's representation or non-representation within democratic nation states is an important one that needs to be addressed. However, beyond challenges to children's representation at the national level, additional questions arise concerning the deficit of representation of children in transnational power struggles, as illustrated by the transnational advocacy campaigns on child soldiering and the use of international legal procedures in advancing climate activism. Where to recruit representatives of children in the transnational public space as counterforces of transnational power entities?

The question of representation is especially salient on a second level that plays out beyond the nation-State. Within the transnational political order, the situation of children and adults is remarkably much more equal: neither adults nor children have much to say in transnational power struggles. Globalisation has created new transnational powers such as transnational private powers or global economic governance structures, leading us to putting on the agenda questions about what the right frame is to ask questions about distribution and recognition. According to Fraser, today's key political question is how to 'integrate struggles against maldistribution, misrecognition and misrepresentation within a postwestphalian frame?' (2009, p. 21). The absence of a transnational public political space indeed poses challenges around how to represent children in global struggles such as against climate change or international legislation on child soldiering. When children are represented in transnational power struggles, it is not always easy to distinguish between innovative forms of international social movement activism and merely pretending doing so.

Discourses on the rights of the world's children tend to complicate rather than facilitate our understanding of children's representation at the transnational level. What strategies could be developed to find ways out of the maze? A first route is offered by Linda Alcoff's (1991) procedural solution to the problem of speaking for others. Alcoff looks for a middle ground between a non-critical, paternalist appropriation of the other (a pitfall in which many present-day children's rights advocacy campaigns are trapped) and a general retreat from speaking for others which would be both illusionary and politically ineffective (prohibiting transnational actors to speak in the name of the world's children). Her series of questions can assist in a concrete analysis and evaluation of specific power relations and discursive practices in transnational affairs concerning children. Looking critically at how much of the motivation to speak for others is about the desire for mastery and domination, or whether it is about something else. Next, we would need to interrogate how social location and context has an impact on what representatives are saying thereby taking care that this act of self-reflection does not make up a simple unanalysed disclaimer that would reinforce, rather than question, the speaker's authority. Finally, remain critical and include an analysis of the actual and probable effects of what is being said on the discursive and material context. Besides the social location of the speaker and the propositional content of the speech, it is important to look at the actual and potential effects of the claims that are being made.

Another possible escape route is to strengthen children's representation within the transnational entities that champion children's rights at the international level. The main strategic and operational decisions made within UNICEF are decided without any formal or informal representation of children. Who represents children within UNICEF? Referring to Stammers (2013), there is a need to strengthen democracy within international intergovernmental organisations that claim to represent children's rights and interests. Can they find ways to include children's standpoints in their internal decision-making processes? In addition, can they make their internal decision-making procedures more transparent and clarify who influences the choices UNICEF makes? For instance, who decided when and how that climate change is an important theme for UNICEF? Increasing transparency about how representation decisions are being made is indeed a precondition to set in motion a series of changes to improve children's representation in transnational affairs. Similar questions about internal democracy also apply to international civil society organisations that are less closely associated with the exercise of state power and can hence be seen as more reliable, independent representatives of children's rights and interests in transnational affairs. Are organisations such as World Vision, Save the Children or Plan International, to name some of the largest global children's rights NGOs, more transparent about how decisions on children's representation are being made?

One of the main challenges for bringing internal democracy within these organisations is that they must deal with similar problems compared to their intergovernmental counterparts, namely that they are very closely related with entities that exercise transnational power. For example, can Save the Children, that in its corporate responsibility actions collaborates with multinational companies which have a revenue up to twenty times higher than their own, speak on behalf of children in transnational matters that are influenced by the entities that fund them? While much of the funding of global NGOs comes from States and intergovernmental donors, will they bite the hand that feeds them? Smaller non-governmental organisations might have greater potential to play an independent role in contesting transnational power. But is their lack of visibility and influence in the transnational political arena compensated by being more independent from the power they contest?

Conclusion

International organisations that represent children's rights and interests, such as UNICEF, the ILO or international NGOs, present themselves as counterforces to transnational power which contribute to struggles for children's rights. Earlier research on priority themes in international children's rights advocacy has shown the pre-eminence of themes that deal with children's basic needs and the protection of their body over emancipatory concerns and children's claims for autonomy (Poretti et al., 2014).

Giving preference to defend these themes rather than others is not a twist of fate nor is it the outcome of a carefully conducted assessment of the rights that children want to focus upon. Making such choices illustrates that 'speaking for others' often originates from a desire for mastery and domination that is part of a political arena where who is speaking on behalf of whom is both the result of and an act of political struggle (Alcoff, 1991).

The present chapter has analysed some of the features of the transnational political arena where childhood and children's rights matters are debated, using the examples of a transnational campaign on child soldiering and international litigation on climate change. It has also explored links between the transnational political forum and the roles and responsibilities of the entities that are claiming to represent children. We have seen that, given their close connection with international policy making on children, childhood and children's rights, transnational campaigns and entities exert a significant part of the transnational public power against which they are struggling. This makes it important to critically assess who is speaking on behalf of children and where their representation is being performed. To find a way out of the transnational mirror maze, it is important to understand its complex and often confusing network of pathways and to design new routes that can help to critically reflect on children's representation in world affairs.

References

Alcoff, L. (1991). The Problem of Speaking for Others. *Cultural Critique, 20*, 5–32.

Barnett, M. N., & Duvall, R. (2005). Power in Global Governance. *International Organization, 59*(1), 39–75.

Becker, J. (2012). *Campaigning for Justice. Human Rights Advocacy in Practice.* Stanford University Press.

Becker, J. (2017). *Campaigning for Children: Strategies for Advancing Children's Rights.* Stanford University Press.

Committee on the Rights of the Child. (2006). *Initial Reports of States Parties on OPAC: France* (UN Doc. CRC/C/OPAC/FRA/1) (6 November).

Committee on the Rights of the Child. (2007a). *Initial Reports of States Parties on OPAC: United Kingdom of Great-Britain and Northern Ireland* (UN Doc. CRC/C/OPAC/GBR/1) (3 September 2007).

Committee on the Rights of the Child. (2007b). *Concluding Observations OPAC: France* (UN Doc. CRC/C/OPAC/FRA/CO/1) (15 October).

Committee on the Rights of the Child. (2013). *Summary Record of the 1835th Meeting. Consideration of Reports of States Parties: China* (UN Doc. CRC/C/SR.1835) (19 November 2013).

Committee on the Rights of the Child. (2021). *Decision adopted under the Optional Protocol to the Convention on the Rights of the Child on a communications procedure in respect of Communication No. 104/2019* (UN Doc. CRC/C/88/D/104/2019) (8 October 2021).

Communication to the Committee on the Rights of the Child. (2019). In the Case of [16 Individuals] v. Argentina, Brazil, France, Germany & Turkey, Submitted Under Article 5 of the Optional Protocol to the Convention on the Rights of the Child on an Individual Communication Procedure, 23 September 2019.

Defence for Children International (DCI) – Belgium. (2018). *Lawyers Defending Children in Conflict with the Law. International Practical Guide*. DCI Belgium. https://lachild.eu/the-projects/mylawyer-myrights/manuals/. Consulted 1 May 2021.

Fraser, N. (2009). *Scales of Justice: Reimagining Political Space in a Globalizing World*. Columbia University Press.

Freeman, R. (2009). What Is 'translation'? *Evidence & Policy: A Journal of Research, Debate and Practice, 5*(4), 429–447.

Hanson, K. (2011). International Children's Rights and Armed Conflict. *Human Rights and International Legal Discourse, 5*(1), 40–62.

Hanson, K. (2015). International Legal Procedures and Children's Conceptual Autonomy. *Childhood, 22*(4), 427–431.

Hanson, K. (2016). Children's Participation and Agency When They Don't 'do the right thing'. *Childhood, 23*(4), 471–475.

Hanson, K. (2021). The State and the World's Children. *Childhood, 28*(1), 3–7.

Hanson, K., & Molima, C. (2019). Getting Tambo Out of Limbo: Exploring Alternative Legal Frameworks That Are More Sensitive to the Agency of Children and Young People in Armed Conflict. In M. A. Drumbl & J. C. Barrett (Eds.), *Research Handbook on Child Soldiers* (pp. 110–131). Edward Elgar.

Hanson, K., & Nieuwenhuys, O. (Eds.). (2013). *Reconceptualizing Children's Rights in International Development. Living Rights, Social Justice, Translations*. Cambridge University Press.

Holzscheiter, A. (2016). Representation as Power and Performative Practice: Global Civil Society Advocacy for Working Children. *Review of International Studies, 42*(2), 205–226.

Kleingeld, P., & Brown, E. (2019). Cosmopolitanism. The Stanford Encyclopedia of Philosophy (Winter 2019 Edition), E. N. Zalta (ed.). https://plato.stanford.edu/archives/win2019/entries/cosmopolitanism/. Consulted 1 April 2021.

Moon, S. (2019). Power in Global Governance: An Expanded Typology from Global Health. *Globalization and Health, 15*(1), 1–9.

Nolan, A. (2021). Democracy Is Failing to Protect the Environment for Future Generations. So the Courts Are Stepping In. *Prospect* June 28, 2021. https://www.prospectmagazine.co.uk/world/democracy-future-generations-environment-climate-german-constitutional-court. Consulted 20 November 2021.

Poretti, M., Hanson, K., Darbellay, F., & Berchtold, A. (2014). The Rise and Fall of Icons of 'stolen childhood' Since the Adoption of the UN Convention on the Rights of the Child. *Childhood, 21*(1), 22–38.

Sheppard, A. (2000). Child Soldiers: Is the Optional Protocol Evidence of an Emerging 'straight-18' Consensus? *The International Journal of Children s Rights, 8*(1), 37–70.

Stammers, N. (2013). Children's Rights and Social Movements: Reflections from a Cognate Field. In K. Hanson & O. Nieuwenhuys (Eds.), *Reconceptualizing Children's Rights in International Development. Living Rights, Social Justice, Translations* (pp. 275–292). Cambridge University Press.

Steinbach, R. (2019). *Growth in Low-Income Countries. Evolution, Prospects, and Policies.* Policy Research Working Paper 8949. The World Bank Group. http://www.worldbank.org/prwp. Consulted 1 February 2021

UNICEF. 2019. Press Release: 16 Children, Including Greta Thunberg, File Landmark Complaint to the United Nations Committee on the Rights of the Child, 24 September 2019. https://www.unicef.org/eap/press-releases/16-children-including-greta-thunberg-file-landmark-complaint-united-nations. Consulted 1 April 2021.

van Daalen, E., & Hanson, K. (2019). ILO's Shifts in Child Labour Policy: Regulation and Abolition. *International Development Policy* 11 – Special Issue on 100 Years ILO, pp. 133–150. http://journals.openedition.org/poldev/3056; https://doi.org/10.4000/poldev.3056

Wewerinke-Singh, M. 2021. Communication 104/2019 Chiara Sacchi et al. v. Argentina et al. *Leiden Children's Rights Observatory*, Case Note 2021/10, 28 October 2021. https://www.childrensrightsobservatory.nl/case-notes/casenote2021-10#introduction. Consulted 10 November 2021.

Open Access This chapter is licensed under the terms of the Creative Commons Attribution 4.0 International License (http://creativecommons.org/licenses/by/4.0/), which permits use, sharing, adaptation, distribution and reproduction in any medium or format, as long as you give appropriate credit to the original author(s) and the source, provide a link to the Creative Commons licence and indicate if changes were made.

The images or other third party material in this chapter are included in the chapter's Creative Commons licence, unless indicated otherwise in a credit line to the material. If material is not included in the chapter's Creative Commons licence and your intended use is not permitted by statutory regulation or exceeds the permitted use, you will need to obtain permission directly from the copyright holder.

PART III

Children's Representation in Times of Inequalities and Injustices

CHAPTER 9

Deliberative Disobedience as a Strategy for Claiming Rights and Representation in the Family: The Case of Accra's Street Children

Yaw Ofosu-Kusi

INTRODUCTION

Ghana is a youthful nation because as at 2018, approximately 39% of the population was below 15 years (Population Reference Bureau, 2018). Culturally, Ghana is a fairly paternalistic society with considerable authority vested in adult males in decision-making processes (Nukunya, 2003), as in many parts of the developing world where patriarchal family models may be found, for example in Brazil (Aptekar and Stoecklin 2014, Moulin & Pereira, 2000); Nigeria (Ayodele, 2016), Mali (Dougnon, 2012), Senegal (Mbaye & Fall, 2000) and India (Gibbon et al., 2014). This entitles adults to assume representational rights over others in society, sometimes even constraining them, especially children, from expressing their

Y. Ofosu-Kusi (✉)
School of Arts and Social Sciences, University of Energy and Natural Resources, Sunyani, Ghana
e-mail: yaw.ofosu-kusi@uenr.edu.gh

© The Author(s) 2023
B. Sandin et al. (eds.), *The Politics of Children's Rights and Representation*, Studies in Childhood and Youth,
https://doi.org/10.1007/978-3-031-04480-9_9

personal views, expectations and directions of their lives. There are however differences in how such representational rights and the authority that accompanies them are applied by adults in children's lives thus bringing to the fore the differential nature of childhood in Ghana. Factors such as family economy, parents' educational and general social background, residence—rural or urban—forms of control and nurturance bring multidimensionality to childhood and the everyday experiences of children.

A central trait in whatever form of childhood one experiences in Ghanaian societies and in many African societies is the tradition of respect and obedience such that some adults are generally enabled to claim an almost religious authority over their children or other subordinates (Ikuomola, 2017; Ofosu-Kusi, 2017a, b). Corresponding to this is a filial obligation to project the wishes and demands of parents. That obligation in its most comprehensive form (in the case of mature children) includes economic support, health and safety needs, sociality, emotional well-being (Caro, 2014), among others. Yet, for many children, adults such as parents, teachers and even NGO officials who purport to represent their interest are unable to constructively articulate their plight when necessary. Nevertheless, while the majority of children accept this authority in homes and schools, others are currently questioning its absoluteness by finding ways to constructively participate in decisions affecting them or assuming some degree of control over their lives. However, in cases where this new form of engagement with those in control of their lives has been disingenuously approached, ensuing criticisms have been swift.

Street children constitute a group of children who have increasingly incurred the wrath of adults and society as a whole for being disobedient, for disregarding the authority of their parents or for daring to stand up to the adults they encounter on the streets. Reasons that motivate them to transgress this deferential expectation are diverse. It could be a bid to escape from domestic privations, verbal or physical abuse, school-related problems, boredom, or even peer pressure (Department of Social Welfare, Ricerca E Cooperazione and Catholic Action for Street Children 2011). Without any intention of glamorising *streetism*, one might be right in hypothesising that street children epitomise a generation of children who are adventurous and courageous enough to disregard the demands of their parents by venturing onto the streets of major cities of the country, often after careful planning and deliberation. The public reaction to such actions is usually disbelief; hence they are often criticised as disobedient, disrespectful, recalcitrant children; and even pejoratively labelled as *kubolor* or good-for-nothing children in pursuit of the elusive attractions of the city (Korboe, 1997).

Yet, as will be argued in the chapter, some street children deliberately defy parents, disengage themselves from families, and assume proto-adult status as a way of claiming decision-making space in order to assert rights and self-representation. We encounter a framing of representation that is personal rather than derived from a third party; a reconfiguration from an external source to an internalized form with its efficacy determined by the actor, in this case the child. That bid is exemplified and given substantive backing by the monetary and in-kind contributions some of them make to their families back at home thus bringing some financial relief. But, while the behaviour on one hand empowers children and elevates their agency, it on the other hand, undermines the authority of parents (or adults) and therefore upends the traditional distribution of power and authority and the accompanying assumption that decisions are made by adults to be unquestionably followed by children.

Rights and Representation in the Context of Urban Informality

One source of street children's claim to independence that enables them to be self-proclaiming individuals is their sojourn in the cities of Ghana, especially Accra and Kumasi, where they are fully or marginally absorbed into the informal sector. The informal sector, as Henry (1987, p. 139) posits is "the generic term for the range of overlapping sub-economies that are not taken into account by formal measures of economic activity". Keith Hart (2000, p. 68) considers it as the "world of economic activities outside the organized labour force…"; while Harris-White (2010, p. 170) describes it as: "Activities outside the regulative ambit of the state"; often atomistic in nature and performed by what Hart calls a "Dickensian mob" of petty traders, hawkers, barbers, repairers, etc. Though a product of developmental challenges (Davis, 2006; Mayne, 2017), the informal sector is an important source of employment, and is even touted as the future of economic growth and development throughout the developing world. For example, according to the African Development Bank (AfDB, 2013), it accounts for 80% of Africa's labour force and contributes over 55% of its gross domestic product (GDP). These characteristics and potential of the informal sector make it attractive and accessible to children. If, as is increasingly predicted, it is the future driving force of African economies, then one would be right in assuming that it would play significant roles in the lives of families and their children. From a child's perspective, the attractiveness of the sector lies in the non-enforcement of labour laws, especially age restrictions, and the ease with which they would be absorbed by the ensemble of small-scale operators. For this reason, it is quite probable that the number of children engaged in its myriad activities will continue to rise as children seek work to earn money, escape rural drudgery, capriciousness of parents and dysfunctional families, poverty-imposed vulnerabilities and dispossession of childhood entitlements (Mizen & Ofosu-Kusi, 2013). Using an elastic definition comprising children born on the streets, migrant children and urban poor children who roam the city to earn money, a census of street children in Greater Accra in 2009 found 61,492 children (Department of Social Welfare, Ricerca E Copoperazione and Catholic Action for Street Children 2011).

Children *on* or *of* the streets (UNICEF), runaway children, homeless children, street-connected children or "Children in Street Situations" are what the Committee on the Rights of the Child (General Comment No. 21, 2017) describes as: "A wider population of children who have formed strong connections with public spaces and for whom the street plays a vital role in their everyday lives and identities" (p. 3). Crucially, these are children who derive their existence and livelihood from such spaces in many cases without the benefit of significant adults as guardians. While we tend to think of street children as a uniform group of people denominated by extreme poverty, jaundiced lifestyles and disoriented childhoods, the reality is that they are a very heterogeneous group of people marked by variations in their backgrounds, experiences and motivations. A thread that binds them is that they might have been ushered into regimes of work when they were quite young as part of their socialization, or possibly what Apterkar and Stoecklin (2014), p. 14) consider, "premature entry into adult roles such as marriage, hazardous labour or combat", or an "initiation … into local activities and knowledge" that was predominated by work (Dougnon, 2012, p. 143). Hence, in contrast to Western societies where, as Myers (2001) argues, there is a clear distinction between childhood and adulthood and for that matter extends children's dependency into adolescence, what pertains in Ghana (as in many parts of the Global South) is a thin, almost imperceptible line, between childhood and adulthood. It is invariable that children, depending on their family background, will make a contribution to the family's economy based on their ability and potential, but not necessarily a legal or bureaucratic age. This may be in the domestic arena, in their community or further afield such as Accra. Street children and what they do to survive is a worthwhile example of differentiated or alternative childhoods in Ghana and raises questions about whether such children should be sent back home if possible to ensure a 'proper' childhood for them, or whether their childhood rights should be reinterpreted to accommodate work as a fulfilment of their aspirations (Liebel, 2012; Bourdillon & Spittler, 2012). After all, as appropriately noted by Apterkar and Stoecklin (2014), p. 2), "…they are actors trying to surmount their difficulties by creating a world that helps them survive."

According to Holzscheiter (2016), p. 209), "Representation is a form of power…it encompasses the possibility and authority to express, defend, and advocate for…others without their immediate involvement or control". In this context, we think of children's representation as one occasioned by others; its actualization is through the generosity of others, principally adults, NGOs and rights-based agencies. An obvious challenge to this notion of representation is ambivalence since the advocates might be torn between their own interest and those of their constituencies, and might therefore motivate a superimposition of their values on those of their subjects. Parents, uncles and aunts, older siblings; extended family members, and teachers are all in this frame and frequently claim to be representing the interest and pursuing the well-being of children. Yet, if as Holzscheiter (2016, p. 209) points out, representation implies power over a particular constituency in the sense that "someone stands in place of another", then whose rights do parents or NGOs for example advocate when they claim to make decisions or influence policies affecting children. We may believe parents, because of the natural tendency to care for their children, although this is sometimes marred by toxic socialization. Similarly, while the intentions of some NGOs may be genuine, those of others are in some cases severely compromised by self-interest. The CRC may suffer the same fate when the competing claims and interests for its development and substance are interrogated. As Droz (2013, p. 116) posits, it "articulates a universalistic catalogue of rights that originates in a culturally specific conception of children: the 'precious child' of twentieth century neo-liberal thought about the self-governing individual…". Its divergence with other cultures' interpretation of childhood and children's experiences especially in the Global South has received considerable attention (see e.g. Boyden, 1997; Ennew, 2000; Ennew, 2005; Myers, 2001).

Thus, the depths of representation, be it personalized or externalized, may vary according to the degree and recognition of the tenets of the CRC. Unsurprisingly, post-colonial thoughts on the CRC point to a new form of cultural imperialism in which traditional adult-child relationship has been supplanted by western concepts of childhood that is deemed to be superior to the latter (Liebel, 2017).

Nevertheless, the spirit of the CRC and its articles have been translated into various national constitutions as well as specific acts such as Ghana's Children Act 560, Kenya's Children's Bill of Rights, Nigeria's Child Rights Act among others. Having achieved this foundational status, the CRC remains the most critical document on comparative discourses on children's lives. For example, Article 12 provides considerable scope on the child's right to express an opinion and be listened to, thus affording children opportunity to participate in decisions or matters that directly affect them. This implies some amount of consultation where the child has the capacity to form an opinion. It is not so easy to operationalise this, especially in spheres where conservative rather than progressive thoughts on childhood are foregrounded. While it is quite easy for African elites and middle class to appreciate a childhood based on the articles of the CRC, it poses considerable challenges to the poor, rural dwellers, illiterates etc. because of the utilitarian value they might place on their children. In the midst of high structural inequalities, households with limited economic resources, limited formal education, unstable sources of employment and income are likely to depend on their children for support in their occupations (Ofosu-Kusi, 2017a). In such situations, children's consent may not be sought, while representation of their interests or recognition of their rights may play second fiddle to their economic contributions. Any form of insistence on what children perceive to be their rights, especially if it is in opposition to the wishes of adults would be interpreted as insolence.

Researching Urban Informal Childhoods

The series of research underlining this chapter was undertaken over a period of three years. Among other objectives, it sought to understand children's street life as labour, engagements and relational challenges with their families and how they reconcile that with their own interests. This was pursued through a programme of qualitative studies in which the researchers variously interacted with 102 core participants, comprising 48 boys and 54 girls, in some of the principal streets, markets, transport stations, and a large slum euphemistically described as an informal settlement, all in Accra. Aged between 8 and 17 years, they had migrated to Accra from all regions of the country and Togo, a neighbouring country to the east of Accra. At arranged and spontaneous encounters, we engaged them in what we called "dialogue with a purpose", during which children were given the opportunity to express themselves through in-depth interviews and focus group discussions. During these sessions they reminisced on their lives back home, reflected on their past and present experiences of street life, as well as speculated on their futures. In addition, we undertook unstructured observations as well as photo-elicitation exercises that empowered the children to capture aspects of their street life on camera so that we could see through their eyes as knowledgeable subjects of inquiry.

Over the course of the research, three sets of interviews were conducted. The first set, based primarily on 72-hour-recall of work experiences, aimed to explore the finer details of children's work such as job descriptions, work patterns, earnings, expenditures, daily aggravations in work, and social life. The second set explored personal backgrounds with emphasis on personal well-being, especially hygiene, infestations and illness, food and hunger, schooling and education, paid and unpaid work, and time use. The third focused on some of the earlier themes but sought greater depth on how they continued to maintain relations with their families, inter-child relations, adult-child relations and their expectations. In all this, the children were positioned as socially capable, and privileged beings, who as "arbiters of their own experience" (Clark, 1999, p. 39), are most qualified to generate discursive constructions that take their origins from their social environments.

The most pressing challenge was the actions of gatekeepers, mostly older street children and adults, who behaved as if they had proprietary rights over the children and therefore had representational rights. Many of them insisted on being interviewed in place of the children. The contradiction here is that whereas these people took for granted children's capacity to work on the streets, paternalistic instincts drove many of them to question the children's capacity to represent themselves by developing and articulating views, processing information and therefore competently participating in research. Representational claims made by the adults is born out of the assumption of their power over children and the presumed social obligation to protect them.

A Quest for Representation and Rights

Children's representation and quest for rights inherent in the CRC are severely hampered by the socio-economic conditions of their families. Hence socio-economic pressures on some families have had the concomitant effect of pushing their children into a premature assumption of adult roles, not simply as workers but as direct financial contributors. But in doing so, they leverage their income-earning potential to chip off some parental authority and bolster their self-representation. As noted earlier, the informal sector is a challenging but welcoming arena for children to engage in all kinds of activities. Considering the amount of time, the hazardous conditions under which they work and the intensity of their labour, their earnings are meagre because their street life is immersed in a net of social relations of exploitation and dispossession by the adults they work for. Nonetheless, the opportunities for paid work regardless of the amount surpass those of the villages they originated from. In this regard, some of the participants claimed to be earning reasonable incomes, with the trend, especially for the 14- to 16-year-olds, who worked for themselves being incomes that exceeded the daily national minimum wage at the time. This enabled them to save some money on good days so that they could occasionally remit their parents back at home. The efforts were small gestures that sporadically helped to alleviate acute hardships or very short-term privations. Arguably, their families could have subsisted without those remittances, nonetheless such monetary contributions brought some relief at times of critical needs. Besides, all children who travel to Accra indirectly lessen the caretaking and monetary burdens on their families since they assume responsibility for themselves while on the streets. This however comes at some social and cultural cost to parents in particular since the financial independence provides them with the wherewithal to contest their parents' authority as well as claim self-representation in matters concerning them.

Assertiveness and Disregard for Parental Authority

Inadequacies and vulnerabilities are in themselves propellants for children to seek alternative forms of representation and relief through migration. Staying put to absorb the uncertainties at home and the shortcomings of parents confirms their obeisance. On the other hand, where such vulnerabilities propel action (Sayer, 2011) and children abandon their parents through migration for example, they would be confirming defiance. A sociocultural implication of the latter especially if children become economic agents either on the streets or at home is an embodied resistance to familial authority; a weakening of parental claim to representation and their ability to exercise control and traditional authority over them. This is manifested in the increasing assertiveness of their children, particularly in taking initiatives, managing, and determining the course of their lives. This trend cannot be attributed to the pervasiveness of the UNCRC or the constitutional rights of children, but circumstantial developments arising from relative deprivation. What sustains this assertiveness is children's realisation that an economic life exists outside domestic and family boundaries as evidenced by the fact that almost all the children in the study left their homes without initially informing their parents of their intentions to seek greener pastures elsewhere. This may look like a benign action but represents a cultural affront to the adults who were ignored when such momentous actions were taken by their children. Bietu (female) symbolizes this assertiveness, when she emphatically noted that:

> I didn't [inform parents] because they wouldn't have let me… sometimes we do things that we shouldn't do but we do them anyway because sometimes we have to do things for ourselves… [15-years-old head-porter]

Though she uses an abstract collective interpretation, presupposing that other children behave as she did, the critical point is that she projected her personal interest to supersede other considerations even if it were unacceptable to others. This shows some deliberation over her action and acknowledgement of a disregard for her parents' authority in preference for personal space and agency. The contextual significance of her reasoning lies in the fact that children from her community in northern Ghana are socialised under a pervasive patriarchal system. Defying a father or even any older male in the household could be a considerable source of familial tension (Assimeng, 1999). Generally, then, although the children were acutely aware of the social strictures on their self-determination, they responded in ways that promoted their personal capacities. Ala (male) for example claimed this tendency to be common to most children on the streets.

> Many children just do what they like…many of them here came without telling their parents that they are going to be here. They only tell them when

they get here and even when they send for them they don't go back home... [14years-old off-loader]

That, children "just do what they like" (Ala) or "have to do things" for themselves (Bietu) underline their estimations of a decline in parental authority in some families but correspondingly raise the stakes for children. There is an opposition of self-interest and parental authority; there is acknowledgement of authority but a refusal to heed it. It connotes a margin of decline in the confidence they can repose in their parents. The traditional perception that views and wishes of parents are sacrosanct may not be fully appreciated by children whose aspirations cannot be actively influenced by parents. Larkins (2014, p. 21) describes such behaviour as "acts of citizenship", in that claims relating to it result in "shifts in rights and responsibilities, new distributions of resources"; and a shifting of boundaries to create new actors who are "claimants of rights and responsibilities". However, the fact that children send messages back to parents demonstrates their recognition of the traditional authority their parents wield over them, even if their actions dilute its efficacy and significance. Thus, for Steve (male) a clear linkage exists between the recalcitrance of some children and the increasing number of children in the cities.

> I think some children are to blame because they don't listen to their parents, they won't pay any heed even if they ordered them not to leave, so they also leave their lives to them, that is why there are so many children on the streets... [15-years-old truck-pusher]

What Steve raises (just like Ala) is the frustration of some parents. In this instance, parents may have been aware of children's decision to travel and therefore "ordered them not to leave". The fact that children act to the contrary symbolises some decline or even failure of that authority. However, while some parents may abandon any hope of influencing the lives of children in such situations as Steve has indicated, the reality is that many parents themselves have limited resources to reverse the situation. For example, many of the children cited parental neglect as a justifiable reason for not informing their parents of their intentions. According to Steve, he did not give prior notice to his parents because "It will worry my mother but not my father. He has been saying all the time that it won't bother him if I weren't one of his children...". For Abe (male)

... it was useless telling my father, he is a hard man and doesn't care about any of us. Sometimes I think it is the work that he used to do (soldier). I don't feel like going to him with my problems [14 years-old truck pusher]

While the emphasis on neglect reflects a weathered parental responsibility and representational claims, it is also symptomatic of a breakdown of the father-child relationship. The cause of this may be more complex but essentially circular. Fathers (and mothers) may neglect their children because of the children's disrespect for their status and authority, which in turn generates the tendency for children to disregard their parents' authority. Although, some children may perceive their parents' inaction as neglect or irresponsibility, the primary reasons may lie in the difficulties they encounter in managing the social, economic and emotional conditions surrounding the exercise of their responsibilities as parents.

The children however were quite aware of the social and moral responsibilities parents had in shaping their future lives. As a result, some were worried about the reactions of their parents to their bold choices and the assertion of their agency. At the same time, they took solace in the physical distance separating them and the realisation that their anger might have subsided by the time they returned home. With this rationalization, there was blatant disregard of entreaties and orders from parents who wanted their children to return home, as the extracts from Otuo (male) and Josh (male) portray.

> Otuo: My father has sent messages for me to come home but I have just come here and I need to get money and some things before I go home again. That way I won't have to come here again...I can't return until I have acquired those things...
> YOK: Are you not disobeying your parents?
> Otuo: [Long pause] Yes, but I'll do what they want when I go back but I am here now so I will just try and get some money and go back. [13 years, barrow pusher]
> According to Josh: "My father wants me to come back to the village but I can't go now because I've just come, I need to get some money first before I can go home..."
> YOK: Even as your father is asking you to come back?
> Josh: I can't do anything about going home now. I will go back but I need to get some things first. [14 years, Truck pusher]

The conflict of interest in both views lies in the recognition of the parents' authority against the need to achieve their primary objectives of travelling to Accra. There is a sound logic to their argument, if the necessary balance can be found between the two contradictory expectations. They, after all, initiated their actions as a result of lapses in the socio-economic roles of their parents. Thus, their firm determination ("I can't return..." (Otuo) and "...I can't go now" (Josh)) diminishes the significance of any immediate response to the wishes of their fathers to return. The parents' reactions to this may depend on the relative degree of impoverishment and the significant difference their acquisitions in Accra will make. It is plausible that parents who consider children's earnings and acquisitions from Accra to be marginal and irrelevant may place more emphasis on the lack of respect for their authority. On the other hand, if the earnings and remittances can make significant differences, the disobedience may be treated as a simple case of the end justifying the means and may therefore be forgiven.

It is obvious that any dislocation of resources, for example through loss of employment, natural or man-made damage to property such as farmlands or means of production, and its ensuing poverty diminishes parents' authority, and impacts their ability to back up their leadership with expectations of obedience and acquiescence. Clearly, the ability to function as the family head cannot be sustained through simple traditional authority; economic resources are needed to back up those responsibilities. The dearth of such resources, especially in the rural areas is the bane of the family and a consequent cause of the dilution in the authority of the father as the family head. There was therefore a sense of pessimism about parental responsibilities as far as some of the participants were concerned and for that reason provided the courage for them to disregard their instructions. In fact, the lack of capacity of their parents to track them because they might not have been to the city themselves or could not contemplate a trip to Accra in search of their children when they had no specific idea of their whereabouts emboldened the children. There is also the added dilemma of whether the children will heed their wishes even if they did manage to locate them in Accra. Bietu exemplifies this:

> ...my father doesn't want me to be here. My elder brother came to trade here and when he told my father about the conditions in which I am living he ordered me to return. He even sent my brother to come for me because he feared for me...Well, I didn't pay any heed...

YOK: And your mother?
Bietu: My mother also disapproves of my presence here and wants me to return to Tamale. My brother told me that she is worried that I will fall into the wrong company and maybe get pregnant... But now that I am here, I must get something before I return, I can't stop everything here simply because they want me to return... [15 years, head porter]

Such direct refusals to heed the demands of parents will be interpreted by most people as disrespect for one's parents. However, within the context of the risks and uncertainties children sustain in Accra, the desire to pursue their aspirations to the limit is powerful enough to justify such behaviours. The single-minded conviction of achieving their objectives for travelling to Accra makes them impervious to the wrath of parents. For some of Accra's street children taking what they perceive to be decisions in their own best interest is a form of mobilization to not only stake a claim to decisions about their lives but also to assert a degree of self-representation and a consequent authority over it. This is evident in the enabling rights to be heard, of association, access to information (of the CRC), and even a form of children's "protagonism" as Myers (2001, p. 51) argues. Leaving home without permission, deciding when to return, or who is remitted is justifiable even if it portends trouble at home or gives signals of disrespect because they are remedying some of the family's challenges while actualising ideas and dreams through their own efforts. As in the case of children of African Movement of Working Children and Youth (AMWCY) in Senegal, their actions may be a way of activating a democratization process that bestows some degree of control over their lives (Fuchs, 2019), especially in their preparation for the future. Their actions therefore simultaneously ignite their own rights and representational abilities while diminishing those of parents.

Although there are instances of defiance, for example departing their villages for Accra without permission or abandoning their education, the children's strategy is not an open contestation of the status quo. It is often a subtle and carefully thought-out re-appropriation of their relationship with other family members. They do not oppose "the moral master frame" of their society but "reinterpret this frame in order to increase their agency within it" (Fuchs, 2019, p. 7). The children therefore concurrently accept their status as children but also claim the right to make decisions about work, friendships, travel etc. It is a quest for liberation from the strictures of parental control, family dysfunction, overexploitation of their labour, poorly resourced schools and abusive teachers so that they can assume representational rights for themselves.

The Conjunction of Children's Remittances, Rights, Representation and Authority

Participants demonstrated a clear desire to help their families in a variety of ways, usually by sending money or provisions. While this altruism can be interpreted as some effort in the alleviation of family poverty, an alternative explanation can be located in the reconciliation of the tension between parental authority and children's agency. As noted in the preceding section, parents may interpret the lack of consultation and refusal to heed their instructions as clear cases of disobedience. Knowing this, children use remittances to pacify and eventually justify their initial action of disregarding their parents. While some parents may contest the economic roles of their children, their impoverished conditions however bring some degree of inevitability to the children's decisions and actions. As evidenced in the following instances, children send home money and provisions upon the assumption that their families would be happy to receive them.

> Chris: Yes, I send them money every now and then. I also buy clothes and provisions for them. I think they like it and are happy to receive from me since their son is working and everybody in the village knows that. It will help them ... it will help them a lot. [male, 14-years old off-loader]
>
> Asmao: Yes, I send money and provisions when somebody is going back to the north...They will be happy to receive those things [money and provisions] in the full knowledge that their daughter is doing well in Accra. [female, 14-years old head porter]
>
> Gabby: I have only been here for six months yet I am able to send them some provisions. It will help somehow and I am sure they will he happy to receive it. They can get food from the farm but sometimes it is difficult to come by money to buy some basic items. [male, 15-years old off-loader]

The three cases project family constraints as the primary motivator for the children's altruism, especially in an environment where they themselves live under adverse conditions. Gabby for example provides a picture of relative deprivation in which rural communities face no food poverty but lack sufficient money to fully participate in the cash economy—purchasing befitting clothes, shelter, health needs, children's education and so on. There may not be any compulsion to remit, but the proto-adult status saddles them with premature economic roles by linking their absence from home to the need to make contributions. And as Asmao and Gabby claim, their parents are "happy to receive" money or other benefits-in-kind. For Ala, remittances will generate approbation since he will be meeting the expectations of his parents. On the other hand, his failure may cause some psychological pain and anxiety.

> Ala: Actually there is no money at home. We have to come and work here before we can send money back home… that money can make a lot of difference back there…
> YOK: Will your parents be annoyed then if you don't send money home?
> Ala: Not annoyed but it will pain them, because their son is in Accra so they will think of me and pray for me, so if I am able to send them something they will be happy and think that I am doing well. If I don't they will think that maybe I am a useless person who spends his money on the wrong things… [14 years, Off-loader]

Apparently, while not mandatory for him to remit, there was still an implied expectation on the part of his parents. There are hints of the family first in the way he anticipates his parents' construction of his life in Accra, since his inability to remit may be construed as a squandering of opportunities. Abebe's (2013, p. 85) studies in rural Ethiopia showed similarly that many children worked because of their 'feelings of responsibility' or because they 'did not want to be dependent'. Thus for Ala, there was solace in his parents' implicit acceptance of what he was doing out of necessity thus giving credence to Verlet's (2000) assertion, in "Growing up in Ghana", that many children have been stepping in the shoes of weak or incompetent male family heads thus usurping their power and authority while boosting their personal claims to self-representation and authority as worthy members of their families.

The traditional provider status of a father suffers if he accepts money from a child he is expected to provide for and therefore contradicts his role as the head of the family. Whereas it is socially acceptable to use child labour in family occupations, for instance farming or herding cattle either as part of the processes of socialization or direct contribution to the family economy, it is illegal to use the same labour in some defined situations under the various ILO conventions. If it is illegal for children to chip stones or spend the whole day selling iced water instead of going to school, then it must be socially and culturally reprehensible for adults to benefit from such activities. While child labour may be appropriated indirectly to support the family (as is usually the case), a contradiction emerges when children earn money in their own right to sustain the family, particularly the father. It compromises the provider status of the father, undermines his paternal role as well as tests his moral authority in directing the affairs of the family. The underlying point here is the authority of the father in relation to the child, which under normal circumstances is supposed to be sacrosanct (Assimeng, 1999). However, in the face of economic and social difficulties, the economic value of some children as independent earners has become an irreversible fact of life because some parents are incapable of preserving the traditional distribution of power and the accompanying roles. In spite of the obvious however, it is still considered irresponsible and shameful by some parents and children themselves if economic roles are reversed this way. Tima (girl) notes:

> I don't think my parents need my money… They don't want me to be here and will never take any money from me even if I gave it. My father in particular will be ashamed to ask me for money… I send money to my grandmother instead; she is old and cannot afford to refuse any help she gets.
> YOK: Do you give them something else?
> Tima: Sometimes I buy some simple things for my mother and even gave her some presents when I went home for the Islamic festival, but not my father… [female, 14-years old, *chopbar* worker]

In contrast to Ala, Tima's parents were perhaps capable of backing up their objection to her presence in Accra through the deed of not accepting any money as 'pacification'. The question of relative impoverishment is evident here since the degree of need may determine parents' ability to maintain their status without compromising the distribution of power. The fact that Tima's grandmother accepts her money on the other hand supports the relative need's view, though the grandmother may have the same moral status in her life as the parents.

In order to deal with the cultural sensitivity of reversing caretaking roles, some children have devised various ways of making contributions to their parents. For instance, instead of sending cash, many send provisions and clothing. Others assume responsibilities for their younger siblings by paying their school fees, providing school uniforms and other materials. In this way, they relieve the father/mother of the direct responsibility and save them the task of finding scarce resources to meet those expectations. Most importantly, they circumvent the embarrassment some parents might feel in accepting money from their young children.

> Dan: Yes, I buy provisions for them. I also buy clothing for my younger brothers; it saves them from having to wait to get one from them [parents]. Just last week I sent some provisions to them, it will help…[male, 14-years old off-loader]
>
> Josh: I am pushing the truck so that I can get the money to enter a trade…still I send them things, I do… I buy soap and other provisions for them but I hardly send money…I also buy school uniforms and other school materials as a way of encouraging my brothers to stay in school… [14-year old truck pusher]

In view of the scarcity of money alluded to earlier for people to regularly purchase basic items, such ostensibly simple non-monetary contributions can prove to be crucial to the family. For instance, the indirect costs of education such as school uniforms, reading and writing materials may exclude some children from regularly attending school. Thus, Josh's contribution is quite a significant one and as he himself indicates might motivate his brothers to remain in school. The significance in both extracts is that children are supporting their families in critical ways, through a mode of payment that will be less embarrassing for their parents. In return they may have greater respect or some amount of leeway or even uncontested rights to participate in decisions concerning them whenever they returned home.

CONCLUSION

Any thoughts on childhood evokes ideological differences that arise from politics that aim to respond to cultural and social expectations of particular geographic areas and policy directions driven by people who are usually far removed from the grassroots. On one hand, cultural diversity and for that matter differentiations in childhood are touted while on the other hand global notions steeped in the economic and social expectations of the developed world are positioned as the models to adopt. In many parts of the developing world, in this particular case Ghana, rights in the formal sense though codified into acts and policies is still seen as elitist, representative of the interest of others and in the majority of households difficult to implement let alone enforce. Nonetheless, as Balagopalan (2019, p. 4) suggests, it is inevitable that we think of "…children's right within the everyday working out of culture, sociality and relationality…"

The presence of children on the streets of the major cities of Ghana, under whichever nomenclature, may be seen as a product of the times characterised by rapid urbanization, rising dysfunctionality in some homes, woeful economic conditions for increasing numbers of families, ubiquitous informality, among other factors. The trend as indicated by recent empirical studies is likely to continue (Department of Social Welfare et al. 2011); but while the foregoing factors may thrust some children onto the streets, others voluntarily decide to find a living on, or association with the streets. Evidence abounds of the consequences such sojourn on the streets may have for children, although useful skills such as "instrumental and symbolic competences" enhance their ability to work and earn incomes, as well as cope better with the stresses of the streets (Lucchini 1993 cited in Apterkar & Stoecklin, 2014, p. 14), and so may prove beneficial to their transition into adulthood. In any case, the relationship between children and parents assumes new dimensions once they get onto the streets.

We discern a clear case of children, especially the relatively older ones, exercising their agency and chipping away some of their parents' power and authority to determine the course of their lives and those of others in the family. The growing importance of such responsibility in the family is a diminution of the representational status and some moral authority that comes naturally with parenthood. If some children can assume such critical roles in the families, then the traditional assumption of unqualified obedience may be undermined, for example, the parent's entreaties to a street child to return home might be problematic and treated with less urgency and deference. It is therefore not surprising that many of the children disregarded or disobeyed instructions from parents to return home, thus claiming a right to a certain degree of self-determination. Ironically though, in cases where the provider role of the child is crucial to their survival, parents cannot afford to assert their authority in the usual paternalistic way when necessary. This might be productive for the child's development if the parents have been abusive in the past. It might on the other hand amount to neglect of parental responsibilities in cases where parents decide to place the child's remittances and contributions above their natural duties, for fear of alienating the child. It is known in this regard that children who work on the streets report improved relations with their family and tend to have more privileges than those who remain at home (Bar-on, 1997). The ostensible reason for this elevated status is that they perform viable socio-economic roles for the family and therefore must be rewarded with special treatment. Or rather, there is no motivation to bite the finger that feeds them.

References

Abebe, T. (2013). Independent Rights and Agency: The Role of Children in Collective Livelihood Strategies in Rural Ethiopia. In K. Hanson & O. Nieuwenhuys (Eds.), *Reconceptualizing Children's Rights in International Development* (pp. 71–92). Cambridge University Press.

African Development Bank (AfDB). (2013). *African Economic Outlook*. AfDB.

Apterkar, L., & Stoecklin, D. (2014). *Children and Homeless Youth: A Cross-Cultural Perspective*. Springer.

Assimeng, M. (1999). *Social Structure of Ghana: A Study in Perseverance and Change*. Ghana Publishing Corporation.

Ayodele, J. (2016). The Realities Surrounding the Applicability of Medical Paternalism in Nigeria. *Global Journal of Social Sciences, 14*(2015), 55–61.

Balagopalan, S. (2019). Why Historicize Rights-subjectivities? Children's Rights, Compulsory Schooling, and the Deregulation of Child Labor in India. *Childhood, 26*(3), 304–320.

Bar-on, A. (1997). Criminalising Survival: Images and Reality of Street Children. *Journal of Social Policy, 26*(1), 63–78.

Bourdillon, M., & Spittler, G. (2012). Introduction. In G. Spittler & M. Bourdillon (Eds.), *African Children at Work: Working and Learning in Growing up for Life* (pp. 1–22). Lit Verlag.

Boyden, J. (1997). Childhood and the Policy Makers: A Comparative Perspective on the Globalization of Childhood. In A. James & A. Prout (Eds.), *Constructing and Reconstructing Childhood: Contemporary Issues in the Sociological Study of Childhood* (pp. 190–229). Falmer Press.

Caro, F. G. (2014). *Family and Aging Policy*. Taylor and Francis.

Clark, C. D. (1999). The Autodriven Interview: A Photographic Viewfinder into Children's Experience. *Visual Studies, 14*(1), 39–50.

Committee on the Rights of the Child, General Comment No. 21. (2017).

Davis, M. (2006). *The Planet of Slums*. Verso.

Department of Social Welfare (DSW), Ricerca e Cooperazione (RC) and Catholic Action for Street Children (CAS). (2011). *Census on Street Children in the Greater Accra Region*. DSW.

Dougnon, I. (2012). Migration of Children and Youth in Mali: Global versus Local Discourses. In G. Spittler & M. Bourdillon (Eds.), *African Children at Work: Working and Learning in Growing up for Life* (pp. 143–168). Lit Verlag.

Droz, Y. (2013). Conflicting Realities: The Kikuyu Childhood Ethos and the Ethic of the CRC. In K. Hanson & O. Nieuwenhuys (Eds.), *Reconceptualizing Children's Rights in International Development* (pp. 115–133). Cambridge University Press.

Ennew, J. (2000). Why the Convention is not about Street Children. Revisiting Children's Rights: 10 years of the UN Convention on the Rights of the Child. In D. Fottrell (Ed.), *Revisiting Children's Rights: 10 Years of the UN Convention on the Rights of the Child* (pp. 169–182). Kluwer.

Ennew, J. (2005). Prisoners of Childhood: Orphans and Economic Dependency. In J. Qvortrup (Ed.), *Studies in Modern Childhood* (pp. 128–146). Palgrave Macmillan.

Fuchs, S. (2019). Towards the Democratization of the Future: The Struggle for Social Recognition and Economic Success of a West African Association of Working Children and Youth. *Childhood*, 1–14. https://doi.org/10.1177/0907568219828807

Gibbon, P., Daviron, B., & Barral, S. (2014). Lineages of Paternalism: An Introduction. *Journal of Agrarian Change, 14*(2), 165–189.

Harriss-White, B. (2010). Work and Wellbeing in Informal Economies: The Regulative Roles of Institutions of Identity and the State. *World Development, 38*(2), 170–183.

Hart, K. (2000). Kinship, Contract, and Trust: The Economic Organisation of Migrants in an African City Slum. In D. Gambetta (Ed.), *Trust: Making and Breaking Cooperative Relations* (pp. 176–193). Dept. of Sociology: University of Oxford.

Henry, S. (1987). The Political Economy of Informal Economies, Annals of American Academy of Political and Social Science. *The Informal Economy, 493*(Sept. 1987), 137–153.

Holzscheiter, A. (2016). Representation as Power and Performative Practice: Global Civil Society Advocacy for Working Children. *Review of International Studies, 42*(2), 205–226.

Ikuomola, A. D. (2017). Child Fosterage Dynamics in Selected Markets in Lagos State, Nigeria. In Y. Ofosu-Kusi (Ed.), *Children's Agency and Development in African Societies* (pp. 33–48). Dakar.

Korboe, D. (1997). *A Profile of Street Children in Kumasi*. Centre for Social Policy Studies, University of Ghana.

Larkins, C. (2014). Enacting Children's Citizenship: Developing Understandings of how Children Enact Themselves as Citizens through Actions and Acts of Citizenship. *Childhood, 21*(1). 7–21.

Liebel, M. (2012). Children's Work, Education and Agency: The African Movement of Working Children and Youth (AMWCY). In G.Spittler & M. Bourdillon (Eds.), *African Children at Work: Working and Learning in Growing up for Life* (pp. 303–332). Lit Verlag.

Liebel, M. (2017). Children Without Childhood? Against the Postcolonial Capture of Childhoods in the Global South. In A. Invernizzi, M. Liebel, B. Milne, & R. Budde (Eds.), *Children out of Place and Human Rights: In Memory of Judith Ennew*. https://doi.org/10.1007/978-3-319-33251-2_6. ISSN: 1879-5196.

Mayne, A. (2017). *Slums: The History of a Global Injustice*. Reaktion Books Ltd.

Mbaye, S. M., & Fall, A. S. (2000). The Disintegrating Social Fabric: Child Labour and Socialization in Senegal. In B. Schlemmer (Ed.), *The Exploited Child* (pp. 292–299). Zed Books.

Mizen, P., & Ofosu-Kusi, Y. (2013). Agency as Vulnerability: Accounting for Children's Movements to the Streets of Accra. *The Sociological Review, 61*(2), 363–382.

Moulin, N., & Pereira, V. (2000). Families, Schools, and the Socialization of Brazilian Children: Contemporary Dilemmas that Create Street Children. In R. A. Mickelson (Ed.), *Children on the Streets of the Americas* (pp. 43–54). Routledge.

Myers, W. E. (2001). The Right Rights? Child Labour in a Globalizing World. *Annals of the American Academy of Political and Social Science, 575*, 38–55.

Nukunya, G. K. (2003). *Tradition and Change in Ghana: An Introduction to Sociology*. Ghana Universities Press.

Ofosu-Kusi, Y. (2017a). Establishing a Foothold in the Informal Sector: Children's Dreams, Agency and Street Life in Ghana. In Y. Ofosu-Kusi (Ed.), *Children's Agency and Development in African Societies* (pp. 15–32). Dakar.

Ofosu-Kusi, Y. (2017b). Conclusion: Agency, Realities and the Future of African Childhoods. In Y. Ofosu-Kusi (Ed.), *Children's Agency and Development in African Societies* (pp. 209–214). Dakar.

Population Reference Bureau. (2018). 2018 World Population Data Sheet with Focus on Changing Age Structure. Retrieved January 23, 2020, from www.prb.org

Sayer, A. (2011). *Why Things Matter to People: Social Science, Values and Ethical Life*. Cambridge University Press.

Verlet, M. (2000). Growing up in Ghana: Deregulation and the Employment of Children. In B. Schlemmer (Ed.), *The Exploited Child* (pp. 67–82). Zed Books.

Open Access This chapter is licensed under the terms of the Creative Commons Attribution 4.0 International License (http://creativecommons.org/licenses/by/4.0/), which permits use, sharing, adaptation, distribution and reproduction in any medium or format, as long as you give appropriate credit to the original author(s) and the source, provide a link to the Creative Commons licence and indicate if changes were made.

The images or other third party material in this chapter are included in the chapter's Creative Commons licence, unless indicated otherwise in a credit line to the material. If material is not included in the chapter's Creative Commons licence and your intended use is not permitted by statutory regulation or exceeds the permitted use, you will need to obtain permission directly from the copyright holder.

CHAPTER 10

Combatting Child Poverty in the Childhood Moratorium: A Representational Lens on Children's Rights

Didier Reynaert, Nicole Formesyn, Griet Roets, and Rudi Roose

Introduction

Over the past decades, child poverty (re-)emerged as a major global problem. Worldwide more than one billion children live in a situation of poverty, having no adequate access to education, health, housing, nutrition, sanitation or water. An estimated of 356 million children are forced to

---

D. Reynaert (✉)
HOGENT University of Applied Sciences and Arts, Ghent, Belgium
e-mail: didier.reynaert@hogent.be

N. Formesyn
SAAMO East-Flanders, Ghent, Belgium
e-mail: nicole.formesyn@saamo.be

G. Roets • R. Roose
Ghent University, Ghent, Belgium
e-mail: Griet.Roets@UGent.be; Rudi.Roose@UGent.be

© The Author(s) 2023
B. Sandin et al. (eds.), *The Politics of Children's Rights and Representation*, Studies in Childhood and Youth,
https://doi.org/10.1007/978-3-031-04480-9_10

survive on less than $1.90 a day, the international measure for extreme poverty. Children are more than twice as likely to be extremely poor as adults (17.5% of children vs. 7.9% of adults) (Silwal et al., 2020). Since the start of the COVID-19 pandemic, the number of children living in poverty has increased by 15%, representing a number that is expected to worsen as the pandemic continuous (Save the Children & UNICEF, 2020). In Europe, an estimated of 22.5% of children are at risk of poverty or social exclusion. Compared with working-age adults (aged 18–64 years; 21.5%) and older people (aged 65 years and over; 18.6%), children have the highest risk of poverty or social exclusion. Generally, children growing up in a single-parent household, children whose parents have a low level of education or children with at least one parent with a migrant background have a higher risk of poverty or social exclusion (Eurostat, 2019). Growing up in poverty is commonly considered as a serious neglect of the realization of the rights of children. As Vandenhole (2013: 612) clearly states: 'Child poverty is an affront to human dignity, and therefore seems to be blatantly in violation of the human rights of children'.

The connection between child poverty and children's rights seems obvious, for a number of reasons. First, child poverty is thought of as a multidimensional problem, affecting almost all areas of children's lives. It has an impact on children's opportunities for equal access of material recourses such as education, health care, recreational activities, adequate food and housing. Moreover, it impacts the psychosocial development of children when confronted with stressful everyday living conditions or systematically having to deal with social exclusion or stigma (see e.g. Ridge, 2011; Morrow, 2010; Attree, 2006; Eamon, 2001). Only an integrated approach has sufficient leeway to deal with the multidimensionality of child poverty. The Convention on the Rights of the Child (hereafter: CRC) is considered as such a holistic framework (Vandenhole, 2013). Second, in all these live domains for children that are affected by child poverty, it is the state that is considered to have a primary obligation to guarantee access to basic resources. So, the state must provide material as well as immaterial resources such as housing, education and health care to guarantee an adequate standard of living for children (Morrow, 2010). More in particular, state parties to the CRC have the obligation to assist parents so they can fulfil their obligations towards their children. According to the CRC, the family is the best setting for a child's development. States must take all necessary measures to assist parents in poverty to raise their children. Third, while poverty undermines the protection, provision and participation rights of children, strategies to combat child poverty might generally be associated with a childhood image of the vulnerable child, overemphasizing protection measures and at the same time underemphasizing participation measures (Vandenhole, 2013). Consequently, growing up in poverty impacts children's representation as poverty limits children's capabilities to be heard and to have their views taken into account on all matters affecting them (FRA, 2018; Ridge, 2006).

In this chapter, we further untangle the relationship between children's rights and child poverty from the lens of representation. We argue that children growing up in poverty are represented differently than their parents living in poverty. A distinction that needs to be understood as the result of a particular interpretation of children's rights. This distinction produces a dichotomy between the interest of children and those of parents. Paradoxically, this can in its turn have a negative impact on realizing children's rights for children in poverty. In a first part of this chapter, we explain how we understand the connection between children's rights and child poverty from a representational approach. From this understanding, we analyse the distinct position of children and parents in the context of poverty. In the next part, we substantiate our theoretical assumptions with empirical data coming from researching parents living and raising their children in poverty.

Child Poverty and Children's Rights: A Representational Approach

Our representational lens on this issue of children's rights and child poverty is for an important part inspired by the work of Nancy Fraser on social justice. We use this lens for a better understanding of the notion of the 'childhood moratorium', that is, the institutionalization of childhood in (Western) societies.

The Childhood Moratorium as the Political Domain for Representational Claims

Fraser (2005) defines social justice as 'parity of participation', consisting of three dimensions. The *economic dimension* is concerned with redistribution, that is, access to material as well as immaterial recourses that support people to participate as peers. Having lack of (im)material resources results in 'distributive injustice or maldistribution'. The situation of children living in poverty, who do not have adequate access to education, health care, adequate food, housing and so on can be considered as a situation of distributive injustice or maldistribution (see e.g. Sarriera et al., 2015). The *cultural dimension* of social justice deals with recognition of status and enables people to interact on terms of parity. Not being recognized because of a person's status can lead to 'status inequality or misrecognition'. Children in poverty generally experience a twofold status inequality: not only are they confronted with the lack of recognition for the active role they play in society 'as a child'; in addition, they have to face the experience of growing up as a 'poor' child who often needs to deal with disrespectful treatment (Lister, 2007). Consequently, child poverty has a severe impact on the citizenship-status of children (O'Brien & Salonen, 2011). The *political dimension* is concerned with the issue of representation and questions of membership. What is at stake here is being in or excluded from those entitled to make claims for social justice. With the words of Fraser: 'The political in this sense furnishes the stage on which struggles over distribution and recognition are played out'. Establishing criteria of social belonging, and thus determining who counts as a member, the political dimension of justice specifies the reach of those other dimensions: it tells us who is included in, and who excluded from, the circle of those entitled to a just distribution and reciprocal recognition' (Fraser, 2005: 75).

This third dimension of social justice as conceived by Fraser is of special importance if we wish to unravel the connection between children's rights and child poverty. This is so, because the political stage for children is fundamentally different than the political stage for parents. As a result, claims for social justice in the context of poverty are particularly different for children than they are for parents. The political stage for children can be understood from what Zinnecker conceives as the 'Bildungsmoratorium' or 'childhood moratorium' (Zinnecker, 2000). Zinnecker used the concept of childhood moratorium to describe the nature of childhood in Western industrialized nations from the second half of the twentieth century. It implies a postponement or time-out for children from adult society and thus a withdrawal from certain responsibilities. Instead of participating in organized adult work, children are expected to engage in learning activities that prepare them to become future adult citizens (Sen, 2013). As Michael-Sebastian Honig (2008) explains, the childhood moratorium can be considered as 'preparatory arenas that implement a principle of integration by means of separation'. The existence of the childhood moratorium goes along with specified institutions, spaces, times and discourses for children, as Zinnecker regards the moratorium as an 'age-specific habitus' (Sen, 2013). Over time, the contours of this childhood moratorium changed. A twin process of antagonistic developments can be observed in relation to this childhood moratorium. On the one hand a process of 'blurring boundaries' occurred whereby the distinction between the world of children and the world of adults is fading out. As a consequence, children can increasingly participate in the adult world. On the other hand, a process of 'strengthened boundaries' arose with childhood domains becoming further separated from the adult world (for further background see Reynaert & Roose, 2014, 2015).

All taken together, the childhood moratorium as the socio-cultural structuring and institutionalization of childhood in Western societies today still shapes the boundaries of the political arena for children. It is the playing field wherein claims for social justice for children are expressed. The childhood moratorium creates a distinction between children and adults where minors are considered as a member of the childhood moratorium and adults are not. Because children are represented differently in society than adults in claims for social justice, they also have a different position in the fight against poverty. In the next session, we explore these different representations of children and parents in relation to the issue of child poverty.

Representational Claims in the Childhood Moratorium: Differences Between Children and Parents

In the fight against child poverty, a distinction is made between the position of children and the position of parents. Strategies to combat child poverty are focused on the living conditions of children as a member of the childhood moratorium. Supportive measures for children living in poverty are located in childhood institutions such as education, childcare, parenting support, youth work and youth care, that is, in those domains of social life that focus almost exclusively on children (Reynaert & Roose, 2016). This is so because the rationality of the childhood moratorium represents children in a two-folded way. First, children are often represented as the victims of poverty (Roets et al., 2013). Children are not thought of as having any responsibility whatsoever for their situation of poverty. On the contrary: a discourse of compassion with children enables a large social mobilization to combat child poverty. So children are represented as the 'deserving' poor' who merit receiving supportive measures to deal with their poverty situation (Sandbæk, 2017). Second, children are represented as future social and economic capital of society (Lister, 2003) and therefore deserve support. In the context of child policies aiming at implementing social investment strategies (Sandbæk, 2017; Kjørholt, 2013), children are thought of as 'investment goods' for future inclusion and success (Olk & Hübenthal, 2009; Lister, 2004).

The way children are represented as the deserving poor contrasts sharply with how parents are represented. Parents are not considered as members of the political arena of the childhood moratorium and therefore are not represented as victims of poverty. Parents are represented as the 'undeserving poor' who do not merit support for their poverty situation. They are not exempt from 'guilt'. On the contrary: parents are being held responsible for the poverty situation in which their children grow up or they are held responsible for the lack of responsibility they take to escape poverty (Gillies, 2008). O'Brien and Salonen (2011) therefore conclude that for parents, there is a rather strong focus on responsibilities rather than on rights.

Two particular problems risk being the result of these different representations of children and parents living in poverty. First is the 'pedagogization' of the poverty problem' (Reynaert & Roose, 2016). A strategy aiming at combating child poverty that is oriented almost exclusively on children, ignoring the living conditions of parents, risks narrowing down the problem of child poverty to an educational problem. Educational problems have their origins as well as their solutions in the womb of the childhood moratorium with interventions directed at children. However, the problem of child poverty is too complex to be locked up in the childhood moratorium. Child poverty is a multidimensional problem with multiple causes. It is not an isolated problem that could exist independently of the poverty situation of parents. In our societies, which are driven by market economies, poverty is primarily a problem of a lack of income (Mestrum, 2011). Since children are unable to earn an income, they are always intrinsically socio-economically dependent on their parents or adults in the household in which they are growing up (Lister, 2003, 2006). When parents deal with a lack of income and material resources, this has direct consequences for the situation of children. In this sense, child poverty should be seen as a product of the general poverty. Disconnecting the two issues could lead to the denial of the multidimensional nature of child poverty (Lister, 2006). Child poverty is indeed much more than creating opportunities in childcare or education. It is at least as much or even more a matter of labour market policy or housing policy, in other words policy areas that are located outside the childhood moratorium. Combatting child poverty with the childhood moratorium as reference point, focusing almost exclusively on children and losing out of sight the position of parents, risks ignoring the structural causes of poverty (Sandbæk, 2017; Featherstone et al., 2011).

Second is the dynamic of social control of parents living in poverty. Parents who are represented as responsible and thus accountable for their alleged lack of parental responsibility in raising their children in poverty risk ending up as objects in measures of social control. Policy measures targeting parents living in poverty are often focused on facilitating parents to entering the workforce and promoting active citizenship behaviour. However, these kinds of measures often strongly emphasize particular parental behaviour and expect parents to accommodate to societal standards of 'good parenthood' (O'Brien & Salonen, 2011; Gillies, 2008). For parents, these kinds of measures are often perceived as a double punishment: there is not only the stigma of being a 'poor parent' living in inhumane circumstances; there is also the stigma of being treated as the 'bad parent' failing to educate his or her children properly.

With the lens of Fraser's approach of representation, both these problems can be considered as 'misrepresentation'. Parents are addressed in a negative way in relation to issues of child poverty. Claims for combatting parental poverty occur isolated from the childhood moratorium. And more important, anti-poverty policies for children risk becoming governing strategies towards parents in which a panoptic eye is turned on their expected behaviour (Van Haute et al., 2018). As a result, parents cannot 'participate on a par'. This misrepresentation of parents in the public debate and discourses on child poverty risks also becoming part of the framework of children's rights. As Sandbæk (2017) states: 'Promoting children's rights and supporting parents may seem easy to combine, but research indicates that there is a risk of giving priority to children without considering how to enable their parents to support them … Children may receive economic support to participate in activities, while their parents, living in deep poverty, receive no such benefits, and may be blamed for failing to meet the expected standards for their children'.

Researching Parental Perspectives on Child Poverty

Focusing on the childhood moratorium as the arena wherein claims for social justice for children in poverty are articulated highlights the political context or setting where the activity of representation is taking place ('where?'). In addition, focusing on the distinct way children are represented in the childhood moratorium—as the deserving poor—in contrast to the representation of parents—the undeserving poor—reveals the discourse on child poverty ('how?'). Besides the *where* and the *how*, Celis et al. (2008), in their conceptual framework for political representation, define two other questions: *who?* and *why?* Particularly the former is of interest for us, as the 'who' question is concerned with identifying those who speak up on behalf of children and child-related issues. Parallel with the re-emerging of child poverty as a social problem in the past decade, scientific research into child poverty has increasingly been uncovering children's own perspectives and experiences of growing up in poverty (Bessell et al., 2020; Fernandez et al., 2015; Roets et al., 2013; Bourdillon & Boyden, 2011; Ridge & Saunders, 2009). What have been less portrayed in recent literature are the perspectives of parents living and raising their children in poverty (see e.g. La Placa & Corlyon, 2016; Ridge, 2009). In representational terms, this means that parents are—at least partly—excluded from having voice in the production of knowledge on child poverty. In its turn, this risks misrepresenting parents in the public discourse on the issue of child poverty. In this contribution, we therefore focus on parental perspectives on child poverty to further entangle the relationship between children's rights and child poverty.

For the present study, 30 families living in a vulnerable situation in Sint-Niklaas, a Flemish town of approximately 80.000 inhabitants in the north of Belgium, were interviewed by a local institution for community development (SAAMO Oost-Vlaanderen). These interviews were part of the development of a local policy for combating child poverty. In order to overcome the dynamic of 'pedagogization' of the poverty problem' where only topics related to the pedagogical arena of the childhood moratorium in combatting child poverty are at stake, the institution for community development used the framework of social rights as recognized in article 23 of the Belgian constitution. Article 23 contains the right to material well-being, the right to housing and a healthy living environment, the right to health, the right to cultural and social development, and the right to participation. These rights were complemented by the right to education as recognized in article 24 of the Belgian constitution.

Selected families were part of the service-user group of the institution for community development or of one of their partner organizations. In addition, snowball-sampling (Noy, 2008) was used. Families in poverty who participated in the study were asked whether they know other families in poverty. The only condition for participation in the study was having experience with raising children in the context of a poverty situation. Of the participating families, 14 were single parents, 12 'traditional' families and 4 extended families. By family size, there were 8 families with 1 child, 7 families with 2 children, 6 families with 3 children, 3 families with 4 children, 5 families with 5 children and 1 family with 6 children. Of the 30 families, 5 were undocumented, 12 families with at least one person working part-time, 13 families receiving financial benefits from the government and 5 families without any income. Half of the families were involved in some form of debt mediation. With regard to the housing situation, there were 19 families who rented on the private rental market, 2 families who were owners, 8 families who make use of social housing and 1 person who was homeless at the time the interview took place. The participants consisted of 27 women and 9 men.

Most of the interviews took place at the homes of the families and were conducted by the second author. The interview guideline was structured according to the themes of the social rights of the constitution. The focus of the in-depth interviews was on exploring how social rights are realized in families in poverty and how the daily living conditions impact the situation of children. The recorded interviews were fully transcribed and thematically analysed by all the authors.

Based on a qualitative content analysis, we discuss in the next part the most important insights that emerged from the interviews. The focus is on the interaction between the interests of children and parents and the areas of tension that arise from these interests. The testimonies of parents often bring these tensions to life in a sharp way. First, we will examine the policy domains that are traditionally associated with the childhood moratorium. Second, we examine the policy areas of housing, health and material well-being.

Child Poverty: An Educational Issue?

Child Poverty and Leisure Time

The domain of leisure is an important feature of the childhood moratorium. According to article 31 of the CRC, participation in leisure, play, recreational activities and cultural and artistic life is a fundamental right of children. Participation in leisure activities is likewise considered as an essential aspect of the fight against poverty. For one reason because it is believed to be a lever for building social capital. Therefore, guiding children who grow up in poverty to leisure activities is a crucial aspect of an anti-poverty policy. Nevertheless, families in poverty often experience all kinds of barriers, hindering access to leisure time activities.

> We have food, drinks, a roof over our heads and clothes. But in terms of leisure time, we are limited. Going to the movie theatre for example ... I really can't afford that.

Many families indicate that leisure time, even with financial support, takes a too big chunk out of the family budget, forcing them to prioritize more basic expenses. As a consequence, children in poverty often do not participate in formal organized leisure activities. However, families in poverty indicate that they frequently organize informal leisure activities themselves. This is an important point of attention because non-participation in formal organized leisure activities does not necessarily imply non-participation in leisure activities. Children in poverty often do participate in self-organized informal leisure activities that are meaningful for them. This should be acknowledged as valuable in itself because these activities produce critical terrains where children also develop social capital.

Although leisure is an important part of the childhood moratorium, its meaning cannot be fully understood without connecting it to the broader living environment in which children grow up. Many families indicate that the housing situation is often an obstacle for inviting friends at home and maintain social relationships with peers.

> Yes, my children have a lot of friends, but they don't come to our house. We live in bad housing conditions and our house is way too small. There is no place to play. We have one bedroom for three children. The room is filled with the three beds. My children sometimes play at others children's home. I always tell my children: don't ask friends to come home to play!

What parents' stories show is that a typical child-related policy domain such as leisure obviously interconnects with domains outside of the childhood moratorium, such as family income or housing. This observation indicates that the rights and interests of children and those of parents in the context of child poverty are interwoven and that these interests cannot be considered separately.

Child Poverty and Parental Support

As mentioned before, an important discussion associated with the issue of narrowing down 'poverty' to 'child poverty' is related to the vulnerability of parents living in poverty to become object of social interventions that interfere in the relationship with their children. Parents in poverty often point to the critical importance of being recognized and respected as a parent (Attree, 2005). Interventions intended to be supportive for parents are not always perceived that way. This is so because these interventions are often focused on parental behaviour in raising their children rather than on the environmental causes of poverty. As a result, the context in which parents raise their children risks getting lost out of sight. Parents in the interviews explain that they want to be acknowledged as primarily responsible for upbringing their children. In order to realize this, they need parental support that is willing to look beyond the behavioural aspects in raising their children. What parents seek for is parental support that takes the effort to cooperate with other welfare organizations to realize structural change in the lives of parents in poverty. Yet, parents reveal that they do not always experience this support.

> You know, I asked for a lot of help, but received only little. The juvenile court is mainly available for criminal offenses. The Youth Assistance Support Centre is difficult to reach and has to deal with long waiting lists, just like mental health care. School social work is confronted with a high work load and schools are too fast in judging my situation, even though they have never been to my place.

A major source of annoyance reported by families in poverty is the fact that organizations for parental support do not give answers to their questions or that they give a kind of support that was not asked for.

I received a letter from an organisation for parental support. I finally thought that they decided something that could help me. I opened the letter. It was saying that they had free tickets for a show of the feast of St. Nicholas and that I could pass by to pick up the tickets. Not only was I very angry about this letter. It made me sick to my stomach. I had to throw up. I was so shocked.... It touched me very deeply at that moment. I don't know about other people, but when I am in deep trouble, having no food, I really don't want to sit and watch a show of the feast of St. Nicholas and receiving some chocolates. This show, I couldn't care less. My children will be distracted for 10 minutes, and afterwards, they are going to see all kinds of things that they want to buy. But I don't have the money to buy that.

Just like leisure time, day care for children is an essential part of the childhood moratorium. But also just like leisure, day care is for an important part connected with other domains of social life of parents, like, for instance, the domain of labour. While organizations for parental support are expecting parents to participate in the labour market, this often conflicts with the support that is organized for children of working parents. Day care for children is not only expensive for parents in poverty. Parents also indicate the lack of places in day care centres with long waiting list as a result. In addition, day care centres are only open from 9 to 5, while parents in poverty, often having a poor job quality, have irregular working hours. All this complicates combining a job with raising children.

I worked in the H&M. I worked on Wednesday, Friday and Saturday with late shifts. There is no day care for my children at these moments. So I quit my job. I can not leave my children all the time home alone. There is no day care after 6PM. But the Public Employment Service does not take that into account. They suspended me for 6 weeks. So, you can not say that you can not do the job because of a lack of day care for my children. They don't accept that.

Also the stories of parents in the domain of parental support show the interconnectedness of, for instance, child care with the domain of labour, and thus the impossibility to 'lock up' the problem of child poverty in the childhood moratorium.

Child Poverty and Education

Education is probably one of the most important levers in the fight against child poverty. The right to education is recognized as an essential child right in all major international children's and human rights instruments (Kjørholt, 2013). A key aspect of the right to education is having access to education. Families in poverty testify that financial accessibility to education in particular is often a barrier. There are not only the direct costs related with attending school, such as buying books or other learning materials. Families are also faced with indirect school costs that often weigh heavily on the family budget, such as the costs of transport to attend parent-teacher conferences.

> I recently went to the parent-teacher conference by train. 11 euros for train and bus. When I arrived at school, I was informed that the meeting has been cancelled. However, they had not notified me. That was a significant financial part from my weekly budget, for nothing. I was so angry … but then they expect you to remain polite and friendly.… They have absolutely no idea what this means to me.

In addition to the financial difficulties, parents in poverty often experience a narrowed view of their poverty situation. They describe how all too often their context of poverty is ignored and how certain problems are too quickly translated into parenting problems.

> The speech therapist and the physiotherapist both diagnosed a delay in the developmental of my child. But if you live in poverty, they immediately think that this delay is caused by our poverty situation. They think it is because of a poor education or because of inadequate food that my children are delayed. While you can just as easily have such problems in a middle class family.

This dynamic of 'pedagogization' of the poverty problem also occurs when children are referred from regular education to the system of special education. The financial argument is often used in these situations because special education can offer extra support without redressing this to the parents.

> I. and M. are both referred to special education. In the first year M. was in a regular school, but grammar and maths were difficult. In special education, there was extra support for free. Until the age of six, M. was in special education. Then, he wanted to go to regular education. But the Pupil Guidance Centre didn't think that was a good idea. Then M. cried. I talked to him and explained him that it might be good to stay in special education,

with smaller classes where they can support you and where you can get good marks, instead of bad marks in mainstream education.

Analysing our findings from the lens of representation, we can observe that *where* representational claims for combatting child poverty are articulated is critical for *how* these representational claims are articulated. When child poverty is mainly dealt with in the domains of the childhood moratorium, a structure characterized by educational frameworks, it is not surprising that mainly educational answers are sought to the problem of poverty. This is inherent to the educational environment in which the problem of poverty manifests itself. The phenomenon of 'pedagogization' of the poverty problem is distinctive for the way the childhood moratorium functions. This has a number of merits, in particular in the recognition that leisure, parenting support and education can be important levers in the fight against child poverty. However, as parents are excluded from the childhood moratorium, parental domains such housing, labour or material support are generally undervalued in the fight against child poverty. This is what we discuss in the next section.

CHILD POVERTY: A SOCIAL ISSUE?

Child Poverty and Housing

While the previous part of the empirical data show that typical childhood domains who are established to take care of children's interests cannot be considered without connecting them to the socio-economic position of parents, this is also true the other way around. Policy domains related to the position of parents have a noticeable impact on the position of children. This is, for instance, the case in the domain of housing. Despite the fact that the right to housing is anchored in national and international legislation, for families living in poverty it is often a major concern. This is particularly the case for households with many children.

> At the time, both my son and my daughter lived with me. So basically, I needed a three bedroom apartment. However, this costs between 700–750 euros.... So I gave my daughter and son a bedroom and I slept here on the couch for a long time. I slept on my couch for many years.

In addition to the cost of housing, the quality of housing is generally experienced by parents as problematic. Growing up in poor housing conditions can have critical health consequences, due to inadequate sanitation or problems with moisture and mould. Poor housing quality also has an effect on the social and cultural development of children, for instance, due to a lack of space to play or do homework. The precarious housing quality of families in poverty often results in difficulties for children to develop and maintain social relations with their peers. Because of the limited space to play or due to embarrassment, children living in poverty don't invite friends to play at their home.

> My home can only be heated in the living room. That's why my daughter's friends can never come to play with us: it is too cold in her room for most of the year. And simply because of the state of our house. Very occasionally in summer time, she can play in the garden. An electric heater could be a solution, but that, I can not afford.

The right to housing is also about the living environment. The place where the house is located is important for families in poverty. It is not only the space where they develop relationships with others. It is also a place that increases their limited housing space. Especially with children playing, the housing environment is of key importance.

> Things are starting to improve with the neighbours. But we are a bit limited in space because we only have a terrace of 20 square meter. The children are not allowed to play with the ball there, because it makes too much noise. 'Cruella De Vil' lives above us and she can't stand children. She really hates them.

The stories of parents about their housing conditions show that their poverty situation, which is often the cause of a precarious living situation, has a major impact on the education and development of children. Furthermore, the topic of housing illustrates how parents almost systematically lock themselves away, trying to compensate the constraints that go together with living in poverty. We see similar mechanisms when it concerns the issue of health.

Child Poverty and Health

Families in poverty are facing increasing health inequalities, even though the right to health care is recognized as a fundamental right for everyone. Families in poverty often seem in a worse health condition while having reduced access to healthcare. Poverty affects health, while health problems also result in more poverty. Medical costs often weigh heavily for families.

> Yes, my youngest should wear glasses. But it costs an immense amount of money. I haven't even been to the ophthalmologist yet. It is scandalous.! That child should have glasses.
>
> I had to stop speech therapy for the eldest because of lack of finances, I just couldn't afford it.

As with housing, issues related to health show mechanisms of parents disqualifying themselves in the benefit of their children. Parents tell us about how they try to save some money by not buying medication for their own health, leaving them with sufficient financial possibilities to take care of their children.

> There were moments when the doctor prescribed me medication. I just didn't go and get them because I couldn't. You can not deprive your children because you need medication for yourself. It will go over if you hold on long enough.

Also the issue of health shows us how deeply intertwined the interests of children and parents are. A pattern emerges in which a lack of financial resources leads parents to put aside their own interests in order to fulfil the interests of their children.

Child Poverty and Material Support

It has already become clear from the above testimonies of parents that child poverty is not just a matter of the direct living conditions of children (i.e. the childhood moratorium) but also of the living conditions of parents. The stories show that an inadequate family budget has far-reaching consequences for raising children. It often concerns fundamental things that are not available to the family, such as (healthy) food, electricity, the possibility to go to the doctor, clothes or shoes. Something that returns in just about every testimony is the difficulty for parents to abandon their freedom of choice with regard to their income. Many parents in poverty are often in a process of debt mediation and budget guidance, resulting in a limited freedom of choice to spend their available budget. In turn, this leads to difficult parenting choices.

> My children asked me: 'Can we go to the fair?' I said: 'what do you prefer? The shoes you need because your feet are practically touching the ground or those 20 euros for the fair?' It puts children in conflict. They would actually rather go to the fair, but they need those shoes more. And they will always choose what they really need. I feel so bad that I force them to make a choice. Also the first of September, friends at school tell about their holidays, where they went, what they have done, etc. My children can just stammer. Spending one day at the sea for them is already going on a trip. But even that is difficult to realize. I feel so sorry that I have to disappoint them so much.

Work remains an important buffer against financial problems and poverty. Households with no adult paid worker face a high risk of poverty. Professional integration into the labour market through activating policy interventions is high on the policy agenda for people living in poverty. However, people in poverty often face long and inflexible working hours, which make it difficult to combine work with care for children. Combining work with children and the household was often mentioned by parents as an extra challenge to find and continue to work, but, above all, to enable a quality of life for the parents.

> I work because then I can keep myself busy. M debt mediator would really like me to work full time. But I already find it difficult to find a part-time job. And honestly, if I go to work full time, I don't think it's going to be that smooth with my household. I have to work all summer without a day off. Half days, five days a week. Five days that I work. So, I have now registered the children for day care. Ultimately, I'm going to invest money in working instead of earning some money.

The stories of parents in poverty show the complex interaction between the low family income, the unstable and often inflexible work situation, the experiences with support and social services, and the impact of all this on family education. The lack of a decent family budget is putting relationships in families under pressure, challenging solidarity within the family. Parents in poverty try to provide their children with the necessary material resources, but often fall short due to lack of means. They often compensate for this by eliminating their own financial needs. The lack of material conditions for building a dignified life with the family is also reflected in the reduced self-determination that parents experience in raising their children. A lack of family budget often results in a lack of freedom to define and realize one's own parenting goals.

Conclusion

In this chapter, we showed that the socio-political arena in which claims for the realization of children's rights are articulated is of fundamental importance if we wish to understand the issue of representation in relation to children's rights. The case of child poverty shows us the distinct way children are represented as the deserving poor on the one hand and parents are represented as the undeserving poor on the other hand. This distinction needs to be understood from the perspective of the childhood moratorium, that is, the socio-political institutionalization of childhood in (Western) societies. The childhood moratorium is constitutive for how representational claims are articulated. Consequently, the problem of child poverty is, above all, considered as an educational problem and therefore primarily addressed by educational means. In terms of Fraser's theory on social justice, our analysis demonstrates how the dimension of representation is inextricably linked with the dimensions of redistribution and recognition. Hence, the childhood moratorium is not only the political arena providing the conditions for defining representational claims. In its turn, it also sets the scene to define who can make claims for redistribution and recognition.

Focusing on the particularity of children and the way their interest are institutionalized in the childhood moratorium can be considered as an important result of the social and political contestation of the children's rights movement, a social movement advocating in the best interest of children. The children's rights movement has the historical merit of representing a group in society (children) that in the past was often ignored as a distinct group with their own interests. Accordingly, children often 'disappeared' in the context of the family (Reynaert et al., 2009). However, the lens of representation in the case of child poverty shows that the pendulum now risks striking back in the other direction. Understanding children's rights in the fight against child poverty as a framework focusing almost exclusively on the best interest of children, while ignoring the position of parents living and raising their children in poverty, not only risks excluding parents in strategies to combat child poverty. In its turn, it also risks impacting children, as important social resources in the fight against child poverty are situated outside the childhood moratorium and are connected to the position of parents, such as housing or labour.

So, a first observation that can be made when analysing the issue of child poverty and children's rights from the representational lens is that *where* representational claims for children's rights are made matters. Therefore, if we wish to overcome the dynamic of educationalization of child poverty, we should interconnect the typical educational domains of the childhood moratorium with the policy domains outside the childhood moratorium. Or interconnect the interest of children with the interest of parents. A second observation to be made is concerned with *who* is articulating claims for children's rights. Our analysis is based on the perspectives of parents living in poverty. They show how their life conditions of poverty have a direct impact on their children living in poverty and thus on the realization of children's rights. Looking for answers to wicked problems such as child poverty should not be left to just one group of representatives such as the children's rights movement or even children. Every representational group in its turn creates blind spots. This is not to suggest that the children's rights movement or children themselves have nothing to say about child poverty. On the contrary. It rather means that we need to involve 'critical actors' who engage in an agonist dialogue (Celis et al., 2008). Until today, scholarship on children's rights has insufficiently explored these pluralist views on child poverty and therefore have insufficiently insight in the ambiguous relation between children's rights and child poverty (O'Brien & Salonen, 2011; Morrow & Pells, 2012).

References

Attree, P. (2005). Parenting Support in the Context of Poverty: A Meta-synthesis of the Qualitative Evidence. *Health & Social Care in the Community*, *13*(4), 330–337.

Attree, P. (2006). The Social Costs of Child Poverty: A Systematic Review of the Qualitative Evidence. *Children & Society*, *20*(1), 54–66.

Bessell, S., Siagian, C., & Bexley, A. (2020). Towards Child-inclusive Concepts of Childhood Poverty: The Contribution and Potential of Research with Children. *Children and Youth Services Review*, *116*, 105118.

Bourdillon, M., & Boyden, J. (Eds.). (2011). *Childhood Poverty: Multidisciplinary Approaches*. Springer.

Celis, K., Childs, S., Kantola, J., & Krook, M. L. (2008). Rethinking Women's Substantive Representation. *Representations, 44*(2), 99–110.

Eamon, M. K. (2001). The Effects of Poverty on Children's Socioemotional Development: An Ecological Systems Analysis. *Social Work, 46*(3), 256–266.

Eurostat. (2019). Children at Risk of Poverty or Social Exclusion. https://ec.europa.eu/eurostat/statistics-explained/index.php/Children_at_risk_of_poverty_or_social_exclusion#Key_findings

Featherstone, B., Broadhurst, K., & Holt, K. (2011). Thinking Systemically—Thinking Politically: Building Strong Partnerships with Children and Families in the Context of Rising Inequality. *British Journal of Social Work, 42*(4), 618–633.

Fernandez, E., Zeira, A., Vecchiato, T., & Canali, C. (Eds.). (2015). *Theoretical and Empirical Insights into Child and Family Poverty: Cross National Perspectives* (Vol. 10). Springer.

FRA (European Union Agency for Fundamental Rights). (2018). *Combating Child Poverty: An Issue of Fundamental Rights*. Publications Office, Luxembourg.

Fraser, N. (2005). Reframing Global Justice. *New Left Review, 36*, 69.

Gillies, V. (2008). Perspectives on Parenting Responsibility: Contextualizing Values and Practices. *Journal of Law and Society, 35*(1), 95–112.

Honig, M.-S. (2008). Work and Care: Reconstructing Childhood Through Childcare Policy in Germany. In A. James & A. L. James (Eds.), *European Childhoods. Cultures, Politics and Childhoods in Europe* (pp. 198–215). Palgrave Macmillan.

Kjørholt, A. T. (2013). Childhood as Social Investment, Rights and the Valuing of Education. *Children & Society, 27*(4), 245–257.

La Placa, V., & Corlyon, J. (2016). Unpacking the Relationship Between Parenting and Poverty: Theory, Evidence and Policy. *Social Policy and Society, 15*(1), 11–28.

Lister, R. (2003). Investing in the Citizen-Workers of the Future: Transformations in Citizenship and the State Under New Labour. *Social Policy and Administration, 37*(5), 427–538.

Lister, R. (2004). The Third Way's Social Investment State. Welfare State Change: Towards a Third Way. In J. Lewis & R. Surender (Eds.), *Welfare State Change: Towards a Third Way* (pp. 157–181). Oxford University Press.

Lister, R. (2006). Children (But Not Women) First: New Labour, Child Welfare and Gender. *Critical Social Policy, 26*(2), 315–335.

Lister, R. (2007). Why Citizenship: Where, When and How Children? *Theoretical Inquiries in Law, 8*(2), 693–718.

Mestrum, F. (2011). Child Poverty. A Critical Perspective. *Social Work & Society, 9*(1), 161–168.

Morrow, V. (2010). Child Poverty, Social Exclusion and Children's Rights: A View from the Sociology of Childhood. In W. Vandenhole, J. Vranken, & K. De Boyser (Eds.), *Why Care?: Children's Rights and Child Poverty* (pp. 33–56). Intersentia.

Morrow, V., & Pells, K. (2012). Integrating Children's Human Rights and Child Poverty Debates: Examples from Young Lives in Ethiopia and India. *Sociology*, 46(5), 906–920.

Noy, C. (2008). Sampling Knowledge: The Hermeneutics of Snowball Sampling in Qualitative Research. *International Journal of Social Research Methodology*, 11(4), 327–344.

O'Brien, M., & Salonen, T. (2011). Child Poverty and Child Rights Meet Active Citizenship: A New Zealand and Sweden Case Study. *Childhood*, 18(2), 211–226.

Olk, T., & Hübenthal, M. (2009). Child Poverty in the German Social Investment State. *Zeitschrift für Familienforschung-Journal of Family Research*, 21(2), 150–167.

Reynaert, D., Bouverne-de-Bie, M., & Vandevelde, S. (2009). A Review of Children's Rights Literature Since the Adoption of the United Nations Convention on the Rights of the Child. *Childhood*, 16(4), 518–534.

Reynaert, D., & Roose, R. (2014). Children's Rights and the Capability Approach: Discussing Children's Agency Against the Horizon of the Institutionalised Youth Land. In *Children's Rights and the Capability Approach* (pp. 175–193). Springer.

Reynaert, D., & Roose, R. (2015). Children's Rights from a Social Work Perspective: Towards a Lifeworld Orientation. In *Routledge International Handbook of Children's Rights Studies* (pp. 110–127). Routledge.

Reynaert, D., & Roose, R. (2016). Children's Rights: A Framework to Eliminate Social Exclusion? Critical Discussion and Tensions. In M. D. Ruck, M. Peterson-Badali, & M. Freeman (Eds.), *Handbook of Children's Rights: Global and Multidisciplinary Perspectives*. Taylor & Francis.

Ridge, T. (2006). Childhood Poverty: A Barrier to Social Participation and Inclusion. In E. K. M. Tisdall (Ed.), *Children, Young People and Social Inclusion: Participation for What?* Policy Press.

Ridge, T. (2009). *Living with Poverty: A Review of the Literature on Children's and Families' Experiences of Poverty*. A Report of Research Carried Out by the Centre for the Analysis of Social Policy, University of Bath on Behalf of the Department for Work and Pensions. Report No 594.

Ridge, T. (2011). The Everyday Costs of Poverty in Childhood: A Review of Qualitative Research Exploring the Lives and Experiences of Low-income Children in the UK. *Children & Society*, 25(1), 73–84.

Ridge, T., & Saunders, P. (2009). Introduction: Themed Section on Children's Perspectives on Poverty and Disadvantage in Rich and Developing Countries. *Social Policy and Society*, 8(4), 499–502.

Roets, G., Roose, R., & Bouverne-De Bie, M. (2013). Researching Child Poverty: Towards a Lifeworld Orientation. *Childhood-a Global Journal of Child Research, 20*(4), 535–549.

Sandbæk, M. (2017). European Policies to Promote Children's Rights and Combat Child Poverty. *International Journal of Environmental Research and Public Health, 14*(8), 837.

Sarriera, J. C., Casas, F., Bedin, L., Abs, D., Strelhow, M. R., Gross-Manos, D., & Giger, J. (2015). Material Resources and Children's Subjective Well-being in Eight Countries. *Child Indicators Research, 8*(1), 199–209.

Save the Children & UNICEF. (17 September 2020). Press Release. https://www.unicef.org/eap/press-releases/150-million-additional-children-plunged-poverty-due-covid-19-unicef-save-children

Sen, H. (2013). *'Time-Out'in the Land of Apu: Childhoods, Bildungsmoratorium and the Middle Classes of Urban West Bengal.* Springer Science & Business Media.

Silwal, A. R., Engilbertsdottir, S., Cuesta, J., Newhouse, D., & Stewart, D. (2020). *Global Estimate of Children in Monetary Poverty: An Update.* Poverty and Equity Discussion Paper, World Bank Group, Washington, DC. http://documents.worldbank.org/curated/en/966791603123453576/Global-Estimate-of-Children-in-Monetary-Poverty-An-Update

Van Haute, D., Roets, G., Alasuutari, M., & Vandenbroeck, M. (2018). Managing the Flow of Private Information on Children and Parents in Poverty Situations: Creating a Panoptic Eye in Interorganizational Networks? *Child & Family Social Work, 23*(3), 427–434.

Vandenhole, W. (2013). Child Poverty and Children's Rights: An Uneasy Fit. *Michigan State International Law Review, 22,* 609.

Zinnecker, J. (2000). Childhood and Adolescence as Pedagogic Moratoria. *Zeitschrift Fur Padagogik, 46*(2), 36–68.

Open Access This chapter is licensed under the terms of the Creative Commons Attribution 4.0 International License (http://creativecommons.org/licenses/by/4.0/), which permits use, sharing, adaptation, distribution and reproduction in any medium or format, as long as you give appropriate credit to the original author(s) and the source, provide a link to the Creative Commons licence and indicate if changes were made.

The images or other third party material in this chapter are included in the chapter's Creative Commons licence, unless indicated otherwise in a credit line to the material. If material is not included in the chapter's Creative Commons licence and your intended use is not permitted by statutory regulation or exceeds the permitted use, you will need to obtain permission directly from the copyright holder.

CHAPTER 11

Child Figurations in Youth Climate Justice Activism: The Visual Rhetoric of the Fridays for Future on Instagram

Frida Buhre

The figure of the child holds a particular place in climate change communication and politics. Admittedly, we already live in a climate changed world, but the conditions of human life will continue to worsen, raising serious concerns about how the contemporary young generation will bear the burden of living in an overheated world (Thiery et al., 2021). This intergenerational injustice has led to the representation of the child to become extra charged in climate change discourse. The adultist discourses of climate politics frame the figure of the child as vulnerable (Tanner, 2010), caught in an intrinsic futurity (Lakind & Adsitt-Morris, 2018), and relatively passive (Lee, 2013, pp. 131–141). In this chapter, I am interested in how contemporary children and youth climate activists utilize or challenge such childhood figurations for their own purposes and, in so doing, help restructure how children's political representation and

F. Buhre (✉)
Department of Literature, Section of Rhetoric, Uppsala University, Uppsala, Sweden
e-mail: frida.buhre@littvet.uu.se

© The Author(s) 2023
B. Sandin et al. (eds.), *The Politics of Children's Rights and Representation*, Studies in Childhood and Youth,
https://doi.org/10.1007/978-3-031-04480-9_11

mobilization might be understood. Through an analysis of images posted on Instagram, the chapter explores how grassroots activists from across the world—both big and small players—use aesthetic representation and visual rhetoric to circumvent some geopolitical obstacles, gain visibility, and contribute to the larger purpose of raising public support for radical climate politics.

In the late summer of 2018, then 15-year-old Greta Thunberg initiated a school strike outside the Swedish parliament in defiance of an adult world that has failed to take climate change seriously. Since then, the Fridays for Future (FFF) movement has grown into the largest climate justice movement ever, with records set in terms of both global spread and number of participants. Notably, the week of 20–27 September 2019 saw an estimated 7.6 million people demonstrating in 185 countries (Martiskainen et al., 2020; de Moor et al., 2020). Imagery of mass-demonstrations holds great potential to attract the attention of the larger public due to the size of the people gathering, the atmosphere of momentum, and the affective outburst of joy and anger in protest. However, this type of visual rhetoric was not equally accessible to all school strikers globally. While traditional media paid most attention to these mass-gatherings in Europe and the United States, the Global South activists struggled against a lack of media representation and restrictions to mobilization. One of the purposes of this chapter is to highlight how Global South activists worked around these obstacles.

Globality, Digital Observation, and Participatory Culture

The FFF is a global movement. Its communicative flows of interaction and mobilization present scholars of youth social movements with important questions about global power hierarchies. As of yet, studies of the demographics of FFF activists have mostly focused on the Global North. They show that the protesters are young, often first-time protesters, girls are more prominent than boys, and they come from well-educated backgrounds (Wahlström et al., 2019; Haunss & Sommer, 2020; Martiskainen et al., 2020; de Moor et al., 2020; Wallis & Loy, 2021). Studies on the mobilization strategies and political implications of the FFF, as well as media responses, have also mostly focused on the Global North (Bergmann & Ossewaarde, 2020; Biswas, 2021; von Zabern & Tulloch, 2021). No quantitative studies on the demographics of the FFF have been conducted in the Global South. However, previous studies on environmental defenders and climate activists in the Global South or in Indigenous communities show that youths are already severely affected by extreme weather events, resource scarcity, and the imperialist politics of extractivism, along with violent repression from governments. Diverse Global South youth therefore work to reduce risk, incite a politics of care, and create spaces for intergenerational learning and solidarity (Tanner, 2010; Trajber et al., 2019; Ritchie, 2021), while struggling under neoliberal paradigms (Muthoni Mwaura, 2018; Hayward, 2020, pp. 39–63). Indeed, environmental concerns in the Global South are often related to direct survival, scarce resources, or communal well-being, making a diverse range of environmental and human rights defenders, indigenous communities, small-scale farmers, and urban poor engage in struggles against environmental degradation, toxic waste, and extractive industries (Anguelovski & Martínez Alier, 2014). The few studies that have focused on the FFF in the Global South or in poor countries show that participants often engage in activism because they face these dangers firsthand (de Moor et al., 2020, pp. 160–165; Kimball, 2021). Many leading Global South activists of the FFF have also reported publicly about experiencing extreme weather events or growing up as climate refugees, as, for example, Indigenous Mexican American leader Xiya Bastida and Ugandan leader Hilda Flavia Nakabuye. The general message of the FFF is focused on *Climate Justice*, a term that highlights the interconnections between race, class, geopolitics, and exposure to risks associated with climate change. The FFF prefers to use the term *Most Affected Peoples and Areas* (MAPA) rather than the Global South, to highlight how a changing climate hits differently across the globe, affects the communities least able to act protectively the most, and where societal structures of racism, imperialism, and capitalism make climate change and environmental degradation disproportionately affect poor people and people of color. In the remainder of the chapter, I use the term MAPA for the activist groups that self-identify as such.

Through digital participant observation, I am present as a (digital) person on Instagram, where I follow all the national FFF accounts, but do not engage in the dynamism of digital striking. The material analyzed are the Instagram groups claiming to represent a national iteration of FFF. Instagram has been chosen because it is the most common platform of FFF—followed by Facebook and Twitter—especially in MAPA countries. Of these three mega platforms, Instagram has a younger user profile and interface design, and it also offers the most pronounced focus on visual rhetoric.[1] I have located 124 pages that assume the role of representing a national group of FFF on Instagram. As Instagram does not allow any scraping of data,[2] I have had to limit my material through a selection of 25 groups.[3] For some countries, multiple pages claim to represent the national FFF page, in which cases I have chosen the group with the most followers. The principles for selecting countries have been (in hierarchal order): (1) Regional spread; (2) Mix of large and small countries; (3) Activity; (4) Followers; and (5) Mix of types of pictures posted.[4] The national groups have been chosen because they are what FFF lists on their website as the "contact" of the movement. Given that this chapter explores material from Instagram, digital access or proxy to someone with digital access is a determinant of the material. Even if these national groups cannot be said to overcome class, racial, or geographic divides in their national context, the material features a high prevalence of small-scale or rural strikes alongside urban strikes, participants of various ages and racial backgrounds, with various religious or non-religious markers. Studies that map and explore these dynamics in the local contexts are much needed.

I am interested in the rhetorical potential that lies in assuming the role of representing the national group of the FFF. This chapter follows Gayatri Chakravorty Spivak in thinking of representation as both *proxy* and *portrait*. The youth activists take on the role of speaking on behalf of a larger constituency through what Spivak calls the proxy of representation—they are part of this constituency and close to their peers. However, their visual rhetoric are also performative speech acts that function as representative portraits that create that same constituency (Spivak, 1990, p. 108). As such, the material both gives voice to youths of diverse backgrounds in the national setting engaged in the struggle for climate justice (proxy), and obscures the divides within that community by visually representing a national cohort (portrait).

In analyzing this body of materials, I recognize the cultural and linguistic difficulties that this global sample of FFF accounts create. Who am I to interpret a Korean or Iraqi FFF account where I cannot understand most of the discursive content (text and speech) of the posts? These are valid concerns, but FFF is also a *participatory culture* (Jenkins, 2009, p. xi) of children and youth from across linguistic and geopolitical boundaries, sustained through politically engaged communicative interaction and the interface design of social media platforms. Given that the activists themselves post in multiple languages and that messages travel across a range of different accounts, a more limited selection criterion would give a skewed image of how the movement operates as a global participatory culture. Finally, this study focuses on the visual imagery, rather than the discursive, which means that the material is more accessible, even if not all cultural details can be considered or read with the care and situated knowledge that a more limited sample would have allowed. Furthermore, the social sciences are heavily skewed to a North Atlantic bias (Cuervo & Miranda, 2019, pp. 2–4), and this includes child studies (de Castro, 2020). As already indicated, the North Atlantic or English bias is also highly tenable in scholarship on FFF countries. A continued and increased attention to the representation of children and youth from the Global South thus seems paramount.

Children's Political Representation and Climate Activism: Literature Review

Childhood scholars have worked hard to challenge reductive notions of children's political lives and rights, and especially how hegemonic discourses portray children and youth as a future potentiality rather than an actuality (Castañeda, 2002; Lee, 2013). Scholars have increasingly argued that young people's political engagement comes through the social networks young people construct online (Kang, 2016; Boulianne & Theocharis, 2020), in what teen scholar Danah Boyd calls *networked publics* (Boyd, 2014, p. 8). However, access to technology and digital skills is a differentiating determinant that affects youth digital participation, especially in the Global South (Lombana-Bermudez, 2015; Cuervo & Miranda, 2019; Boulianne & Theocharis, 2020). Largely, these findings are applicable to FFF, which is composed of politically motivated children and youth, engaged in networked publics that use do-it-yourself digital methods.

Scholarship on children and youth's climate activism is growing. Although still a small field, the role of youth activism for international climate politics and governance has gained increased attention (Foran et al., 2017; Thew et al., 2020). By foregrounding children and youth as political agents, this scholarship questions the narrative of children as simply climate change victims or future inheritors of a warmer world (Tanner, 2010; Trajber et al., 2019). Other scholars emphasize the importance of youth activism for sharpening ambitions in climate politics (Trott, 2021), and the importance of the activism for the youth themselves (Fisher, 2016). Scholars also stress the multiple factors—such as education, friends, and local belonging—that motivate children and youth to engage in climate activism (Buttigieg & Pace, 2013; Börner et al., 2020). Again, this picture is applicable to the FFF that moves between the public spheres of international climate governance to local social or educational activities—all with the aim of sharpening climate politics.

Uneven Possibilities of Image Events: *The Child Speaking Truth to Power*

This chapter explores the visual representation of childhood figurations in FFF Instagram posts, through what rhetorician and environmental humanities scholar Kevin M. DeLuca calls *image events* (2012). Image events are a type of rhetorical strategy used by climate activists, not to solve an immediate problem (close a specific mine, save an individual whale, plant that specific tree, etc.), but to create attention for a larger issue and thus stir public awareness. If we assume that environmental and climate activists attempt to attract attention, it becomes necessary to ask under what conditions the activists of FFF can create dramatic images. With what aesthetic and rhetorical compositions do the global FFF activists seek to create stunning images or videos and how do they use creative aesthetic play to circumvent eventual restrictions to their right to strike?

The most iconic image event of the FFF is arguably the first image of Greta Thunberg in front of the Swedish parliament, posted on Instagram and Twitter by herself on August 20, 2018. The method of school striking was inspired by students in Parkland, Florida, who used it to protest US gun laws after a school shooting (Watts, 2019). Almost instantly, Thunberg's strikes were covered by Swedish mass media and her Twitter post was retweeted by prominent Swedish individuals. The news of her strike spread throughout the fall of 2018.

Photo: Greta Thunberg

In the image, Thunberg is dressed in a blue hoodie, cheetah pants, and her hair is parted in two braids. She is sitting with her back against the stone wall of the Swedish parliament, with a hand-made sign that reads "Skolstrejk för klimatet" ("School Strike for Climate") and a stack of printed papers next to her, held to the ground by a stone. All in all, the image presents a physically small, white girl who looks like an older child or young teen, sitting alone in front of a building that represents the sedimentation of political power in Sweden. The image was explosive. Not only does Thunberg look vulnerable and determined at the same time, but the parliament—with its classical architecture that echoes Roman stateliness—represents imposing and grandiose power. The Swedish viewer of this image also knows that the parliament is situated next to the Royal Castle, thus signaling centuries of centralized political power. The contrast between the body of Thunberg and this public space very much reads as a David versus Goliath image event. The fact that this image gained so much traction in both mass and social media reinforces what digital network theorist Manuel Castells calls "the symbolic power" of state or financial buildings. These iconic places are condensed sites of meaning, memories, and political expectations, and protesters gather there to create a sense of togetherness in opposition to institutional power and to recover the rights of representation from the dominant elites (Castells, 2015).

For this image to "work" as an image event—that is, do the rhetorical work of spurring the public to take notice—it is of importance that Thunberg is read as a child. As mentioned in the beginning of this chapter, children represent a certain position in climate change discourse closely linked to hegemonic notions of children as more vulnerable to climate impacts (Tanner, 2010), as representing futurity rather than a present actuality (Lakind & Adsitt-Morris, 2018), and as passive in relation to climate politics (Lee, 2013, pp. 131–141). Childhood scholar Claudia Castañeda uses the concept of *childhood figurations* to consider "why the child as a figure has been made a resource for wider cultural projects" (Castañeda, 2002, p. 2). The childhood figuration of Thunberg holds together an array of contradicting values and affects connected to adult values and political governance: Thunberg represents both the brave child speaking truth to (overwhelming) adult power, and the vulnerable child worthy of adult protection. As noted by a number of childhood scholars (Higonnet, 1998; Castañeda, 2002; Wall, 2012; Dyer, 2019), such images of children are often represented in a sentimental frame: the child embodies a higher moral value that needs protection by adults, while also figuring as the embodiment or potentiality of a better society—the promise of a better future adult. Thinking with Spivak, we can say the adult audience can look at the image of Thunberg and see a portrait that "stands in" for an entire young generation and the political hopes attached to it. For the young audience, the image clearly functioned differently as Thunberg came to represent by proxy: by being part of that generation and working as an extension of its anger and disappointment in the face of the public eye. Ryalls and Mazzarella argue that Thunberg represents a combination of fierceness and childhood, creating an alternative form of girlhood political agency (Ryalls & Mazzarella, 2021). Indeed, her anger and agonistic rhetorical style can be understood as what Wendy Hesford calls *children's rhetorical agency*, or a claim to political subjectivity (Hesford, 2011, p. 153). Thunberg's representation of herself turns into a childhood figuration of anger, bravery, competence, and intergenerational injustice in the present rather than future moment, not easily coopted for adult values and projects, even if there have been plenty of attempts. The imagery of Thunberg and the FFF movement in its entirety must be understood in this dynamic space of representation at the intersection of (adult imaginaries of) childhood figurations and the activists' representation of their own political agenda, childhood subjectivity, and aesthetic choices.

Childhood Figurations of the Global Mass-movement

Not all activists of the FFF movement have the same possibilities of striking that Thunberg has, which prompts the need to explore what aesthetic strategies the global activists of the FFF use to stage image events. Here, I wish to propose that one strategy is of representing something bigger than the individual children and youth participating: of shouldering the representative position of speaking on behalf of a generation in its global entirety. FFF can be critiqued for such representative claims: even if children and youth tend to be somewhat more concerned about climate change than the older cohort (Corner et al., 2015; Lee et al., 2020), such claims neglect the complicated social ecology around children and youth's perception of climate politics (Stevenson et al., 2019). Nonetheless, the combination of hegemonic notions of children as society's future potentiality and the global and intergenerational injustices of climate change enables a position for these climate activists to represent both the future and the young generation of the world. For that representative position to hold legitimacy, I suggest, the FFF movement needs to construct a visual rhetoric of mass-demonstrations across the globe.

Many of the strikes begin as lone-strikes and then grow and unfold into large mass-demonstrations. For example, the first strike in the United States was staged by then 13-year-old Latina Alexandria Villaseñor, who sat down outside the Headquarters of the United Nations in New York. Similarly, the Indian FFF begins with a lone strike but moves into the aesthetics of mass quickly. The caption of the second image, posted on March 15, 2019, is indicative of the mood: "Way to go Delhi and Mumbai!! We will arise again, all over India and the world." Here, the dimension of an escalation of the movement is emphasized. The Indian FFF also forefronts the contrast by returning to the importance of the lone-striker in later posts: "Here's to everyone who went on climate strike all alone! 🌍✊ Y'all are brave climate strikers!! Hope to see you lead the upcoming strikes. IN🌍💚 "[5] This post contains a series of images of lone strikers from across different places in India, thus signaling a sense of inclusion of rural strikers or strikers who are not part of a larger movement. For all such posts on initial lone strikes, the childhood figuration is like that of Thunberg's initial strike: the brave and politically engaged child or youth who speaks truth to institutional power. Of course, none of them have attracted the same type of media attention as Thunberg, and as noted by Hannah Dyer, certain childhood figurations are "not assigned to all children in equal amounts" but instead, such "rhetorical maneuvers are permeated by the elisions and attempted disavowals along the lines of race, class, gender, and sexuality" (Dyer, 2019, p. 1). Childhood figurations—even if similar on the surface—are unevenly distributed, circulated, and the adultist affective response is different or absent depending on the child's race, gender, age, and nationality.

Many of the accounts of FFF on Instagram showcase the narrative arc from small-scale to the aesthetics of mass, and often on symbolic sites. The Argentinian FFF begins by posting infographics on climate change and small-scale strikes, and it is only when they have gathered a mass of demonstrators that they post pictures outside the Palace of the Argentine National Congress. The below image is one such example, where large masses of school strikers have gathered outside the symbolically important building, and where the organizers are standing on a stage, facing opposite the Congress, and are lit up by headlamps. The visual aesthetics invites the viewer to both see the mass and the building from the perspective of these leading activists, while it also forefronts their determination and literal and metaphoric "facing up" to power.

Photo: Tobías Skarlovnik

Similarly, in the Mexican Instagram account, the first strike images do not center any particular site, but as the strikers begin to amass large numbers, they march to the *Angel of Independence* on May 24, 2019, which is a landmark monument in Mexico City and a site of previous protests. Both the German and the Australian accounts also begin by posting pictures of small-scale strikes, leading up to larger strikes. It is difficult to speak of trends as there are so many and large regional varieties, but European and North and South American FFF accounts use this visual rhetoric extensively. These images of mass-demonstrations provide for the exciting and joyful narrative arc of being part of something at the forefront of the movement; something that is unfolding and snowballing right now in the eruption of ever-larger protest. They also tend to be the images that attract the most likes. Entering the public in this way—in a large mass, in front of symbolically charged buildings—makes a claim on a political activist subjectivity, usually not granted children. The visual rhetoric of these images clearly challenge adult power and inaction on climate change by questioning passive figurations of children and youths simply being affected by politics, instead claiming to be doing politics. These strikers are making a bodily demand to be seen and heard, thus restructuring what counts not only as a political voice but also as a political body with rhetorical agency.

I would suggest that the aesthetics of mass is dependent on the contrast: only if the movement is grounded in local and small-scale strikes, do the big strikes come forth as a culmination. Such assemblages of mass are clearly read as exciting, joyful, and unstoppable. To a large extent, the FFF is characterized by its lack of "hopeful" climate change communication, but if there is a "positive" message from the FFF, it is this one: that activism, large masses, and the ability to speak as one angry generation hold great power and joy. One might call it a childhood figuration of the performative joy of activism. In a similar fashion as Thunberg's anger, these images present a childhood figuration that does not easily lend itself to adult values. As noted by Nick Lee, the stereotypical positions given to children in climate discourse—such as the child who needs climate change education or the child who will become a future leader or innovator in the fight against climate change—tend to figure the child as relatively passive (Lee, 2013, pp. 131–141). Or, in other words, such figurations retain agency and power in the hands of the adult cohort. I suggest that such divisions of power between adults and children are challenged through these images of children and youth that march in masses in front of seats of power and do so with defiant joy.

Alternative Childhood Figurations: Mass-by-Proxy and Globality-by-Proxy

The aesthetics of mass is not equally accessible in countries that suppress the freedom of assembly. For example, in Singapore, protest is made near-impossible due to strict laws regulating permits for protest, arrestment of activists, and confiscation of their belongings, as well as strong pressure from police to close down social media accounts and websites (Han, 2020). In India, protest is often allowed, but not in front of symbolically important places like the parliament (350.org, 2020). In Afghanistan, protests have taken place before the Taliban seize of power in 2021 but with armed troops protecting the protesters (Glinski, 2019). The strikers in Russia are mostly staging lone or very small-scale strikes because single-person strikes do not need permission in a country that otherwise regularly rejects permission to large strikes and demonstrations. Arguably, the Russian activists' childhood vulnerability is accentuated even further given the authoritarian responses from the political regime: the lead organizer in Russia, Arshak Makichyan, then 24-year-old and of Armenian descent, has been arrested for his school strikes. Even if the images of Makichyan being arrested by Russian police are dramatic, he has not received the same media attention as other activists, pointing to the aspect of age (he is too old), gender (he is a young man), nationality (he is Russian and Armenian and thus outside the media bias toward Western activists), in the inscription of childhood innocence. Similar arrests have taken place against FFF activists in India, Colombia, and Kenya, to just mention a few. The lack of general outrage from the global adult public against the violence and repression that some climate activists face further supports Dyer's claim that childhood innocence is inscribed in asymmetrical ways according to race, age, gender, and geopolitical position. Following Dyer, adultist discourses of childhood innocence also "constitute material conditions of possibility and violence for children" (Dyer, 2019). In other words, the lack of emotional, political, and ethical outrage against such violence in global media indicates that the hegemony of certain childhood figurations is part of a circulation of discourses that allow violence against some children and youth to take place.

For some FFF groups, a combination of restrictions makes image events of large masses hard or impossible: it might be dangerous to strike both for immediate security risks and for repression by authoritarian governments, the climate movement might not be that large, or the protest culture might take other forms than street protest. In the FFF, many non-Western activist groups had only just begun their organization at the time of the biggest marches globally on March 15 and September 20–27, 2019. Therefore, many of these groups "missed" the opportunity to participate in these events of global mass-demonstrations. For example, the FFF in the Philippines started their account in December 2019, which meant that they were too late to participate in the biggest demonstrations and that they only had a few months before the Covid-19 pandemic restricted physical demonstrations. The visual rhetoric of mass and momentum—communicated through the dramatic narrative of the lone child whose rightful cause attracts a mass of people— is thus unequally available.

One common strategy in such cases is to repost pictures of large masses of demonstrations elsewhere. This might come across as strange but is a form of image activism that gestures to the transposability of youth climate activism. As such, it flattens out differences between youth across the world, masking differences but reinforcing the category of "youth" and "climate activism" as the common denomination. Through the sheer number of such posts, the mass of pictures also grows, and the aesthetics of mass is redistributed into online spaces and for activist groups that might otherwise not have access to them: it becomes an aesthetics of mass-by-proxy. Similarly, North-based groups regularly post pictures of small-scale strikes from the Global South, with the clear signal that FFF is a global movement and with youth protesting in every part of the world.

Such images create an aesthetics of globality-by-proxy. It is a visual rhetoric that de-emphasizes the racial dynamics on the on-site strikes (which are usually more homogenous) and creates a sense of racial diversity within the Instagram networked public. The map on FFF's website with pins for each strike also communicates this aesthetics of globality. I would suggest that the aesthetics of mass-by-proxy and globality-by-proxy become part of the remix participatory culture of FFF, in which the transposability of global activists is visually emphasized.

Childhood Figurations of Competence and Assuming Responsibility

Other visual strategies consist of challenging perceptions of, on the one hand, children as lacking agency and, on the other, of adults assuming appropriate political responsibility. One example of such visual rhetoric is that activists from the FFF use imagery responding to climate and environmental degradation directly, such as tree-planting activities, emergency relief during extreme weather events, or plastic clean-ups. For example, the FFF in the Philippines have engaged in food and water emergency relief after a typhoon in 2020 and Brazil engages in a continuous campaign to support environmental defenders in the Amazons, mostly indigenous and highly vulnerable communities. According to childhood political theorist Sana M. Nakata, the question is not whether children are mature and competent enough to make political decisions or act, but the point is that they do (Nakata, 2008, p. 23). However, it is clear that the FFF activists attempt to challenge adultist perceptions of children as less competent or less responsible than adults.

Many of the African FFF groups participate in direct campaigns, often targeting plastic or toxic waste, for example through the campaign #Africaisnotadumpster, highlighting how Northern and Western countries dump waste in various parts of the African continent. These images create a different form of place-making than mass-protest: one that is situated in smaller groups of activists, in a place near home or school, and where the visual narrative is that of being directly affected by climate change or environmental harms.

Photo: Fridays for Future Uganda

On the surface, these images look similar to victimizing images of vulnerable Global South children circulated by NGOs (Wells, 2008), and they represent childhood figurations that might be co-opted for adult purposes as they can be read to figure the child as passive and in need of adult protection. It is perhaps also the reason why the responses from the activist communities are mixed: some of these images create a comparatively high number of likes whereas others tend to be on the lower side. However, these images can also be read as a visual representation of asserting agency and leveling a political critique. The children and youth depicted in these images are active and by their own initiative, thus asserting agency rather than passivity. They are also performing tasks that ought to have been handled otherwise, and by someone else: either by a government responsible for cleaning up waste, or by global capital not dumping on Africa. Some of these images also show elderly people, signaling a sense of intergenerational solidarity and communal action, but most only show children and youth. These images can thus be read as a critique of an adult world that does not accurately address economic, social, or environmental wrongs and thus displaces that burden unto young activists. It is hard to generalize, but pictures that forefront either joy in such direct action or a high-level of competence tend to receive more likes than the ones that mostly signal emergency relief. As the above picture from Uganda shows, these images are part of creating a different type of image event, less about the small child speaking truth to power or the aesthetics of mass, and more about the child assuming the role and responsibilities of government. But crucially, the activists are also smiling and posing happily for the camera. As such, these images become part of the visual rhetoric that shows the performative joy of activism.

This visual rhetoric indicates a childhood figuration of a high level of political competence and sense of responsibility. It can also be seen in the extensive posting of educational material (mostly on climate change and climate politics, but also on intersectionality, gender, racism, indigenous rights, and other justice-oriented themes, along with mental health information and resources) that clearly signals a competent child figuration that can take on the role of teaching and learning. A sense of political competence and responsibility is also shown in instructions on how to strike including information about safety for strikers in the face of repressive states, and in educational posts on geopolitical questions, such as FFF Croatia posting about the Yemen crises. It can also be seen in the ways that almost all groups closed down physical strikes during the Covid-19 pandemic and posted extensively on protective measures and particularly vulnerable communities, signaling a responsible child figuration that puts people's health before the movement's own political momentum. As the pandemic was most seriously affecting the elderly cohort, the FFF's protective stance also posits the question of intergenerational responsibility and such images reversed adultist understandings that it is the role of grown-ups to take care of children. John Wall discusses children's representation and the democratic move in many countries to secure arenas where children can voice their concerns. However, Wall concludes that "In no case are children democratically represented to the same extent as adults" (Wall, 2012, p. 89). Children and youth worldwide do not enjoy political suffrage, and these images prompt us to consider the legitimacy of this democratic limitation circumventing children: If children are not granted political power and representation based on the assumption that they lack competence, as well as on the assumption that adults take care of children's best interest, what happens when children use visual aesthetics that clearly state that they are competent? And when the adult world clearly does not measure up to that assumed responsibility?

Childhood Figurations of the Creative Play of Activism

The last visual strategy that I wish to explore is that of creative uses of beautiful or dramatic imagery. It is a strategy that might be used when mass-demonstrations outside symbolically charged buildings are not possible, and it is a strategy that grew under the Covid-19 pandemic. It can be to stage small-scale strikes with dramatic costumes, alternative strike formats such as shoe-strikes or die-ins, or it can be to post visually salient illustrations.

One rhetorical strategy is to use beautiful or funny costumes. The strikers of the Afghan FFF were mostly focusing on greening Kabul to ease human health harms caused by air pollution. Even if they seem to have been a sizable number of strikers, the activists used a rhetorical tactic of humor, beautiful costumes, large sculptors, or theater performances.

Photo: Fridays for Future Afghanistan

In this strike, the costumes are not only humorous but also quite beautiful: the activists dressed as trees lead the march, followed by activists carrying green signs and green foliage, together creating a visually coherent design of a green movement. The visual aesthetics of this strike is using a different affective register than the angry child speaking truth to power, the mass-demonstrating child challenging political representatives, or the responsible child having to assume the tasks of government. This visual rhetorical strategy is more hopeful in the sense that it represents a generation that uses creative play to showcase what the alternative to air pollution might look like. It can be argued that such tactics are unrealistic: planting trees will not solve air pollution in Kabul, nor climate impacts in Afghanistan, but I do not think that these strategies were meant to be realistic solutions in that sense. Instead, the activists were using humor, hope, and beautiful costumes to assert a critique of the present and invite alternative futures. This type of childhood figuration has similarities with the performative joy of activism, discussed above, because the sheer creative play of the activism itself is a "hopeful" or "optimistic" message, even if it does not provide any concrete solution to the climate crises. These images are, I suggest, a form of political action in which the child does not simply figure as the victim of climate change, but as the rhetorical agent who might represent an alternative world-making.

During the Covid-19 pandemic, many school strikers posted images of themselves striking online, and often the FFF national account inserts these into one large frame to make use of the aesthetics of mass in digital form. However, such images—although very common—lack a sense of place-making and of the strikes dimension of happening right now, in the rise of the momentum. To counter these weaknesses of digital striking, the South Korean FFF staged an online strike that was digital, but still simultaneously on-site outside the National Assembly in Seoul and synchronous in the moment. With a banner of water signaling ocean rise, the activists put a large screen on a platform with videos of school strikers.

Photo: Youth 4 Climate Action in Korea

I would suggest that this is a childhood figuration that makes use of many of the above discussed figurations: they strike outside the symbolically important parliamentary building, they signal a sense of here-and-now through the synchronous videos, and they make use of the aesthetics of mass through the number of people in the video. The images also clearly state that these activists are organized and competent in their mobilization. In many ways, it is also using humor and the performative joy of protest through its display of a sense of creativity and play. It is in all seriousness a strike, but it is also humorous that they use such innovative means of creating image events. Together, these examples show that the activists of the FFF use creativity to challenge the restrictions on physical, large-scale strikes, and where the visual aesthetics represents a young generation that is angry and disappointed with the adult world, but that can mobilize though high-competence, humor, and beautiful aesthetics.

Conclusion: Climate Action When There Is No Time to Grow Up

This chapter analyzes the visual rhetoric of the FFF movement and how it makes use or challenges dominant childhood figurations for the movement's own purposes. The political activism of the young climate protesters radically challenges two childhood figurations: the child as political only in the sense of its future potentiality rather than its present actuality, and the child as lacking in political agency. The discussion indicates a few aspects about the uneven possibilities of staging certain childhood figurations and spectacular imagery: (1) The right to public assembly and public protest. (2) Urbanity: Proximity to the symbolic sites of power indicates the uneven possibilities for rural children and youth to stage spectacular images. (3) Nationality: kids from various countries are charged with the burdens of geopolitical power play. (4) Race and gender: the availability for hegemonic childhood figuration of innocence and a child worthy of protection is not distributed to boys, non-binary children, or children of color in the same way as to white girls. Building on Dyer, we can say that "despite the familiar rhetorical insistence that children are the future," not all children are equal in their possibilities of representing the future. I am not pointing out these inequalities to criticize individual strikers of the FFF, but to suggest that FFF is a global movement unfolding in transnational flows of interactions, where the possibilities of staging image events are uneven. As my analysis show, the activists use various rhetorical strategies to counter these inequalities and to create visually dramatic image events, ranging from humor to competence, from anger to joy, and from mass-demonstrations to small-scale strikes. The FFF movement invites a rethinking of established concepts of political representation and agency, as well what a just division of power between young and old would mean in the face of dangerous climate change.

Acknowledgment This publication is a deliverable of The Seed Box program, which is funded by MISTRA—The Swedish Foundation For Strategic Environmental Research—and Formas—a Swedish Research Council for Sustainable Development.

Notes

1. Problems with Instagram are plenty, most notably that it is not allowed in some very important countries, such as China, which limits the material's global reach. Another key problem is the possibility of surveillance of the activists themselves on these platforms.
2. Instagram's algorithms prioritize certain posts and as a user, it is impossible to get a chronological feed. To remedy these problems, I have gathered my data from each FFF group's wall, which has allowed for chronological data from each group.

3. Afghanistan (fridaysforfuture.afg); Argentina (jovenesporelclimarg); Australia (schoolstrikeforclimate); Bangladesh (fffbangladesh); Brazil (Fridaysforfuturebrasil); Canada (climatestrikecanada); Costa Rica (fridaysforfuture_costarica); Germany (fridaysforfuture.de); India (fridaysforfuture.india); Iraq (fridaysforfuture.iq); Israel (strike4future_israel); Italy (fridaysforfutureitalia); Lebanon (fridaysforfuture.lb); Mauritius (fridaysforfuture.mauritius); Mexico (fridaysforfuturemx); Nigeria (fridaysforfuturenigeria); Peru (fridaysforfutureperu); Romania (fridaysforfutureromania); Russia (fridaysforfuture.russia); Senegal (fff_sn); South Korea (youth4climateaction.kr); Tunisia (Youthforclimatetunisia); Turkey (fridaysforfuture_tr); Uganda (fridays4futureug); UK (youthstrike4climate); and USA (fridaysforfutureusa).
4. An alternative principle could have prioritized criterion 4, which would have given a sample of the biggest and most successful players. I have instead prioritized criteria 1–2 that enable a sample of big and small players globally, and criterion 3, because it captures the self-representation of these groups.
5. I have not seen a quantitative study of the use of emojis in FFF, but nonetheless it is clear that a combination of the green heart and the planet holds a particular place in the aesthetic repertoires of the movement.

References

350.org. (2020). *Profile: Ridhima Pandey, 12, India. Global Climate Strike.* Retrieved October 28, 2020, from https://globalclimatestrike.net/ridhima-pandey-12-india/

Anguelovski, I., & Martínez Alier, J. (2014). The "Environmentalism of the Poor" Revisited: Territory and Place in Disconnected Glocal Struggles. *Ecological Economics, 102*, 167–176.

Bergmann, Z., & Ossewaarde, R. (2020). Youth Climate Activists Meet Environmental Governance: Ageist Depictions of the FFF Movement and Greta Thunberg in German Newspaper Coverage. *Journal of Multicultural Discourses*, 1–24. https://doi.org/10.1080/17447143.2020.1745211

Biswas, T. (2021). Letting Teach: Gen Z as Socio-Political Educators in an Overheated World. *Frontiers in Political Science, 3*. https://doi.org/10.3389/fpos.2021.641609

Börner, S., Kraftl, P., & Giatti, L. L. (2020). Blurring the "-ism" in Youth Climate Crisis Activism: Everyday Agency and Practices of Marginalized Youth in the Brazilian Urban Periphery. *Children's Geographies, 19*, 1–9. https://doi.org/10.1080/14733285.2020.1818057

Boulianne, S., & Theocharis, Y. (2020). Young People, Digital Media, and Engagement: A Meta-Analysis of Research. *Social Science Computer Review, 38*(2), 111–127. https://doi.org/10.1177/0894439318814190

Boyd, D. (2014). *It's Complicated: The Social Lives of Networked Teens*. Yale University Press.
Buttigieg, K., & Pace, P. (2013). Positive Youth Action Towards Climate Change. *Journal of Teacher Education for Sustainability, 15*(1), 15–47.
Castañeda, C. (2002). *Figurations: Child, Bodies, Worlds*. Duke University Press.
Castells, M. (2015). *Networks of Outrage and Hope: Social Movements in the Internet Age*. John Wiley & Sons.
Corner, A., et al. (2015). How Do Young People Engage with Climate Change? The Role of Knowledge, Values, Message Framing, and Trusted Communicators. *WIREs Climate Change, 6*(5), 523–534. https://doi.org/10.1002/wcc.353
Cuervo, H., & Miranda, A. (2019). *Youth, Inequality and Social Change in the Global South*. Springer.
de Castro, L. R. (2020). Why Global? Children and Childhood From a Decolonial Perspective. *Childhood, 27*(1), 48–62. https://doi.org/10.1177/0907568219885379
de Moor, J., et al. (2020). *Protest for a Future II: Composition, Mobilization and Motives of the Participants in Fridays for Future Climate Protests on 20–27 September, 2019, in 19 Cities Around the World*. Gothenburg. Retrieved August 17, 2020, from https://gup.ub.gu.se/publication/290509
DeLuca, K. M. (2012). *Image Politics: The New Rhetoric of Environmental Activism*. Routledge.
Dyer, H. (2019). *The Queer Aesthetics of Childhood: Asymmetries of Innocence and the Cultural Politics of Child Development*. Rutgers University Press.
Fisher, S. R. (2016). Life Trajectories of Youth Committing to Climate Activism. *Environmental Education Research, 22*(2), 229–247. https://doi.org/10.1080/13504622.2015.1007337
Foran, J., Gray, S., & Grosse, C. (2017). "Not yet the end of the world": Political Cultures of Opposition and Creation in the Global Youth Climate Justice Movement. *Interface: A Journal for and About Social Movements, 9*(2), 353–379.
Glinski, S. (2019). Fridays for Future Afghanistan: Combating Climate Change in a War Zone. *The National*, 25 December. Retrieved October 28, 2020, from https://www.thenationalnews.com/world/mena/fridays-for-future-afghanistan-combating-climate-change-in-a-war-zone-1.953935
Han, K. (2020). Climate Change Activists Test Strict Singapore Protest Laws. *Al Jazeera*, 10 April. Retrieved October 28, 2020, from https://www.aljazeera.com/news/2020/4/10/climate-change-activists-test-strict-singapore-protest-laws
Haunss, S., & Sommer, M. (2020). *Fridays for Future—Die Jugend gegen den Klimawandel: Konturen der weltweiten Protestbewegung*. transcript Verlag.
Hayward, B. (2020). *Children, Citizenship and Environment: #SchoolStrike Edition*. Routledge.
Hesford, W. (2011). *Spectacular Rhetorics: Human Rights Visions, Recognitions, Feminisms*. Duke University Press.

Higonnet, A. (1998). *Pictures of Innocence: The History and Crisis of Ideal Childhood*. Thames and Hudson.

Jenkins, H. (2009). *Confronting the Challenges of Participatory Culture: Media Education for the 21st Century*. The MIT Press. Retrieved April 20, 2021, from https://library.oapen.org/handle/20.500.12657/26083

Kang, J. (2016). *Igniting the Internet: Youth and Activism in Postauthoritarian South Korea*. University of Hawaii Press.

Kimball, G. (2021). *Climate Girls Saving Our World*. Equality Press.

Lee, K., et al. (2020). Youth Perceptions of Climate Change: A Narrative Synthesis. *WIREs Climate Change, 11*(3), e641. https://doi.org/10.1002/wcc.641

Lee, N. (2013). *Childhood and Biopolitics: Climate Change, Life Processes and Human Futures*. Springer.

Lombana-Bermudez, A. (2015). Re-thinking Youth Participation and Civic Engagement in the Digital Age. In U. Gasser & S. Cortesi (Eds.), *Digitally Connected: Global Perspectives on Youth and Digital Media* (pp. 88–91). Berkman Center Research Publication.

Martiskainen, M., et al. (2020). Contextualizing Climate Justice Activism: Knowledge, Emotions, Motivations, and Actions Among Climate Strikers in Six Cities. *Global Environmental Change, 65*, 102180. https://doi.org/10.1016/j.gloenvcha.2020.102180

Muthoni Mwaura, G. (2018). "Professional Students Do Not Play Politics": How Kenyan Students Professionalise Environmental Activism and Produce Neoliberal Subjectivities. In S. Pickard & J. Bessant (Eds.), *Young People Re-Generating Politics in Times of Crises* (pp. 59–76). Springer International Publishing (Palgrave Studies in Young People and Politics). https://doi.org/10.1007/978-3-319-58250-4_4

Nakata, S. M. (2008). Elizabeth Eckford's Appearance at Little Rock: The Possibility of Children's Political Agency. *Politics, 28*(1), 19–25. https://doi.org/10.1111/j.1467-9256.2007.00306.x

Ritchie, J. (2021). Movement from the Margins to Global Recognition: Climate Change Activism by Young People and in Particular Indigenous Youth. *International Studies in Sociology of Education, 30*(1–2), 53–72. https://doi.org/10.1080/09620214.2020.1854830

Ryalls, E. D., & Mazzarella, S. R. (2021). "Famous, Beloved, Reviled, Respected, Feared, Celebrated": Media Construction of Greta Thunberg. *Communication, Culture and Critique* [Preprint], (tcab006). https://doi.org/10.1093/ccc/tcab006

Spivak, G. C. (1990). *The Post-colonial Critic: Interviews, Strategies, Dialogues*, Psychology Press.

Stevenson, K. T., Peterson, M. N., & Bondell, H. D. (2019). The Influence of Personal Beliefs, Friends, and Family in Building Climate Change Concern Among Adolescents. *Environmental Education Research, 25*(6), 832–845. https://doi.org/10.1080/13504622.2016.1177712

Tanner, T. (2010). Shifting the Narrative: Child-led Responses to Climate Change and Disasters in El Salvador and the Philippines. *Children & Society*, 24(4), 339–351. https://doi.org/10.1111/j.1099-0860.2010.00316.x

Thew, H., Middlemiss, L., & Paavola, J. (2020). "Youth is not a political position": Exploring Justice Claims-Making in the UN Climate Change Negotiations. *Global Environmental Change*, 61, 102036. https://doi.org/10.1016/j.gloenvcha.2020.102036

Thiery, B. W., et al. (2021). Intergenerational Inequities in Exposure to Climate Extremes. *Science*, 374, eabi7339. https://doi.org/10.1126/science.abi7339

Trajber, R., et al. (2019). Promoting Climate Change Transformation with Young People in Brazil: Participatory Action Research Through a Looping Approach. *Action Research* [Preprint]. https://doi.org/10.1177/1476750319829202

Trott, C. D. (2021). What Difference Does It Make? Exploring the Transformative Potential of Everyday Climate Crisis Activism by Children and Youth. *Children's Geographies*, 19, 1–9. https://doi.org/10.1080/14733285.2020.1870663

von Zabern, L., & Tulloch, C. D. (2021). Rebel with a Cause: The Framing of Climate Change and Intergenerational Justice in the German Press Treatment of the Fridays for Future Protests. *Media, Culture and Society*, 43(1), 23–47. https://doi.org/10.1177/0163443720960923

Wahlström, M., et al. (2019). *Protest for a Future: Composition, Mobilization and Motives of the Participants in Fridays For Future Climate Protests on 15 March, 2019 in 13 European Cities*, p. 121.

Wall, J. (2012). Can Democracy Represent Children? Toward a Politics of Difference. *Childhood*, 19(1), 86–100. https://doi.org/10.1177/0907568211406756

Wallis, H., & Loy, L. S. (2021). 'What Drives Pro-environmental Activism of Young People? A Survey Study on the Fridays For Future Movement. *Journal of Environmental Psychology*, 74, 101581. https://doi.org/10.1016/j.jenvp.2021.101581

Watts, J. (2019). Greta Thunberg, Schoolgirl Climate Change Warrior: "Some people can let things go. I can't". *The Guardian*, E-version, 11 March. Retrieved August 25, 2020, from https://www.theguardian.com/world/2019/mar/11/greta-thunberg-schoolgirl-climate-change-warrior-some-people-can-let-things-go-i-cant

Wells, K. (2008). Child Saving or Child Rights. *Journal of Children and Media*, 2(3), 235–250. https://doi.org/10.1080/17482790802327475

Open Access This chapter is licensed under the terms of the Creative Commons Attribution 4.0 International License (http://creativecommons.org/licenses/by/4.0/), which permits use, sharing, adaptation, distribution and reproduction in any medium or format, as long as you give appropriate credit to the original author(s) and the source, provide a link to the Creative Commons licence and indicate if changes were made.

The images or other third party material in this chapter are included in the chapter's Creative Commons licence, unless indicated otherwise in a credit line to the material. If material is not included in the chapter's Creative Commons licence and your intended use is not permitted by statutory regulation or exceeds the permitted use, you will need to obtain permission directly from the copyright holder.

CHAPTER 12

Political Strategies of Self-representation: The Case of Young Afghan Migrants in Sweden

Jonathan Josefsson

INTRODUCTION

The recent mass mobilization of children and youth on issues such as climate change, democracy, racism, labor, peace, and migration has garnered considerable attention in public debate and research. Despite what could be described as an unprecedented international diffusion and institutionalization of children's rights norms in the last decades, we have witnessed a growing unease among young people who have been contesting the regimes under which they are governed and politically represented (Bessant, 2021, p. 1ff; Cummings, 2020; Holzscheiter, 2016; Josefsson & Wall, 2020; Taft, 2019). Yet, while a growing body of scholarship has highlighted how children and youth are subject to systems of governance as much as they can shape these systems (Holzscheiter et al., 2019), still

---

J. Josefsson (✉)
Department of Thematic Studies—Child Studies, Linköping University, Linköping, Sweden
e-mail: jonathan.josefsson@liu.se

© The Author(s) 2023
B. Sandin et al. (eds.), *The Politics of Children's Rights and Representation*, Studies in Childhood and Youth,
https://doi.org/10.1007/978-3-031-04480-9_12

we have scarce empirical knowledge about the actions and strategies that are used by children and youth to claim political representation, how these are shaped by institutional, societal, and cultural contexts, what the political effects of them are, and how we theoretically can make sense of them.

One of the domains in global politics where questions around rights and political representation of children and youth has been particularly pressing is migration. The fact that children constitute one third of the roughly 90 million forcibly displaced persons around the world has not only revealed some of the challenges involved in finding well-functioning systems of governance at national and international level (Bhabha, 2014, 2019), but has also resulted in long-standing political controversies around how and by whom the rights of young non-citizens are represented (Heidbrink, 2016; Josefsson, 2019). In many recipient countries in the Global North, young migrants have contested and refused the ways in which they have been politically represented. By using extra-parliamentary actions such as street protests, mobilizing in social media, and blockades (Corruncer, 2012; Josefsson, 2017, 2019; Nicholls & Fiorito, 2015; Patler & Gonzales, 2015; Rosenberger et al., 2018), children and youth have made what Michael Saward would refer to as 'representative claims' of rights in seeking new forms of political representation (Saward, 2010, 2020).

In this chapter, I explore how children and youth make use of particular *strategies of self-representation* to seek political representation. I do so by taking my point of departure in a group of young Afghan migrants in Sweden and their political mobilization for their right to stay. In dialogue with political theoretical debates around democracy and representation, I examine how young political actors contest and recast dominant regimes of political representation to claim political space and a voice of their own. The focus is put on the ways in which various actors struggle over the authority to represent and give meaning to the interests, rights, and well-being of young migrants, and how these processes of representing children and youth become politically productive. The empirical observations of the mobilizations of young non-citizens against deportations spur more careful investigations into how their strategies of self-representation disrupt current legal and political orders and open up new avenues for political representation. By situating the chapter in a Swedish context of global migration and anti-deportation protests, it aims to present an empirical illustration of and theoretical framework for the study of children and youth strategies of self-representation. It thus contributes to our understanding of politics by and for children and youth in global politics while at the same time offering a vital impetus to the more general theoretical debate around the concept of political representation.

In the first section, I provide an overview of ongoing theoretical debates around the concept of political representation in light of children and youth. In the second section, I focus on global youth migration to elaborate on the governing power of representing rights of young people and how certain forms of representation have become tools for liberal democratic states to exclude and undercut the fundamental rights of young migrants. In the third section, the political mobilization by young Afghan migrants for their right to stay is used to analyze four strategies that I suggest constitute a politics of self-representation: *Rejecting previous forms of representation; establishing, shaping and controlling political identity; creating political space; making opponents and allies.* In the concluding section, I reflect on the limits and potentials of these strategies for contesting dominant regimes of representation and how these strategies can open up spaces for political actions and agendas.

THE POLITICAL REPRESENTATION OF CHILDREN AND YOUTH

The concept of political representation has played a central role in the theory and organization of representative democracies throughout the twentieth century (Disch et al., 2019; Pitkin, 1967, 2004; Runciman, 2007; Saward, 2010). In their struggles for justice, rights, and equality, scholars have been seeking to find effective forms of political representation to ensure the 'continuing responsiveness of the government to the preferences of its citizens' (Dahl, 1971, p. 1; Pitkin, 1967). In recent years, we can note a revitalized theoretical discussion which also, as this chapter suggests, has implications for how we understand political responsiveness as it relates to children and youth. What is referred to as the 'constructive turn' in political theory has rejected a traditional understanding of political representation as a 'transmission of pre-constituted interests' from a constituency via elections and that rests on an understanding where the constituents are logically prior to the representative (Disch et al., 2019; Disch, 2019, p. 7; Saward, 2020). In contrast, it has been argued that political representation must be regarded as a constitutive and mobilizing force that 'facilitates the formation of political groups and identities' (Urbinati, 2006, p. 37) and that 'contribut[es] to the identity of what is represented' (Laclau, 1996, p. 86ff). At the same time, attention has been called to how the political representation of interests and groups also takes place in a broad range of other contexts such as social movements, philanthropic and business networks, NGOs, individual citizens and media that 'mobilize, educate, and aggregate constituent perspectives and interests in the process of representing them' (Disch, 2019, p. 4; see also Brito Vieira, 2017; Saward, 2020). The case of the Afghan youth mobilizing for a right to stay, as analyzed in this chapter, is thus not about political representation in the sense of elections for representatives in parliaments, but is about social movement activism and how the claims of the young people to represent themselves challenge core mechanisms of authorization and accountability beyond territoriality and the traditional institutions of representative democracies (Disch, 2019, p. 9). Building on critical democratic theory, my analysis of these processes is based on an understanding of political representation as 'a space between the representative and the represented' in which children and youth enter in order to disrupt dominant forms of political representation through claims and strategies of self-representation (Disch, 2019; Holzscheiter, 2016; Laclau, 1996, pp. 84–104; Saward, 2010, 2020).

To the dominant strands of political theory, and to most constitutional and institutional constructions of modern democracies, people under a certain age have simply been absent or explicitly excluded from full political citizenship, for instance by consistently being denied the right to vote or to stand for elections (Cummings, 2020; Josefsson, 2016, p. 34ff; Schrag, 1975; Wall, 2012, 2021). Similar restrictions to full political citizenship apply also to non-citizens (Beckman, 2009). In these ways, the group of young migrants in focus here have for long been barred from what are commonly regarded as key instruments of representative democracy by virtue of their ages and citizenships. Instead, political representation of children and youth in representative democracies has been following a distinct path. In the latter part of the twentieth century, we can note an increasing interest in children as citizens and rights subjects (Archard, 1993; James et al., 1998). The civil rights movements and other societal transformations in the 1960s and 1970s were accompanied by the 'discovering' of children and youth as rights holders (Margolin, 1978; Verhellen & Spiesschaert, 1989; see also Sandin's chapter in this volume), which was in turn followed by a global diffusion of children's rights norms following the adoption of the United Nations Convention on the Rights of the Child in 1989 (Hallett & Prout, 2003; Josefsson, 2016, p. 23ff; Reynaert et al., 2012; Vandenhole, 2015). This development forced governments to be legally, morally, and politically responsive, no longer only to the rights and interests of the electorate (i.e., the adult part of the population), but also to the rights and interests of young and underaged citizens (Goddard et al., 2005; Verhellen & Spiesschaert, 1989, p. 1). However, this 'responsiveness' was not based on the granting of political rights to the underaged, but rather on the fact that their rights and interests were being protected by other actors like governmental authorities, and through legislative frameworks.

A new landscape of actor constellations involved in protecting the rights and interests of children resulted in 'new defining features' of the link between the representative and the represented that did not follow the ordinary trajectories of a reciprocal relationship between the elected and the electorate. The political representation of children and youth was carried out through a complex playing field of professionals, NGOs, international organizations, corporations, a plurality of state agencies, families, and certainly, young people themselves (Holzscheiter et al., 2019). Yet, as I will suggest below, the global mainstreaming of children's rights and the emergence of new systems of governance for children and youth also limited what forms of political representation were possible, and turned out to be a productive tool for controlling young people and advancing other political interests and agendas, not least in the field of migration.

The Governing Power of Representing Children and Youth

When the new systems of child rights governance emerged at national and international levels in the latter part of the twentieth century (Holzscheiter et al., 2019; Smith, 2014; Wells, 2011), the political representation of children and youth was reshaped (see e.g., Sandin and Balagopalan in this volume). In the welfare states of the Global North, like Sweden, civil society organizations, political parties, and government-initiated inquiries and legislative processes have resulted in the implementation of new legal provisions, policy frameworks, and the establishment of 'child rights' institutions like national children's ombudspersons and agencies specialized in child protection (Hallett & Prout, 2003; Quennerstedt, 2015; Sandin, 2012). While national and local authorities in areas like education, social services, health, and migration were given the responsibility of implementing new catalogues of rights, inspecting authorities, courts, child ombudspersons, NGOs, and 'child experts' took on the role of representing children and youth by monitoring the implementation processes. These national developments were framed by the period's more general trend of global mainstreaming of human rights (Koskenniemi, 2009).

The mainstreaming of human rights, as was observed by international legal scholar Martti Koskenniemi, meant that a wide range of institutions increasingly came to make use of the concept of human rights in official documents. This mainstreaming opened up the possibility for human rights experts to pronounce whether particular rights were being upheld or violated in 'apparently neutral language' (Koskenniemi, 2009, p. 13), which obviously had implications for political representation of children and youth. Certain actors, organizations, and institutions now claimed the authority to represent the rights of children and youth in the public sphere or vis-á-vis the government. At the same time, the act of representing younger people became a powerful tool for mobilizing constituencies and building narratives to pave the way for various political actions (Hallberg & Sandin, 2021; Holzscheiter, 2016; Peacock, 2014; Wells, 2011). These observations connect to what democratic theorists have discussed as the problematic relationship between rights, representation, and democracy (Pitkin, 2004; Runciman, 2007). Hanna Pitkin notes apparently critically, some three decades after her seminal work 'The Concept of Political Representation' (1967), that '[d]espite repeated efforts to democratize the representative system, the predominant result has been that representation has supplanted democracy instead of serving it. Our governors have become a self-perpetuating elite that rules—or rather, administers—passive or privatized masses of people. The representatives act not as agents of the people but simply instead of them' (Pitkin, 2004, p. 339).

Against this backdrop, the point of analysis for this chapter is not *if* the rights or interests of children and youth are sufficiently implemented or properly transmitted from represented to representative (as has dominated much scholarly work in the field of children's rights, see for example Josefsson, 2016; Quennerstedt, 2013; Reyneart, 2009; Vandenhole, 2015), but rather, an inquiry into *the ways in which various actors and political forces struggle over the authority* to fill rights and interests with meaning, and how claims of representing children and youth become *politically productive*. It is in this context that scholarship on the performativity of representation is helpful for our analysis (Disch, 2019; Holzscheiter, 2016; Laclau, 1996; Saward, 2010, 2020). Holzscheiter noted (2016, p. 207) that, while scholarly focus on representative claims has been particularly productive for the empirical study of governance in a global setting, scholars have been strangely silent on performativity and the 'exclusionary effects of representational power' when it comes to drawing the boundaries between actors with legitimate and illegitimate representative claims (e.g., politicians, state authorities, civil society organizations, professionals, or young people that self-organize) and between citizens and non-citizens (like young migrants).

In this regard, the context of global child and youth migration requires closer examination. Although children's rights frameworks have largely become an integrated part in administrative and legal procedures of child migration, child rights' principles and provisions, such as the best interest of the child, have in fact been a very weak normative force in decision-making and policy, while state interests in restricting immigration has been given more weight (Bhabha, 2019; Josefsson, 2017). In addition, studies demonstrate that rights language and 'protections discourse' have become tools in legal decision-making and political discourse for legitimizing migration governance and undercutting access to fundamental rights of non-citizen children and youth (Andersson, 2012; Josefsson, 2016; Lind, 2019; Stretmo, 2014). Court procedures, evidence requirements, legal doctrines and case law have all been used to limit the conditions for the possibility of giving asylum-seeking children rights, and used to such an extent that deportations are motivated as being in 'their best interest' and with reference to a right to 'family reunification' in their home country (Josefsson, 2017). As a result, the legal and political institutionalization of representing young migrants rights and interests often runs contrary to how young migrants themselves perceive of their rights and best interests, namely, to reside in the recipient country and to access fundamental rights of security, education, a private life, and health (Josefsson, 2019). In political discourse, scholars have forcefully demonstrated how the 'ethically comfortable' public framing of protecting children from trafficking and harm has been a rhetorical device used by officials and politicians to make undocumented migrants appear before welfare authorities, which, in a next step, enabled the enforcement of immigration control and deportation (Andersson, 2012, p. 1255; Lind 2019; Stretmo 2014). In this way, the representation of young migrants' rights has converged into migration governance and a representational politics of domination and exclusion.

Political Strategies of Self-representation: The Case of Young Migrants in Sweden

In late summer 2017, a group of young Afghan migrants started a sit-in strike outside the Swedish Parliament in Stockholm with the goal of stopping all deportations to Afghanistan. In a few days, the group grew to a couple hundred protesters and received considerable attention in leading newspapers and in social media. A couple of years before, in the wake of an increasing number of asylum seekers in 2015/2016, the Swedish government (like other European governments) had taken a range of extraordinary measures to restrict immigration (Stern, 2018). The turn towards a more restrictive immigration regime significantly reduced the chances that 30,000–35,000 young unaccompanied minors that arrived during the period would be granted a residence permit (Swedish Migration Agency 2016). The protest in front of the Swedish parliament became the start of a contentious struggle in the streets, outside detention centers, at airports and in social media to compel the Swedish government and leading politicians to give amnesty for this group. At an early stage, these youths, who called themselves *Ung i Sverige* ('Young in Sweden'), made it clear that the protest was arranged by themselves and that they did not want to be represented by others. They claimed a voice of their own independent from NGOs, networks of professionals, guardians, or the state agencies that traditionally had been representing them.

In the following section, I will explore how the claims and strategies for self-representation turned out to be key for advancing a more radical political agenda. I develop my analysis around four strategies that I suggest constitute a politics of self-representation: *Rejecting previous forms of representation; establishing, shaping and controlling political identity; creating political space; making opponents and allies.* The four strategies should not be seen as an exhaustive list, but rather as a way to outline directions and provide starting points for future studies of the political representation of children and youth.

Rejecting Previous Forms of Representation

A first strategy for establishing self-representation is to refuse or oppose previous forms of representations. For the group of young migrants in the square in front of Parliament, the refusal to be represented by others was, as some of the organizers described it, 'essential to establish a direct link to the Swedish public' and to counter dominant discourses around young Afghans that had been in circulation for some time (interview, 9 October 2018).[1] Evidently, the forms of representation by NGOs, legal representatives, government officials, professional organizations and child ombudspersons had not been sufficient. In an interview for a newspaper, one of the spokespersons stressed that they appreciated the support of other organizations but that they wanted to do this by themselves (Feministiskt perspektiv, 7 August 2017). The distancing from other organizations seemed at the time necessary to create room for political maneuvering and to take control over the identity that was communicated to the Swedish public. The distancing had also obvious internal political functions for the group. At a later point, when I asked one of the organizers about why the claim to represent themselves was so important to them, he explained:

> *There was a distrust among young people. And organizations are not really working [...] We said that from the beginning. That we are a group to represent the young people. We should be close to the young people. We shall represent them. We should be their voice. Like this. We are not going to be a bureaucratic organization that has a lot of paperwork and stuff. In this way, we tried to be closer to the young people and represent them. We said no older Afghans would be among us. And no big organizations from the beginning. We represent ourselves.* (Interview, 9 October 2018)

The quote makes it clear how creating distance from 'bureaucratic' and 'big' organizations as well as 'older Afghans' was a way to demonstrate proximity among group members and build an identity as youth. It was also a way to create credibility internally and 'gather the forces', and to make a claim on the *authority* to represent the group. Through the quote, we can sense what Saward has pointed to before, namely, the close connection between the rejecting of an old and the making of a new representative claim (Saward, 2020, p. 8). If we, as I suggested at the start of this chapter, regard representation as 'a space between the representative and the represented', it is this space that Ung i Sverige entered and claimed. By rejecting previous forms of political representation through internal and external identity work, they made possible a *regrouping*, to use the words of critical democratic theorists (Disch, 2015, p. 490; Laclau, 1996, p. 40). This regrouping served as a political strategy for producing new political subjects, and in so doing, doors were opened to political spaces that had hitherto been closed to them. Historically, the rejection of young people of the ways that they have been politically represented has been a recurrent first step in creating political space and paving the way for new political actions and agendas. School strikes, mass mobilizations in the streets, protests in workplaces, and a variety of more subtle strategies of civil disobedience are just a few examples of how children and youth have been using contentious repertoires (Bessant, 2021; Cummings, 2020; Holzscheiter, 2016; Josefsson & Wall, 2020; Pickard & Bessant, 2018), like many protests movements before them (Tilly & Tarrow, 2015, p. 49ff), to break into the space between the representative and represented.

Establishing, Shaping, and Controlling Identities

If rejecting previous forms of representation, as described above, is an essential first step for children and youth to open up political space, the establishing, shaping, and controlling of group identity serves as a key mechanism for filling this space with representative claims. The group of young Afghan migrants protesting outside the Swedish parliament established an identity at the very start of the sit-in strike by posting a statement at their homepage and Facebook page.

> *We are young in Sweden who moved here from violence and persecution. Many of us came in 2015 and have tried to find a home here. Some go to school and others play soccer in some team, some are dreaming of studying at university and having a safe future. We came here because we had to. You do not choose to flee, to be chased by the Taliban or to be close to losing your life on the Mediterranean. The trip has been very difficult from the start. To grow up under threat in Afghanistan, to be forced to flee on dangerous roads and to come here and realize that we are not welcome after all. Most were born as refugees. But we want security and a future. To make it possible, we must stay and continue to build a life here and build this country more strongly. We are young in Sweden with the hope of having a future.* (Ung i Sverige, 2017b)

The statement illustrates how representing the 'we' provides the backdrop to the problems at stake ('moved here from violence and persecution'), why the group is protesting ('we want security and a future'), and the urgency of the issue ('we came here because we had to… [yet] realize we are not welcome after all'). At the same time, the statement comprises identity markers to create links to the surrounding society by displaying belonging and sameness, the quintessence of the phrase 'we are young in Sweden'.

As the strike continued in time and space, the identity of the group was shaped by a continuous back and forth movement between internal and external performances and claims of representation (Saward, 2020, p. 58). What constituted the core identity of the group, its claims, and the authority of its leadership was contested from within the group as well as from outside the group. About one month after the sit-in strike started, the organizers posted a statement at their Facebook page with the header *Respektera Ung i Sverige* ('Respect Young in Sweden'). In the statement, the leaders of the strike positioned themselves in the context of the attacks and proclaimed what constituted the core identity of the movement.

> *What we do is bigger than most and we are therefore also a target for mistrust, criticism, hatred and coup attempts [...] Above all, we want to ask adults to let us run our strike with your support or completely without you [...] We do not think it is possible to just appeal to politicians and they will give us a residence permit, because they have already heard all the arguments, they have already decided and are not listening. But we can have a broad and sharp movement to stop the deportations to Afghanistan that bring people together widely and that right now makes the government afraid to meet us at all.* (Ung i Sverige, 2017a, 15 September)

This and similar statements of the group illustrate how claims of self-representation require a constant performance and negotiation over representation and identity formation vis-à-vis the state, its agencies, NGOs, and Swedish society, as well as towards its own constituency, the group of young Afghan migrants. The group sought to create an authoritative leadership, which, as Saward notes, if successful, can also create new audiences and political spaces for further mobilization (Saward, 2020, p. 58). The staging of new subjectivities is a way to 'appear' before the public (Arendt, 1958, p. 50–51) as a group that can recast the defining features of representational power and transform the identity of what is represented (Laclau, 1996, p. 98), and, in turn, lay the groundwork for further political claims and actions. We can note how the establishment of a 'we' has also been a central component in current children and youth mobilizations from young workers fighting for decent working conditions to mass mobilizations against racism, police violence, and intergenerational climate injustice (March for our Lives, 2021, Fridays for Future, 2021,

Movimiento de Adolescentes y Niños Trabajadores Hijos de Obreros Cristianos 2021; Black Lives Matter, 2021; see also Buhre, Van Daalen, and Nakata and Bray in this volume). Yet the public appearance of new group identities and the act of regrouping does not come without conflict and is in constant need of negotiation, reformulation, and defense in relation to other actors. Dominant notions of childhood as a condition, sphere, or life phase in need of particular protection has affected the opportunities, and needs, for the reformulation of identities in democratic politics (Bessant, 2020; Goddard et al., 2005; Nakata & Bray, 2020).

Creating (New) Political Space

A third key strategy of self-representation is creating a political space from which one can act and raise claims of representation. This space is physical as well as virtual and symbolic, and from which one can hold other actors accountable, recast dynamics of who is an authoritative representative, and position oneself as a political actor. For *Ung i Sverige*, the struggle over space became essential for the resistance against deportations. As the protests moved between central public places in Stockholm, outside detention centers, airports, schools, and into news reporting and social media, these sites were fundamental for raising the group's claims. These sites were used, for example, for holding leading politicians, the Swedish government, and migration authorities accountable, for approaching political opponents and allies, and for working out the authority of individuals to be credible representatives for this group of young migrants.

One central geographical site was the public square. While the group started the sit-in strike at Mynttorget just outside the Swedish parliament, the local police ordered protesters to move among various central squares of Stockholm. Five days after the strike started, the group called for a press conference at the square Medborgarplatsen ('the citizen square'), about two kilometers from Mynttorget, to make a public statement. This episode illustrates how the physical and symbolic space of the square, similar to many historical protest movements in Stockholm and elsewhere, was used as a platform for creating a political space, a platform from which one could reach out to a wider audience and shape a political agenda. The press conference was covered by the major Swedish news media (Sveriges Television, Svenska Dagbladet, Dagens Nyheter, Expressen) and was live-streamed at the group's Facebook page (11 August 2017) with significant outreach (1400 comments, 3100 likes and 525 shares). At the press conference, the spokesperson Fatemeh Khavari read from a prepared statement in front of cameras and microphones with a couple hundred young Afghan migrants sitting on the stairs behind her. In the statement, which was signed by Ung i Sverige, the protesters first described some of the experiences and obstacles the group had to overcome during the first days of the strike. But the larger part of the statement was devoted to making direct, specific calls and questions to a list of key actors in Swedish society, holding them accountable for not taking their proper responsibility to respond or meet the demands of the group. They detailed the inaction of actors such as the general director and the head of justice at the migration board, to each political party in the parliament and to the Swedish government and Prime Minister Stefan Löfven.

> *On Thursday after five days of strike, representatives from the government Gustav Fridolin, Maria Ferm and Minister of Migration Helene Fritzon arrived. We said welcome, we have been waiting for you. But no one gave us an answer to our demand—to stop the deportations to Afghanistan. Why? Everyone has said that someone else has to do it. Who takes responsibility? Several have said that we are right, that Afghanistan is not safe. Why do you do nothing? [...] You cannot fool us. We know you can stop the deportations to Afghanistan. The Swedish Migration Agency makes assessments of the security situation in other countries. Fredrik Beijer you are the Head of Justice, you can take a legal position on Afghanistan. You've done it before, why can you not do it now? Afghanistan is not safe and your own report states that it will deteriorate. Mikael Ribbenvik you are responsible at the Swedish Migration Agency, how do you guarantee our safety? Politicians you have the power. To stop deportations to Afghanistan, you can grant amnesty to unaccompanied minors. Do not pretend that it is someone else who has the role of pursuing politics in Sweden, it is you who can make political decisions.* (Ung i Sverige, 2017a, 11 August)

By staging this specific event at the public square of Medborgarplatsen and having a significant amount of outreach, Ung i Sverige not only used the square as a platform to (re)present themselves as a group to a wider public, but also started to craft a political space in the Swedish political landscape. As time went on, this space in turn opened room for new actions and political maneuvering. The public square was obviously a key site of political intervention at the start of the strike, but as it developed, other geographical sites in Stockholm and around Sweden like classrooms, detention centers, town halls, streets, and other official buildings were also frequently used for taking political action. Not the least important in this process were the public appearances of the group at these sites combined with making virtual and symbolic political space of greater outreach through the active use of social media. Frequent use of videos, public statements, photos, sharing of news reporting, and scientific reports were some of the tools used to approach opponents and allies, hold authorities accountable, and communicate substantive claims.

While the first two strategies discussed above (rejecting of previous forms of representations and establishing, shaping, and controlling of identities) are critical for paving the way for such political space, a rich catalogue of protest repertoires have been used throughout history by children and youth and in other fields of politics to intervene in preexisting political spaces and to create new ones. Schools, streets, official buildings, neighborhoods, parliaments, commercial buildings, news reporting and social media are just some examples of spaces that recurrently have been used by children and youth for making representative claims and which underlines the centrality of spatial dimensions for the crafting of political representation (Bessant, 2021; Hinton, 2021; Josefsson & Wall, 2020; Pickard & Bessant, 2018; Taft, 2019). Although it has been neglected in much liberal political theory, the critical role of spatiality for citizenship and democratic politics has been previously discussed in studies of citizenship and contentious politics (Isin, 2002; Lindahl, 2013; Mainwaring & Walton, 2018; Tilly & Tarrow, 2015) and in the politics of childhood (Kallio & Häkli, 2011; Skelton, 2013). If we follow Isin's argument that 'space is a condition of being political' and that citizenship is bounded and expressed through various buildings, forums and assemblies (Isin, 2002, p. 3), it appears as if spatiality will remain a key dimension in the study of political representation by and for children and youth.

Making Opponents and Allies

A fourth key strategy of self-representation is to navigate the political landscape by approaching opponents and allies. At an early stage of the protests, Ung i Sverige used public appearances by its members in streets, social media, press conferences, open letters and statements in mainstream media to approach agency officials, individual politicians, fractions of parties or party coalitions, and government representatives to oppose their lack of action and to hold them accountable. By criticizing conflicting positions and acts, Ung I Sverige built the political pressure needed to enable decision-makers to take new directions. In this way, the group entered as a new player into a political playing field comprising a complex set of actors, interests, alliances, agendas, public opinions, and trends that constituted Swedish politics at that particular time. In addition, the group used press conferences and social media to defend itself from counter-protesters. In the early phases of the strike, members of the group were verbally and physically attacked by a right-wing youth organization *Nordisk Ungdom* ('Nordic Youth') (Nordisk Ungdom, 2017; Ung i Sverige, 2017a, 8 August; Expressen, 2017) and by more loosely connected anti-immigrant networks protesting the public presence of Ung i Sverige. These right-wing groups posed a threat to the very existence of Ung i Sverige, as they continually contested the public presence of the group in squares and streets. During these confrontations, the media tactics of Ung i Sverige were to publicly condemn the attacks and fiercely defend its right to assembly by positioning the opposition as 'racists' and 'nazis', as a main enemy and threat. At the same time, group members met physical attacks with nonviolent acts like sitting down, building circles, and countering and contrasting 'hateful' speech by explicitly using a language of love and a heart as a symbol of their struggle (Sydsvenskan, 2017). These confrontations were concrete and at the same time symbolic conflicts around access to and control of public places that manifested a continuum of disputes around claiming space and territory.

The press conference described above and the plethora of political actions and public statements by the group in the following years illustrates how Ung i Sverige developed a sophisticated strategy for approaching party politics. The group pushed the Swedish government for not taking its proper responsibility while simultaneously approaching other political parties in Parliament to build alliances and find support for its cause, for finding a place in the parliamentary agenda, and for proposing new legislation and policy. In its statements it became clear that Ung i Sverige would not accept mere rhetorical support or vague political responses, but sought to force the parties to take a stand on the issues. In Sweden, this period was characterized by political instability because the government was supported by a minority in Parliament and the imminent risk of an extra election made the government dependent on the opposition for approving key decisions. Following a significant increase in the number of asylum applicants in autumn 2015, the government coalition parties and several others were internally torn between the previous, more liberal immigration politics (especially for the group of children and unaccompanied minors) and the current, more restrictive asylum politics. At a press conference, Ung i Sverige started to confront the opposition and what they apparently knew spoke to the parties' ambivalences in their political agendas and different factions.

> *The Liberals have said that deportations to Afghanistan should be stopped. Good, but why do you not support the demand for amnesty? The Center Party wanted at one point to pause the deportations to Afghanistan and at another moment thinks that it is a safe country. What do you want? Give us an answer. The Moderates say nothing to us. Why do you not say anything when we call for help? Why do you let us be sent to death? The Christian Democrats have said that more young Afghans should be allowed to stay. How do you want to make it possible? What are you doing to make it happen?* (Ung i Sverige, 2017a, 11 August)

In its next step Ung i Sverige addressed the government parties (the Green Party and the Social Democrats) and their supporting party (the Left Party).

> *The Green Party says that they do not want to deport us but that they have to because of public opinion in the Riksdag. Are you martyrs or are we the victims of your policies? The Social Democrats say over and over again that it is the Migration Board's decision. Does not Löfven lead this country? Why do you refuse to take responsibility for the consequences of your policies? Why do you not want to grant us amnesty? The Left Party wants to stop deportations to Afghanistan and grant amnesty. You agree with us, but what actions do you take for it? Why are not more of your leaders here?* (Ung i Sverige, 2017a, 11 August)

After a couple months, strategically approaching the political parties through statements and meetings with political representatives, publicly and informally, started to have an effect on activities in Parliament. Even though Parliament never decided on full amnesty for the entire group of up to 35,000 young Afghans that arrived in 2015, the political action of the group propelled a line of debates, legislative proposals, political agreements, and adoption of legislation (Ung i Sverige, 2017a, 28 November; Ung I Sverige 2018, 4 March; 25 April; 7 June).

In addition to approaching opponents, the actions of seeking allies and establishing links in solidarity with other groups in society appeared to be just as important in the strategy of formulating a politics of self-representation. For Ung i Sverige, seeking allies was particularly salient about a month after the sit-in strikes started, when the group launched a new campaign to support other high-profile struggles against injustices in Sweden. Under the banner 'We build the country', the group initiated a series of Sweden-wide protest events in which it bundled together its cause with protests against actions like reduction of assistance to disabled people, closures of rural maternity wards, and the fight to raise pensions (Ung i Sverige, 2017a, 12 September). By naming the campaign 'We build the country' and starting the campaign just outside the headquarters of the Swedish labor movement, the group alluded to a classical labor movement hymn and the fact that popular movements historically have been key for building Swedish society. In addition, Ung i Sverige created alliances with party politicians and with factions of parties and political youth organizations, many times through the sharing of news or statements at its Facebook page. Another way of seeking alliances was to systematically make public lists of NGOs, artists, athletes, teachers and corporations that formally agreed to support the group in their fight against deportations (Ung i Sverige, 2018, 6 June).

The political strategy for approaching opponents and allies is something we encounter in various struggles of children and youth around the world. In this volume, we see examples in the politics of young climate activists (see the chapter in this volume by Buhres), first nation youth against discriminatory policing (see chapter by Nakata and Bray), and in child labor movements (see the chapter by Van Dalen). Central to this strategy is to position the group against unjust political orders and opponents that hold oppressive power, or adversaries that pose a direct threat to the existence of the movement. At the same time, links of solidarity and building of alliances with other parts of society outside one's own group appears to be just as fundamental. This enemy and friend distinction, the agonistic nature of politics, has obviously been ideologically prominent in what constitutes the political in modern political theory (see e.g., Honig, 2003; Mouffe, 2005). However, while these thinkers have mainly regarded children and youth as apolitical (or simply excluded them from analysis), in contrast (and what informs this paper) is the view that children and youth play a constitutive role 'as temporary outsiders who present both renewal and risk to the demos' (Nakata & Bray, 2020), seeming to produce the very conditions for why agonism and the enemy/friend distinction is so central to a politics of childhood and for claims of self-representation of children and youth.

CONCLUSION

This chapter began with the observation that, despite the unprecedented diffusion of human rights and the emergence of new systems of governance for children and youth at the turn of the twenty-first century, we have witnessed growing unease among young people, who have been contesting the regimes under which they are governed on issues such as climate, labor, gun violence, racism, and migration. The analytical focus has been on scrutinizing the ways that various actors and political forces struggle over the authority to fill rights and claims of young people with meaning and how these representations become politically productive. If political representation is conceptualized as 'a space between the representative and the represented', it is in this space that children and youth enter and disrupt dominant regimes of political representation through strategies of self-representation and representative claims. In turn, strategies of self-presentation enable what can be referred to as a *regrouping* (Disch, 2015; Laclau, 1996), to appear as political subjects and open up new avenues for political actions and agendas. The strategies of self-representation can recast logics of where, when, and how political representation take place from a traditional focus on political institutions (party politics, parliaments, elections) to streets, squares, schools, news reporting, and social media. But just as important, and as noted by scholars before, 'to speak on behalf of', to represent, a constituency does not necessarily pave the way for emancipation, democratic inclusion, or the protection of human rights, but certainly works as a means for controlling and administering certain practices and groups (Alcoff, 1991; Pitkin, 2004; Spivak, 1988).

Through the example of a group of young Afghan migrants in Sweden, who started a group called Ung i Sverige, and their political mobilization for a right to stay, I have in this chapter identified and analyzed four key strategies that I suggest constitute a politics of self-representation. A first strategy is *rejecting previous forms of representation*. For the group of young migrants that initiated a sit-in strike at the square in front of the Swedish parliament, the refusal to be represented by others enabled a first step to appear as political subjects, and with that, to open the doors to new political spaces that hitherto had been closed to them. A second strategy is *establishing, shaping, and controlling the identity of the group*. By staging new subjectivities for the public and the appearance of a new 'we', the group could recast the defining features of representational power and transform the identity of who and what was represented. These actions in turn laid the groundwork for further political claims and action. A third strategy is *creating political space* from which a group can act and raise claims of representation. This space exists in physical, virtual, and symbolic senses and was crafted through the use of a rich catalogue of extra-parliamentary protest repertoires and sites such as schools, streets, official buildings, neighborhoods, parliaments, commercial buildings, news reporting, and social media as a means to hold other actors accountable and to position the group as a political actor. A fourth strategy of self-representation is *approaching opponents and allies*. Central to this strategy, as the case of Ung i Sverige illustrates, is positioning the group against unjust political orders and opponents that hold oppressive powers, or that pose direct threat existential threats. At the same time, the strategy seeks to build links of solidarity and alliances with other parts of society outside the group.

For this group of young Afghans, the political strategies of self-representation were needed to disrupt and critique the current regime of democratic and representational politics and to stake out new political routes for redrawing the normative boundaries of inclusion and exclusion (Fraser, 1990; Disch, 2011, 2015; Lindahl 2013). The mobilizations of these young non-citizens against deportations spoke to the need for more careful investigations into how child and youth strategies of self-representation contest current legal and political orders more generally. Their protests exposed a central landscape of representational and democratic politics for children and youth that has largely been neglected by political sociologists and political theorists. The claims and strategies of political self-representation, I suggest, cannot be reduced to a form of politics that is complementary to institutionalized processes of representation through elections, parliaments, government authorities and court systems, as is commonly held in liberal theory (Rawls, 1997), and from which children and youth have largely been excluded. Rather, as the empirical analyses in this chapter has demonstrated, the claims and strategies are situated at the center of politics. In these disruptive forms of politics, strategies of self-representation are a critical component for reconstituting groups (Disch, 2015, p. 490; Laclau, 1996, p. 98) and redefining the conditions under which political representation takes place (Disch, 2019). This view of political representation and politics of childhood contrasts with the global mainstreaming of international law in which focus is put on standard-setting, institutional implementation, and monitoring of well-established legal and political processes. Instead, by shifting our focus to representative claims and strategies of self-representation, we direct the analytical lens to that which disrupts such processes.

Note

1. One salient public discourse at the time depicted young male migrants from Afghanistan as threats, perpetrators who harassed young women in public spaces (Hedlund, 2015; Dagens Nyheter, 11 January 2016).

References

Alcoff, L. (1991). The Problem of Speaking for Others. *Cultural Critique, 20*, 5–32.

Archard, D. (1993). *Children: Rights and Childhood*. Routledge.

Andersson, B. (2012). Where's the Harm in That? Immigration Enforcement, Trafficking and the Protection of Migrants' Rights. *American Behavioral Scientist, 56*(9), 1241–1257.

Arendt, H. (1958). *The Human Condition*. University of Chicago Press.

Beckman, L. (2009). Alienated From the Vote: The Case of Non-Citizens. In *The Frontiers of Democracy*. London: Palgrave Macmillan.

Bessant, J. (2020). From Denizen to Citizen: Contesting Representations of Young People and the Voting Age. *Journal of Applied Youth Studies, 3*, 223–240.

Bessant, J. (2021). *Making-up People: Youth, Truth and Politics*. Taylor & Francis.

Bhabha, J. (2014). *Child Migration and Human Rights in a Global Age*. Princeton University Press.

Bhabha, J. (2019). Governing Adolescent Mobility: The Elusive Role of Children's Rights Principles in Contemporary Migration Practice. *Childhood, 26*(3), 369–385.

Black Lives Matter. (2021). Retrieved October 22, 2021, from https://blacklivesmatter.com/about

Brito Vieira, M. (Ed.). (2017). *Reclaiming Representation: Contemporary Advances in the Theory of Political Representation*. Routledge.

Corruncer, L. (2012). Coming Out of the Shadows: Dream Act Activism in the Context of Global Anti-deportation Sctivism. *Indiana Journal of Global Legal Studies, 19*(1), 143–168.

Cummings, M. (2020). *Children's Voices in Politics*. Peter Lang.

Dagens Nyheter. 2016, January 11. Questions and Answers on DN's Handling of Events in the Kungsträdgården. Retrieved August 12, 2021, from www.dn.se/nyheter/sverige/questions-and-answers-on-dns-handling-of-events-in-the-kungstradgarden/

Dahl, R. (1971). *Polyarchy*. Yale University Press.

Disch, L. (2011). Toward a Mobilization Conception of Democratic Representation. *American Political Science Review, 105*(1), 100–114.

Disch, L. (2015). The "Constructivist Turn" in Democratic Representation: A Normative Dead-End? *Constellations, 22*(4), 487–499.

Disch, L. (2019). Introduction: The End of Representative Politics? In L. Disch, van de S. Mathijs, & N. Urbinati (red.) (Ed.), *The Constructive Turn in Political Representation*. Edinburgh University Press.

Disch, L., van de Sande, M., & Urbinati, N. (Eds.). (2019). *The Constructive Turn in Political Representation*. Edinburgh University Press.

Expressen. 2017, August 8. Flyktingar attackerade under demonstrationen. Retrieved August 12, 2021, from www.expressen.se/nyheter/flyktingar-attackerade-under-demonstration/

Fraser, N. (1990). Rethinking the Public Sphere: A Contribution to the Critique of Actually Existing Democracy. *Social Text, 25*(26), 56–80.

Fridays for Future. (2021). Retrieved October 22, 2021, from https://www.fridaysforfuture.org/what-we-do/who-we-are/

Goddard, J., McNamee, S., & James, A. (Eds.). (2005). *The Politics of Childhood: International Perspectives, Contemporary Developments*. Palgrave Macmillan.

Hallberg, M., & Sandin, B. (2021). Pictured Political Projects: Sunshine Over a Welfare State in the Shadow of War. *Journal of the History of Childhood and Youth, 14*(1), 85–112.

Hallett, C., & Prout, A. (Eds.). (2003). *Hearing the Voices of Children: Social Policy for a New Century*. Routledge.

Hedlund, D. (2015). "Beard boys": Standing in the Way of a Transformation of the Self. In C. Hällgren, E. Dunkels, & G. M. Frånberg (Eds.), *Invisible Boy: The Making of Contemporary Masculinities*. Umeå University.

Heidbrink, L. (2016). *Migrant Youth, Transnational Families, and the State Care and Contested Interests*. University of Pennsylvania Press.

Hinton, E. (2021). *America on Fire: The Untold History of Police Violence and Black Rebellion Since the 1960s*. Liveright.

Honig, B. (2003). *Democracy and the Foreigner*. Princeton: Princeton University Press.

Holzscheiter, A. (2016). Representation as Power and Performative Practice: Global Civil Society Advocacy for Working Children. *Review of International Studies, 42*(2), 205–226.

Holzscheiter, A., Josefsson, J., & Sandin, B. (2019). Child Rights Governance: An Introduction. *Childhood, 26*(3), 271–288.

Isin, E. F. (2002). *Being Political: Genealogies of Citizenship*. University of Minnesota Press.

James, A., Jenks, C., & Prout, A. (1998). *Theorizing Childhood*. Polity Press.

Josefsson, J. 2016. *Children at the Borders*, Dissertation, Linköping University.

Josefsson, J. (2017). Children's Rights to Asylum in the Swedish Migration Court of Appeal. *The International Journal of Children's Rights, 25*(1), 85–113.

Josefsson, J. (2019). Non-citizen Children and the Right to Stay: A Discourse Ethical Approach. *Ethics & Global Politics, 12*(3), 32–49.

Josefsson, J., & Wall, J. (2020). Empowered Inclusion: Theorizing Global Justice for Children and Youth. *Globalizations, 17*(6), 1043–1060.

Kallio, K. P., & Häkli, J. (2011). Are There Politics in Childhood? *Space and Polity, 15*(1), 21–34.

Koskenniemi, M. (2009). The Politics of International Law – 20 Years Later. *The European Journal of International Law, 20*(1), 7–19.

Laclau, E. (1996). *Emancipation(s)*. Verso.

Lindahl, H. (2013). *Fault Lines of Globalization: Legal Order and the Politics of A-Legality*. Oxford University Press.

Lind, J. (2019). Governing Vulnerabilised Migrant Childhoods Through Children's Rights. *Childhood, 26*(3), 337–351.

Mainwaring, C., & Walton, R. M. (2018). Governing Migration from the Margins. *Social & Legal Studies, 27*(2), 131–141.

March for Our Lives. (2021). Retrieved October 22, 2021, from https://www.marchforourlives.com/mission-story/

Mouffe, C. (2005). *On the Political*. Routledge.

Margolin, C. R. (1978). Salvation Versus Liberation: The Movement for Children's Rights in a Historical Context. *Social Problems, 25*(4), 441–452.

Movimiento Latinoamericano y del Caribe de Niñas, Niños y Adolescentes Trabajadores (MOLACNAT). (2021). ('Latin American and Caribbean Movement of Working Children and Adolescents'). Retrieved October 22, 2021, from http://www.molacnats.com/

Nakata, S., & Bray, D. (2020). The Figure of the Child in Democratic Politics. *Contemporary Political Theory, 19*(1), 20–37.

Nicholls, W., & Fiorito, T. (2015). Dreamers Unbound: Immigrant Youth Mobilizing. *New Labor Forum, 24*(1), 86–92.

Nordisk Ungdom. (2017). Film: Motdemonstration på Mynttorget. Retrieved August 12, 2021, from http://www.nordiskungdom.com/film-motdemonstration-pa-mynttorget/

Patler, C., & Gonzales, R. G. (2015). Framing Citizenship: Media Coverage of Anti-deportation Cases Led by Undocumented Immigrant Youth Organisations. *Journal of Ethnic and Migration Studies, 41*(9), 1453–1474.

Pickard, S., & Bessant, J. (Eds.). (2018). *Young People Re-generating Politics in Times of Crises*. Palgrave Macmillan.

Pitkin, H. F. (1967). *The Concept of Representation*. University of California Press.

Pitkin, H. F. (2004). Representation and Democracy: Uneasy Alliance. *Scandinavian Political Studies, 27*(3), 335–342.

Peacock, M. (2014). *Innocent Weapons: The Soviet and American Politics of Childhood in the Cold War*. Chapel Hill: The University of North Carolina University Press.

Quennerstedt, A. (2013). Children's Rights Research Moving into the Future – Challenges on the Way Forward. *The International Journal of Children's Rights, 21*(2), 233–247.

Quennerstedt, A. (2015). Mänskliga rättigheter som värdefundament, kunskapsobjekt och inflytande: en läroplansanalys. *Utbildning & Demokrati, 24*(1), 5–27.

Rawls, J. (1997). *The Law of Peoples: With 'The idea of public reason revisited'*. Harvard University Press.

Reynaert, D., Bie, M. B., & Vandevelde, S. (2009). A review of children's rights literature since the adoption of the United Nations Convention on the Rights of the Child. Childhood: *A Global Journal of Child Research, 16*(4), 518–534.

Reynaert, D., Bie, M. B., & Vandevelde, S. (2012). Between 'believers' and 'opponents': Critical discussions on children's rights. *The International Journal of Children's Rights, 20*(1), 155–168.

Rosenberger, S., Stern, V., & Merhaut, N. (eds.). (2018). *Protest Movements in Asylum and Deportation*. IMISCOE Research Series. https://doi.org/10.1007/978-3-319-74696-8

Runciman, D. (2007). The Paradox of Political Representation. *Journal of Political Philosophy, 15,* 93–114.

Sandin, B. (2012). Children and the Swedish Welfare State: From Different to Similar. In P. Fass & M. Grossberg (Eds.), *Reinventing Childhood After World War II*. Pennsylvania University Press.

Saward, M. (2010). *The Representative Claim*. Oxford University Press.

Saward, M. (2020). *Making Representations: Claim, Counterclaim and the Politics of Acting for Others*. Rowman & Littlefield.

Schrag, F. (1975). The Child's Status in the Democratic State. *Political Theory, 3*(4), 441–457.

Skelton, T. (2013). Young People, Children, Politics and Space: A Decade of Youthful Political Geography Scholarship 2003–13. *Space and Polity, 17*(1), 123–136.

Smith, K. (2014). *The Government of Childhood: Discourse, Power and Subjectivity*. Palgrave Macmillan.

Spivak, G. C. (1988). Can the Subaltern Speak? In C. Nelson & Grossberg l. (Eds.), *Marxism and the Interpretation of Culture* (pp. 21–78). University of Illinois Press.

Stretmo, L. (2014). *Governing The Unaccompanied Child – Media, Policy and Practice*. Doctoral dissertation at the Department of Sociology and Work Science, University of Gothenburg, Gothenburg.

Stern, R. (2018). Proportionate Or Panicky? On Developments in Swedish and Nordic Asylum Law in Light of the 2015 "refugee crisis". In E. Karageorgiou & V. Stoyanova (Eds.), *The New Asylum and Transit Countries in Europe During and in the Aftermath of the 2015/2016 Crisis* (pp. 233–262). Brill Academic Publishers.

Swedish Migration Agency (Migrationsverket). (2016). *Inkomna ansökningar om asyl*. Retrieved October 22, 2021, from http://www.migrationsverket.se/Om-Migrationsverket/Statistik.html

Sydsvenskan. (2017, August 21). Att hata andra är inte att stå upp för Sverige. Retrieved October 22, 2021, from www.sydsvenskan.se/2017-08-21/att-hata-andra-ar-inte-att-sta-upp-for-sverige

Taft, K. J. (2019). *The Kids Are in Charge: Activism and Power in Peru's Movement of Working Children*. New York University Press.

Tilly, C. & Tarrow, S. (2015). *Contentious Politics*. New York: Oxford University Press.

Ung i Sverige. (2017a). Retrieved October 22, 2021, from www.ungisverige.nu

Ung i Sverige. (2017b). Retrieved October 22, 2021, from http://www.facebook.com/ungisverige.nu

Urbinati, N. (2006). *Representative Democracy: Principles and Genealogy*. University of Chicago Press.

Vandenhole, W. (2015). Children's Rights from a Legal Perspective: Children's Rights Law. In E. Vandenhole, E. Desmet, D. Reynaert, & S. Lembrechts (Eds.), (pp. 27–42). *Routledge International Handbook of Children's Rights Studies*, Routledge.

Verhellen, E., & Spiesschaert, F. (Eds.). (1989). *Ombudswork for Children*. Acco Academic Publishing Company.

Wall, J. (2012). Can Democracy Represent Children? Towards a Politics of Difference. *Childhood, 19*(1), 86–100.

Wall, J. (2021). *Give Children the Right to Vote: On Democratizing Democracy*. Bloomsbury Academic.

Wells, K. (2011). The Politics of Life: Governing Childhood. *Global Studies of Childhood, 1*(1), 15–25.

Open Access This chapter is licensed under the terms of the Creative Commons Attribution 4.0 International License (http://creativecommons.org/licenses/by/4.0/), which permits use, sharing, adaptation, distribution and reproduction in any medium or format, as long as you give appropriate credit to the original author(s) and the source, provide a link to the Creative Commons licence and indicate if changes were made.

The images or other third party material in this chapter are included in the chapter's Creative Commons licence, unless indicated otherwise in a credit line to the material. If material is not included in the chapter's Creative Commons licence and your intended use is not permitted by statutory regulation or exceeds the permitted use, you will need to obtain permission directly from the copyright holder.

CHAPTER 13

Political Representation of Aboriginal and Torres Strait Islander Youth in Australia

Sana Nakata and Daniel Bray

INTRODUCTION

Proportionally, we are the most incarcerated people on the planet. We are not an innately criminal people. Our children are alienated from their families at unprecedented rates. This cannot be because we have no love for them. And our youth languish in detention in obscene numbers. They should be our hope for the future.—*Uluru Statement from the Heart, 2017*

On the continent now known as 'Australia', Aboriginal and Torres Strait Islander[1] children represent the descendants of the world's longest, continuing civilisation. These children have inherited a deep past and a highly uncertain yet hopeful future. The words that open this chapter were read

---

S. Nakata (✉)
School of Social and Political Sciences, The University of Melbourne, Melbourne, VIC, Australia
e-mail: snakata@unimelb.edu.au

D. Bray
Department of Politics, Media and Philosophy, La Trobe University, Melbourne, VIC, Australia
e-mail: D.Bray@latrobe.edu.au

© The Author(s) 2023
B. Sandin et al. (eds.), *The Politics of Children's Rights and Representation*, Studies in Childhood and Youth,
https://doi.org/10.1007/978-3-031-04480-9_13

out loud for the first time on 26 May 2017 as part of the *Uluru Statement from the Heart* (National Constitutional Convention, 2017). This statement was crafted at the National Constitutional Convention involving 1200 Aboriginal and Torres Strait Islander delegates who gathered to discuss recognition of Indigenous peoples in the Australian Constitution. It agreed on recommendations for a constitutionally enshrined Voice to Parliament, and a Makarrata[2] Commission to facilitate treaty-making and processes for truth-telling. Despite the high level of consensus in the six-month long deliberative process that preceded the Convention, conservative Liberal-National governments responded by dismissing any prospect of constitutional reform (*Response to Referendum Council's report on Constitutional Recognition*, 2017). The election of a Labor government in May 2022, five years after the Uluru Statement, has seen the federal government commit for the first time to a constitutional referendum, and establishment of a Makarrata Commission. As of publication, the language of the referendum question and a referendum date yet to be announced.

This long and uncertain path toward a constitutionally protected mechanism for Indigenous representation to the Commonwealth of Australia, is a product of historical and mainstream narratives that depict the lives of Indigenous people as deficient (Walter, 2010; Walter, 2016) and a history of population management policies that prioritise government interventions in childhood, including removing Indigenous children from their families (see Davis, 2019; Dunstan et al., 2019). Indeed, Aboriginal and Torres Strait Islander people have often been characterised as a primitive, uncivilised peoples who belong to the past and not the future. It is within this deficit discourse that Aboriginal and Torres Strait Islander children have become represented within the Australian policy-making landscape as a problem to be solved rather than a source of democratic potential and renewal (Nakata, 2018). As will become evident in this chapter, the focus on deficits tends to ignore the representations that Indigenous peoples, globally and within Australia, have always made in resisting and responding to the violence of colonization. Indigenous people have never been passive and agentless subjects of colonial power. Their histories are fuelled by resistance, political strategy, and sustained kinship systems that bond them to one another despite generations of intervention into family life. Aboriginal peoples and Torres Strait Islanders have always been the makers of the future in Australia, even (and especially) during the period of violent oppression that has been experienced since colonization. This future-making necessarily occurs within a complex apparatus of power in which Aboriginal and Torres Strait Islander people, and especially children, have limited capacity to affect political decision-making. And yet, Aboriginal and Torres Strait Islander people continue to work in careful, strategic, and diverse ways to give effect to the futures they imagine for themselves.

The Australian government's suppression of Indigenous self-representation is the political context in which this chapter examines the political claims made by Aboriginal and Torres Strait Islander young people. Our central argument is that the transformative potential of these representations is deliberatively foreclosed through the infantilization of all Indigenous people as children of the colonial state who can never grow up. This infantilization serves to undermine claims that Indigenous children can be a source of democratic renewal and strengthens representations of them as a risk to the *demos*. In order to make this argument, we first outline our theorisation of children as constitutive of the political realm, despite formal modes of exclusion, which represent both risk and renewal to the *demos* (Bray & Nakata, 2020). Second, we contextualise this work by considering the modern and colonial context of childhood and the function of a child/human binary (Rollo, 2018) that enables the infantilization of Indigenous peoples. Third, we turn to contemporary examples in Australian politics that exemplify representations of Aboriginal and Torres Strait Islander children as a source of risk and renewal to democratic life. We demonstrate the salience of risk by considering both the treatment of Dylan Voller at the Don Dale Youth Detention Centre in the Northern Territory in 2016 and the more recent case of a youth curfew policy proposed in the late weeks of the Queensland 2020 state election.

We argue that these contemporary debates represent a historical continuity from first contact in which representations of Aboriginal and Torres Strait Islander children are used and contested in the ongoing process of 'settling' colonial Australia. While our empirical analysis is specific to the continent of Australia, we sustain a theorisation of childhood that adds to critical scholarship on racialized and colonised children globally (Alanamu et al., 2018; Alexander, 2016; Balagopalan, 2014; Hinton, 2021; Meiners, 2016). As this theorisation of childhood reveals, efforts to exclude Indigenous peoples and their children from democratic politics out of fear of the risks they pose to the polity restricts their transformative potential in renewing democracy over successive generations. And yet, as we will argue, representations made by Aboriginal and Torres Strait Islander young people about their futures have important transformative potential in shaping Australian politics.

THEORISING CHILDHOOD AS RISK AND RENEWAL TO THE *DEMOS*

Our approach to the politics of childhood is centred on the role of children as new individuals that must remake democratic life. We undertake this approach as political theorists trained in the Western tradition, taking the view that democracy is conceived as an unfinished project in which freedom and plurality must be continually regenerated in response to new social conditions. As John Dewey (2008, p. 299) puts it: 'Every generation has to accomplish democracy over again for itself…its very nature, its essence cannot be handed from one person to another, but has to be worked out in terms of the needs, problems and conditions of social life'. The political socialisation and education of children is therefore at the heart of the collective task of regenerating democracy. While temporarily excluded from formal politics, we argue that children nevertheless constitute democracy through their appearance as future adult citizens that are indispensable to imagining and realising democratic futures. Because they are constituents of an unknown future polity, children are represented in a wide range of political debates where competing idealisations of democratic society are at stake.

From this perspective, the politics of childhood is grounded in the ontological presence of children as *new citizens with indeterminate potential* (Bray & Nakata, 2020). The children that are born into the world are new and unique individuals and, as such, have the potential to initiate new action that interrupts and alters existing political cultures, norms and institutions. From the moment of birth, children literally embody new possibilities for politics. As perennial newcomers, they 'produce an unending stream of automatic and singular interruptions to the world that create new possibilities for action', against which existing institutions and laws intended to bound politics 'can never reliably withstand the onslaught with which each new generation must insert itself' (Arendt, 1958, p. 9, 191). For Hannah Arendt (1958, p. 247), this human individuality is necessary for sustaining democratic freedom and plurality because it brings forth diverse individuals capable of new beginnings no matter the extent of political socialisation or oppression. Yet, this same radical potential of children poses inherent challenges to the established democratic order, which must maintain a relatively stable set of norms and institutions through which politics can be conducted. Hannah Arendt struggled with and never fully resolved this tension in her work. We have previously argued that this tension produces a special challenge for democracy to strike a balance between an *openness* to the new required to harness each child's potential for originality and initiative in response to changing social conditions, and a *closure* in political norms and institutions that can sustain collective values and protect the existing democratic order against the constant influx of new individuals (Bray & Nakata, 2020, p. 25).

Based on this theorisation, a central facet of democratic politics involves the unending task of conditioning and representing children during their period of temporary exclusion from the formal political realm. As part of this upbringing, the newness of children is disciplined and steered toward a future adult-subject that must be educated to intelligibly operate within a desired (democratic) political order. This simultaneous presence and absence of children (as temporary outsiders that constitute a democratic future) means that the political representation of childhood and children is a central dynamic of democratic politics (Bray & Nakata, 2020). We can see the constitutive effects of representations of children and the ways in which they are used and contested for political purposes in a range of debates and decision-making institutions where the normative fabric of society is at stake. Below, we demonstrate this with respect to representations about Aboriginal and Torres Strait Islander children. However, such constitutive effects of representation have also been established in numerous other contexts, including child migration (Josefsson, 2017), environmental politics (Hayward, 2012) and international rights and governance (Holzscheiter et al., 2019). Our undertaking here is to strengthen our understanding of the politics of childhood by taking seriously the experience of Indigenous children in political life. Across a range of normative contests, competing representations of children and childhood struggle for influence in order to achieve present political objectives that shape the future. And that this takes place in distinct and specific ways for Indigenous children.

Children are at the heart of this representative politics because their indeterminate political potential means they present both risk and renewal to the *demos*. In this sense, they can be represented as holding either fear or hope for democracy to come. Their newness brings forth different forms of subjectivity and action that can challenge and reshape old political frontiers in both threatening and progressive ways. In terms of *risk*, children can be characterised as potential adversaries that prefigure new bases of conflict and radical opposition to the interests, institutions and imagined futures of older generations (Bray & Nakata, 2020, pp. 33–34). We argue in the examples below that this figure of the child as a source of risk to the *demos* is especially evident in representations of Aboriginal and Torres Strait Islander young people. The diverse, unpredictable and ultimately threatening possibilities that arise from the existence of children representing different races, classes, ethnicities, gender identities etc. are posed as risks to the existing normative scope of political futures (Hinton, 2021; Stewart, 2019).

Yet, as indicated above, children are also a social group essential to *renewing* democracy across successive generations in order to meet the different conditions, needs and interests of the changing polity. As new individuals born into an old world, the interests and experiences of children are unique and as such they embody new possibilities for improving democracy and its capacity to address social problems. In this sense, democratic societies must avoid foreclosing capacities for critical inquiry, innovation and political action that are required to regenerate freedom and plurality in a new social context. Preserving the radical potential of children is vital to both guarding against social homogenisation and authoritarian politics that is ultimately fatal to democratic life, and also to overcoming the problems of democracy and transforming it for new social conditions. From this perspective, children can be represented as figures of renewal and hope or as figures of risk and threat, and this representative terrain impacts on policy debates across a range of sites (Hallberg & Sandin, 2021; Lee-Koo, 2011; Pruitt, 2021).

Childhood in Colonial Contexts: The Infantilization of Indigenous Peoples

The above theorisation presents a broad and ahistorical outline of the transformative potential of children's representation grounded in Western political thought. However, by contextualizing our conceptualization of the 'child' that figures in this theorization, we can further illuminate what is at stake for Indigenous children in these forms of representative politics. As Zhao argues, childhood 'is often a reflection of the constructors rather than a reflection of children themselves' (Zhao, 2011, p. 241). Zhao wants to understand the relationship between the construction of the modern subject and the child, arguing that 'modern constructions of childhood have constructed children in the category of the other. Children are consigned with other groups of "deficiency" for whom different treatment is warranted' (Zhao, 2011, p. 254). He makes an exception for modern constructions of childhood that emphasize active growth, but is still cautious due to concern that 'even in this construct, the child's agency and voice are systematically undermined by the hidden agenda of social control' (Zhao, 2011, p. 254).

In a similar vein, more recent work helps further our understanding of the relationship between modernity and childhood in a manner that is specifically useful for racialized and Indigenous contexts. In Toby Rollo's theorisation of childhood, race and Indigeneity are not subcategories of an already-determined category of 'child' but rather an outcome of a preceding child/human binary that aligns the child with the Other. He writes that 'the idea of a *telos* of progress from animal child to human adult is both a historical and conceptual antecedent of the idea of European civilisation, prefiguring its stories about maturation and progress from cultural ignorance to enlightenment' (Rollo, 2016, p. 61). Furthermore, Erica Meiners, writing in the context of child criminalization in the United States, provides historical examples demonstrating how '[d]emocracy required both consent and adulthood, and, therefore, also nonconsent and nonadulthood. Racialized from inception, childhood concurrently shaped forms of association and life beyond the figure of the adult and the child' (Meiners, 2016, p. 34). Whether race is theorised as a precedent or antecedent to the category of child, this work highlights the interrelationship between boundaries of race and boundaries of age, and it becomes possible to see more clearly how modernity and coloniality comes to position Indigenous peoples (and other racialized groups) as *infantilized* subjects (Nakata, 2018; see also Vallgårda, 2015).

It is well established that Indigenous peoples have long been dehumanised. Historically, this dehumanisation was achieved through theories of evolution grounded in Social Darwinism and eugenics which figured the Indigenous person as 'primitive' and closer to animals on a scale of evolutionary development to white Europeans. In the Torres Strait Islands, for example, it was reported that:

> 'The islanders [sic] have not yet reached the state where they are competent to think and provide for themselves; they are really overgrown children, and

can be best managed, for their own welfare, as a prudent parent would discipline his family.' (1915 Queensland State Government Protector's Report quoted in Nakata, 2007, p. 129)

Even at the point that Indigenous peoples are able to be seen as *human*, the subjugation of Indigenous peoples' and the paternalistic frameworks that have governed and regulated life and movement has long been predicated upon this infantilized status: lacking the maturity, autonomy and the rational capacities sufficient to be extended any rights (Nakata, 2015, p. 21). Given these assumptions, the argument for a more respected and protected civil and political status is built upon the demonstration of our 'rational' capacities, which in practice underpins paternalistic and assimilationist policies that align the 'fully developed' and the 'rational' with the European.

Thus, the relationship of the Indigenous person to state is that of the *child* of the state. More than a paternalistic relationship, however, which retains some possibility for 'growing up', the Indigenous adult is infantilized: constructed as a child that can never grow up. It is in this context that we can understand the infantilization of Indigenous peoples as a logic that arises in the very formation of modernity itself. This is not simply a conceptual claim; an examination of Enlightenment liberal philosophers such as John Locke, Jean-Jacques Rousseau and others reveals that they emphasize the necessity of rational adult citizens to the project of modernity and democracy (see Nakata, 2015). In *On Liberty*, John Stuart Mill is careful to place conditions on the recognition of an individual's freedoms:

'It is, perhaps hardly necessary to say that this doctrine is meant to apply only to human beings in the maturity of their faculties. We are not speaking of children, or of young persons below the age which the law may fix as that of manhood or womanhood'. (Mill, 2011, p. 22)

Excluded alongside children in this very same passage are 'barbarians' and 'consideration [of] those backward states of society in which the race itself may be considered as in its nonage' (Mill, 2011, p. 23). That is, the 'primitive' races of Indigenous peoples around the globe are excluded from Mill's theorisation of sovereignty and individual freedom because those very races are childlike (nonage).

With this in mind, it is possible revisit the policy contexts—historical and contemporary—that shape Aboriginal and Torres Strait Islander peoples' lives on this continent and see how the logic of infantilization informs the transformative potential of Aboriginal and Torres Strait Islander young peoples' representation in public and political debates. Representation has both a discursive role in making, receiving and accepting/rejecting representative claims (Saward, 2010), as well as an institutional role in structuring political power and distributing the right to represent and make decisions about one's own interests. While social norms and recognition of civil, cultural and political rights have transformed markedly in the twentieth century, we argue that the infantilized Indigenous subject remains present in some contemporary colonial contexts. Most significantly, we argue that this colonial figure of the Indigenous child, as one who never grows up, operates to strengthen representations of Aboriginal and Torres Strait Islander children as a source of risk to the *demos*. As we demonstrate below, this severely limits the transformative potential of representations of Aboriginal and Torres Strait Islander children by undermining their claims to be a source of democratic renewal.

Representing Aboriginal and Torres Strait Islander Children as Sources of Risk

This section considers how Aboriginal and Torres Strait Islander children are represented as *risks* to the demos in the context of two public controversies: the overincarceration of Indigenous children and young people; and election campaign proposals for youth curfews in the Queensland towns of Cairns and Townsville. Across both these cases, representations of children as a source of risk are focused on sites of criminalisation, and are consistent with literature on criminality and childhood in both contexts of moral panics and race (Bernstein, 2011; James & Jenks, 1996; Meiners, 2016; Nakata, 2015). The cases below demonstrate the representation of young Aboriginal and Torres Strait Islander people as sources of risk, but also involve representations of their parents as inadequately equipped to usher their children in adulthood.

In Australia, the most recent national level data (June 2020) shows that 48% of all young people in youth detention on any given night are Aboriginal and/or Torres Strait Islander young people despite representing just 6% of the national population aged between 10–17 (Australian Institute of Health and Welfare, 2021, p. 3) On any given night, the children detained in the Northern Territory are most likely to be all Aboriginal.

This overrepresentation is attributed to the same factors of Indigenous overincarceration generally; that is, greater police contact rather than higher crime rates. For young people, this contact can arise as a result of school disengagement, poverty and homelessness, or residing in out-of-home care. These factors all reflect sites of systemic inequity and injustice in which historical conditions continue to shape contemporary experiences.

It is in this context that the significance of the 2016 reporting by the public, national broadcaster Australian Broadcasting Corporation (ABC) of the mistreatment of a number of teenagers at the Don Dale Youth Detention Centre in Darwin is to be understood. There were no especially notable events leading up to the exposure of alleged human rights breaches that might have acted as a catalyst for either the events within Don Dale, or the impact of the Four Corners reporting itself. In an episode titled, 'Australia's Shame' (2016), the national broadcaster ABC's Four Corners program broadcast footage taken between 2010 and 2015 that included the stripping, hooding and use of teargas on teenage detainees, all of whom were Aboriginal. Graphic video footage was broadcast as evidence of the brutalization of these young people, and the morning after the program aired the then Prime Minister, Malcolm Turnbull, announced a Royal Commission into the Detention and Protection of Children in the Northern Territory. This announcement was made despite the fact that numerous other reviews and reports into the detention system in the Northern Territory had already taken place, including the 2012 Northern Territory's Children's Commissioner Howard Bath's report into the sustained maltreatment of Dylan Voller which had remained secret for two years. These reports included the previous identification of 21 significant incidents at Don Dale Youth Detention Centre, which included one report of detainee assault on staff and five reports of staff assaults on detainees.

Kate Fitz-Gibbon undertook a media analysis of coverage following the Don Dale controversy, analysing 281 news articles between 2012 and 2016 (Fitz-Gibbon, 2018, p. 104). It demonstrates that the Four Corners episode was a transformative moment that created a national conversation around Indigenous youth detention. It found that of 281 news articles over four years about the Don Dale Detention Centre, 223 news articles appeared in 2016 following the Four Corners episode. Fitz-Gibbon's media analysis was focused upon the impact of reporting, including in shaping responses from advocates such as the Children's Commissioner, and highlights that much media commentary expressed outrage and calls for reform. Indeed, her analysis demonstrates the important role the media plays in making allegations of human rights abuses public. However, Fitz-Gibbon gives less attention to the ways in which the mainstream media traditionally reports (or more precisely, *fails* to report) on matters of concern to Aboriginal and Torres Strait Islander communities. This point has been emphasized by Indigenous scholars in recent decades, who demonstrate both the ways in which the media fails to report on Indigenous issues, or that when it does so it often risks further damage by perpetuating harmful racial stereotypes especially in the context of criminal justice (Porter, 2015; McQuire, 2019). The Don Dale Royal Commission's Final Report specifically implicated the role of media in the context around Indigenous youth crime, stating that it 'received evidence throughout the relevant period, [that] media reporting "heightened the public's concern for personal and community safety"' (White & Gooda, 2017, p. 119). And that in the Northern Territory that the media 'regularly published articles in the nature of "youth crime waves" and "gangs out of control"', including the "names and photographs of children on many occasions"' (White & Gooda, 2017, p. 119). This is to say that as well as being able to expose sites of Indigenous injustice, the media are often as likely to be implicated in manufacturing representations of young Aboriginal people and Torres Strait Islanders that contribute to heightened surveillance, over-policing and violence.

Below we highlight examples of representative claims made following the publication of allegations of human rights breaches at Don Dale Detention Centre to demonstrate how a discourse of Aboriginal children as a source of risk emerged from key actors to defend those allegations. While much of the public response was one of shock and outrage, it remains that the representations of key actors below were presented to the Australian public to minimise that shock and outrage, and indeed to justify the actions of corrections officers against young Aboriginal detainees. While not part of Kate Fitz-Gibbon's analysis, it was also the case that much formal news reporting of the Don Dale controversy that was republished and promoted on social media outlets, such as Facebook, produced racist and defamatory comments from members of the broader public which would later become subject to litigation (Byrne, 2021).

The day following the 2016 Four Corners episode, the then (Country Liberal Party) Chief Minister of the Northern Territory Mr Giles said:

> 'There are kids who are trying to deliberately cause cranial issues by bashing their head against the wall. Prison officers need the ability to be able to de-

escalate issues when children are not in … a calm environment within themselves and at all times those kids' wellbeing is being put at the best possible place.'

He continued that the Northern Territory community:

'was sick of youth crime … they have had a gutful. They've had a gutful of cars getting smashed up, houses getting broken into, people being assaulted. There's no doubt. And the majority of the community is saying let's lock these kids up' (Dunlevie, 2016).

The Four Corners broadcast included video footage of six young people being tear-gassed, and showed a seventeen-year-old Dylan Voller handcuffed and hooded in a mechanical restraint chair, being thrown across the cell, stripped naked, and kept in solitary confinement. Despite clear evidence of breaches of human rights, including children's rights, which would later be confirmed in the findings of the Royal Commission, it is revealing that the Chief Minister of the Northern Territory chose to emphasize Aboriginal youth crime.

Furthermore, in the lead national broadsheet, *The Australian*, commentator Janet Albrechtson (Albrecthson, 2016) further transformed the representation of Aboriginal children's experiences of state-sanctioned violence into the failures of Indigenous Australian parents, writing:

'But where were, where *are* the parents of these broken boys? Where are the fathers and mothers? This is the gaping hole in this horribly sad story. That we haven't heard from the mothers and fathers of the boys in Don Dale tells its own story. It's a story of generational dysfunction that a royal commission into Don Dale won't fix… The reality is that not every parent is up to the job. We have become so hopeless, so scared of making judgments about other parents, we would rather turn our eyes away from children whose life chances are dashed by dysfunction than ask parents to do the best they can by their child. We seem more at ease making judgments about the owners of mistreated greyhounds than parents who mistreat their kids.'

Against a historical conceptualisation of Indigenous peoples as infantilized subjects, what we see in this shift is not a fear to make judgment of parents, as Albrechtson accuses, but rather a sustained judgment against Aboriginal and Torres Strait Islander adults as incompetent, uncaring and ultimately unfit parents. If Indigenous adults are childlike, best governed by paternalistic structures and policies, then their capacity to parent their own children is too easily called into question. As a result, their children are removed into institutions where they are kept out of view from society and from their own families (see also Hinton, 2021). In doing so, children are also disappeared from the public discourse and discussion becomes about the personal responsibilities of adult carers and not about the context, conditions and decisions that lead so many young Aboriginal and Islander girls and boys into youth detention. And the capacity of the young people who experience the effects of Indigenous social policy on a daily basis find themselves even more distanced from the public, their capacity to self-represent their interests ever more restrained by representations of them by adult Australians.

Dylan Voller was incarcerated in Don Dale Detention Centre for serious offences. In a handwritten letter in July 2016, he wrote: 'I would just like to thank the whole Australian community for the support you have showed for us a [sic] boys as well as our families. I would also like to apologise to the community for my wrongs and I can't wait to get out and make up for them' (Graham, 2016). Dylan Voller also sought a personal apology from the Northern Territory Chief Minister for the treatment of himself and other boys. The Chief Minister declined to do so (Wild, 2016). He was released from the Don Dale Detention Centre in February 2017, having served three years and eight months from the age of fifteen. As we write, not only do the NT Royal Commission's recommendations remain unimplemented, the current Labor government has recently announced legal amendments to create new offences and legislation to make it more difficult for magistrates to divert young offenders away from prison (Breen, 2021). Instead, in 2021, the Northern Territory reached a financial settlement for all youth detainees mistreated between 2006 and 2017, understood to be up to 1200 individuals (Gooley, 2021). Also in 2021, the majority bench of the High Court of Australia held that media companies could be held liable for defamatory posts made by commentators on Facebook pages that they controlled: the claimant in that case was Dylan Voller.

In a representative terrain that reported the breaches of human rights that young Aboriginal detainees were subjected to, representative claims emphasizing Aboriginal youth crime and the purported inability of Aboriginal people to properly parent their own children were used to defend and justify the law-and-order policies of the Northern Territory that today remain broadly unchanged. Despite the outcry from many, representative claims of Aboriginal children as source of risk in this policy context prevailed.

The power of these claims was also evident in the proposed youth curfew policy in Cairns and Townsville during the 2020 Queensland state election. On 31 October 2020, the election in the state of Queensland took place. Late in the election campaign, the leader of the state Opposition Deb Frecklington announced a youth curfew policy for two northern Australian towns, Cairns and Townsville, should the LNP form government. This had previously been proposed for implementation in Townsville at the 2017 state election, but the Opposition did not win government. It was proposed that the policy would be enforced by issuing $250 AUD fines to parents of any unaccompanied children who were found outside at night 'without a reasonable excuse'. The policy additionally sought to impose mandatory detention for third convictions (three-strikes policy), and establish 'community payback farms' in which young people were to be sent to labour as a form of punishment for their crimes (Zillman, 2020).

For context, these towns are both marginal electorates, and contain large, young communities of Indigenous people. Cairns is a state electorate that was held by the Australian Labor Party by a margin 3.4% at the 2017 election; this increased by 2.2% as a result of the 2020 election. The Townsville electorate was held by the Australian Labor Party by a margin of 0.4% at the 2017 election among the tightest in the state; this increased by 2.7% as a result of the 2020 election. Nonetheless, both seats remain classified as marginal being held by a margin of less than 6%. The 2020 election results can be interpreted in part as the electorate's refusal to be swayed by the youth curfew policy. However, the use of a youth curfew policy as a key platform heavily promoted by the Opposition in the final stages of campaign also points to the ways in which a youth curfew policy was employed in pursuit of political victory, related as it is to perceptions of youth crime as a 'wicked problem' and its capacity to induce 'moral panics'. Tackling youth crime is seen to be an effective platform upon which to move voters, and in marginal seats each and every vote matters.

The youth curfew policy in these two electorates can also be contextualised by its demographic particularities. The nearest statistical age band we can produce from the most recent census data for Indigenous/non-Indigenous comparison is 0–19 years (though the policy related to age 16 years and younger). However, even across this slightly more expansive age band we are able to demonstrate the relative 'youth' of the Indigenous Australian population compared with the non-Indigenous population in

Cairns and Townsville. In Cairns and Townsville, approximately 10% of the population identified as Aboriginal and, or Torres Strait Islander in the 2016 national census. Nationally, Aboriginal and, or Torres Strait Islander people represent 2.8% of the population. This is to say, Cairns and Townsville are towns that have a visibly higher population of Aboriginal and Torres Strait Islander people. In these towns, all policies affect a greater proportion of Aboriginal and Torres Strait Islander people than in other parts of the Queensland state and Australia. Policies, such as the youth curfew, that are proposed to be specifically implemented in these towns alone have a direct and greater impact on Aboriginal and Torres Strait Islander people. This is further underscored by the relatively young age profile of Aboriginal and Torres Strait Islander people: 42% and 43% of the Aboriginal and Torres Strait Islander population is aged under nineteen years compared to 21% and 18% of the non-Indigenous population in Cairns and Townsville, respectively. A policy intended to apply only to the towns of Cairns and Townsville is one that in practice disproportionately and deliberately affects Aboriginal and Torres Strait Islander young people. The youth curfew policy proposed by the Opposition party as part of its electoral campaign was, for these reasons, a racialized and racist policy.

The state parliament in Queensland is comprised of a single chamber composed of 93 members representing a little over 3.3 million registered voters.[3] Historically, Queensland has been known for being a particularly racist and anti-democratic state within the Australian federation, particularly during the period of the controversial Bjelke-Petersen government (1968–1987) in which a range of democratic rights were placed at risk, including the right to association and assembly. In the 1990s, the rise of the right-wing politician Pauline Hanson (current Federal Senator) would result in the formation of the One Nation Party on anti-immigration and anti-multiculturalism platforms, with huge success in Queensland at the time. Both Senator Hanson, the One Nation Party and other small anti-multiculturalist parties have come to shape the contemporary political landscape, with much of their approach to multiculturalism and Indigenous affairs slowly becoming reflected in major party rhetoric across the nation.

It is in this context that we interpret the 2020 youth curfew policy proposal in the towns of Cairns and Townsville. The policy itself was formally difference-blind, in that it was proposed to apply to all youth aged up to 16 years. However, as we have shown it is also a policy proposal that disproportionately targets and affects Aboriginal and Torres Strait Islander youth. At the time, Opposition Leader Ms Frecklington was reported as saying that 'she made no apologies for being "tough on crime"' arguing that 'An 11-year-old—what is he doing on the streets at that time at night? He's got to be back at home, safely tucked into bed' (McKenna, 2020). She continued that:

> It is a terrible indictment when every time I come to Townsville, I have to meet with another community member who has had their house broken into, their car flogged ... it's just got to stop. (McKenna, 2020)

While Townsville is known for higher rates of crime than elsewhere (and a higher unemployment rate), the policy was challenged at the time for a number of reasons, including that it risked breaching international law and that at the time crime was in decline and the age trend was such that offenders were increasingly aged 25 and older (Dennien & Lynch, 2020). Nonetheless, the public stage in the final weeks of the Queensland state election was clearly set to frame young people, and Aboriginal and Torres Strait Islander young people especially, as the source of criminal behaviour and an ongoing risk to social order.

Beyond the demographic implications of a youth policy in towns with high Aboriginal and Torres Strait Islander populations is a broader national context concerning the policing and incarceration practices relating to Indigenous peoples. This context brings into sharper relief the racialized impacts of the proposed youth curfew. Representing young people and, implicitly Indigenous young people, as a source of risk to social order and future governance sits at odds with the starker reality that Aboriginal and Torres Strait Islander people, including youth, are more likely than non-Indigenous Australians to be subjected to violent policing and death within the criminal justice system as has been evidenced in the Northern Territory example above.

Australia is already a country that disproportionately criminalizes and incarcerates Aboriginal and Torres Strait Islander people. So much so that in 1987, the Commonwealth of Australia initiated a Royal Commission into Aboriginal Deaths in Custody ('RCIADC'), which delivered its final report four years later composed of 339 recommendations that largely remain unimplemented (Johnston, 1991). Since the report, hundreds of Aboriginal and Torres Strait Islander people have died in custody and the number rises every month. It is now broadly acknowledged that the key contributor to these deaths is the overincarceration of Aboriginal and Torres Strait Islander people (see Cuneen & Porter, 2017). A youth curfew policy in towns with very high populations of young Aboriginal and Torres Strait Islander people is the making of the very conditions that contribute to this overincarceration and deaths in custody. While the thirty-year old RCADIC remains broadly unimplemented, we remain in electoral campaign cycles that continue to produce the conditions that sustain over-policing, overincarceration and ultimately, disproportionately high rates of deaths in custody for Aboriginal and Torres Strait Islander people.

In broader public discourse, sustained efforts by Aboriginal and Torres Strait Islander people to draw attention to the harms and violence experienced at the hands of police demonstrate alternative representations of victims rather than perpetrators of crime. As Darumbal and South Sea Islander journalist, Amy McQuire, wrote during the 2020 Black Lives Matters protests, 'There cannot be 432 victims and no perpetrators' in Australia's *The Saturday Paper*, referring to the then number of documented Aboriginal Deaths in Custody since the 1991 RCIADC (as of April 2021 that number was 474). She observed at this time that in contrast to the global outpouring of support for African Americans dying at the hands of police, 'We have never seen this in Australia, where Aboriginal people continue to die on the floor of watchhouse, in the back of paddy wagons and in handcuffs locked to hospital beds. When Aboriginal people die in custody, there is a national silence' (McQuire, 2020). It is a silence that sits in stark contrast to the politicisation of youth crime that disproportionately targets Aboriginal and Torres Strait Islander young people. That these competing representations exist is testament to labour of Indigenous peoples to continue to testify to their experiences of violence, and it is within this context that *The Guardian Australia*'s recent series on 'Childhood in Custody' can be located as a rare example of mainstream media attention to the experiences of young Aboriginal and Torres Strait Islander people (The Guardian Australia, 2021).

Having set out the fuller context of the proposed youth policy, in electoral and demographic terms, we argue that Aboriginal and Torres Strait Islander youth crime is used to represent Aboriginal and Torres Strait Islander young people as source of *risk* to the demos. In this case, the risk is represented in terms of violent crime, but the subtext is a judgement about dysfunctional parents and communities that require state intervention because they can never grow into adequate parental figures, let alone ideal Australian citizens. This representation persists notwithstanding the high rates of violence and targeted policing against Aboriginal and Torres

Strait Islander people that result in their status as the most incarcerated people on the planet, with disproportionately high rates of our people dying in custody. We argue that representing risk to the voting public in these terms, operates to further position Aboriginal and Torres Strait Islander people as a legitimate site of racialized policing and surveillance in order to produce a sense of security for the broader Australian public.

These illustrative cases are not intended to be an exhaustive account of representations of Aboriginal and Torres Strait Islander young people as a source of risk. Rather, they are recent examples that are consistent with decades and centuries of the colonial governance of Indigenous lives. While there are real harms and challenges surrounding the lives of young people which are deserving of informed and thoughtful response from governments, this example highlights the ways in which discourses about youth crime coincide with race and Indigeneity in ways intended to secure political power and to 'settle' the colonial state by continuing to represent Aboriginal and Torres Strait Islander young people as an existential threat. By doing so, opportunities are missed to better understand the social, cultural, economic and political experiences that shape those young peoples' lives and the positive and negative impacts it has upon them.

Conclusion: Renewal and the Transformative Potential of Indigenous Children's Representation

What we have presented here is the argument that the representation of Aboriginal and Torres Strait Islander young people as sources of risk to the *demos* encompasses more than just how those young people appear in the media or are spoken about by politicians. In colonial contexts, the interplay between law, economy, politics and policy is predicated upon conceptualisations of Indigenous people as infantile, deficient, still-not-fully-human subjects. This is not just a matter of individual psychologies of bias but reflects a conceptualisation that was integral to the very foundation of liberal, democratic, colonial nation-states. This conceptualisation cannot be relegated to the historical record. The subjugated status of infantilized races, including those of Indigenous peoples, is embedded in the systems and institutions of colonial states. Intergenerational inequity and political powerlessness continue to shape the lives of young Indigenous peoples and limit the conditions of justice that liberal democratic colonies such as Australia can imagine. The transformative potential of representation, then, is shown here to not just be about making visible the positive (alongside the negative) representatives of young Aboriginal and Torres Strait Islander people, but also a claim to representation that might work to legitimize and redistribute political power to them.

On viewing the ways in which Aboriginal and Torres Strait Islander young people are represented in Australian public discourse, it is easy to become disheartened at its bleakness: crime, incarceration, deaths in custody, and beyond the context of this chapter, the disproportionate removal of young people from their families into out-of-home care. These are important, urgent sites of Indigenous social policy that reflect just how preoccupied the colonial state remains with Indigenous young peoples' lives. However, to view these representations as comprehensive and immutable is misplaced. Aboriginal and Torres Strait Islander young people have always been a source of radical potential across the continent of Australia, and each generation has resisted and navigated their conditions of their colonisation, in ways that work to cleave open other possible futures for the Australian nation. The *Uluru Statement from the Heart* expressed such possible futures, and two years later a youth delegation at the national Garma Festival pleaded for 'the freedom to write a new story' (Garma Youth Forum, 2019). These normative orientations are not without their own politics and risks, specifically, projecting onto Aboriginal and Torres Strait Islander young people the ideals and hopes of an old generation. But we remind our readers here that alongside the representations of risk presented in this chapter, the possibility for democratic renewal persists in Aboriginal and Torres Strait Islander young people. Indeed, the transformative potential of their representations in renewing Australian democracy lies in their ability to contest the figure of the risky, infantile Indigenous subject. And that for Indigenous and all racialized people world over, this is a tension that weaves the very fabric of democratic states.

Notes

1. Aboriginal peoples and Torres Strait Islanders are distinct ethnic groups who were both colonized by the British as part of the creation of 'Australia'. They are sometimes described together as "Indigenous Australians" but it is increasingly preferred to use the term Aboriginal and Torres Strait Islander peoples to respect those members of the community who do not consider themselves Australian. Within Australia, we also increasingly use language

names to describe ourselves and the communities or nations to which we belong of which there are hundreds across the continent. Within this chapter we use 'Aboriginal and Torres Strait Islander' and 'Indigenous Australian' interchangeably, and sometimes refer only to Aboriginal people where the subject is specific to that community. We also use the term 'Indigenous' when locating our regional experience in the broader context of global Indigenous peoples' political claims. The first author of this chapter, Sana Nakata, is a Torres Strait Islander woman.
2. *Makarrata* is a Yolgnu word and concept with a multilayered meaning. Here, it can be interpreted to mean the 'coming together after struggle'.
3. Voting in Australia is compulsory for all citizens from 18 years onwards.

References

Alanamu, T., Carton, B., & Lawrance, B. (2018). Colonialism and African Childhood. In M. S. Shanguhyia & T. Falola (Eds.), *The Palgrave Handbook of African Colonial and Postcolonial History* (pp. 389–412). Palgrave Macmillan.

Albrecthson, J. (2016). Deadbeat Parents Failed the Don Dale Detention Centre Boys. *The Australian*.

Alexander, K. (2016). Childhood and Colonialism in Canadian History. *History Compass, 14*, 397–406. https://doi.org/10.1111/hic3.12331

Arendt, H. (1958). *The Human Condition*. Chicago: University of Chicago Press.

Australian Institute of Health and Welfare. (2021). Youth Detention Population in Australia 2020.

Balagopalan, S. (2014). *Inhabiting 'Childhood': Children, Labour and Schooling in Postcolonial India*. Palgrave Macmillan.

Bernstein, R. (2011). *Racial Innocence: Performing American Childhood from Slavery to Civil Rights*. New York University Press.

Bray, D., & Nakata, S. (2020). The Figure of the Child in Democratic Politics. *Contemporary Political Theory, 19*, 20. https://doi.org/10.1057/s41296-019-00319-x

Breen, J. (2021). Mandatory Refusal of Youth Bail Included in NT Labor's Tough-on-Crime Crackdown. ABC News Online.

Byrne, E. (2021). High Court to Decide Whether News Outlets Responsible for Facebook Comments at Centre of Dylan Voller Defamation Case. ABC News Online.

Cuneen, C., & Porter, A. (2017). Indigenous Peoples and Criminal Justice in Australia. In A. Deckert & R. Sarre (Eds.), *The Palgrave Handbook of Australian and New Zealand Criminology* (pp. 667–682). Palgrave Macmillan.

Davis, M. (2019). Family Is Culture: Final Report. Independent Review of Aboriginal Children in OOHC.

Dennien, M., & Lynch, L. (2020). LNP Warned Youth Curfew Plan Could Breach International Law. *The Brisbane Times*.

Dewey, J. (2008). *The Middle Works of John Dewey, Volume 10: 1899-1924*. Edited by Boydston, Jo Ann. Carbondale: Southern Illinois University Press.

Dunlevie, J. (2016). John Elferink Sacked from Corrections in Wake of Four Corners Report; Adam Giles Alleges Culture of Cover-up. ABC News Online.

Dunstan, L., Hewitt, B., & Nakata, S. (2019). Indigenous Family Life in Australia: A History of Difference and Deficit. *Australian Journal of Social Issues*, ajs4.90. https://doi.org/10.1002/ajs4.90

Fitz-Gibbon, K. (2018). *The Treatment of Australian Children in Detention: A Human Rights Law Analysis of Media Coverage in the Wake of Abuses at Don Dale, 41*, 100–129.

Garma Youth Forum. (2019). Imagination Declaration.

Gooley, C. (2021). Don Dale Child Inmates to Share in Record $35 Million Settlement. The Sydney Morning Herald (Online).

Graham, C. (2016). *NT Juvenile Detention Abuse: Dylan Voller Writes Letter of Thanks to Oz Community*. New Matilda.

Hallberg, M., & Sandin, B. (2021). Pictured Political Projects: Sunshine Over a Welfare State in the Shadow of War. *Journal of the History of Childhood and Youth, 14*, 85–112.

Hayward, B. (2012). *Children, Citizenship and Environment: Nurturing a Democratic Imagination in a Changing World*. Routledge.

Hinton, E. (2021). *America on Fire: The Untold History of Police Violence and Black Rebellion Since the 1960s*. Liveright.

Holzscheiter, A., Josefsson, J., & Sandin, B. (2019). Child Rights Governance: An Introduction. *Childhood, 26*, 271–288.

James, A., & Jenks, C. (1996). Public Perceptions of Childhood Criminality. *The British Journal of Sociology, 47*, 315–331.

Johnston, E. (1991). *Royal Commission into Aboriginal Deaths in Custody National Report*. Australian Government Publishing Service.

Josefsson, J. (2017). 'We beg you, let them stay!': Right Claims of Asylum-Seeking Children as a Socio-political Practice. *Childhood, 24*, 316–332.

Lee-Koo, K. (2011). Horror and Hope: (Re)presenting Militarized Children in Global North-South Relations. *Third World Quarterly, 32*, 725–742.

McKenna, K. (2020). LNP's Queensland Election Pitch to Enforce Townsville Youth Curfew Branded "a dog pound for kids" by Katter's Australian Party. ABC News Online.

McQuire, A. (2020). There Cannot Be 432 Victims and No Perpetrators…. The Saturday Paper.

Meiners, E. (2016). *For the Child? Protecting Innocence in a Carceral State*. University of Minnesota Press.

McQuire, A. (2019). 'White Justice, Black Suffering: extracting false confessions'. *Griffith Review*, 65, 213–227.

Mill, J. S. (2011). *On Liberty [1839]*. Cambridge University Press.

Nakata, M. N. (2007). *Disciplining the Savages: Savaging the Disciplines*. Aboriginal Studies Press.

Nakata, S. (2015). *Childhood Citizenship, Governance and Policy: The Politics of Becoming Adult*. Routledge.

Nakata, S. (2018). The Infantilisation of Indigenous Australians: A Problem for Democracy. *Griffith REVIEW*, 104–116.

National Constitutional Convention. (2017). Uluru Statement from the Heart.

Porter, A. (2015). 'Riotous or Righteous Behaviour? Representations of Subaltern Resistance in the Australian Mainstream Media'. *Current Issues in Criminal Justice*, 26(3), 289–304.

Pruitt, L. (2021). Children & Migration: Political Constructions and Contestations. Global Policy Online First. https://doi.org/10.1111/1758-5899.13011

Response to Referendum Council's Report on Constitutional Recognition (Media Release). (2017). Office of the Prime Minister of Australia.

Rollo, T. (2016). Feral Children: Settler Colonialism, Progress, and the Figure of the Child. *Settler Colonial Studies*, 8, 60–79.

Rollo, T. (2018). The Colour of Childhood: The Role of the Child/Human Binary in the Production of Anti-black Racism. *Journal of Black Studies*, 49, 307–329.

Saward, M. (2010). *The Representative Claim*. Oxford: Oxford University Press.

Stewart, C. (2019). The Future Is Queer Kids: Queering the Homonormative Temporalities of Same-Sex Marriage. *Politics*, 40, 265–280.

The Guardian Australia. (2021). Childhood in Custody.

Vallgårda, K. (2015). *Imperial Childhoods and Christian Mission: Education and Emotions in South India and Denmark*. Palgrave Macmillan.

Walter, M. (2016). Data Politics and Indigenous Representation in Australian Statistics. In T. Kukutai & J. Taylor (Eds.), *Indigenous Data Sovereignty: Toward an Agenda* (pp. 79–98). ANU Press.

Walter, M. M. (2010). The Politics of the Data: How the Australian Statistical Indigene Is Constructed. *International Journal of Critical Indigenous Studies*, 3, 45–56.

White, M., & Gooda, M. (2017). Final Report of the Royal Commission and Board of Inquiry into the Protection and Detention of the Children in the Northern Territory (No. Vol. 1).

Wild, K. (2016). Four Corners: Juvenile Detainee Dylan Voller Asks NT Chief Minister Adam Giles for Personal Apology. ABC News Online.

Zhao, G. (2011). The Modern Construction of Childhood: What Does It Do to the Paradox of Modernity? *Studies in Philosophy and Education, 30*, 241–256. https://doi.org/10.1007/s11217-010-9213-8

Zillman, S. (2020). Queensland Opposition Says Youth Crime Out of Control and Vows to Get Tough on Offenders. ABC News Online.

Open Access   This chapter is licensed under the terms of the Creative Commons Attribution 4.0 International License (http://creativecommons.org/licenses/by/4.0/), which permits use, sharing, adaptation, distribution and reproduction in any medium or format, as long as you give appropriate credit to the original author(s) and the source, provide a link to the Creative Commons licence and indicate if changes were made.

The images or other third party material in this chapter are included in the chapter's Creative Commons licence, unless indicated otherwise in a credit line to the material. If material is not included in the chapter's Creative Commons licence and your intended use is not permitted by statutory regulation or exceeds the permitted use, you will need to obtain permission directly from the copyright holder.

Index

A

Aboriginal, 301–319
Aboriginal residents, 21
Abuse, 32, 35, 36, 40–45, 48, 49
Abusive treatment, 32–35, 40, 44, 46, 50
Access to justice, 106–109, 111–114
Accountability, 278
Accountable, 286–288, 293
Accra, 205–223
Act, 2–6, 11, 13
Acting on behalf of, 2, 3
Action, 1, 2, 4, 6, 7, 11, 12, 17, 19, 22, 276, 277, 280, 284, 285, 287–293
Active citizenship, 107
Additional Protocols to the Geneva Conventions, 165, 166
Adoption, 34
Adultist, 251, 260, 264, 266
Adult legal actors, 106
Advocacy, 181–183, 185, 186, 189, 191, 192, 194–197
Aesthetic representation, 252
Affect, 253, 255, 258
Afghan, 275–294
Afghanistan, 262, 267, 270n3
African Development Bank (AfDB), 207
African Movement of Working Children and Youth (AMWCY), 140, 217
Afrikaans, 71, 72
Agarwal, Ashok, 89, 94, 98n3
Age, 33–36, 39, 40, 42, 43, 49, 50, 161, 163, 166–169, 176, 278
Agency, 60, 63, 65–67, 69, 70, 74, 75, 123, 207, 209, 213, 215, 217, 218, 222, 258, 261, 263, 265, 269
Allies, 277, 282, 286, 288–291, 293
Ambivalence, 174

Amnesty International, 191
Amsterdam Child Labour Conference (1997), 141, 143
Angel of Independence, 261
Anger, 252, 258, 261, 269
Anticolonial, 19
Apartheid, 6, 12, 61, 71, 74
Apartheid government, 71
Apartheid State, 71, 73, 75
Argentina, 132, 188, 270n3
Armed conflict, 183, 185
Article 12 (of the Convention), 65
Australia, 301–319
Australian Labor Party, 314
Authorities, 4, 6, 10, 15, 17, 205–207, 209, 212–222, 276, 279–281, 283, 285, 286, 288, 292, 293
Autonomous, 4, 11, 16, 44
Autonomous individuals, 33

B
Ball, Stephen, 87
Bal Mazdoor Union (India), 140
Barnens rätt i samhället, 44
Bastida, Xiya, 253
Battered child syndrome, 41, 44
Beah, Ishmael, 173, 177
Beijer, Fredrik, 287
Best interests, 110, 121, 123
Best interests of children, 68
Best interests of the child, 188, 190
Bhima Sangha (India), 140
Black children, 71
Black Conscious movement, 73
Born into Brothels, 1, 2
Bottom-up approaches (to participation), 69
Bray, Daniel, 97
Brazil, 188, 205
BRIS, 44, 45, 48, 50

Briski, Zana, 1–3
Buenos Aires, 131, 132, 152, 153

C
Cairns, 309, 314, 315
Cape Town Principles, 166, 167
Capitalism, 253
Caste, 18
Cause lawyers, *see* Lawyers
Chaplin, Charlie, 182
Chastise, 38, 40, 50
Child abuse, 39, 41, 42, 44–46, 48
Childcare, 33, 41, 44, 50
Child figurations, 265, 266
Child-friendly, 107, 109–110, 113
Childhood, 2–4, 6–17, 19–22, 206, 208–211, 221, 286, 288, 291, 293
Childhood entitlement, 208
Childhood figurations, 251, 256, 258–269
Childhood moratorium, 18, 229–234, 240, 244, 245
Childhood studies, 8, 20–22
Child labour, 5, 6, 8, 15, 131–153, 181, 194
Child liberationists, 62, 63
Child ombudsperson, 279–280, 283
Child participation, 59–69, 75, 76
Child participation framework, 61
Child poverty, 227–245
Child protection, 31–53
Child-rearing, 35, 43, 47, 48, 51
Child-rearing practices, 33, 52
Child removal/'out-of-home care,' 310, 319
Children, 1–22, 275–282, 284, 285, 288, 289, 291–293
    having responsibilities, 64, 65
    of the streets, 208
    on the streets, 208, 213, 214, 222

Children's citizenship, 70
Children's dependency, 208
Children's everyday lives, 70
Children's involvement decision-making, 60, 62
Children's ombudsman, 45, 52
Children's representation, 2–9, 12–22
Children's rights, 1, 3, 7–18, 20, 22, 31–53, 60–65, 67, 68, 75, 84, 86–89, 96, 98n1, 98n2, 183, 184, 186–198, 227–245, 275, 278–281
  governance, 107, 109
  in society, 44
Children's views, 60, 62
Children's voice, 4, 11, 15, 186
Child rights governance, 165, 168, 279
Child rights movement, 9
Child slavery, 138, 139, 146, 148, 151
Child soldiering, 182–187, 191, 194–196, 198
Child studies, 34
Child trafficking, 139, 148
Child Welfare Act, 36, 39, 40, 42, 44
Child welfare boards, 36, 40–42, 50
China, 184, 185
Circulation, 262
Citizenship/citizen, 68–70, 84–89, 91, 92, 97, 98, 277–279, 281, 286
Civil rights movement, 278
Civil society, 279, 281
Claim, 4, 8, 15–21, 276, 278, 280–286, 288, 291–294
Class, 5, 8, 18, 33–35, 40, 41, 49, 50
Climate activism, 195
Climate change, 182, 187–193, 196–198, 251–253, 255, 258–261, 264, 265, 267, 269
Climate justice, 251–269
Climate strikes, 19

Coalition, 183–187
Colonial exploitation, 10
Coloniality, 307
Committee on the Rights of the Child, 184, 185, 188, 190, 192, 193
Communication, 188, 190–193
Competence, 258, 263–266, 268, 269
Competent, 2, 5
Comprehensive school, 40
Concept of participation, 62
Constituency, 277, 280, 285, 292
Constructive turn, 277
Control, 7, 10–13, 17
Controlling, 50
Control of children's participation, 60, 65
The Convention, 59–66, 69, 76
Convention on the Rights of the Child, *see* United Nations Convention on the Rights of the Child
Coomaraswamy, Radhika, 171
Corporal punishment, 31–53
Correction, 38, 46
Cosmopolitanism, 189
Counterforce, 195, 197
Court, 12, 13, 106–125
Court of Appeal of Skåne and Blekinge, 42
Covid-19, 81
Creativity, 268
Criminal justice, 39
Criminal Justice Committee, 39
Criminal law, 32, 39–41, 44
Cultural values, 47, 51
Culture, 45, 47–49

D
Dallaire, Roméo, 170
Defence for Children International (DCI), 191

Defiance, 213, 217
Delhi High Court, 12, 13, 81–98
Deliberative disobedience, 205–223
Democracy/democratize, 5, 8, 15, 20, 86
Democratic, 47, 51
Democratic deficit, 195
Democratic inclusion, 292
Democratic Republic of the Congo (DRC), 185, 186
Democratic theory, 278
Demonstration(s), 72–74
Department of Justice, 38
Dependent, 4, 12
Depictions, 3, 7, 22
Deportation, 276, 281, 282, 285–287, 290, 291, 293
Deserving poor, 232, 234, 244
Deviation, 169
Dialogue with a purpose, 211
Dickensian mob, 207
Diffusion, 275, 278, 292
Digital strike, 253, 268
Discipline/disciplining, 33, 45, 50, 86, 91
Discourses, 33, 164, 165, 169, 171, 172, 176, 177n1
Division of power, 269
Domination, 281
Don Dale Youth Detention Centre, 303, 310
Dysfunctional families, 208

E
Education, 2, 7, 8, 10, 12, 13, 33, 34, 36, 47, 227, 228, 230, 231, 233, 235, 238–241, 243
EHRC, *see* European Court of Human Rights
Elections, 191, 195, 277, 278, 289, 292, 293
Elementary schools, 33, 36, 38, 40, 50

Elementary School Statute, 38, 40, 43, 44
Emancipation, 107, 108, 292
Emancipatory, 48
Emergency, 161–177
Emotional, 44, 45, 51
Emotional well-being, 206
Empowering, 66
Empowerment, 66, 69
Enhetsskola, 40
Epistemological domination, 107
Epistemological imperialism, 122
Equality, 17, 44, 50, 51, 98
Equity, 83, 87, 88, 90, 96, 97
Ethics, 190
Ethnicity, 8
European Convention on Human Rights, 118
European Court of Human Rights (EHRC), 107, 114, 118–120, 122
Everyday acts of participation, 75
Exceptional, 169, 173, 177
Exclusion, 13, 16, 281, 293

F
Facebook, 253
Family, 2, 3, 10, 11, 15, 17, 18, 32–35, 39–46, 49–52
Family economy, 206, 219
Family law, 32
Feared perpetrator, 172
Figure of the child, 19
Filial obligation, 206
First Nation Youth, 21
Folkskola, 36
Formal processes of participation, 67
Formal representation, 5
Foster care, 34
Frame, 169–171, 177
France, 184, 185, 188
Frecklington, Deb, 314, 315

Freedom, 11
Fridays for Future (FFF), 19, 251–269
Future citizens, 68, 69
Future generations, 187
Future responsible citizens, 68

G
Gatekeepers, 211
Gender, 8, 11, 18, 33–35, 40, 43, 44, 49, 50
Generations, 5–7
Geneva, 115, 116, 119
Geneva Declaration of 1924, 14
Genuine participation, 59
Genuine transformational impact, 60, 64
Germany, 187, 188
Ghana, 17, 205–210, 213, 219, 221, 222
Ghertner, Asher, 93
Girlhood, 258
Global childhood, 182, 186, 187
Global discourse, 187
Global governance, 15, 16, 20, 181
Globalisation, 187, 194, 195
Globality, 252–255
Global March Against Child Labour, 132, 134, 146–147
Global migration, 276
Global North, 5, 10, 19, 252, 276, 279
Global politics, 276, 277
Global power, 181, 182
Global South, 3, 6, 10, 18, 19, 22, 64, 187, 194, 252, 253, 255, 263, 265
Gornitzka, Charlotte Petri, 188
Governance, 9–11, 14–16, 20, 22, 31, 35, 255, 256, 258, 275, 276, 279, 281, 292

Government, 34–36, 46–52, 53n1, 277–280, 282, 283, 285–290, 293
Greater Accra, 208
Grundskola, 40
Gun violence, 5

H
Hanson, Pauline, 315
Hart, Roger, 85
Harvey, David, 86
Hazardous labour, 208
Headquarters of the United Nations, 259
Health, 227, 228, 230, 234, 235, 237, 241, 242
Health care, 34
Hegemonic, 255, 258, 259, 269
Hines, Lewis, 6
Homeless children, 208
Homogeneous, 33
Housing, 227, 228, 230, 233–237, 240–242, 245
Humanitarianism, 116
Humanitarian organisations, 186
Human rights, 31–53, 182, 189–191, 194
Human rights law, 12
Human Rights Watch, 191
Humiliating treatment, 50, 52
Humor, 266–269

I
Iconic symbols, 3
Identity, 277, 282–286, 288, 292, 293
ILO Convention 138 on the Minimum Age to Employment (C138), 134
ILO Convention 182 on the Worst Forms of Child Labour (C182), 134, 146–149

Image events, 256–259, 262, 263, 265, 268, 269
Imageries, 5
Images, 3, 6, 16
Immigrant, 45–49, 51, 52
Immigrant groups, 47
Immigrant policy, 47
Immigrant population, 33, 46, 48, 51
Immigration, 281, 282, 289
  control, 281
  courts, 109
  policy, 49
Imperialism, 253
Implementation, 279, 280, 294
"Implementation gap", 113
Incarceration/overincarceration, 309, 310, 316, 317, 319
Incompetency, 190
Incompetent, 2
Independent individual, 40, 44, 47, 48
India, 1, 5, 12, 190, 205, 259, 262
Indigeneity, 307, 318
Indigenous, 5, 19–21, 301–319
Inequalities, 4, 9, 12, 16–21
Infantilization, 303, 306–309
Informal representation, 5
Injustices, 4, 8, 9, 16–21
In loco parentis, 36, 41, 50
Innocence, 171, 175, 176
Innocent victim, 164, 177
Inquiry, 38, 44–46, 49, 51
Instagram, 19, 251–269
Institutions, 7, 10, 11, 14–16
Integrity, 35, 41, 44, 46, 48, 49, 51
Interdependence, 4, 18
Intergenerational, 251, 253, 258, 259, 265, 266
Intergovernmental organisations, 196
International Confederation of Free Trade Unions (ICFTU), 137, 142, 145, 146, 148, 153
International Criminal Court (ICC), 161–163, 166, 173
International humanitarian law, 183
International human rights law, 194
International jurisprudence, 192
International Labour Conference (ILC), 143, 146–150, 155
International Labour Organization (ILO), 15, 131, 133–144, 146, 148–153, 155, 181, 182, 194, 197
International Labor Organization Worst Forms of Child Labor Convention, 165
International litigation, 198
International Monetary Fund (IMF), 87
International politics, 9, 14–17
International Programme on the Elimination of Child Labour (IPEC), 136–139
International relations, 11
International Working Group on Child Labour (IWGCL), 141, 154
Intersectionalities/intersectional differences, 85
Intervention, 164, 169, 173, 174, 176
Irrationality, 171, 176
IV Global Conference on the Sustained Eradication of Child Labour (2017), 131

J
James, Allison, 84
Job market, 184
Joy, 252, 261, 265, 267–269
Justice, 13, 17–19
Justice-making, 106, 111, 114, 122
Juvenile delinquency, 33, 34

K

Kabul, 266, 267
Kauffman, Ross, 1
Kenya's Bill of Rights, 210
Key, Ellen, 6, 34
Khadr, Omar, 171, 172, 177
Khavari, Fatemeh, 287
Kolkata, 1
Kony, Joseph, 162
Kubolor, 206
Kumasi, 207
Kundapur Meeting, 140–141, 154

L

Latin American and Caribbean Movement of Working Children and Adolescents, 132
Law, 10, 13, 17, 162, 164, 165, 168, 169, 176, 281, 294
Lawyers, 107–109, 114–123
League of Nation's Child Welfare Committee in 1919, 14
Legal capacity, 106–109, 113
Legal knowledge, 113, 122, 125
Legal pedagogy, 125
Legal procedures, 182, 187, 189, 190, 195
Legal professionals, 107, 113, 115, 116, 122, 124
Legal representation, 13, 112–114, 117, 125, 190
Legal scholars, 51
Legal standing, 107, 109, 111
Legislation, 32, 34–36, 38, 39, 41, 42, 46, 48, 49, 52
Legitimate claims, 5
Leisure, 236–238
Liberation, 10, 11
Liberia, 163, 172
Listen to children, 46, 52
Litigation, 13
Löfvén, Stefan, 287

M

Machel, Graça, 162, 163, 165, 177n1
Mainstreaming, 279, 280, 294
Makichyan, Arshak, 262
Mali, 205
Maltreatment, 45
Management of adults, 60, 65
Mandate, 191, 192
Manipulation, 190
Marginal children/childhood, 82–84, 90, 92, 93, 96–98, 99n8
Mass-demonstration, 252, 259, 261, 263, 266, 269
Material support, 240, 242–244
Maturity, 308
Maze, 181–198
Medborgarplatsen, 286, 287
Medical Board, 36
Melithafa, Ayakha, 190
Mental, 35–38, 44
Mexico, 261, 270n3
Migrants, 275–294
Migration, 275–277, 279, 281, 286, 287, 292
Militarization, 166, 167
Minimum age, 182–186, 191, 194
Ministry of Justice, 42
Minor assaults, 39
Misrecognition, 60, 61, 74, 76
Misrepresentation, 61, 195, 196, 233
Mobilization, 275–277, 284, 285, 292, 293
Modernity, 307, 308
Modes of representation, 52
Monitoring, 184, 189, 193, 280, 294
Monster, 162, 169, 171–175, 177
Most Affected Peoples and Areas (MAPA), 253
Movement of Working Adolescents and Children of Christian Workers (Peru), 139

Multicultural society, 33
Multinational corporations, 192
Municipal social welfare board, 39
Mynttorget, 286

N
Nakabuye, Hilda Flavia, 253
National Board of Social Welfare, 37, 44, 50
National identity, 31
National Movement of Street Boys and Girls (Brazil), 140
National sovereignty, 185–187
Nation states, 189, 192, 193, 195
Neglect, 40
Neo-liberal, 209
Neoliberalism, 86, 88
New York, 1, 5
NGO coalition, 185
NGOs, 278–280, 282, 283, 285, 291
Nigeria, 205, 210
Nigeria's Child Rights Act, 210
The 1924 Declaration on the Rights of the Child, 60–62, 65
1959 Declaration on the Rights of the Child, 60–62, 65
1960s, 10, 14
1970s, 10, 11, 14
Nineteenth century, 33, 35
Non-citizen, 276, 278, 281, 293
Non-governmental organisations (NGOs), 6, 181, 183, 185, 190, 191, 197
Nordic countries, 31
Normality, 34
Norms, 13, 14, 164, 176, 275, 278
Northern Territory, 303, 309–313, 316

O
Obeisance, 212
One Nation Party, 315
Ongwen, Dominic, 161–164, 166, 171–173, 177
Opponents, 277, 282, 286, 288–291, 293
Optional Protocol to the Convention on the Rights of the Child on the Involvement of Children in Armed Conflict, 166
Optional Protocol to the CRC on a communication procedure (OPIC), 188–190, 192
Optional Protocol to the CRC on the involvement of children in armed conflict (OPAC), 183
Organisation of African Unity (OAU), 6
Oslo Child Labour Conference (1997), 143

P
Padatik, Amra, 2, 3
Palace of the Argentine National Congress, 260
Pandemic Classroom, 81, 82
Pandey, Ridhima, 190
Paradox of institutionalisation, 138–139, 154
Parental code, 32, 38, 39, 42, 43, 45, 47
Parental education, 44, 47, 51
Parental rights, 35, 39–41, 44
Parental support, 237–238
Parent-child relations, 34
Parenthood, 34
Parents, 31–35, 38–45, 47–51, 228–235, 237–245
  capability, 51
  right, 38, 41–46

Paris Principles, 166, 167
Parliament, 36, 38, 41–43, 49, 278, 282, 284, 286–290, 292, 293
Parliamentary bill, 48
Parliamentary debates, 32
Participation, 3, 5–14, 18, 59–76, 81–98, 229, 235, 236
Participatory culture, 252–255
Participatory initiatives, 60, 63, 66–68, 76
Participatory processes, 59–77
Participatory rights, 52, 66, 67
Particular or universal rights, 49–53
Passive, 2, 6, 19
Paternalist, 196
Paternalist framing, 69
Paternalistic, 48, 52
Paternalistic society, 205
Pathology, 164, 169
Patriarchal, 205, 213
Pedagogization, 232, 234, 239, 240
Penal Code, 39, 45
Percy-Smith, Barry, 85
Performance, 4, 5, 7, 14–17, 19, 21, 285
Performative act, 3
Performativity, 280, 281
Peru, 187
Petitioner, 188–190
Philanthropists, 6, 9
Phoenix, Anne, 97
Photo-elicitation, 211
Photographs, 2, 6
Physical, 35, 37, 38, 41, 46, 49–51
Physical and psychological violence, 41
Physical punishment, 31, 37, 44, 45, 47
Plan International, 197
Police, 110, 116, 119, 120, 122, 123
Policing, 291
Policy, 279, 281, 289

Political action, 277, 280, 284, 287, 289, 290, 292
Political citizenship, 278
Political identity, 277, 282
Political mobilization, 276, 277, 292
Political participation, 113, 195
Political representation, 4, 7–9, 14–19, 21, 22, 251, 255–256, 269, 276–280, 282, 283, 288, 292, 293
Political space, 276, 277, 282–285, 288
Political struggle, 198
Political subject, 164, 174, 175
Political subjectivities, 7, 19, 258, 261
Political theory, 277, 278, 288, 291
Politics, 3–5, 7–14, 21, 22, 276, 277, 281, 282, 286–293
Poor relief, 32, 34
Portrait, 254, 258
Portrayals, 2–5, 7, 14, 15, 17, 19, 21, 22
Post-colonial, 210
Postwestphalian, 196
Potential, 302–306, 309, 318–319
Potentiality, 255, 258, 259, 269
Poverty, 3, 8, 18
Power, 181, 186, 189, 191, 195–198, 277, 279–281
Power hierarchies, 110
Power over children, 211
Preschool, 47
Prime minister, 287
Professional representation, 106–108, 113, 121
Professionals, 6, 13, 14
Prohibiting, 40
Protagonism, 217
Protagonismo infantile, 140
Protecting, 33, 41, 45, 50
Protection, 164–166, 169, 171, 176, 177

Protection of children, 31, 34, 50
Protests, 71–73, 252, 256, 261, 262, 268, 269
Proto-adult status, 207, 219
Proxy, 254, 258
Psychological maltreatment, 48
Public authority, 32, 36, 50
Public place, 39, 40
Public protest, 269
Public shaming, 50
Punish, 33, 35, 38, 42, 50, 52
Punishment, 31–53

Q
Queensland, 303, 309, 314–316

R
Race, 306–309, 318
Racism, 253, 265
Ratification, 184, 194
Recognition, 107, 112, 120, 193–196, 230, 240, 244
Recruitment, 183–185
Red Cross, 46
Redeemed hero, 164, 169, 172, 174, 177
Redistribution, 107, 112, 193, 229, 244
Referral bodies, 48
Reformatories, 41
Regimes, 275–277, 282, 292, 293
Regimes of power, 4
Regrouping, 283, 286, 292
Regulate and control children, 67
Regulated and controlled by adults, 60, 69
Regulation of families, 35
Relational meanings of children's rights, 35
Religion, 18

Remittances, 212, 216, 218–221
Renewal, 302–306, 318–319
Represent, 2–8, 10–12, 15, 19, 21
Representation, 2–4, 7–22, 84, 89, 95–97, 181–198, 275–294, 301–319
  discourses that articulate, 164, 172
  understandings of the world and how to behave in this world, 176
  understood as narratives, 164, 174
Representational power, 15, 16, 134, 150, 152, 191, 281, 285, 292
Representational rights, 205, 206, 211, 218
Representative, 182, 189–192, 195–197, 276–280, 283, 284, 286–288, 290, 292, 294
Representative claim, 276, 280, 281, 283, 284, 288, 292, 294
Representative democracy, 277, 278
Represented, 275–280, 282–285, 292, 293
Representing (state representing), 33
  role of the state, 33
Reprimand, 38, 42, 43
Reprove, 38
Resilience, 173, 177
Resources
  immaterial, 228, 229
  material, 228, 229, 232, 244
Responsibility, 10, 11, 230–233, 263–266
Responsiveness, 277
Ribbenvik, Mikael, 287
Right holders, 9, 10, 15
Rights, 2, 3, 5–22
Rights and representation, 205–223
Right to education, 81–98
Right to vote, 195
Riis, Jacob, 6
Risk, 303–306, 309–319

Roma, 114–117, 119, 120, 122, 124
Rome Statute, 165, 167, 168
Royal Commission into Aboriginal Deaths in Custody (RCIADC), 316, 317
Royal Commission into the Detention and Protection of Children in the Northern Territory, 310
Runaway children, 208
Russia, 262, 270n3

S
Satyarthi, Kailash, 131, 146
Save the Children, 44–46, 48, 50–51, 197
School, 2, 6, 7, 10, 12, 17, 18
School children, 72–74
School law, 32, 41
Schools/schooling, 81–84, 86–98, 98–99n4, 99n5, 99n7, 99n8, 99n9, 100n12, 100n14, 100n15, 100n16, 284, 286, 288, 292, 293
School strike, 252, 257, 262
Secretary of state, 38
Security Council, 184–186
Self-determination, 63, 213, 222
Self-representation, 4, 12, 18, 20, 61, 69, 74, 76, 207, 212, 217, 219, 275–294
Sen, Amartya, 88
Senegal, 205, 217
Sex workers, 1–4
Sites of power, 269
Skyddshem, 36, 37
Smokey Mountain Project, 136, 138, 139, 148
Social control, 233
Social environment, 211
Social exclusion, 228
Sociality, 206, 222
Socialization process, 64, 75

Social Jurist, 91, 93
Social justice, 107, 112, 113, 115, 124, 125, 182, 193–195, 229–231, 234, 244
Social law, 32, 41
Social location, 196
Social media, 253, 257, 262
Social movement, 182, 189–191, 196
Social relations of exploitation and dispossession, 212
Social rights, 34, 50, 52
Social Welfare Board, 36
Societal transformation, 59–77
Socio-economic rights, 118–120
Solidarity, 2, 290, 291, 293
South, 64
South Africa, 12, 61, 64, 71, 75, 187, 190
South Asia, 82
South Korea, 187
Soweto, 72–75
Soweto Uprising 1976, 6, 19, 70–76
Spatial, 20
Speaking for others, 182, 190, 191, 196, 198
Speaking on behalf of, 16, 21
Spokesperson, 182, 190, 191
Square, 282, 286, 287, 289, 292
Standard-setting, 294
Standing Committee on Law, 43
State sovereignty, 186, 187, 193
Status inequality, 60, 61, 74, 76
Stay aways, 73, 75
Stockholm, 282, 286, 287
Straight-eighteen, 183–186, 195
Strategic litigation, 189, 190
Strategic targets, 109
Strategies, 183, 196, 275–294
Strategies of self-representation, 275–294
Street-begging, 115, 117, 119
Street-connected children, 208

Streetism, 206
Streets, 276, 282, 284, 287–289, 292, 293
Street urchins, 5
Structural inequalities, 210
Subjectivities, 285, 292
Subjects, 2–4, 7, 8, 12, 14
Sub-Saharan Africa, 64, 76
Surveillance, 51
Sustainable Development Goals (SDGs), 151
Sweden, 31–34, 41, 47, 49, 51, 52, 190
Swedish Migration Agency, 282, 287
Swedish parliament, 252, 256, 257
The Swedish Poor Law and Child Welfare Association, 36
Swedish Poor Relief and Child Welfare Association, 38
Swedish values, 51
Systems of governance, 275, 276, 279, 292

T
Target 8.7, 151, 155
Temporal, 20
Thomas, Nigel, 85
Three formats of legal representation, 125
legal representation, 125
Thunberg, Greta, 190, 252, 256–259, 261
Tillrättavisa, 38
Togo, 211
Tomesveski, Katarina, 88
Torres Strait Islander, 21, 301–319
Townsville, 21, 309, 314–316
Toxic socialization, 209
Trade unions, 134, 139, 141, 142, 145, 148, 153, 155
Traditional distribution of power and authority, 207
Tradition of respect and obedience, 206
Trafficking, 133, 151
Transform, 285, 293
Transformation, 8, 10
Transformational impact, 69
Transformative, 61, 69, 74, 76, 77
Transformative potential, 69
Translation, 118, 120–122, 191
Transnational advocacy, 181, 182, 185, 186, 192, 195
Transnational networks, 186
Transnational political order, 195
Transnational power, 195–197
Transparency, 197
Tukta, 38
Turkey, 188
Turnbull, Malcolm, 310
Twentieth century, 277–279
Twitter, 253, 256

U
Uganda, 162, 163, 264, 265, 270n3
Uluru Statement from the Heart, 301, 302, 319
Unaccompanied minors, 282, 287, 289
UN Convention on the Rights of the Child (UNCRC), *see* United Nations Convention on the Rights of the Child
UN Declaration on the Rights of the Child, 14
Undeserving poor, 232, 234, 244
UNESCO, 87
Ung I Sverige, 282–293
UNICEF, 81, 82, 88, 96, 97, 166–168, 188, 189, 192, 193, 196, 197

UN International Year on the Elimination of Child Labour (2021), 151
United Kingdom of Great-Britain and Northern Ireland (UK), 184, 185
United Nations Convention on the Rights of the Child (UNCRC), 9, 11–14, 61–69, 76, 84, 94, 106, 108, 110, 123, 165–168, 183, 188, 193, 209, 210, 212, 213, 217, 228, 236, 278
United Nations Framework Convention on Climate Change, 188
United Nations General Assembly, 9
United States of America (USA), 184, 185, 188, 190, 270n3
Universal, 186, 187, 189
Universal values, 51
Unstructured observation, 211
Uprising, 71, 73–75
Urban informality, 207–211
Urbanity, 269
Urbanization, 18
Utilitarian value, 210

V
Victimization, 3, 4
Victims, 2, 6, 18
Villaseñor, Alexandria, 188, 190, 259
Violence, 284, 285, 292
Visibility, 252
Visual rhetoric, 251–269
Voice, 51, 52
Voice-based participation, 64
Voice-centred notion of child participation, 65
Voller, Dylan, 303, 310, 312, 313

Vulnerability, 164, 165, 170, 171, 175–177, 185–187, 189, 194
Vulnerable, 251, 257, 258, 264–266

W
War crime, 161, 167, 168, 172
We are foot soldiers, 2, 4
Welfare, 2, 8–11, 13, 22, 279, 281
Welfare institutions for children, 35, 37, 50
Welfare states, 10, 31, 32, 41, 44, 51
Westphalian, 186, 195
Whyte, Jessica, 86
Women's employment, 50
Working children, 182
Working children's movements, 132, 134, 139–145, 150, 152, 153
Working-class, 33
World Bank, 87
World's children, 188–191, 193, 196
World Vision, 197
Worst forms of child labour, 133, 136, 137, 139, 144–146, 148–149, 151, 154

Y
Young migrants, 276–278, 281, 282, 286, 292
Young people, 4, 5, 7–10, 14–16, 18–22
Youth, 4, 5, 8, 9, 14–22, 275–285, 288, 289, 291–293
Youth activism, 255, 263
Youth climate activism, 255
Youth crime/child criminalization, 307, 311–314, 317, 318
Youth curfew, 303, 309, 314–317

Made in United States
Troutdale, OR
08/11/2024

21913751R00199